Student Guide and Workbook

for use with
MACROECONOMICS
EIGHTH EDITION
N. Gregory Mankiw

Roger T. Kaufman
Smith College

WORTH PUBLISHERS

Student Guide and Workbook
by Roger T. Kaufman
for use with
Mankiw: Macroeconomics, Eighth Edition

Printed in the United States of America

ISBN-13: 978-1-4641-0493-0
ISBN-10: 1-4641-0493-x

First printing 2012

Worth Publishers
41 Madison Ave.
New York, NY 10010
www.worthpublishers.com

Contents

Preface

To the Student

Gregory Mankiw's *Macroeconomics* is an exciting textbook in which you will learn how to apply a variety of economic models to some fascinating macroeconomic questions. Although these models are not complicated, it is easy, initially, to become confused about the relationships they represent, and consequently fail to appreciate fully their power and usefulness. I have found that students understand the underlying concepts much better if they actively take part in constructing economic models and applying them. This Student Guide provides a variety of ways to engage you in this type of active learning. Each chapter of the Student Guide is divided into five or six sections:

The **Fill-in Questions** give you the opportunity to review and check your knowledge of the key terms and concepts presented in the chapter. Note that some of the terms are used more than once.

The **Multiple-Choice Questions** allow you to test yourself on the chapter material. There are 12 to 30 multiple-choice questions for each chapter, ranging from easy to difficult.

The bulk of the Student Guide consists of a series of **Exercises** for each chapter. These exercises contain step-by-step presentations and applications of the models discussed in the textbook. You will be asked to complete tables of data, plot graphs, and illustrate shifts in curves. The exercises can be answered entirely in the Student Guide. When you are given a choice of two or more underlined alternatives, circle the correct one. After you complete each exercise, I strongly encourage you to spend two minutes reviewing it to reinforce the concepts. I also suggest that you try to work through some of the exercises *before* the lecture material is discussed. The only mathematics required in this section is simple algebra and an understanding of the slopes of lines. A mathematical review of these concepts is contained in the Exercises for Chapter 1.

The **Problems** ask you to apply the models on your own. I have made a concerted effort to include problems on policy-oriented questions from both the United States and abroad. These problems are similar to the questions you might be asked on an examination. You should complete them on a separate sheet of paper. Several of these problems require the use of calculus, and these are marked **C** (see the Key to Symbols table on page xiii). Some problems that are more challenging are marked with a **CH**. The symbol **A** is used to designate a question, exercise, or problem discussed in the appendix to the textbook chapter. Although the answers to most of the problems appear at the back of the Student Guide, the problems marked **■** have been suggested to your instructor as prime candidates for homework assignments and exams; their answers are not given here.

Most chapters include one or two **Data Questions**, in which you are required to find actual economic data to answer the question. Because I am aware of your busy schedules, the data for almost all of these questions are available from one source—the latest edition of the *Economic Report of the President*. This very useful book, published every Febuary, is undoubtedly in your college library and is also available at either http://gpoaccess.gov/eop or at http://www.whitehouse.gov/administration/eop/cea/economic-report-of-the-President on the Internet. Other Web sites that provide useful domestic and international macroeconomic data are listed at the end of this Preface. Because the data are frequently revised, I have not provided answers to the data questions in this student guide.

Questions to Think About often go beyond the material presented in the textbook and ask you to think critically about the model itself or some application of the model. This material will probably not be covered in class and it will almost never appear on an examination, but your professor would be thrilled if you told him or her that you were interested in discussing it (and he or she believed you!). I should warn you, however, that good economists disagree about the correct answers to some of these questions. Consequently, no answers are provided. However, developing your ability to think critically will enhance your education in macroeconomics, so I encourage you to tackle some of these questions.

The answers to all but the specially marked Problems, the Data Questions, and the Questions to Think About are printed at the back of the Student Guide.

Although you may want to complete all the questions for each chapter, you may be limited by time constraints. The Exercises have been especially helpful for most of my students, but you should decide which of the sections of questions and problems are most helpful for you. I can assure you, however, that your understanding of macroeconomics will be substantially deeper and longer-lasting if you complete most of the Student Guide. If you have any specific comments, please send them to me at Smith College, Northampton, MA 01063 or e-mail me at rkaufman@smith.edu.

To the Instructor

This Student Guide is designed to involve students in active learning. I have found that students who have reconstructed the economic models themselves and applied them independently have a much deeper and longer-lasting understanding of the material.

The difficulty many students have with the models taught in intermediate macroeconomics precludes their appreciation of the usefulness of these models in answering important macroeconomic questions. This situation leads some instructors to spend more time than they would like on the formal models and less time on important applications. Others respond by glossing over the models. It is my hope that Greg Mankiw's innovative textbook and this Student Guide will allow you to teach a course in which students understand both the relevant macroeconomic models and their applications.

The Student Guide is printed on perforated pages. With the exception of the **Problems,** the answers to all of the questions can be written directly into the Student Guide. Consequently, instructors may wish to make parts of the Student Guide required assignments. (You should be aware, however, that the answers to all but the specially marked Problems, the Data Questions, and the Questions to Think About are printed at the back of this Student Guide.)

Each chapter of the Student Guide includes five or six sections:

The **Fill-in Questions** review the Key Concepts listed at the end of each chapter of the textbook. I have made these questions a bit more challenging by using some of the concepts more than once.

The 12 to 30 **Multiple-Choice Questions** for each chapter range in difficulty from easy to difficult. Several of these questions are suitable for examinations.

The bulk of the Student Guide consists of a series of **Exercises** for each chapter. In this section, students are guided step-by-step through the models presented in the chapter. I have found that students benefit greatly from solving simple algebraic models, plotting data on grids, and illustrating the comparative statics results themselves. Because the Exercises for some chapters are quite long, you may wish to give your students guidance about which exercises you consider most important. I urge students to spend an extra two minutes reviewing each exercise after they complete it to reinforce the concept. I have also experimented successfully with assigning exercises *before* the material is covered in class. This forces the student to read the assignment and engage the material, albeit at an elementary level. Each exercise begins with a brief description. The only mathematics required in this section is simple algebra and an understanding of the slopes of lines. A mathematical review of these concepts is contained in the Exercises for Chapter 1.

The questions in the **Problems** section are similar to those in the Problems and Applications section of the textbook. In these problems, students are asked to apply the models on their own. Many of the problems concern policy applications involving the United States or specific foreign countries. Several of these problems require the use of calculus, and these are marked **C** (see the Key to Symbols table on page xiii). Others are more challenging and noted by a **CH**. The symbol **A** is used to designate a question, exercise, or problem containing material presented in the appendix to the textbook chapter. Although the answers to most of the problems appear at the back of the Student Guide, the answers to those problems marked with a **■** are printed only in your *Solutions Manual*. Consequently, they can be used for homework assignments and exams.

Most chapters include one or two **Data Questions**, in which students are required to obtain actual economic data to answer the question. I believe students should be able to make reasonable estimates of the current inflation rate, unemployment rate, and gross domestic product. The data for all of these questions are contained in the *Economic Report of the President*, which is available at http://gpoaccess.gov/eop or at http://www.

whitehouse.gov/adminstration/eop/cea/economic-report-of-the-President. Although many students will have access to computerized databases, I will be satisfied if my students know how to use this valuable reference by the end of the course. Because the data are frequently revised in subsequent editions of the *Economic Report of the President*, answers to the data questions are not included in the Student Guide to avoid confusion. Instead, answers using the *2012 Economic Report of the President* are included in the *Solutions Manual*. Other useful Web sites are listed on the next two pages.

In the last section, several **Questions to Think About** go beyond the material presented in the textbook. By including this section, I hope to motivate talented and industrious students to think more deeply about the models themselves and their applications. Although I rarely have enough time to cover this material in class, I have a number of special lunches each term and invite any students who wish to discuss these questions. You may want to cover some of them if time permits.

I hope you and your students find the Student Guide to be useful in developing their knowledge and skills. If you have any specific comments, please send them to me at Smith College, Northampton, MA 01063 or email me at rkaufman@smith.edu.

Roger Kaufman
March 2012

Economics Data on the Internet

During the past decade there has been an explosion of economics data available on the Internet. Insofar as the sites and addresses change literally every day, any compilation becomes obsolete very quickly. In this section, I list 13 Web sites that I have found to be especially useful in obtaining economics data. I have divided them into three groups. The first group consists of two sites that provide excellent gateways to the Internet. They include links to all sorts of national and international economics data, and they are easy to use. The second group lists the addresses of seven sites specializing in U.S. data, and the third group concentrates on international data.

Gateways to the Web

1. *http://www.rfe.org* This is the oldest, most well-known, and probably most comprehensive site for economics data and economics information in general. It is maintained and updated regularly by Bill Goffe, sponsored by the American Economic Association, and is easy to use.

2. *http://www.economy.com/freelunch* Once you register (for free) you will gain access to literally millions of data series, each of which you can easily export as an Excel file

Sources of U.S. Data

3. *http://www.access.gpo.gov/eop* This site contains the most recent *Economic Report of the President*. Almost all of the data questions in this Study Guide can be answered using this source. The entire report can be browsed or parts of it can be downloaded. Make sure to check the table of contents for the Statistical Tables that are located about two-thirds of the way through the report. Sometime in 2012 this site will be replaced by http://www.whitehouse.gov/administration/eop/cea/economic-report-of-the-President

4. *http://www.fedstats.gov* This site includes data for over 100 federal agencies and can be searched by topic or by agency.

5. *http://www.bea.gov/* This is one of the best sources for locating the most recent monthly and quarterly U.S. GDP data.

6. *http://www.bls.gov/* This gateway to the Bureau of Labor Statistics has a wealth of earnings, employment, and unemployment data.

7. *http://www.census.gov/compendia/statab/* This is the on-line edition of the latest *Statistical Abstract of the United States*, the traditional workhorse for many reference librarians. Unfortunately, the publication is being discontinued, but the 2012 edition is still useful.

8. *http://www.federalreserve.gov* The homepage of the Federal Reserve Board of Governors contains extensive information on monetary issues.

9. *http://research.stlouisfed.org/fred2* A great source of monetary and macroeconomic data, this site is maintained by the Federal Reserve Bank of St. Louis. It has a program that automatically calculates the growth rates for its data series.

Sources of International Data

10. *http://unsats.un.or/unsd/default.htm* This homepage of the Statistical Division of the United Nations Department of Economic and Social Affairs contains a wealth of economic and socioeconomic data for hundreds of countries.

11. *http://www.imf.org* The gateway to the International Monetary Fund is another excellent source of international data and reports.

12. *http://data.worldbank.org* The World Bank's gateway has thousands of international socioeconomic time series.

13. *http://www.cia.gov/cia/publications/factbook* Called the *CIA World Factbook*, this site has useful information about many countries, although it isn't as lurid as you might imagine.

Acknowledgments

I would like to thank Greg Mankiw for writing such an excellent and enjoyable textbook. We have worked together for over twenty years, and it has been a pleasure. I also thank Geoffrey Woglom for stimulating my interest in macroeconomics and for his numerous suggestions and support. Yan Zhang, Tanya Luthra, Robin Drouin, Nayantara Mukerji, Alka Srivastava, Eileen King, Ling Zhang, Dorothy Cratty, Muneeba Kayani, Kanta Murali, Katrina Cokeng, and Sarah Anders provided assistance in writing, editing, and proofreading the manuscript; I could not have completed it without their help. In preparing this edition of the Student Guide, I wish to thank Lukia Kliossis, Thomas Acox, Edgar Bonilla, and Stacey Alexander of Worth Publishers for their helpful editorial and production assistance and guidance. Finally, I want to thank my children, Rebecca and Joshua, for making it all worthwhile.

Key to Symbols

C   This problem requires the use of calculus.

CH   This problem is especially challenging.

A   This question, exercise, or problem includes a topic discussed in the appendix to the textbook chapter.

▪   This problem does not have its answer printed in the Student Guide.

CHAPTER 1

The Science of Macroeconomics

Fill-in Questions

Use the key terms below to fill in the blanks in the following statements. Each term may be used more than once.

deflation
depression
endogenous
exogenous
inflation
macroeconomics
market-clearing

microeconomics
models
price flexibility
price stickiness
real GDP
recession
unemployment

1. _____ is the study of the economy as a whole. It focuses on issues such as economic growth, inflation, and unemployment.

    _____ is the study of the economy in the small. It focuses on the individual firm, industry, or consumer.

2. _____ measures the total income of everyone in the economy. A period in which this measure is falling is called a(n)

    _____ if the decline is small, and a

    _____ if the decline is severe.

3. During depressions many people lose their jobs, so _____ rises substantially.

4. An increase in the general level of prices is called _____.

5. Economists construct _____ to assist them in understanding the real world.

6. One purpose of an economic model is to show how the _____ variables affect the _____ variables, where the former come from outside the model and the latter are determined within the model.

7. With regard to prices, most macroeconomists believe that _____ is a reasonable assumption for studying long-run issues but that _____ is a better assumption for studying short-run issues.

8. Models that exhibit price flexibility are examples of _____ models.

Multiple-Choice Questions

1. Macroeconomists study all of the following issues EXCEPT the:

    a. determinants of inflation.
    b. relative market shares of General Motors and Ford.
    c. growth of total production in the United States.
    d. amount of imports and exports between the United States and Japan.

2. An example of a controlled experiment is:

    a. astronomers formulating the "big bang" theory of the origin of the universe by making observations through the Hubble telescope.
    b. economists analyzing the effects of an increase in the money supply by examining output, interest rates, and inflation following a large increase in the money supply.
    c. biologists modifying Darwin's original theory of evolution after examining newly found fossils.
    d. physicians testing the effects of aspirin on the incidence of heart disease by following two groups of men who differ only in their intake of aspirin.

3. If real GDP is growing rapidly, which of the following is most likely to occur?

    a. a recession
    b. a depression
    c. higher unemployment
    d. inflation

4. The variable that is likely to be exogenous in a model that explains production in a small firm within a large industry is the:

    a. amount of output produced by the firm.
    b. price of the firm's inputs.
    c. number of workers hired by the firm.
    d. amount of machinery employed by the firm.

5. All of the following are reasons why wages and/or prices may be sticky in the short run EXCEPT:

    a. long-term labor contracts often set wages in advance for up to three years.
    b. many firms leave their product prices unchanged for long periods of time in order to prevent current customers from "shopping around."
    c. it is costly for firms to print new price lists and advertise frequently changing prices.
    d. firms are already charging the highest prices people will pay, so there is no reason to change them.

6. The market in which the assumption of continuous market clearing seems to be LEAST applicable is the:

   a. stock market.

   b. market for wheat.

   c. labor market.

   d. market for U.S. Treasury bonds.

Exercises: Review of Basic Math

In this first set of exercises, we review some basic mathematical concepts that are an essential part of this course. If you have any difficulty with these concepts, you should discuss your math background with your instructor as soon as possible.

1. **Percentage Change** *In this exercise we review the calculation of percentage change.*

   The percentage change in a variable Q that changes in value from Q_0 to Q_1 may be calculated by using the equation

   $$\text{Percentage change in } Q = 100 \times \frac{Q_1 - Q_0}{Q_0} \qquad \text{(1-1)}$$

   Use the equation to calculate the percentage changes in the following examples:

   a. $Q_0 = 100$; $Q_1 = 120$

   b. $Q_0 = 20$; $Q_1 = 85$

   c. $Q_0 = 50$; $Q_1 = 40$

2. **Graphs, Slopes, and Simultaneous Equations** *In this exercise, we review how to plot pairs of points on a graph, calculate slopes and intercepts of lines, and solve two linear equations simultaneously.*

   a. Consider the equation

   $$Y = \tfrac{1}{2}X + 3. \tag{1-2}$$

   In Table 1-1, list the values of Y according to Equation 1-2 for each of the stated values of X.

   Table 1-1

(1) X	(2) Y
0	$Y = (1/2)(0) + 3 = 3$
1	$Y = $
2	$Y = $ _____
3	$Y = $ _____

   b. Plot these four pairs of points on Graph 1-1 and connect them.

   Graph 1-1

   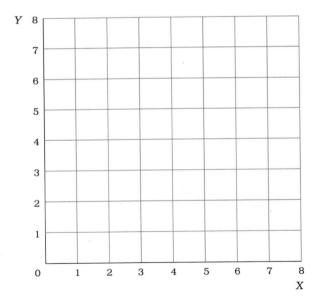

c.   Recall that the *slope* of a curve indicates the amount by which the variable measured on the vertical axis increases when the variable measured on the horizontal axis increases by one unit. The slope may be measured by "rise over run," or $\Delta Y/\Delta X$, that is, the change in Y divided by the change in X. What is the numerical value of the slope of this curve? Explain how you derived this result.

d.   The *Y intercept* of a curve is equal to the value of the variable measured on the vertical axis when the curve intersects that axis. Alternately, it is the value of Y when $X = 0$. What is the numerical value of the Y intercept of this curve? How did you derive this answer?

e.   Now consider the equation

$$Y = -2X + 8 \qquad\qquad \textbf{(1-3)}$$

In Table 1-2, list the values of Y according to Equation 1-3 for each of the stated values of X.

Table 1-2

(1) X	(2) Y
0	$Y = (-2)(0) + 8 = 8$
1	$Y = $ _____
2	$Y = $ _____
3	$Y = $ _____

f. Plot the preceding four pairs of points on Graph 1-1 and connect them.

g. Calculate the slope and Y intercept of the equation in Part e.

h. Determine algebraically the values of X and Y that satisfy both equations by setting Equations 1-2 and 1-3 equal to each other. Check your answer by determining visually where the two curves intersect.

i. Explain why setting these two equations equal to each other yields the coordinates at the intersection.

3. **Exponents** *In this exercise, we review the use of positive and negative exponents, which are used occasionally in the text.*

a. When n is a whole number that is greater than or equal to 1, the expression y^n is equal to the product of n y's multiplied by each other. Thus, $y^1 = y$, and $y^3 = y \times y \times y$. By convention, $y^0 = 1$.

Calculate each of the following:

$2^3 = $ _____.

$3^2 = $ _____.

$5^1 = $ _____.

b. The expression y^{-n} is equal to $1/y^n$. Therefore, $y^{-2} = 1/y^2$ and $y^{-3} = 1/y^3$.

Calculate each of the following:

$2^{-3} = $ _____.

$3^{-1} = $ _____.

$10^{-3} = $ _____.

c. Finally, recall that the expression $y^n \times y^p = y^{n+p}$, that is, we add exponents when we multiply. Thus, $2^2 \times 2^3 = 2^5$. This can easily be confirmed by noting that $2^2 \times 2^3 = 4 \times 8 = 32 = 2^5$. (Remember, however, that $y^n \times z^p$ *does not equal* $(yz)^{n+p}$).

Compute each of the following using the multiplication rule for exponents and confirm your answers by calculating the product directly:

$5^2 \times 5^3 =$ _____.

$6^3 \times 6^{-1} =$ _____.

$4^{1/2} \times 4^{1/2} =$ _____.

(Recall that $y^{1/2}$ is equal to the square root of y.)

Problems

Answer the following problems on a separate sheet of paper.

1. According to the textbook, natural scientists often conduct research via controlled experiments, whereas macroeconomists typically rely on natural experiments.

   a. What is a controlled experiment, and how does it differ from a natural experiment?

   b. Why are controlled experiments considered to be preferable for scientific research?

   c. Why can't macroeconomists typically perform controlled experiments?

2. Consider the market for coal.

   a. Draw market supply and demand curves for coal, label them S_1 and D_1, and illustrate the initial equilibrium price and quantity.

   b. Suppose that the price of oil, which is an alternative fuel, triples. Draw the new supply and demand curves for coal on your preceding graph and label them S_2 and D_2. (*Hint:* One of the curves does not shift from its original position.) What happens to the equilibrium price and quantity of coal?

   c. Now return to the initial equilibrium price and quantity for coal. Suppose that the government imposes restrictions on strip mining that significantly increase the cost of producing coal. Draw the resulting supply and demand curves for coal on your graph and label them S_3 and D_3. What happens to the equilibrium price and quantity of coal?

Questions to Think About

1. The textbook discusses how economists build models—simplified representations of reality—to explain how the world works. How important do you think each of the following criteria should be in evaluating whether a model is good? (Note that there is no single correct answer to this question.)

    a. Accuracy in prediction.

    b. Reasonableness of the assumptions.

    c. Simplicity of the model.

    d. Consistency with other models.

The Data of Macroeconomics

Fill-in Questions

Use the key terms below to fill in the blanks in the following statements. Each term may be used more than once.

consumer price index
consumption
core inflation
depreciation
disposable personal income
flow
GDP deflator
government purchases
imputed value
investment
labor force

labor-force participation rate
Laspeyres
national income accounts identity
net exports
nominal gross domestic product
nominal gross national product
Paasche
real gross domestic product
stock
unemployment rate
value added

1. _____ measures the current dollar value of the final goods and services produced in a given time period within a country's borders. _____ measures the value of final goods and services measured at constant prices.

2. The _____ is the percentage of the _____ that does not have a job.

3. A firm's _____ is equal to the value of its output minus the value of the intermediate goods it purchases.

4. The _____ traces the price of a fixed market basket of goods over time. Because the basket remains fixed as we move forward in time, this measurement is an example of a _____ index.

5. The _____ compares the price of the current mix of output in GDP with what the current mix of output would have cost in a particular base year. It is calculated as _____ divided by _____. Because the mix of output changes as we move forward in time, this measure is an example of a _____ index.

6. One of the more important distinctions in macroeconomics is the one between stocks and flows. Your personal wealth is an example of a
_____ whereas your income is an example of a

_____ .

7. _____ measures the reduction in value of the economy's stock of plants, equipment, and residential structures as these wear out.

8. The _____ measures the percentage of the economy's adult, noninstitutional population that is in the labor force.

9. The amount of income consumers have available to spend or save after paying taxes and receiving government transfer payments is called _____ .

10. Since homeowners do not pay rent, when the national income accounts estimate consumption they use a(n) _____ of what the rent on their house would be.

11. There are two measures of income for an open economy.
_____ is the nominal income earned by domestic citizens both here and abroad. _____ is the nominal income earned domestically by both domestic citizens and foreigners.

12. According to the _____ , GDP is equal to the sum of
_____ , _____ ,
_____ , and _____ .

13. _____ measures the increase in price of a consumer market basket that excludes food and energy prices. It is viewed as a better measure of ongoing inflation trends than the CPI.

Multiple-Choice Questions

1. All of the following are flow variables EXCEPT:
   a. disposable personal income.
   b. consumption expenditures.
   c. personal wealth.
   d. gross domestic product.

2. During periods of inflation:
   a. nominal GDP rises at the same rate as real GDP.
   b. nominal GDP rises at a faster rate than real GDP.
   c. nominal GDP rises at a slower rate than real GDP.
   d. one cannot infer anything about the relative rates of growth of nominal and real GDP.

3. In 2011 General Motors experienced a large increase in its inventories of unsold cars. Thus in 2011:

   a. total income exceeded the total expenditure on goods and services.

   b. total income was less than the total expenditure on goods and services.

   c. total income was still equal to the total expenditure on goods and services because increases in inventories were counted both as part of expenditure and as part of income.

   d. General Motors' investment was negative.

4. Suppose U.S. Steel sells steel to Chrysler for $10,000 and then this steel is used in a Voyager van that is sold to a new car dealer for $25,000. The car dealer then sells the van to a family for $30,000. In this scenario, GDP has risen by:

   a. $50,000.

   b. $40,000.

   c. $30,000.

   d. $15,000.

5. The value added of a particular company is equal to:

   a. its sales.

   b. its profits.

   c. its sales minus its cost of intermediate goods.

   d. zero in the long run.

6. Suppose you purchase a new home for $250,000 and move in. In the national income accounts, consumption expenditures:

   a. rise by $250,000.

   b. rise by $250,000 divided by the number of years you expect to live in the house.

   c. rise by the imputed rent on the house, which is equal to what the market rent would be if it were rented.

   d. are unchanged.

7. The GDP deflator is defined as:

   a. nominal GDP/real GDP.

   b. nominal GDP × real GDP.

   c. nominal GDP – real GDP.

   d. nominal GDP + real GDP.

8. On occasion the GDP deflator can rise while real GDP falls. When this phenomenon occurs, nominal GDP:

   a. must also rise.

   b. must also fall.

   c. remains constant.

   d. can rise, fall, or remain constant.

9. In the national income accounts, investment is divided into three subcategories that include all of the following EXCEPT the:

   a. purchase of new plants and equipment by firms.

   b. purchase of stocks on the New York Stock Exchange.

   c. purchase of new housing by households and landlords.

   d. increase in firms' inventories of goods.

10. All of the following would be counted as a government purchase of a good or a service EXCEPT:

    a. the purchase of a new stealth bomber.

    b. your grandmother's receipt of her monthly Social Security benefit.

    c. the construction of a new dam by the U.S. Army Corps of Engineers.

    d. the hiring of a new police officer by New York City.

11. The largest component of GDP in the United States is typically:

    a. consumption.

    b. investment.

    c. government purchases.

    d. net exports.

12. If OPEC were to collapse and the price of imported oil were to fall dramatically, then:

    a. the GDP deflator and the consumer price index (CPI) would fall at the same rate.

    b. the GDP deflator would probably fall at a faster rate than the CPI.

    c. the CPI would probably fall at a faster rate than the GDP deflator.

    d. nothing would happen to either the CPI or the GDP deflator.

13. All of the following could reduce the unemployment rate EXCEPT a(n):

    a. reduction in the number of people who are unemployed.

    b. increase in the number of people who are employed.

    c. decrease in the labor force unaccompanied by any change in the number of people who are unemployed.

    d. increase in the number of people who have given up looking for work.

14. Male and female labor force participation rates have converged for all of the following reasons EXCEPT:

    a. women now earn as much as men.

    b. new technologies have reduced the time it takes to do household tasks.

    c. improved birth control methods have led to a reduction in the number of children per family.

    d. political and social attitudes about working women have become more favorable.

15. Occasionally, the establishment survey indicates a decline in total employment while the labor force survey shows an increase. All the following might help to explain this discrepancy EXCEPT:

    a. people who had two jobs before the current surveys were conducted were laid off from one of them.

    b. more new small businesses were started since the last surveys than had been anticipated based on past trends.

    c. both surveys are imperfect and collect information from different sources.

    d. employees over the age of 65 are not counted in the employment survey.

16. If a U.S. citizen is employed by a U.S. company in Brazil, the income that she earns is:

    a. part of U.S. GDP and Brazil's GNP.

    b. part of U.S. GDP and Brazil's GDP.

    c. part of U.S. GNP and Brazil's GNP.

    d. part of U.S. GNP and Brazil's GDP.

17. If the GDP deflator grows by 4 percent from one year to the next and real GDP grows by 3 percent, then nominal GDP will:

    a. rise by approximately 1 percent.

    b. fall by approximately 1 percent.

    c. rise by approximately 7 percent.

    d. rise, but by somewhere between 1 percent and 7 percent, depending on the initial level of GDP.

18. If labor productivity Y/L falls from one year to the next, then:

    a. output Y must have fallen.

    b. labor input L must have risen.

    c. the percentage change in L must have been less than the percentage change in Y.

    d. the percentage change in L must have been greater than the percentage change in Y.

19. If the U.S. government wants to increase Social Security benefits to the elderly each year by an amount that allows the elderly to maintain the same standard of living, the percentage change in benefits should be:

    a. equal to the percentage change in the CPI.

    b. somewhat smaller than the percentage change in the CPI.

    c. somewhat greater than the percentage change in the CPI.

    d. equal to the percentage change in the GDP deflator.

20. Percentage changes in the CPI tend to overstate inflation because:

    a. people substitute away from goods whose relative price has risen.

    b. the continual introduction of new goods makes consumers better off even if prices do not fall.

    c. improvements in product quality tend to be underestimated by government agencies.

    d. All of the answers are correct.

Exercises

1. **Intermediate and Final Goods, Value-Added, and GDP** *In this exercise, we review the distinction between intermediate and final goods and illustrate how GDP can be calculated by totaling the production of final goods and services or by totaling firms' value added.*

    a. Suppose that an economy consists of only four firms: Intel, Princeton Graphic Systems, IBM, and Anheuser-Busch. Suppose that this year Intel manufactures 1 million computer chips, which it then sells to IBM for $200 each for IBM to use in the manufacture of its computer systems. Similarly, Princeton Graphic Systems produces 1 million computer monitors, which it sells for $300 each to IBM, again to use in its computer systems. IBM uses these components and its own to manufacture and sell 1 million computer systems at a price of $1,200 each. Anheuser-

Busch, on the other hand, produces 200 million six-packs of Busch beer, which it sells for $1.50 per six-pack. Assume, furthermore, that Anheuser-Busch does not buy any new computer systems during the year. The GDP for this simple economy is the dollar value of the final goods produced during the year. Identify each of the following as a final or an intermediate good. (Circle the correct answer.)

- Intel computer chip: final/intermediate good.
- Princeton Graphic Systems computer monitor: final/intermediate good.
- IBM computer system: final/intermediate good.
- Anheuser-Busch beer: final/intermediate good.

b. GDP is calculated by multiplying the unit price of each final good by the number of units produced. Calculate the GDP for this simple economy.

c. Recall that the value added for each firm is equal to its sales minus the cost of its intermediate products. Calculate the value-added for each of the four firms in Table 2-1 and confirm that the total is equal to GDP. (Use the space provided after the table for your work.)

Table 2-1

	(1) Value Added per Unit	(2) Number of Units	(3) Company Value Added
Intel	——————	——————	——————
Princeton Graphics	——————	——————	——————
IBM	——————	——————	——————
Anheuser-Busch	——————	——————	——————
Total			——————

2. **Nominal and Real GDP** *In this exercise, we calculate nominal and real GDP for a simple economy. We then calculate real GDP growth using two base years and discuss the differences.*

   a. Consider a country that produces only two products: computers and automobiles. Sales and price data for these two products for two different years are as follows:

Table 2-2

(1) Year	(2) No. of Computers Sold	(3) Price per Computer	(4) No. of Automobiles Sold	(5) Price per Automobile
2002	500,000	$6,000	1,000,000	$12,000
2012	5,000,000	$2,000	1,500,000	$20,000

Nominal GDP in any year is calculated by multiplying the quantity of each final product sold by its price and summing over all final goods and services. Algebraically, this can be written as $\sum_i P_i Q_i$, where P_i and Q_i represent the price and quantity sold of the ith final good or service. Assuming that all computers and automobiles are final goods, calculate nominal GDP in 2002 and in 2012.

   b. Real GDP in any year is calculated by multiplying that year's quantities of goods and services by their prices in some base year. Using 2002 as the base year, real GDP in 2002 is equal to nominal GDP in 2002. From Part a, this equals

   _____.

   c. Calculate real GDP in 2012 using 2002 as the base year.

   d. Calculate the percentage change in real GDP between 2002 and 2012 using 2002 as the base year.

    e.   Calculate real GDP in 2002 and 2012 using 2012 as the base year.

    f.   Calculate the percentage change in real GDP between 2002 and 2012 using 2012 as the base year.

    g.   Explain why your answers to Parts d and f are different.

3.   **Using the New Chain-Type Measures to Calculate Changes in Real GDP** *In this exercise we use the data from Table 2-2 in Exercise 2 to illustrate the method of calculating real GDP using chain-type weighted measures. This method is described but not presented formally in the textbook.*

    Partially in response to criticism about substitution biases and other problems, the U.S. Bureau of Economic Analysis has begun using a more sophisticated measure of changes in real GDP. This method uses a (geometric) average of two ratios. The first is the ratio of real GDP in the current year to real GDP in the preceding year, using current-year prices. The second is the ratio of real GDP in the current year to real GDP in the preceding year using last year's prices. To illustrate this method we shall use the data from Table 2-2 but assume that they now refer to two adjacent years, 2011 and 2012:

Table 2-3

(1) Year	(2) No. of Computers Sold	(3) Price per Computer	(4) No. of Automobiles Sold	(5) Price per Automobile
2011	500,000	$6,000	1,000,000	$12,000
2012	5,000,000	$2,000	1,500,000	$20,000

Of course, it is unlikely that relative prices and quantities would change so dramatically from one year to the next.

a. As we saw in Exercise 2, real GDP in 2012 using (in this case) 2011 as the base year is calculated by multiplying the year 2012 quantities by the year 2011 prices for each good and summing. Calculate this amount and compare it with your answer for Exercise 2, Part c.

b. Now calculate real GDP in 2011 using 2011 as the base year, which is merely equal to nominal GDP in 2011, and compare your answer with Exercise 2, Part a.

c. Using the answers to Parts a and b, the percentage change in real GDP between 2011 and 2012 using year 2011 prices is _____. The first ratio we need is the ratio of real GDP in 2012 to real GDP in 2011, using 2011 as a base year. Using the answers to Parts a and b, this ratio is _____. Note that this ratio is equal to 1.0 plus the precentage change in real GDP (expressed as a decimal).

d. Now, use 2012 as the base year to calculate the percentage change in real GDP from 2011 to 2012. The former is calculated by multiplying the year 2011 quantities by the year 2012 prices for each good and summing. The latter is merely equal to nominal GDP in 2012. (Compare your answers with those from Exercise 2, Part e.)

e. The second ratio we need is that of real GDP in 2012 to real GDP in 2011, using 2012 as a base year. Using the numbers in Part d, this ratio is _____. Note that this ratio is equal to 1.0 plus the percentage change in real GDP (expressed as a decimal) you calculated in Part d.

f. The chain-type measure uses a geometric mean of the ratios calculated in Parts c and e. It has many desirable, but rather complicated properties. The geometric mean of two numbers is the square root of the product of the two numbers. The square root of the product of these two ratios is _____. This ratio is 1.0 plus the percentage change in the chain-type measure of the percentage change in real GDP between 2011 and 2012 (expressed as a decimal). The percentage change in real GDP using this measure is therefore _____, which lies in between the estimates in Parts c and d.

4.   The GDP Deflator and the Consumer Price Index *In this exercise, we calculate the consumer price index and GDP deflator using the data in Table 2-2 from Exercise 2. We then illustrate how and why the percentage changes in these two price indices can differ.*

a.   The CPI in a given year is equal to the cost of a fixed market basket of consumer purchases in that year divided by the cost of that same market basket in a base year. Although the cost of the basket changes, its composition remains the same. For ease in reporting, the official CPI is equal to this ratio multiplied by 100. Note that the ratio of these costs in the base year necessarily equals 1. Thus, if 2002 is the base year, the reported CPI for 2002 would equal $1 \times 100 = 100$. If the fixed market basket is the total amounts of computers and automobiles purchased in 2002, use the data in Table 2-2 to calculate the CPI in 2012, using 2002 as the base year (which is often denoted as "2002 = 100").

b.   The GDP deflator for any year is equal to nominal GDP in that year divided by real GDP. Again, it is common practice to multiply this ratio by 100. Calculate the GDP deflator in 2012, using 2002 as the base year (2002 = 100).

c.   The GDP deflator is often used to "deflate" nominal GDP in order to calculate real GDP. This is obvious from your calculations in Part b. If we did not know real GDP but did know both nominal GDP and the GDP deflator, we could calculate it by dividing nominal GDP by the GDP deflator (divided by 100). Using the numbers from Part b, this gives us _____/ _____ = _____. Economists often use price indices, like the GDP deflator or the CPI, to calculate real (inflation-adjusted) values.

d. Calculate the percentage changes in CPI and the GDP deflator between 2002 and 2012.

e. Explain why your answers in Part d are so different from each other, and relate your explanation to the difference between Laspeyres and Paasche indices.

5. **Working with Percentage Changes** *In this exercise, we illustrate how to approximate the percentage changes in products and quotients.*

a. Economists often find it useful to examine percentage changes in variables. The percentage change in real GDP from one year to the next, for example, represents economic growth during the year. The percentage change in the CPI or GDP deflator represents the rate of inflation during the year. The percentage change of the product of two variables is approximately equal to the sum of the percentage changes in each variable. (This approximation is valid only for relatively small percentage changes.)

b. Recall that nominal GDP = $P \times Y$, where P is equal to the GDP deflator and Y equals real GDP. Consequently, the percentage change in nominal GDP is approximately equal to the percentage change in P *plus* the percentage change in Y. Consider the data in Table 2-4:

Table 2-4

(1) Period	(2) Nominal GDP (PY)	(3) % Change in PY	(4) P	(5) % Change in P	(6) Y	(7) % Change in Y
1	100		1.00		100	
		_____		_____		_____
2			1.02		103	

Calculate the percentage changes in Y and P between Periods 1 and 2 in Table 2-4 and complete Columns 5 and 7.

c. Recall that % Change in PY (nominal GDP) is approximately equal to % Change in P + % Change in Y. Using your answers in Columns 5 and 7,
    % Change in PY = _____ % + _____ % = _____ %.
    Place this number in Column 3 in Table 2-4.

d. Now compute Nominal GDP in Period 2 exactly by calculating PY in Period 2 =
    _____ × _____ = _____ . Consequently, the actual % Change in nominal GDP is equal to 100 × (_____ − 100)/100 = _____ %.

Note the accuracy of our approximation.

e. If % Change in PY = % Change in P + % Change in Y, one can subtract % Change in Y from both sides to obtain:

    % Change in PY − % Change in Y = % Change in P.

    This is another application of percentage changes. Recall that the GDP deflator = (Nominal GDP)/(Real GDP), or $P = PY/Y$. The percentage change in a quotient is approximately equal to the % Change in the numerator *minus* the % Change in the denominator. Suppose you did not know the level of P in Table 2-4, but you knew the percentage changes in PY and Y in Columns 3 and 7. You could then calculate

    % Change in P = % Change in PY − % Change in Y = _____ %.

f. As another example, consider labor productivity Y/L, which represents output per worker. Its percentage change from one year to the next is approximately equal to % Change in Y plus/minus % Change in L. Consequently, if Y grew by 5 percent in a year and L grew by 2 percent, then labor productivity would grow by approximately _____ percent.

6. **The Differences between GDP and GNP** *In this exercise, we discuss the differences between GDP and GNP by examining a series of transactions.*

   a. In an open economy, there are two different measures of total income: gross domestic product (GDP) and gross national product (GNP). GDP defines output according to geographical boundaries. It includes the output produced (and the income received) by everyone within the borders of the country. GNP, on the other hand, includes the output produced (and the income received) by every citizen of that country, regardless of whether he or she is currently living in the country. With these differences in mind, complete Table 2-5.

   Table 2-5

(1) Event	(2) Included in U.S. GNP	(3) Included in U.S. GDP
1. Lady Gaga performs a rock concert in New York	Yes	Yes
2. Lady Gaga performs a rock concert in London	_____	_____
3. The Rolling Stones perform a rock concert in New York	_____	_____
4. The Rolling Stones perform a rock concert in London	_____	_____
5. Toyota earns profits from its car factory in California	_____	_____
6. Ford earns profits from its car factory in Germany	_____	_____

7. **Semilogarithmic Graphs** *In this exercise, we graph the growth of real GDP on a semilogarithmic graph and illustrate how straight lines on a semilog graph represent constant percentage (rather than absolute) changes over time.*

a. Economists often use semilogarithmic graphs to make some interesting comparisons. In this exercise we shall see how these graphs work. Consider the following hypothetical economy:

Table 2-6

(1) Year	(2) Real GDP ($ in billions)
1970	100
1980	150
1990	200
2000	280
2010	420

Plot and graph these five points on Graph 2-1.

Graph 2-1

Note that the slope of the line connecting the points is greatest between 2005 and 2010, the time period during which real GDP rose by $140 billion. Similarly, the slope is smallest between 1970 and 2000, when real GDP rose by only $50 billion in each decade. The point to be remembered is that on a conventional graph, segments having equal slopes reflect equal *absolute* changes in the variable that appears on the vertical axis.

b. In economics we frequently want to compare *percentage changes* rather than absolute changes. For this purpose, semilogarithmic graphs can be very helpful. In conventional graphs the numbers on the vertical axis are spaced proportionately. Consequently, the distance between 150 and 100 is the same as the distance between 200 and 150. In semilogarithmic graphs, however, the numbers on the vertical axis are spaced proportionately according to their *logarithms*. You don't need a calculator to calculate logarithms. As you can see from Graph 2-2 below, the numbers are already marked on the vertical axis. Plot and connect the data from Table 2-6 on this graph.

Graph 2-2

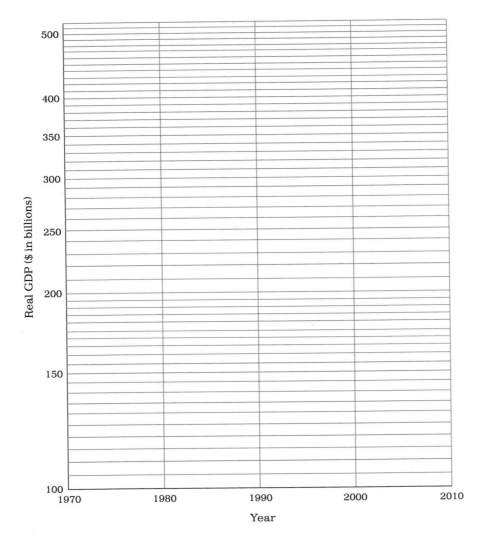

Note that the slope of the line now reaches a maximum on two segments: 1970–1980 and 2000–2010. This is true because the slope of a line segment in a semilogarithmic graph is directly related to percentage changes. The percentage change in real GDP is 50 percent in each of these two decades; hence, the slopes of the segments are equal. The percentage changes in real GDP in the other decades were smaller (33 percent in the 1980s and 40 percent in the 2000s). Consequently, the slopes of their line segments on a semilogarithmic graph are smaller, even though the absolute change of $140 billion during the 2000s was the second highest.

One obvious question you may have is, which graph is better? This depends on the particular question you are addressing. If you are interested in comparing absolute changes, use a conventional graph. If you are interested in comparing percentage changes, use a semilogarithmic graph.

Problems

Answer the following problems on a separate piece of paper.

1. Consider the following preliminary data for 2011:

	($ in billions)
Gross Domestic Product	$15,094.0
Factor Payments from Abroad	779.3
Factor Payments to Abroad	533.8
Consumption of Fixed Capital	1,950.1
National Income	13,437.3
Indirect Business Taxes and Related Items	1,153.9
Corporate Profits and Related Items	1,942.8
Social Insurance Contributions	926.4
Net Interest	535.1
Dividends	791.9
Government Transfers to Individuals	2,336.2
Personal Interest Income	998.1
Personal Tax and Nontax Payments	1,400.3

    a. Calculate net national product.

    b. Calculate personal income.

    c. Calculate disposable personal income.

2. When computing gross domestic product, economists multiply the price of individual goods by the quantity in order to compare apples and oranges. Why do you think they use prices rather than another common measure, such as the weight of each unit of the good?

3. In the national income accounts, expenditures on one's education (for example, college tuition) are treated as consumption. Some economists believe these should be treated as investment. Why?

4. In 2010, GDP per capita in the United States was about $47,000 per person. In the same year, GDP per person was $642 in Bangladesh, $350 in Ethiopia, and $180 in Burundi. Does this mean that the standard of living in the United States was 73 times as great as that in Bangladesh, 134 times that in Ethiopia, and 261 times that in Burundi? Why or why not?

5. For *each* of the following transactions, indicate whether it represents an increase in the U.S. gross domestic product, and, if so, state whether it represents U.S. consumption, investment, government purchases of goods or services, or net exports.

   a. You buy a new Ford Mustang automobile.

   b. You buy a used computer from a friend.

   c. You buy 100 shares of Google stock.

   d. IBM builds a new factory in Massachusetts.

   e. General Motors' inventories of steel rise by 50,000 tons.

   f. The government sends your grandmother her monthly Social Security check.

   g. The government buys a new submarine for $1 billion.

6. Suppose a family purchases a new home for $300,000. The house would rent for $1,000 per month, or $12,000 per year. How are these amounts included in the national income accounts?

7. Some Americans are concerned about Chinese investment in the United States, especially when Chinese firms buy existing U.S. firms. Suppose that a Chinese firm buys an existing U.S. firm and sends some of its Chinese managers to run the firm with U.S. workers. If the firm's output is unchanged and the former U.S. managers remain unemployed, what happens to:

   a. U.S. GNP?

   b. U.S. GDP?

8. Suppose the entire economy consists of only two types of products: computers and motorcycles. Sales and price data for these two products for two different years are shown below.

Year	Quantity of Computers Sold	Price per Computer	Quantity of Motorcycles Sold	Price per Motorcyle
2002	2	$10,000	10	$5,000
2012	15	$ 4,000	20	$8,000

   a. Assuming that all computers and motorcylces are final goods, calculate nominal GDP in 2012.

   b. Calculate *real* GDP in 2012 in 2002 dollars.

   c. Use the relationship between nominal and real GDP to calculate the GDP deflator in 2012 using 2002 prices (i.e., using 2002 as the base year).

Data Questions

The questions in these data sections require you to obtain actual macroeconomic data. All of the data should be included in the latest issue of the Economic Report of the President, *which can be obtained at http://www.gpoaccess.gov/eop/ on the Internet. Other Internet sources appear in the Preface.*

1. **a.** Obtain the appropriate data to complete the following table for the latest calendar year. For each series state your statistical source and table number.

Table 2-7

(1)	(2) ($ in billions)
Gross Domestic Product	_____
EQUALS	
Consumption	_____
+ Investment	_____
+ Government Purchases of Goods and Services	_____
+ Exports	_____
– Imports	_____

   b. Confirm that GDP = $C + I + G + NX$.

2. **a.** Collect the relevant data for the consumer price index and the GDP deflator for the years 2007 and 2008, and complete the following table.

Table 2-8

(1) Year	(2) CPI	(3) % Change in CPI from Preceding Year	(4) GDP Deflator	(5) % Change in GDP Deflator from Preceding Year
2007	_____		_____	
		_____		_____
2008	_____		_____	

b. Between 2007 and 2008 oil prices almost doubled. How does this help to explain the relative differences in the percentage changes in the two indices?

3.   a. Complete the following table.

Table 2-9

(1) Year	(2) Real GDP ($ in billions)	(3) Total U.S. Population (in millions)	(4) Real GDP per Capita	(5) % Change in Real GDP per Capita from Preceding Decade
1981	_____	_____	_____	
				_____
1991	_____	_____	_____	
				_____
2001	_____	_____	_____	
				_____
2011	_____	_____	_____	

b. In which decade did real GDP per capita grow the fastest in the United States? In which decade did it grow the slowest?

4. **a.** Complete Columns 2–5 in the following table.

Table 2-10

(1) Year	(2) GDP Deflator (*P*)	(3) % Change in *P*	(4) Real GDP (*Y*)	(5) % Change in *Y*	(6) Nominal GDP (*PY*)	(7) % Change in *PY*
2010	_____		_____		_____	
		_____		_____		_____
2011	_____		_____		_____	

b. According to the text,

% Change in nominal GDP (*PY*) = % Change in *P* + % Change in *Y*.

Using this approximation, the % Change in nominal GDP between 2010 and 2011 was approximately equal to _____ percent.

c. Now use the exact data for nominal GDP to complete Column 6. Calculate the exact percentage change in Column 7 and verify your approximation in Part b.

Questions to Think About

1. If you had to choose only one measure to represent the level of economic well-being in a country, which of the following would you choose? Why?

real gross domestic product per capita

real gross domestic product per working hour

the literacy rate

the infant mortality rate

life expectancy

the degree of income inequality

the unemployment rate

the average level of education

2. How do you think economists might estimate the size of the underground economy?

National Income: Where It Comes From and Where It Goes

Fill-in Questions

Use the key terms below to fill in the blanks in the following statements. Each term may be used more than once.

accounting profit
Cobb–Douglas production function
competition
constant returns to scale
consumption function
crowding out
diminishing marginal productivity
disposable income
economic profit
Euler's theorem
factors of production
factor prices

loanable funds
marginal product of capital
marginal product of labor
marginal propensity to consume
national saving
nominal interest rate
private saving
production function
public saving
real interest rate
real rental price of capital
real wage

1. _____ are the inputs used to produce goods and services.

2. _____ are the amounts paid (per unit) to the factors of production.

3. If a firm hires an additional unit of labor while keeping other inputs constant, its production increases by the _____; if it hires an additional unit of capital while keeping other inputs constant, its production increases by the _____.

4. The _____ expresses mathematically how the factors of production determine the amount of output produced.

5. If we double the amounts of labor and capital and output also doubles, the production function is said to have _____.

6. Under perfect _____, profit-maximizing firms hire labor until the _____ equals the real wage. They hire capital until the marginal product of capital equals the _____.

7.   The _____ is what a worker is paid (per hour) measured in units of output rather than in dollars.

8.   _____ includes both economic profit and the return to capital.

9.   According to _____, if a production function has constant returns to scale and each factor of production is paid its marginal product, then the sum of these factor payments equals total output. Consequently, _____ equals zero.

10. One special production function that exhibits a constant ratio of labor income to capital income is $Y = F(K, L) = AK^{\alpha}L^{1-\alpha}$. This is called the _____.

11. Most production functions exhibit _____, whereby each additional unit of input increases total output by smaller and smaller increments, all other things being equal.

12. The _____ depicts the relationship between consumption and disposable income. Its slope, called the _____, represents the fraction of each additional dollar of _____ that people spend on consumption.

13. The _____ is the rate investors pay to borrow money. It is equal to the _____ plus the rate of inflation.

14. According to the national income accounts identity, _____ equals investment.

15. Disposable income minus consumption equals _____.

16. An increase in government purchases decreases _____. If private saving remains unchanged, the interest rate increases and investment decreases. Consequently, an increase in government purchases results in the _____ of investment.

17. The interest rate may be viewed as the equilibrium price in the market for _____. Saving represents the supply of _____, and investment represents the demand for _____.

Multiple-Choice Questions

1. The production function is a mathematical law that:
   a. relates factor prices to the amounts of inputs demanded.
   b. relates marginal products of factors of production to factor prices.
   c. relates factors of production to the amount of output produced.
   d. always has constant returns to scale.

2. The variable that is held constant for a given production function is the:
   a. amount of labor input.
   b. amount of output.
   c. amount of capital input.
   d. production technology.

3. An economy's aggregate income equals:
   a. the total number of dollars earned by workers.
   b. aggregate output.
   c. the number of dollars received by producers as profits.
   d. the total rent collected by the owners of capital.

4. A competitive firm takes:
   a. the prices of its outputs as given, but not the prices of its inputs.
   b. the prices of its inputs as given, but not the prices of its outputs.
   c. the prices of both its inputs and its outputs as given.
   d. neither the prices of its inputs nor the prices of its outputs as given.

5. Profit is:
   a. total revenue minus total cost.
   b. the price of output minus the price of input.
   c. the amount of money paid by a company to its stockholders as dividends each year.
   d. the amount of money earned by firm managers.

6. Constant returns to scale occurs when:
   a. output doubles when the amounts of all factor inputs double.
   b. output remains constant over time.
   c. the marginal productivity of labor equals the marginal productivity of capital.
   d. the marginal products of capital and labor do not change.

7.   The production function that illustrates diminishing marginal product of labor is:

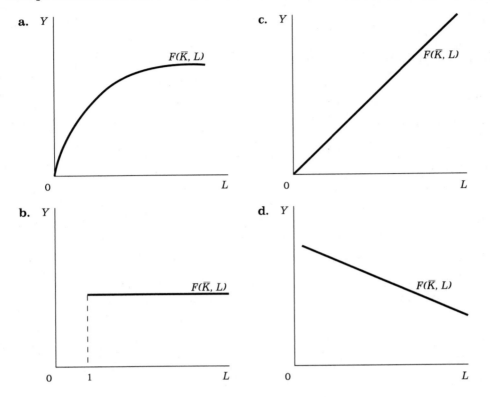

8.   A profit-maximizing firm will hire labor up to the point at which:

a.   the marginal product of labor equals the marginal product of capital.
b.   the marginal product of labor equals the real wage.
c.   marginal revenue equals zero.
d.   the real wage equals the real rental price of capital.

9.   The FALSE statement below is:

a.   the extra revenue a firm gets from an extra unit of capital equals the marginal product of capital times the price of output.
b.   the extra revenue a firm gets from an extra unit of labor equals the marginal product of labor times the wage.
c.   a perfectly competitive firm's labor demand curve is the *MPL* schedule.
d.   constant returns to scale and profit maximization together imply that economic profit is zero.

10.   According to Euler's theorem, the sum of all factor payments will equal total output if each factor of production is paid its marginal product and if:

a.   the production function has constant returns to scale.
b.   the production function displays diminishing marginal productivity.
c.   the amounts of capital and labor employed are equal.
d.   accounting profits equal zero.

11. Which of the following transactions is viewed as investment in the national income accounts?

    a. You buy 100 shares of stock in Apple Inc.
    b. You buy an Apple iMac computer to help your children do their homework.
    c. Apple Inc. builds a new factory in the United States to manufacture computers.
    d. You eat an apple.

12. Which of the following transactions is viewed as investment in the national income accounts?

    a. You buy $1,000 of U.S. Treasury bonds.
    b. Richard, a carpenter, builds himself a log cabin.
    c. The Museum of Modern Art buys a painting by Picasso for $20 million.
    d. Your family buys a newly constructed home.

13. The interest rate on a loan depends on:

    a. the term of the loan.
    b. the riskiness of the loan.
    c. the tax treatment of the loan.
    d. All of the answers are correct.

14. The FALSE statement about national saving is:

    a. national saving is the total amount of savings deposits in banks.
    b. national saving is the sum of private saving plus public saving.
    c. national saving reflects the output that remains after the demand of consumers and the government has been satisfied.
    d. national saving equals investment at the equilibrium interest rate.

15. With total output fixed and national saving unrelated to the interest rate, an increase in government purchases increases:

    a. national saving.
    b. public saving.
    c. the equilibrium interest rate.
    d. private saving.

16. With total output fixed and national saving unrelated to the interest rate, an increase in taxes will:

    a. shift the vertical saving schedule to the left.
    b. decrease investment.
    c. increase consumption.
    d. decrease the equilibrium interest rate and increase investment.

17. If national saving is positively related to the interest rate, a technological advance that increases investment demand will:

   a. have no effect on the amount of national saving.
   b. shift the investment demand curve to the left.
   c. increase both investment and the equilibrium interest rate.
   d. have no effect on consumption.

18. Public saving is equal to:

   a. taxes plus government transfers minus government purchases.
   b. taxes minus government transfers minus government purchases.
   c. taxes plus government transfers plus government purchases.
   d. the government budget deficit.

19. If the nominal interest rate is 8 percent and prices are rising at 5 percent per year, the real interest rate is:

   a. 8 percent.   **c.** 13 percent.
   b. 3 percent.   **d.** –3 percent.

20. If consumption $C = 100 + 0.8(Y - T)$, disposable income equals 1,000, and $Y = 2,000$, then the marginal propensity to consume is:

   a. 0.5.   **c.** 0.8.
   b. 900.   **d.** 0.9.

21. All the following are characteristic of the Cobb–Douglas production function EXCEPT:

   a. constant returns to scale.
   b. diminishing marginal productivity of labor.
   c. constant marginal productivity of capital.
   d. a constant ratio of labor income to capital income.

Exercises

1. **Labor Demand and the Nominal Wage** *In this exercise, we derive the demand curve for labor in terms of the nominal wage by equating the nominal wage to the marginal product of labor multiplied by the price of output.*

   Continuing the example introduced in the textbook, consider the data in Columns 1 and 2 for a fictitious bakery—we'll call it the Bread and Butter Bakery.

Table 3-1

(1) No. of Workers (L)	(2) No. of Loaves Baked per Hour	(3) Marginal Product of Labor (MPL)	(4) Price per Loaf	(5) Price per Loaf × MPL	(6) Nominal Wage Rate (W)	(7) Real Wage Rate (W/P)
0	0				$8	8
		20	$1	$20		
1	20				_____	_____
		_____	_____	_____		
2	36				_____	_____
		_____	_____	_____		
3	48				_____	_____
		_____	_____	_____		
4	56				_____	_____
		_____	_____	_____		
5	60				_____	_____
		_____	_____	_____		
6	62				_____	_____

This company has a fixed amount of capital equipment. As it hires additional workers, total bread production increases, but by smaller and smaller increments.

a. Using the data from the first two columns of Table 3-1, graph the production function for the Bread and Butter Bakery on Graph 3-1.

Graph 3-1

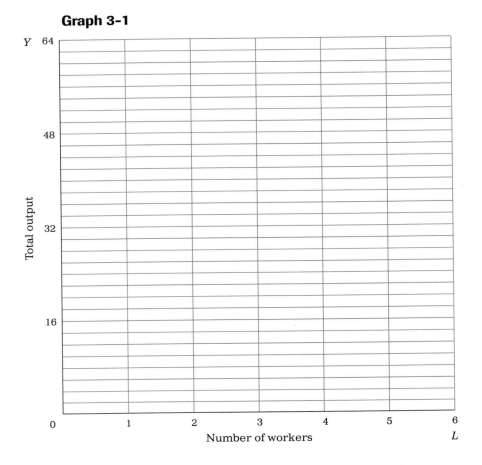

This curve has a positive slope. What does this tell us about the production function of this firm?

The slope decreases as the firm hires additional workers. What does this tell us?

The phenomenon just described is called the property of *diminishing marginal productivity*. As more inputs (here, labor) are added to a fixed amount of other inputs (here, capital), output will rise by smaller and smaller increments. (At some point, the bakery could become so crowded that total output might even fall.)

b. Recall from the text that the *marginal product of labor (MPL)* is defined as the extra amount of output the firm gets from hiring an additional unit of labor. When the Bread and Butter Bakery hires its first worker, bread production rises from 0 to 20 loaves per hour. Consequently, the marginal product of labor of the first worker is 20. These data are shown in Column 3 of Table 3-1. Using the definition of *MPL*, complete the remainder of Column 3.

c. Now, use the data from Columns 1 and 3 of Table 3-1 to complete Graph 3-2. The point for $L = 1$ is already shown on this graph. Note that this curve has a negative slope, illustrating that the marginal product of labor declines as more workers are hired. This is another example of the law of diminishing marginal productivity.

Graph 3-2

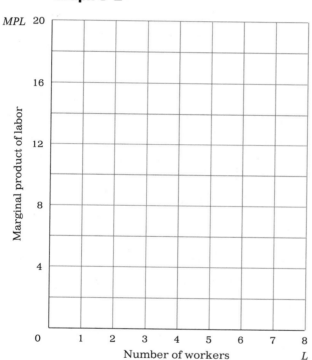

d. The number of workers that the Bread and Butter Bakery will hire depends on the production function and on two additional items: the wage rate the bakery must pay and the price it receives for each loaf of bread. As in the textbook, we assume that the firm operates in perfectly competitive input and output markets. Consequently, the bakery will not drive up the wage of bakers if it hires additional employees or drive down the price of bread if it sells more bread. Assume initially that the market price for a loaf of bread is $1. Thus, as the firm hires additional workers, its revenues from sales will rise by $1 multiplied by *MPL*. For the first worker this will equal $1 × 20 = $20. Use this information to complete Columns 4 and 5 of Table 3-1.

e. Now assume that the market wage for each baker is $8 per hour. Complete Column 6 of Table 3-1 appropriately.

The Bread and Butter Bakery will hire an additional baker only when the extra sales revenue she generates exceeds or equals her wage of $8 per hour. (Although the bakery's profits will also be the same if it hires one fewer baker, we shall assume throughout this exercise and the next that more laborers will be hired as long as profits either increase or do not decrease.) Consequently, how many bakers will the bakery hire?

f. Note that when the fourth baker was hired, bread production rose by eight loaves, which were sold for an additional $8. This increase exactly offsets the baker's wage of $8, so she was hired. Algebraically, at this equilibrium

$$W = P \times MPL. \qquad \textbf{(3-1)}$$

A fifth baker was not hired because his wage of $8 would have exceeded the $4 in extra revenue he would have generated. Indeed, he would be hired only if the nominal wage rate fell to $4. Similarly, a sixth baker would be hired only if the nominal wage rate fell to $2. Using all of this information, we can now draw the Bread and Butter Bakery's demand curve for labor on Graph 3-3. For each of the wage rates depicted on the vertical axis, plot the number of bakers who will be hired by using the rule $W = P \times MPL$ and connect the points.

Graph 3-3

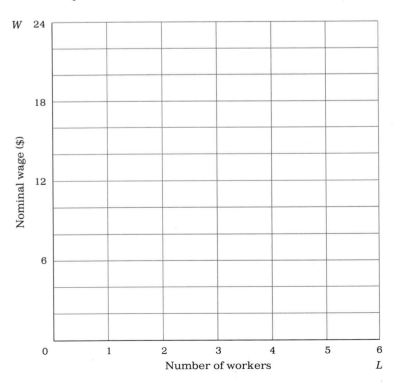

2. **Labor Demand and the Real Wage** *In this exercise, we derive the labor demand curve in terms of the real wage.*

   a. As the textbook describes, one can divide $W = P \times MPL$ by P to rewrite the profit-maximizing rule as

$$\frac{W}{P} = MPL, \tag{3-2}$$

   where W/P is defined as the real wage. Whereas the nominal wage represents a worker's remuneration in dollars, the real wage represents her remuneration in terms of the amount of goods and services (in this case, loaves of bread) she can purchase. To illustrate this, complete Column 7 of Table 3-1 in Exercise 1. Since $P = \$1$, $W/P = W/\$1$; therefore, the numbers in Column 7 of the table are the same as those in Column 6, although the units are now loaves of bread. Similarly, since $P = \$1$, we could also write W/P instead of W on the vertical axis on Graph 3-3.

   b. Now suppose that the price of bread rises to $2 per loaf and the nominal wage rate doubles to $16 per hour. Assuming that the amount of bread produced by each worker remains the same, complete Table 3-2.

Table 3-2

(1) No. of Workers (L)	(2) No. of Loaves Baked per Hour	(3) Marginal Product of Labor (MPL)	(4) Price per Loaf	(5) Price per Loaf × MPL	(6) Nominal Wage Rate (W)	(7) Real Wage Rate (W/P)
0	0				$16	8
		20	$2	$40		
1	20				_____	_____
		_____	_____	_____		
2	36				_____	_____
		_____	_____	_____		
3	48				_____	_____
		_____	_____	_____		
4	56				_____	_____
		_____	_____	_____		
5	60				_____	_____
		_____	_____	_____		
6	62				_____	_____

c. How many workers would the Bread and Butter Bakery now hire?

d. We can illustrate this new labor demand curve graphically in two ways. One way is to find the number of bakers the firm would hire at each nominal wage (just as we did in Exercise 1a). For example, the bakery would hire the first baker only if the wage rate fell to $40 because this is the amount by which revenues rise when the first baker is hired. Similarly, the second baker would be hired only if the nominal wage fell to $_____. Use this type of analysis to draw the Bread and Butter Bakery's demand curve for labor on Graph 3-4. Assume that the price of bread equals $2 per loaf and remember that bakers will be hired according to the rule $W = P \times MPL$. Note that this curve lies to the right/left of the demand curve in Exercise 1f.

Graph 3-4

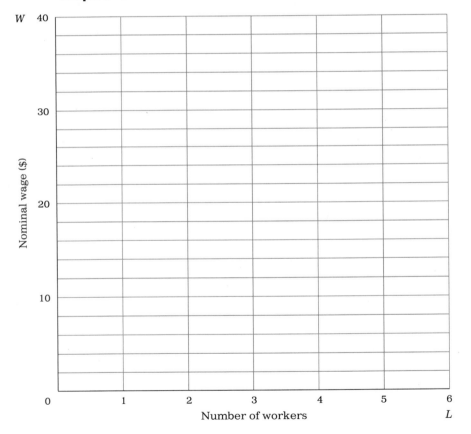

e. A second way to illustrate the labor demand curve graphically is to use the real wage W/P as the variable on the vertical axis and to draw the labor demand curve as a function of the real wage. Use the data from Column 3 of Table 3-2 to complete Table 3-3 and find the number of bakers hired at varying real wages.

Table 3-3

(1) Nominal Wage (W)	(2) Price of Bread (P)	(3) Real Wage (W/P)	(4) Number of Bakers Hired
$20	$1	_____	_____
40	2	_____	_____
16	1	_____	_____
32	2	_____	_____
12	1	_____	_____
24	2	_____	_____
8	1	8	4
16	2	8	4
4	1	_____	_____
8	2	_____	_____

From the data in this table, draw the labor demand curve in terms of the real wage on Graph 3-5. Note that this curve will not shift when inflation increases W and P by the same proportion.

Graph 3-5

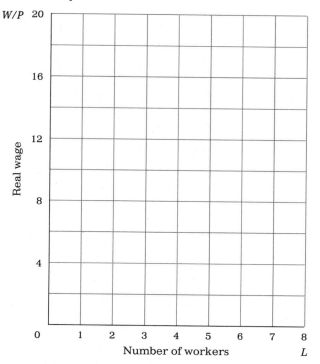

f. In Exercises 1 and 2, we derived the labor demand curve in terms of its nominal and real factor prices, that is, the nominal and real wages. Other factor inputs can be treated in an analogous fashion. For example, we could just as easily draw a table depicting the increase in bread production when the bakery adds more ovens (capital) while holding the number of bakers (labor) constant. This table would allow us to compute the marginal product of capital (*MPK*). We would then equate the *MPK* to the real factor price of capital, *R/P*—called the *real rental price of capital*—in order to determine how many ovens the Bread and Butter Bakery would need to maximize its profits. The curve representing the demand for capital would then be a downward-sloping function of the real rental price of capital.

3. **The Cobb–Douglas Production Function**   *This exercise utilizes a simple Cobb–Douglas production function to illustrate some of the concepts discussed in the textbook—constant returns to scale, diminishing returns, and Euler's theorem. Students who know calculus may choose to do Problem 3 instead of, or in addition to, this exercise.*

a. Consider the following Cobb–Douglas production function:

$$Y = K^{1/2}L^{1/2} = \sqrt{KL}. \tag{3-3}$$

Compute the value of Y for $K = 100$ and $L = 25$.

b. Define the term *constant returns to scale*.

Now show that the production function depicted by Equation 3-3 has constant returns to scale by completing Table 3-4. (You will need a calculator.)

Table 3-4

(1)	(2)	(3)
K	L	$Y = K^{1/2}L^{1/2}$
100	25	_____
200	50	_____
2,500	625	_____

When you doubled the amounts of capital and labor to 200 and 50, respectively, total output <u>doubled/remained constant/fell by half</u>. When you increased the amounts of capital and labor 25-fold to 2,500 and 625 (from 100 and 25), respectively, total output <u>increased 25-fold/doubled/remained constant/fell</u>. This phenomenon, called *constant returns to scale,* is characteristic of all Cobb–Douglas production functions. Mathematically, this occurs because the exponents on the inputs in the Cobb–Douglas production function sum to 1.0. You may wish to prove this.

c. Using the original values, where $K = 100$ and $L = 25$, compute the marginal product of labor at $L = 25$ by calculating how much output would rise if an additional worker were employed. This can be done by substituting $L = 26$ and $K = 100$ in the production function and noting the increase in Y. Note that in this exercise, as in the textbook, the *MPL* is calculated as the change in output when 1 unit of labor is *added*. This is different from Exercises 1 and 2 where the *MPL* is calculated as the change in output when 1 unit of labor is *subtracted*. (You will need a calculator to solve for $26^{1/2}$. Round off your answer to the nearest hundredth.)

Recall that, in equilibrium, firms will hire workers until the *MPL* equals the real wage W/P. Given your answer to the first part of Part c, if firms in the economy had decided to employ 25 workers, what would the equilibrium real wage have to be?

d. Start again at the original values of $K = 100$ and $L = 25$, and compute the marginal product of capital at $K = 100$ by calculating how much output would rise if an additional unit of capital were employed. This can be done by substituting $K = 101$ and $L = 25$ in the production function and noting the increase in Y. (You will again need a calculator. Round off your answer to the nearest hundredth.)

Recall that, in equilibrium, firms will hire capital until the *MPK* equals the real rental price of capital *R/P*. Given your answer to the first part of Part d, if firms in the economy had decided to employ 100 units of capital, what would the equilibrium real rental price of capital have to be?

e. Now we will compute the constant factor shares in this Cobb–Douglas production function.

Step 1   From Part a you found that when $K = 100$ and $L = 25$, $Y = $ _____.

Step 2   From Part c you discovered that the marginal product of labor and the equilibrium real wage at $L = 25$ were both equal to _____. Consequently, total real labor payments, $(W/P) \times L$, are equal to _____.

Step 3   Labor's share of total output is equal to total labor payments divided by total output, or $[(W/P) \times L]/Y = $ _____.

Step 4   From Part d you found that the marginal product of capital and the equilibrium real rental cost of capital at $K = 100$ were both equal to _____. Consequently, total real payments to capital, $(R/P) \times K$, are equal to _____.

Step 5   Capital's share of total output is equal to total payments to capital divided by total output, or $[(R/P) \times K]/Y = $ _____.

Step 6   Note that in a Cobb–Douglas production function, labor's share is always equal to the exponent on the labor input variable in the production function, and capital's share is equal to the exponent on the capital input variable.

Step 7   To see how Cobb–Douglas production functions yield constant factor
CH   shares even as inputs vary, verify that the relative shares would remain constant if *K* remains equal to 100 but *L* equals 625. To see this, it is necessary to recompute *Y, MPL, W/P, MPK, R/P*, and total factor payments for both capital and labor when $L = 625$. If you know calculus, it is easier to see this by answering Problem 3g.

f. Finally, add up the total factor payments from Part e, Steps 2 and 4, and compare the sum with your answer to Part a to illustrate Euler's theorem. This theorem states that, if a production function has constant returns to scale and each factor of production is paid its marginal product, then the sum of these factor payments equals total output.

4.   **The Consumption Function** *In this exercise, we introduce the marginal propensity to consume and the simple consumption function.*

a.   As described in the textbook, consumption expenditures may be specified as a function of disposable income, where the latter is equal to GDP minus taxes, $Y - T$. Even if disposable income equals zero, people still need to eat, so they will consume out of their wealth, and consumption will still be positive. For each $1 increase in disposable income, consumption rises by $MPC, where MPC represents the *marginal propensity to consume,* defined as the fraction of each additional dollar of disposable income that is spent on consumption. Consider the following *consumption function:*

$$C = 125 + 0.75(Y - T).\qquad\text{(3-4)}$$

Use Equation 3-4 to complete Table 3-5.

Table 3-5

(1) Disposable Income $(Y - T)$	(2) Consumption
$ 0	_____
100	_____
200	_____
500	_____
800	_____
1,000	_____

b.   Plot the points from Table 3-5 on Graph 3-6 and connect them.

Graph 3-6

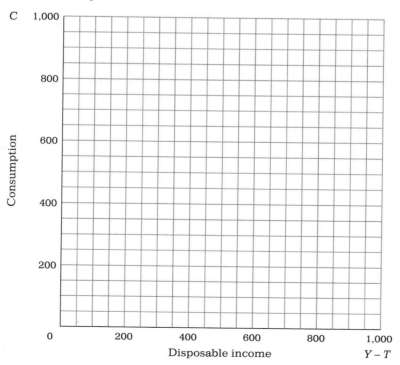

c. What is the value of the *y* intercept of this line?

d. The slope of this line is _____. Explain why the numerical value of the slope is also equal to the marginal propensity to consume.

5. **Taxes, Transfers, Budget Surpluses, and Budget Deficits** *In this exercise, we illustrate how the government budget surplus (or deficit) is related to government purchases, taxes, and transfers.*

a. As the textbook suggests, in most economic models, *T* is equal to total taxes minus government transfer payments. Some economists refer to T as net taxes, which are equal to what households pay to the government in total taxes minus what they receive from the government in the form of transfer payments.

   According to this definition:

   If total taxes = 100 and government transfers = 0, net taxes *T* = _____.

   If total taxes = 100 and government transfers = 50, net taxes *T* = _____.

   If total taxes = 100 and government transfers = 150, net taxes *T* = _____.

b. The *government budget surplus* is equal to total government tax revenues minus total government outlays, where the latter consist of both transfer payments and government purchases of goods and services. Since net taxes *T* already equals total taxes minus transfers, then the

$$\text{Budget Surplus} = T - G. \qquad \textbf{(3-5)}$$

   The *budget deficit* is equal to the negative of the budget surplus:

$$\text{Budget Deficit} = -(T - G) = G - T \qquad \textbf{(3-6)}$$

   Use Equations 3-5 and 3-6 to complete Table 3-6.

Table 3-6

(1) Net Taxes (*T*)	(2) Government Purchases	(3) Budget Surplus	(4) Budget Deficit
200	100	_____	_____
200	200	_____	_____
100	200	_____	_____
−100	100	_____	_____

6. **The Saving-Investment Identity** *In this exercise, we assume, as in the textbook, that the total output of the economy is fixed and that the factors of production are fully utilized. We then show that national saving is equal to investment.*

Assume that there are two factors of production, K and L, and that they are both fully employed at $K = \bar{K}$ and $L = \bar{L}$. Furthermore, assume that the economy is described by the following set of equations:

$$Y = \bar{Y} = F(\bar{K}, \bar{L}) = 1{,}200, \tag{3-7}$$
$$Y = C + I + G, \tag{3-8}$$
$$C = 125 + 0.75(Y - T), \tag{3-9}$$
$$I = I(r) = 200 - 10r, \tag{3-10}$$
$$G = \bar{G} = 150 \text{ and} \tag{3-11}$$
$$T = \bar{T} = 100. \tag{3-12}$$

Equation 3-7 represents the production function and the fact that the economy is operating at full employment when $Y = 1{,}200$.

Equation 3-8 is the national income accounts identity.

Equation 3-9 is the consumption function, whereby consumption is a function of disposable income, $(Y - T)$.

Equation 3-10 is an investment equation in which investment falls by 10 whenever the interest rate rises by 1 percentage point.

Equations 3-11 and 3-12 imply that government purchases and net taxes are set exogenously at 150 and 100, respectively.

a. Substituting these values for Y and T in the consumption function, solve for the level of consumption.

$$C = 125 + 0.75\,(Y - T) = \underline{\hspace{4cm}}.$$

b. Rearranging Equations 3-7 and 3-8, we obtain

$$\bar{Y} - C - G = I. \tag{3-13}$$

As the textbook describes, the left-hand side of Equation 3-13 is equal to national saving S:

$$S = \bar{Y} - C - G. \tag{3-14}$$

This is the amount of saving that remains after the demands of consumers and the government have been satisfied. As Equations 3-13 and 3-14 illustrate, national saving must equal investment I:

$$S = I. \tag{3-15}$$

Substitute the values for Y, C, and G in Equation 3-14 and solve for the initial equilibrium values of both S and I.

$$S = I = \bar{Y} - C - G = \underline{\hspace{4cm}}.$$

Finally, substitute this value of I in the investment equation and solve for the real interest rate.

$$I = 200 - 10r = \underline{\hspace{3cm}}.\; r = \underline{\hspace{3cm}}.$$

c. In the model we developed in Parts a and b, national saving is assumed to be a fixed amount that is unrelated to the interest rate. Consequently, it is depicted as a vertical line on Graph 3-7. Complete the graph by drawing the curve representing the investment equation. (This is most easily done by solving the investment equation for r—that is, by isolating r on the left-hand side of the equation.) Indicate the slope of the investment curve, the initial equilibrium interest rate, and the initial levels of saving and investment.

Graph 3-7

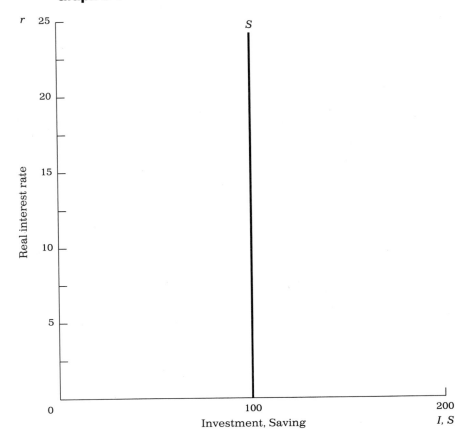

d. Economists often divide national saving into two parts in order to separate the saving of the private sector from that of government. This is done by subtracting and adding net taxes T to the right-hand side of Equation 3-14. Therefore,

$$S = I = (Y - T - C) + (T - G). \qquad \textbf{(3-16)}$$

The term in the first set of parentheses is equal to disposable income minus consumption. This is called *private saving*. Recall that the term in the second set of parentheses is the government budget surplus, which is equal to *public saving*. Given your answers in Part b, calculate the initial levels of public and private saving and verify that their sum is equal to national saving.

7.   **Shifts in the Saving and Investment Curves**   *In this exercise, we use the saving-investment identity to analyze the effects of changes in government purchases, taxes, and technology on the level of investment and the equilibrium interest rate.*

Assume the same model as in Exercise 6.

$$Y = \bar{Y} = F(\bar{K}, \bar{L}) = 1{,}200$$
$$Y = C + I + G$$
$$C = 125 + 0.75(Y - T)$$
$$I = I(r) = 200 - 10r$$
$$G = \bar{G} = 150 \text{ and}$$
$$T = \bar{T} = 100.$$

Using the same initial equilibrium values, let us now see what happens when there is a change in fiscal policy or in the investment equation.

a.   Graph 3-8 depicts the same initial equilibrium as in Exercise 6. Suppose that government purchases increase by 50 to 200. If $\bar{Y}$ and T remain fixed at 1,200 and 100, respectively, consumption would remain constant at $C = 950$. Consequently, saving S would have to <u>rise/fall</u> by _____ to have

$$S = Y - C - G = \text{_____}$$

Graph 3-8

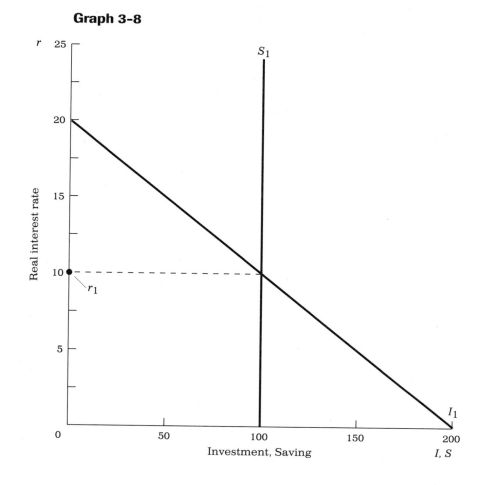

This would shift the vertical saving line to the <u>left/right</u> by _____.
Illustrate this shift on Graph 3-8 and label the new line S_2.

b. For the supply of output to remain equal to the demand for output,
    investment would also have to <u>rise/fall</u> by _____ to
    _____. This would be accomplished by a <u>shift in/move-</u>
    <u>ment along</u> the investment curve. Consequently, the interest rate would <u>rise/fall</u>.
    Solve for the new level of the interest rate by substituting this new value for
    investment into the investment equation; illustrate the new equilibrium interest
    rate on Graph 3-8 and label this point r_2.

c. In Parts a and b you found that if GDP is fixed at full employment $\overline{Y}$, an increase
    in government purchases would <u>increase/decrease</u> national saving. This would
    <u>increase/decrease</u> the real interest rate and thereby <u>increase/decrease</u> invest-
    ment. Thus, an increase in government purchases is said to crowd out invest-
    ment.

d. Now suppose that we start again at $G = 150$ and taxes are reduced by 20 to 80.
    Given a value of $\overline{Y} = 1,200$, this would <u>increase/decrease</u> the level of consumption
    to

$$C = 125 + 0.75(1,200 - 80) = \text{_____}.$$

Consequently, national saving would <u>increase/decrease</u> to

$$S = Y - C - G = \text{_____}.$$

This would shift the vertical saving line to the <u>left/right</u> by _____.
For output to remain in equilibrium, investment would also have to
<u>rise/fall</u> by _____ to _____. This would be accomplished
by a <u>shift in/movement along</u> the investment curve. Consequently, the interest
rate would <u>rise/fall</u>. Thus, a decrease in taxes also crowds out investment.

e. Finally, suppose that a technological breakthrough increases investment demand such that investment rises by 100 at each interest rate. Consequently, on Graph 3-9, the investment curve shifts to the right/left by 100. Draw the new curve and label it I_2.

Graph 3-9

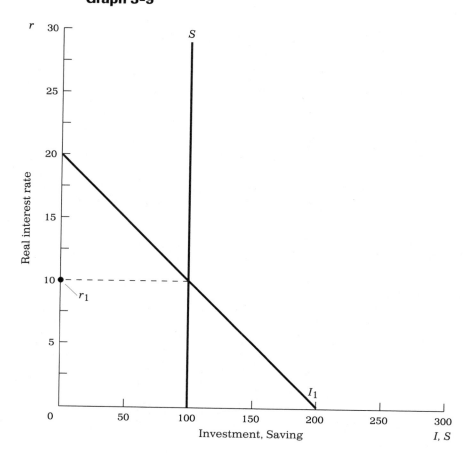

If $\overline{Y}$ initially remains unchanged, national saving will increase/remain constant/decrease and the vertical saving line will shift right/not shift/shift left. As a result, the interest rate would rise/fall, and we would move along the new investment demand curve until investment equaled _____.

f. The result in Part e would be different if saving were positively related to the interest rate. A higher interest rate might reduce consumption and increase saving. If this were true, the saving schedule would have a <u>positive/negative</u> slope, as in Graph 3-10.

Graph 3-10

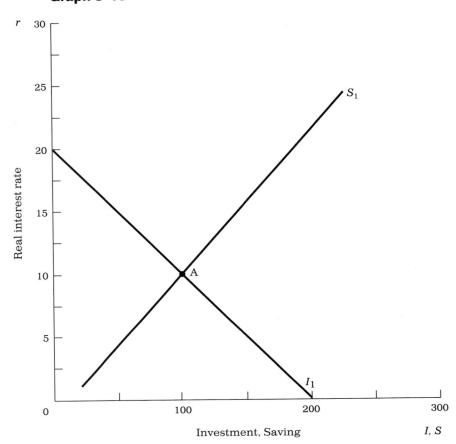

Now suppose that a technological breakthrough increases investment demand at each interest rate by shifting the investment demand curve to the <u>right/left</u> by 100, as in Part e. Draw the new investment curve on Graph 3-10, label it I_2, and label the new equilibrium Point B. The technological break-through would now tend to <u>increase/decrease</u> both the interest rate and the level of investment.

8. **The Identification Problem** *In this exercise, we illustrate Problem 14 from the text-book, which is sometimes called the "identification problem."*

Consider the situation depicted below, in which the saving schedule is positively sloped, as in Exercise 7f, rather than vertical.

Graph 3-11

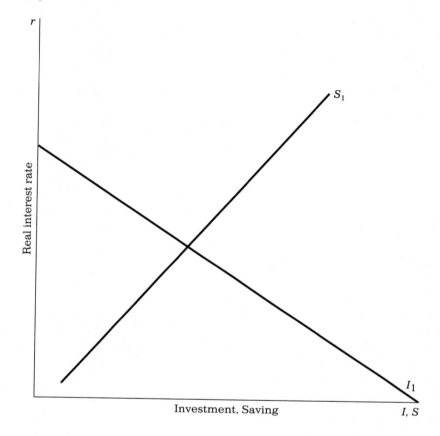

a. In Exercises 7b and 7d, we saw that an increase in government purchases or a reduction in taxes would <u>increase/have no effect/decrease</u> national saving. Starting from the initial position S_1 on Graph 3-11, these policy changes would shift the saving schedule to the <u>right/left</u>. Draw the new saving schedule and label it S_2. The investment demand curve would not shift, but we would move along it to the new equilibrium. Consequently, the interest rate would <u>rise/remain constant/fall</u>, investment would <u>rise/remain constant/fall</u>, and we would observe a <u>positive/negative</u> relationship between the interest rate and investment.

b. Similarly, a reduction in government purchases or an increase in taxes would <u>increase/decrease</u> national saving. Starting again from S_1 on Graph 3-11, this set of policy changes would shift the saving schedule to the <u>right/left</u>. Draw the new saving schedule on Graph 3-11 and label it S_3. The investment demand curve would not shift, but we would move along it to the new equilibrium. Consequently, the interest rate would <u>rise/fall</u>, investment would <u>rise/fall</u>, and we would again observe a <u>positive/negative</u> relationship between the interest rate and investment.

c. Reviewing Exercise 7f, however, we see that a technological breakthrough that increases investment demand would shift the investment curve to the <u>right/left</u> and <u>increase/decrease</u> both the interest rate and investment. Similarly, a reduction in investment demand would shift the investment curve to the <u>right/left</u> and <u>increase/decrease</u> both the interest rate and investment. This would result in a <u>positive/negative</u> relationship between the interest rate and investment.

d. After putting the results from Parts a through c together, we see that one cannot predict whether the relationship between the interest rate and investment will be positive or negative. If the economy experiences shifts primarily in its saving schedule, the relationship will be <u>positive/negative</u>, but if it experiences shifts primarily in its investment demand curve, the relationship will be <u>positive/negative</u>.

Problems

Answer the following problems on a separate sheet of paper. Complete tables in the spaces provided.

1. How would Graphs 3-1 and 3-2 in Exercise 1 look if each additional worker added the same amount to total output, that is, if there were constant rather than diminishing returns?

2. Oranges grown in California and Florida are sold at the same price. Farm workers in both states work in a perfectly competitive labor market and receive identical wages. Suppose, however, that economists have discovered that the *average* product of labor in California orange groves is 50 percent greater than in Florida. The average product of labor is defined as total output divided by the number of workers (or worker-hours).

a. Explain why the following statement could easily be false: Since the average product of labor is different in these two states, California and Florida orange groves obviously follow different economic rules in hiring workers; the firms in Florida must not be maximizing profits.

b. Suppose that all groves in the two states are currently maximizing profits and evaluate the following statement: Because the average product of labor is higher in California, U.S. orange production would increase if farm workers moved from Florida to California orange groves.

3.
C This problem uses calculus to derive the same results as Exercise 3 concerning the Cobb–Douglas production function.

Consider the following Cobb–Douglas production function:

$$Y = 60K^{1/3}L^{2/3}.$$

a. Complete Table 3-7. (You will need a calculator.)

Table 3-7

(1) K	(2) L	(3) $Y = 60K^{1/3}L^{2/3}$
64	8	_____
128	16	_____
192	24	_____

Explain how these results illustrate the property of constant returns to scale.

b. Derive the algebraic expression for the marginal product of labor by differentiating the right-hand side of the production function with respect to L.

c. Evaluate the expression you just derived—that is, find the numerical value of *MPL*—when $K = 64$ and $L = 8$.

Recall that, in equilibrium, firms will hire workers until their *MPL* equals the real wage W/P. Given your answer to the first part of Part c, if firms in the economy had decided to employ eight workers, what would the equilibrium real wage have to be?

d. Derive the algebraic expression for the marginal product of capital by differentiating the right-hand side of the production function with respect to K.

e. Evaluate the expression you just derived—that is, find the numerical value of *MPK*—when $K = 64$ and $L = 8$.

Recall that, in equilibrium, firms will hire capital until the *MPK* equals the real rental price of capital R/P. Given your answer to the first part of Part e, if firms in the economy had decided to employ 64 units of capital, what would the equilibrium real rental price of capital have to be?

f. Illustrate how Cobb–Douglas production functions result in constant factor shares that are equal to the exponents on the respective factors of production. To show this, calculate total real labor payments, total real payments to capital, and labor's and capital's shares of total output when $K = 64$ and $L = 8$.

g. Use the algebraic expressions you derived for the marginal products of capital and labor (your answers to Parts b and d) to prove your result from Part f algebraically.

h. Finally, show that this production function satisfies Euler's theorem.

4. Soon after his election in 1992, President Clinton proposed to reduce government spending and increase taxes.

   a. What effect would this have on the government budget deficit?

   b. State and explain what the long-run effects of this policy would be on private saving, public saving, and national saving.

   c. Use the *I,S* diagram to state and illustrate what the long-run impact of this program would be on national saving, investment, and the real interest rate.

5. At some point during the next decade it is likely that Congress and the president will reduce Social Security *benefits*. Suppose benefits were cut by $100 billion per year and the marginal propensity to consume is ¾. According to the model presented in Chapter 3, explain what the exact long-run effects would be on:

   a. real GDP?

   b. public saving?

   c. private saving?

   d. national saving?

   e. investment?

   f. Use a graph to illustrate the effects on national saving, investment, and the real interest rate.

6. Many Congressional Republicans have often suggested cutting both government purchases and taxes.

   a. If both taxes and government purchases were cut by equal amounts, state and explain what the long-run effects of this policy would be on private saving, public saving, and national saving.

   b. Use the *I,S* diagram to state and illustrate what the long-run impact of this program would be on national saving, investment, and the real interest rate.

   c. Explain how the magnitude of the changes you depicted in Part b depends on the size of the marginal propensity to consume.

7. During his first term, President Obama increased government spending and cut taxes. Given these developments,

   a. what happened to the government budget surplus?

   b. state and explain what the *exact* long-run effects were on private saving, public saving, and national saving.

   c. use the *I,S* diagram to state and illustrate the long-run impacts on national saving, investment, and the real interest rate.

8. When the prices of stocks and houses plummeted between 2008 and 2011, Americans experienced a dramatic decline in their wealth. As a result, they began to save a greater portion of their incomes. Graphically illustrate what a permanent increase in saving would do in the long run to the real interest rate and investment.

The Monetary System: What It Is, and How It Works

Fill-in Questions

Use the key terms below to fill in the blanks in the following statements. Each term may be used more than once.

100-percent-reserve banking	interest on deposits
balance sheet	leverage
bank capital	medium of exchange
capital requirement	monetary base
central bank	monetary policy
commodity money	money
currency	money multiplier
currency–deposit ratio	money supply
demand deposits	$M1$
discount rate	$M2$
double coincidence of wants	open-market operation
excess reserves	quantitative easing
Federal Reserve	reserve–deposit ratio
fiat money	reserve requirements
financial intermediation	reserves
fractional-reserve banking	store of value
gold standard	unit of account
high-powered money	

1. _____ is the stock of assets used for making transactions. It serves three functions: it is a _____, a _____, and a _____.

2. In a barter economy, all trade requires the _____—the unlikely occurrence of two people each having a good that the other wants.

3. Money that has no intrinsic value is called _____ since it is established as money by government decree.

4. Gold is an example of _____ because it has some intrinsic value. An economy in which gold serves as money is said to be on a _____.

5. The quantity of money available is called the _____. In many countries the control of the money supply is delegated to a partially independent institution called the _____. In the United States this institution is called the

    _____.

6. The control of the money supply is called _____. In the United States the primary way in which the _____ controls the supply of money is through _____—the purchase and sale of government bonds.

7. The most frequently used measure of the quantity of money—_____— includes _____, which consists of paper money and coins, and the funds that individuals hold in their checking accounts, called _____. A some-what broader measure of the quantity of money, called _____, includes all of the preceding items plus money market deposits, savings accounts, and several other categories.

8. A bank's _____ is a statement of its assets and liabilities.

9. The deposits that banks receive but do not lend out are called _____. Under a _____ system, banks hold all deposits as reserves and are, there-fore, unable to create money by making loans.

10. Under a _____ system, banks keep a fraction of their deposits in reserve.

11. The _____ represents the fraction of deposits banks keep in reserve. The _____ reflects the preferences of the public about how to apportion their money holdings between currency and deposits.

12. Institutions that act as go-betweens for those individuals who wish to save some of their income for future consumption and those individuals who wish to borrow engage in _____.

13. The financial resources bank owners use to start a bank are called the equity of the bank's owners, or _____.

14. The process by which banks use borrowed money to create and acquire assets that greatly exceed the amount of bank capital is called _____.

15. In order to ensure that banks have enough capital to pay their depositors if their assets lose some of their value, bank regulators establish a _____.

16. The _____ is the sum of currency and bank reserves. It can easily be con-trolled by the Fed, and it sometimes called _____.

17. The money supply is equal to the monetary base multiplied by the _____, where the latter is equal to (one plus the _____) divided by (the _____ plus the _____).

18. The Fed uses three tools to control the money supply. The tool most often used is an _____, by which the Fed purchases and sells government bonds. The Fed may also alter _____, which regulate the minimum reserve–deposit ratio. Finally, the Fed may change the _____, which is the interest rate it charges banks that wish to borrow reserves from the Fed.

19. When the reserve–deposit ratio exceeds the reserve requirements, banks are holding _____.

20. Between 2007 and 2011 the Fed increased the monetary base substantially as a result of its policy of _____. Banks decided to lend out only a small portion of the increase in reserves, partly because the Fed began to pay

_____.

Multiple-Choice Questions

1. Money is:

    a. the stock of assets used for transactions.
    b. the number of dollars in the hands of the public.
    c. a store of value, a unit of account, and a medium of exchange.
    d. All of the answers are correct.

2. Barter economies require:

    a. the use of fiat money.
    b. the use of commodity money.
    c. a double coincidence of wants.
    d. money to serve as a store of value but not as a medium of exchange.

3. Fiat money:

    a. is backed by gold.
    b. is established as money by an Italian automobile manufacturer.
    c. includes currency and gold stored in bank vaults.
    d. is a type of money that has no intrinsic value.

4. The money supply increases when:

    a. there is an increase in government purchases.
    b. the Federal Reserve buys Treasury bonds from the public.
    c. a private citizen buys a bond issued by General Motors.
    d. Facebook sells stock to the public and uses the proceeds to finance the construction of a new office building.

5. All of the following are included in *M*1 EXCEPT:

    a. currency
    b. demand deposits
    c. savings deposits
    d. traveler's checks

6. All of the following statements about credit cards are true EXCEPT:

    a. Credit card balances are included in $M2$ but not in $M1$.

    b. Credit card balances are not part of the money supply.

    c. Credit cards may affect the demand for money.

    d. Credit cards are a means of deferring payment, unlike debit cards.

7. In a 100-percent-reserve banking system, if someone deposits $500 of currency in a bank:

    a. the bank's assets will increase by $500.

    b. the bank's liabilities will increase by $500.

    c. the money supply will not change.

    d. All of the answers are correct.

8. In a fractional-reserve banking system in which there is no currency and the reserve–deposit ratio is 25 percent, a $500 new deposit will eventually increase the money supply by:

    a. $125.

    b. $500

    c. $2,000

    d. $12,500.

9. A bank's capital, or owner's equity, is calculated as:

    a. reserves minus deposits.

    b. assets minus liabilities.

    c. reserves and loans minus deposits.

    d. assets plus liabilities.

10. A bank's leverage ratio is the ratio of its:

    a. assets to liabilities.

    b. deposits to reserves.

    c. assets to bank capital.

    d. assets to debt.

11. A bank's capital requirement is calculated as the minimum acceptable ratio of its:

    a. assets to liabilities.

    b. reserves to deposits.

    c. bank capital to assets.

    d. assets to debt.

12. The monetary base is equal to:

    a. currency held by the public plus bank reserves.

    b. currency held by the public plus bank deposits.

    c. $M1$.

    d. total bank deposits.

13. In a fractional-reserve banking system, if the reserve–deposit ratio is 30 percent and the currency–deposit ratio is 40 percent, then the money multiplier equals:

    a. 1.
    b. 0.5
    c. 1.5
    d. 2

14. If the monetary base is $60 billion and the money multiplier is 3, then the money supply equals:

    a. $20 billion.
    b. $60 billion.
    c. $63 billion.
    d. $180 billion.

15. If the monetary base doubles and both the currency–deposit and reserve–deposit ratios remain constant, the money supply will:

    a. fall by half.
    b. remain constant.
    c. double.
    d. increase by a factor of $2 \times [(1 + cr)/(cr + rr)]$.

16. An increase in the currency–deposit ratio leads to a(n):

    a. increase in the money supply.
    b. decrease in the money supply.
    c. increase in the money multiplier.
    d. increase in the reserve–deposit ratio.

17. An open-market operation occurs when:

    a. there is an emergency appendectomy at the farmers' market.
    b. the Fed buys government bonds from the public.
    c. the Fed sells government bonds to the public.
    d. Both b and c are correct.

18. A reduction in reserve requirements will not significantly affect the money supply if:

    a. banks do not change their reserve–deposit ratios.
    b. the currency–deposit ratio does not change.
    c. the amount of excess reserves held by banks does not change.
    d. the monetary base does not change.

19. The discount rate is the:

    a. difference between the price of a good sold at Walmart and the price of the same good sold at Bloomingdale's.
    b. interest rate charged by banks on loans to their best customers.
    c. interest rate charged by the Fed to banks that borrow reserves from the Fed.
    d. difference between the interest rate on Treasury bonds and the interest rate on Walmart bonds.

20. If the Fed wishes to increase the money supply, it may:

    a. perform an open-market purchase.
    b. decrease the discount rate.
    c. decrease reserve requirements.
    d. All of the answers are correct.

21. A decrease in the discount rate will increase the money supply by:

    a. increasing the money multiplier.

    b. increasing the amount of reserves banks borrow from the Fed.

    c. decreasing the reserve–deposit ratio.

    d. increasing the currency–deposit ratio.

22. A decrease in the reserve–deposit ratio will increase the money supply by:

    a. increasing the monetary base.

    b. increasing the money multiplier.

    c. decreasing the currency–deposit ratio.

    d. decreasing the discount rate.

23. Between 2007 and 2011 the Fed's practice of quantitative easing almost tripled the monetary base. The money supply, however, rose by a much smaller percentage because there was a dramatic increase in:

    a. the currency–deposit ratio.

    b. the reserve–deposit ratio.

    c. banks' excess reserves.

    d. Both b and c are correct.

24. Between 1929 and 1933, during the Great Depression, the money supply fell for all of the following reasons EXCEPT the:

    a. reserve–deposit ratio increased.

    b. currency–deposit ratio increased.

    c. monetary base decreased.

    d. money multiplier decreased.

Exercises

1. **Fractional-Reserve Banking** *In this exercise, we illustrate how money is created by an open-market purchase in a fractional-reserve banking system.*

   a. Imagine an economy with three banks, each of which has the following initial balance sheet:

   Initial Balance Sheet of
   First, Second, and Third National Banks

Assets		Liabilities	
Reserves	$250 million	Deposits	$1,000 million
Loans	$750 million		

   If there is no currency held outside the three banks, the total initial money supply will equal total deposits, or 3 × $_____ million = $_____ million. The reserve–deposit ratio in this economy is _____ percent. Note that this percentage may or may not equal the <u>discount rate/reserve requirements</u>, which mandate the minimum legal reserve–deposit ratio.

b. Suppose that the Fed makes an open-market purchase of $10 million by buying $10 million in government bonds from Tara, a typical citizen. It pays Tara with a $10 million check, which Tara takes to her bank, the First National Bank. When the bank presents the check to the Fed, the Fed credits the First National Bank with an additional $10 million in reserves, and Tara's deposits at the First National Bank officially increase by the amount of the check, or by $_____ million. At that point, the bank's balance sheet will be:

First National Bank

Assets			Liabilities		
Reserves	$_____ million		Deposits	$_____ million	
Loans	$_____ million				

The balance sheets of the two remaining banks have not yet changed.

c. If the First National Bank wishes to maintain its initial reserve–deposit ratio of _____ percent, it must keep _____ percent of the additional $_____ million in reserves, and it can lend out the remaining $_____ million. Suppose it lends all this money to Fred, who is not a depositor at the bank. When it makes the loan, its reserves fall and its loans rise by the same amount, and its deposits do not change. Thus, the First National Bank's balance sheet becomes:

First National Bank

Assets			Liabilities		
Reserves	$_____ million		Deposits	$_____ million	
Loans	$_____ million				

d. Now suppose that Fred takes his $_____ million loan and either deposits it in the Second National Bank or buys a minor league baseball team, and the seller of the team deposits the proceeds in the Second National Bank. In either case, both the reserves and deposits of the Second National Bank will rise by $_____ million above their initial levels in Part a, and its balance sheet will be:

Second National Bank

Assets			Liabilities		
Reserves	$_____ million		Deposits	$_____ million	
Loans	$_____ million				

e. If the Second National Bank wishes to maintain its initial reserve–deposit ratio of _____ percent, it must keep _____ percent of the additional $_____ million in deposits (and reserves) obtained from Fred, and it can lend out the remaining $_____ million. Suppose it lends this amount to Eileen, who is not a depositor at the bank. Consequently, its reserves fall and its loans rise by the same amount, and the Second National Bank's balance sheet becomes:

Second National Bank

Assets			Liabilities		
Reserves	$_____ million		Deposits	$_____ million	
Loans	$_____ million				

f. Eileen takes her $_____ million loan and either deposits it in the Third National Bank or donates it to her college, and the college deposits it in the Third National Bank. In either case, both the reserves and deposits of the Third National Bank will rise by $_____ million above their initial levels in Part a, and its balance sheet will be:

Third National Bank

Assets			Liabilities		
Reserves	$_____ million		Deposits	$_____ million	
Loans	$_____ million				

g. The money supply has now grown by more than the $10 million open-market purchase that the Fed made in Part b. From Parts c, e, and f, total deposits in the three banks now equal $_____ million, compared with the initial level of 3 × $_____ million = $_____ million. Thus, the money supply has increased by $_____ million.

h. The process is not yet over. The Third National Bank will now increase its loans, and deposits at one of the three banks will rise even more when the borrower deposits the proceeds of his or her loan in the bank. According to the textbook, the total increase in deposits is equal to the initial infusion of reserves, or $10 million, multiplied by $1/rr$, where rr is the reserve–deposit ratio expressed as a decimal. (In this exercise, we implicitly assume that the currency–deposit ratio cr equals zero.) In this exercise, $rr =$ _____; thus, deposits (and the money supply) will eventually increase by $_____ million.

i. Note that reserves in all three banks increased by a total of $_____$ million above their initial level. Thus, when $cr = 0$, an open-market purchase of $10 million will increase bank reserves by <u>more than/exactly/less than</u> $10 million, while it eventually increases the money supply by <u>more than/exactly/less than</u> $10 million.

2. **Bank Capital, Leverage, and Capital Requirements** *In this exercise, we develop a more realistic bank balance sheet to illustrate the relationships among bank capital, leverage, and capital requirements.*

In Exercise 1, we considered a simple balance sheet in which a bank's assets consisted solely of its reserves and loans, and its only liabilities were its deposits. Furthermore, we made the simplifying assumption that assets always equal liabilities. In order to understand the bank crisis of 2008–2009, we present the following, more realistic initial bank balance sheet for State Bank:

Initial Balance Sheet for State Bank

Assets		Liabilities and Owner's Equity	
Reserves	$50	Deposits	$300
Loans	$250	Debit	$180
Securities	$200	Capital (Owner's Equity)	$20

As described in Chapter 4, a bank obtains resources from its owners, who provide capital, and also by taking deposits and issuing debt. Some of these resources are held as bank reserves. The remaining amounts are used either to make loans or to buy financial securities, such as government and corporate bonds. Total assets on the left-hand side of the balance sheet must equal the sum on the right-hand side of the balance sheet, which is equal to total liabilities (deposits plus debt) plus bank capital. Bank capital is also called owner's equity. If the bank's assets grow faster than its liabilities, the value of the bank's capital (or equity) will also grow. If the bank's assets grow less rapidly than its liabilities, the value of the bank's capital (or equity) will fall.

a. In the initial balance sheet, State Bank's total assets equal $_____$. Its total liabilities, consisting of its deposits and debt, equal $_____$. The value of its capital (or equity) is calculated as Assets minus Liabilities, which equals $_____$.

b. A bank's capital ratio is calculated as the total value of its capital divided by its assets. State Bank's capital ratio is $_____/\$_____ = _____$ percent. Bank regulators require banks to maintain a minimum capital ratio to ensure that the bank can pay its depositors.

c. Clearly, State Bank's assets greatly exceed the value of its capital. The bank has used leverage to purchase assets by borrowing from its depositors and its creditors. A bank's leverage ratio is calculated by dividing its total assets by the value of its capital. State Bank's leverage ratio is equal to $_____/\$_____ =$

_____.

d. Now suppose that some of State Bank's securities were bonds whose value was linked to risky (subprime) mortgages. (These were called residential mortage-backed securities, or RMBS.) When some homeowners could not pay their monthly mortgage payment, the value of these bonds fell. Suppose the value of State Bank's securities fell by $10 to $190. In this case State Bank's balance sheet would become:

Second Balance Sheet for State Bank

Assets		Liabilities and Owner's Equity	
Reserves	$50	Deposits	$300
Loans	$250	Debit	$180
Securities	$190	Capital (Owner's Equity)	_____

Note that the value of State Bank's other assets and liabilities remains the same. Since the total value of its assets, including its securities, falls to $_____, while its total liabilites remain equal to $_____, the value of its capital, or owner's equity, calculated as Assets minus Liabilities, will now equal $_____. (Put this number in the appropriate spot in the balance sheet.) Because of its high leverage ratio, the _____ percent reduction in the value of its securities led to a _____ percent reduction in the value of its capital. This is exactly what happened to many banks in 2008–2009.

e. Furthermore, now suppose that some of State Bank's car loans could not be repaid because the car owners lost their jobs during the recession. If the value of State Bank's loans also fell by $10, its balance sheet would be:

Third Balance Sheet for State Bank

Assets		Liabilities and Owner's Equity	
Reserves	$50	Deposits	$300
Loans	$240	Debit	$180
Securities	$190	Capital (Owner's Equity)	_____

The value of State Bank's assets have now fallen to $_____, while its total liabilities remain equal to $_____. Thus, the value of its capital, or owner's equity, calculated as Assets minus Liabilities, now equals $_____. (Put this number in the balance sheet.) Consequently, State Bank is now insolvent. It could be taken over by the FDIC (Federal Deposit Insurance Corporation), or it might acquire new bank capital by issuing stock to private investors or the government.

f. In order to ensure that banks can pay their depositors, bank regulators require banks to maintain a minimum ratio of bank capital to assets, called capital requirements. Suppose State Bank's capital requirement was 4 percent. In the initial balance sheet, State Bank's actual ratio of capital to assets was $_____/$_____ = _____ percent, so its capital requirements were/were not met. In the second balance sheet, State Bank's actual rate of capital to assets was $_____/$_____ = _____ percent, so its capital requirements were/were not met. As in Part e, State Bank could acquire new bank capital by issuing stock to private investors or the government.

3.   **The Money Multiplier** *In this exercise, we review the determinants of the money multiplier.*

According to the model of the money supply presented in Chapter 4 of the textbook, the money supply can be written as

$$M = [(cr + 1)/(cr + rr)] \times B, \tag{4-1}$$

where *M* equals the money supply, *B* is the monetary base, and the term in brackets is called the money multiplier.

a.   The money supply consists of currency plus reserves/deposits/loans. The monetary base consists of currency plus reserves/deposits/loans, and it is sometimes called high-powered money. The reserve–deposit ratio is equal to *rr*, and *cr* is the currency–deposit ratio.

b.   Complete Table 4-1.

Table 4–1

(1) Currency–Deposit Ratio *cr*	(2) Reserve–Deposit Ratio *rr*	(3) Money Multiplier [(cr + 1)/(cr + rr)]
0.2	0.2	_____
0.2	0.4	_____
0.6	0.4	_____
0.2	1.0	_____
0.6	1.0	_____
0	0.2	_____

c.   From Table 4-1, note that an increase in the reserve–deposit ratio *rr* will increase/decrease the money multiplier, and an increase in the currency-deposit ratio *cr* will increase/decrease the money multiplier in a fractional-reserve banking system. If *rr* = 1.0, all deposits are held as reserves, there are no loans, and we have a 100-percent-reserve banking system. In this case, the money multipler is equal to _____, and the money supply is greater than/less than/equal to the monetary base. Finally, if *cr* equals 0, the formula for the money multiplier becomes _____. In this case, the entire money supply would be in the form of currency/deposits.

4. **The Three Instruments of Monetary Policy** *In this exercise, we describe the three instruments of monetary policy and discuss their effects on the money supply and the federal funds rate.*

   a. As Chapter 4 of the textbook states, the Fed has three instruments of monetary policy: open-market operations, reserve requirements, and the discount rate. If the Fed buys $1 million in bonds from the public, it makes an open-market <u>purchase/sale</u> of $1 million. If bank deposits initially increase by an amount equal to $1 million, then total bank deposits will eventually <u>increase/decrease</u> by an amount that is <u>greater than/less than/equal to</u> $1 million, and the money supply <u>increases/decreases</u> by an amount that is <u>greater than/less than/equal to</u> $1 million. Conversely, when the Fed sells existing government bonds to the public, total reserves, deposits, and the money supply will <u>rise/fall/remain constant</u>.

   b. Since 1993, the Fed has conducted monetary policy by setting a target for the federal funds rate, which is the interest rate that banks pay when they borrow short-term funds from each other. If the federal funds rate rises above the Fed's target, the Fed can make an open-market <u>purchase/sale</u>, which will <u>increase/decrease</u> bank reserves and push the federal funds rate down toward its target. If the federal funds rate falls below the Fed's target, the Fed can make an open-market <u>purchase/sale</u>, which will <u>increase/decrease</u> reserves and push the federal funds rate up toward its target.

   c. A reduction in reserve requirements lowers the minimum reserve–deposit ratio. If banks respond by reducing the actual reserve–deposit ratio, they will <u>increase/decrease</u> the amount of loans, and both deposits and the money supply will <u>increase/decrease/remain constant</u>. Conversely, an increase in reserve requirements will <u>increase/decrease</u> the money supply, if banks respond by increasing the actual reserve–deposit ratio.

   d. The discount rate is the interest rate that the Fed charges when it makes loans to banks. If the Fed reduces the discount rate, banks will usually borrow <u>more/fewer</u> reserves from the Fed. Consequently, total bank reserves will <u>rise/fall/remain constant</u>, total deposits will eventually <u>increase/decrease/ remain constant</u>, and the money supply will <u>increase/decrease/remain constant</u>.

Problems

Answer the following problems on a separate piece of paper.

1. Which of the three functions of money is satisfied by each of the following?

   a. a $50 traveler's check

   b. a $10 food stamp

   c. a vacation home in the Caribbean

2. In the absence of money, we would have a barter economy. In this type of economy, the price of each good X would be a ratio indicating the number of units of every other good in the economy for which one could trade one unit of good X. It there were two goods, X and Y, in the economy, we would have two price ratios. For example, if one can trade one unit of good X for three units of good Y, the price of good X is 3Y and the price of good Y is (1/3)X.

   a. How many price ratios would there be in an economy with three goods?

   b. How many price ratios would there be in an economy with four goods?

   c. When the future mathematician Carl Friedrich Gauss was 10 years old, he derived a formula that determined the number of price ratios in an economy with any given number of goods. Letting n represent the number of goods, try to write that formula.

3. In the simple fractional-reserve model of the banking system, in which the currency–deposit ratio is zero, how much would the money supply eventually rise if someone received an additional $1,000 in currency and the reserve–deposit ratio were 0.10? Explain.

4. Reexamine State Bank's initial balance sheet in Exercise 2. If the value of its securities fell by $30 to $170, what would happen to the value of its bank capital?

5. Although most bank assets have explicit market prices, some do not. In 2011, many economists believed banks were still overvaluing the assets on their balance sheets in order to maintain their capital requirement. If these economists were correct, explain how more realistic valuations would affect the banks' actual capital ratios.

6. What is the mathematical relationship between a bank's capital ratio and the percentage by which the value of its assets could fall before the bank became insolvent?

7. Calculate the money multiplier for the following values of the currency–deposit ratio cr and the reserve–deposit ratio rr:

   a. $cr = 0.5$; $rr = 0.25$

   b. $rr = 1.0$; cr = any fraction less than 1. Explain the result.

8. **C** a. Differentiate the formula for the money multiplier with respect to rr and determine whether an increase in the reserve–deposit ratio will increase or decrease the money supply.

   b. Differentiate the formula for the money multiplier with respect to cr and determine whether an increase in the currency–deposit ratio will increase or decrease the money supply.

Data Questions

Locate the necessary economic data and apply them to answer the following data questions. All of the relevant data may be found in the Economic Report of the President (http://www.gpoaccess.gov/eop/).

1. a. Complete Columns 2, 3, and 5 of Table 4-2 in billions of current dollars. Use data for December of each year.

Table 4-2

(1) Year	(2) Monetary Base ($ in billions)	(3) M1 ($ in billions)	(4) M1 Money Multiplier	(5) M2 ($ in billions)	(6) M2 Money Multiplier
1987	_____	_____	_____	_____	_____
1997	_____	_____	_____	_____	_____
2007	_____	_____	_____	_____	_____

   b. Now compute the money multipliers in Columns 4 and 6. Round off to one decimal place.

   c. If the Fed has preset targets for $M1$ and $M2$, how did the changes in the money multipliers between 1987 and 2007 complicate its job?

   d. Now complete Table 4-3. Note that the data in the first row of Table 4-3 are the same as those for the year 2007 in Table 4-2.

Table 4-3

(1) Year	(2) Monetary Base ($ in billions)	(3) M1 ($ in billions)	(4) M1 Money Multiplier	(5) M2 ($ in billions)	(6) M2 Money Multiplier
2007	_____	_____	_____	_____	_____
2011	_____	_____	_____	_____	_____

   e. According to Chapter 4 in the textbook, why did the Fed increase the monetary base by so much between 2007 and 2011? What did banks do to reduce the money multiplier so dramatically?

2. What was the average federal funds rate for the years 2007, 2009, 2011, and the most recent year for which you have data? Has it risen from its lows in 2009 and 2011? Why or why not?

Inflation: Its Causes, Effects, and Social Costs

Fill-in Questions

Use the key terms below to fill in the blanks in the following statements. Each term may be used more than once.

classical dichotomy

ex ante real interest rate

ex post real interest rate

Fisher effect

Fisher equation

hyperinflation

income velocity of money

inflation

menu cost

monetary neutrality

money demand function

nominal interest rate

nominal variables

quantity equation

quantity theory

real interest rate

real money balances

real variables

seigniorage

shoe-leather cost

transactions velocity of money

1. The overall increase in prices is called _____.

2. An episode of extraordinarily high inflation is known as a

   _____.

3. The link between transactions and money is expressed in the equation $MV = PT$, which is called the _____. In this equation V is called the _____. This equation can be turned into a useful theory— called the _____ of money—by making the additional assumption that V is constant.

4. Economists also use a similar equation, $MV = PY$, that replaces the number of transactions T with the total output of the economy Y. Because Y is also total income, the variable V in this equation is called the _____.

5. When analyzing the effects of money on the economy, it is often convenient to express the quantity of money in terms of the quantity of goods it can buy, M/P, which is called _____.

6. A _____ is an equation that shows what determines the quantity of real money balances people wish to hold.

7. The revenue raised by the government through the printing of money is called _____.

8. The interest rate banks pay to depositors is called the _____. According to the _____, it is equal to the _____ plus the inflation rate. This one-for-one relation between the inflation rate and the _____ is called the _____.

9. The real interest rate that the borrowers and lenders expect when a loan is made is called the _____; the real interest rate actually realized is called the _____.

10. One cost of inflation, which is metaphorically called the _____ of inflation, is the inconvenience of reducing money holding. A second cost of inflation, which is called the _____, arises because high inflation causes firms to change their posted prices more often.

11. Chapters 1–3 of the textbook focus on quantities and relative prices, which are called _____. Those variables that are expressed in terms of money, on the other hand, are called _____.

12. The phrase that macroeconomists use to describe the theoretical separation of real and nominal variables is the _____. It arises in models in which changes in the money supply do not influence _____. This irrelevance of money in determining _____ is called _____.

Multiple-Choice Questions

1. Suppose that potatoes are the only product in the economy and that 1,000 pounds of potatoes are sold in a given year at $0.15 per pound. The quantity of money in the economy is $50. The transactions velocity of money is:

    a. 5.

    b. 3.

    c. 1.5.

    d. 0.33.

2. If the nominal money supply rises by 6 percent, the price level rises by 4 percent, and output rises by 3 percent, then, according to the quantity equation, income velocity rises by:

   a. 13 percent.
   b. 7 percent.
   c. 3 percent.
   d. 1 percent.

3. Suppose that the money supply increases by 1 percent in one year and then remains constant at this higher level thereafter. According to the quantity theory of money, the inflation rate:

   a. is 1 percent in the first year and thereafter.
   b. increases by 1 percent in the first year and remains constant at the higher level thereafter.
   c. increases by 1 percent in the first year and returns to its former value thereafter.
   d. is unaffected.

4. According to the Fisher equation, the nominal interest rate is:

   a. equal to the real interest rate plus inflation.
   b. equal to the real interest rate minus inflation.
   c. always greater than the real interest rate.
   d. constant.

5. According to the Fisher effect, a higher inflation rate leads to:

   a. higher real money balances.
   b. a higher nominal interest rate.
   c. a higher real interest rate.
   d. All of the answers are correct.

6. If inflation falls from 6 percent to 4 percent and nothing else changes, then, according to the Fisher effect:

   a. both the nominal and the real interest rates fall by 2 percent.
   b. neither the nominal interest rate nor the real interest rate changes.
   c. the nominal interest rate falls by 2 percent and the real interest rate remains constant.
   d. the nominal interest rate does not change, but the real interest rate falls by 2 percent.

7. Expected inflation hurts:

   a. money holders.
   b. people who receive their pensions in fixed nominal terms and who bargained for their pensions before the inflation was expected.
   c. restaurant owners.
   d. All of the answers are correct.

8. Suppose that the nominal interest rate equals 9 percent, the expected inflation rate is 5 percent, and actual inflation turns out to be 3 percent. In this case, the:

    a. *ex ante* real interest rate is 4 percent.
    b. *ex post* real interest rate is 4 percent.
    c. *ex ante* real interest rate is 6 percent.
    d. *ex post* real interest rate is 2 percent.

9. During a period of inflation, the cost of holding money equals:

    a. the nominal interest rate.
    b. the *ex ante* real interest rate plus the expected rate of inflation.
    c. both a and b.
    d. the *ex post* real interest rate.

10. The quantity of real money balances demanded depends on:

    a. the *ex ante* real interest rate.
    b. the nominal interest rate.
    c. real income.
    d. both b and c.

11. During periods of unexpected inflation, lenders are hurt while borrowers gain because the:

    a. *ex post* real interest rate exceeds the *ex ante* real interest rate.
    b. *ex post* real interest rate is lower than the *ex ante* real interest rate.
    c. real interest rate falls.
    d. nominal interest rate falls.

12. At the end of a period of hyperinflation, real money balances rise because the:

    a. Federal Reserve stops hyperinflation by printing more money.
    b. reduction in expected inflation decreases the nominal interest rate, and this raises the quantity of real balances demanded. This allows the real money supply to rise even as prices stabilize.
    c. reduction in inflation decreases the expected real interest rate, which increases the quantity of money demanded.
    d. real interest rate rises, so people put more of their assets into money.

13. If the money demand equation is $(M/P)^d = 0.4Y$, then:

    a. the income velocity of money is constant.
    b. money demand is unrelated to the interest rate.
    c. the income velocity of money equals 2.5.
    d. All of the answers are correct.

14. According to the classical dichotomy:

    a. the money supply does not affect any real variables.
    b. the price level and all other nominal variables are influenced by the equilibrium in the money market.
    c. money is neutral.
    d. All of the answers are correct.

15. Almost all economists agree that the classical model is most relevant in discussions concerning:

   a. economic recessions.

   b. the short run.

   c. the long run.

   d. economic recoveries.

Exercises

1. **The Quantity Equation and the Percentage Change Rule** *In this exercise, we examine the quantity equation and review the percentage change rule.*

   a. Income velocity V is the number of times per year an average dollar in the money supply changes hands in transactions involving final goods and services. It is equal to

$$V = PY/M. \qquad (5\text{-}1)$$

Multiplying both sides of this equation by money M yields the quantity equation:

$$MV = PY. \qquad (5\text{-}2)$$

Using preliminary data for 2011, for example,

> real GDP = Y = \$13,313 billion
> the GDP deflator = P = 1.133 (= 113.3/100)
> $M2$ = \$9,120.8 billion (on June 30, 2011).

Consequently, the income velocity for $M2$ in 2011 was equal to $V = PY/M =$

_____.

   b. Multiply this value of V by the value for M in 2011 and verify that $MV = PY$.

   c. Recall from Chapter 2 that the percentage change in the product of two variables is approximately equal to the sum of the percentage change in each of the variables. Applying this approximation to both sides of Equation 5-2 yields

% Change in M + % Change in V = % Change in P + % Change in Y. **(5-3)**

To confirm this approximation, consider the data in Table 5-1.

Table 5-1

(1)	(2)	(3) % Change in M	(4)	(5) % Change in V	(6)	(7) % Change in P	(8)	(9) % Change in Y
Period	M		V		P		Y	
1	100		2.0		1.0		200	
2	104		2.02		1.03		204	

Calculate the percentage changes in each of the variables in Table 5-1. Now substitute the percentages into Equation 5-3 and verify that the percentage change version of the quantity equation is accurate (to within two decimal places).

d. Starting again at Period 1, calculate *V* for Period 2 in Table 5-2. Compute the percentage changes. Substitute the percentages into Equation 5-3 and once again verify that the percentage change version is a reliable approximation.

Table 5-2

(1)	(2)	(3) % Change in M	(4)	(5) % Change in V	(6)	(7) % Change in P	(8)	(9) % Change in Y
Period	M		V		P		Y	
1	100		2.0		1.0		200	
2	108				1.06		194	

2. **The Quantity Theory and Long-Run Growth in GDP** *In this exercise, we examine the quantity theory when real GDP is rising at its trend rate of growth.*

   a. The simple quantity theory of money assumes that velocity is relatively constant and that real GDP increases at its long-run rate of growth. Over the past few decades, the long-run growth rate of real GDP has been about 3 percent per year. This 3 percent figure is the result of changes in population, resources, and technology, which are all typically viewed as exogenous. Substituting these values into the percentage change version of the quantity equation yields

   % Change in M + _____ = % Change in P + _____ .

   Or, upon rearranging,

   % Change in P = % Change in M − _____% .   **(5-4)**

   This equation indicates that, according to the quantity theory, the rate of inflation will be equal to the growth rate of the money supply minus the long-run rate of growth of output.

   b. Given the assumptions in Part a concerning velocity and real GDP growth, complete Columns 4, 5, 8, and 9 in Table 5-3 for four *successive* periods (the values for V and Y in Period 2 are already entered).

Table 5-3

(1)	(2)	(3) % Change in M	(4)	(5) % Change in V	(6)	(7) % Change in P	(8)	(9) % Change in Y
Period	M		V		P		Y	
1	100		2.0		1.0		200	
		3		0		_____		3
2	103		2.0		_____		206	
		_____		_____		_____		_____
3	97.85		_____		_____		_____	
		_____		_____		_____		_____
4	101.76		_____		_____		_____	

   c. Use the data in Column 2 of Table 5-3 to complete Column 3. Now use Equation 5-4 to complete Column 7. Finally, use your approximations of the percentage changes in P in Column 7 to estimate the price levels in Column 6.

d. Using the exact quantity equation $MV = PY$ and the levels of M, V, and Y in Columns 2, 4, and 8, calculate the exact price level in each period and compare these answers with your estimates in Column 6. Note how the percentage change version of the quantity equation is a good approximation of the percentage changes in Table 5-3.

3.   Nominal Interest Rates, Real Interest Rates, and the Fisher Effect *In this exercise, we analyze the distinction between nominal and real interest rates and discuss the Fisher effect.*

   a. The real interest rate r is equal to the nominal interest rate i minus the inflation rate π, or

$$r = i - \pi. \tag{5-5}$$

Use this equation to complete Table 5-4.

Table 5-4

(1) Real Interest Rate (%)	(2) Nominal Interest Rate (%)	(3) Inflation Rate (%)
_____	10	4
_____	10	8
_____	10	12
4	7	_____
−2	12	_____
3	_____	5
−2	_____	9

The Fisher equation is obtained by rearranging the preceding equation to obtain an equation expressing i, that is, by putting i on the left-hand side. Thus, the Fisher equation is

$$i = \text{_____}. \tag{5-6}$$

b. Recall from Exercise 2 that if the long-run annual growth of real output is 3 percent and velocity is constant, then the quantity equation implies that

$$\% \text{ Change in } P = \% \text{ Change in } M - \underline{\hspace{2cm}}\%. \tag{5-7}$$

Since the percentage change in P is equal to the rate of inflation, this fact suggests that an increase in the rate of money growth of 1 percent causes a 1 percent increase in inflation. According to the Fisher equation, this 1 percent increase in inflation causes a 1 percent increase in the nominal interest rate i because the real interest rate r is presumed to be affected only by real variables. Use all of this information to complete Table 5-5.

Table 5-5

(1) % Change in P	(2) % Change in M	(3) Inflation Rate (%)	(4) Real Interest Rate (%)	(5) Nominal Interest Rate (%)
0	3	0	3	3
___	4	___	3	___
___	5	___	3	___
___	2	___	3	___
___	8	___	3	___

This one-for-one relation between the inflation rate and the nominal interest rate is called the *Fisher effect*. Almost all economists agree that the Fisher effect holds in the long run.

4. ***Ex Ante* versus *Ex Post* Real Interest Rates and Unexpected Inflation** *In this exercise, we introduce the distinction between the* ex ante *and* ex post *real interest rates and illustrate how unexpected inflation hurts lenders and benefits borrowers.*

a. Because the actual inflation rate during a year may be different from the inflation rate that was expected at the beginning of the year, the actual real interest rate during that year may turn out to be different from the real interest rate that was expected at the beginning of the year. To account for this difference, a distinction is made between the *ex ante* real interest rate and the *ex post* real interest rate. The *ex ante* real interest rate is the real interest rate that people expected to prevail at the beginning of the year. It is equal to $i - E\pi$, where $E\pi$ is equal to the expected rate of inflation. After the year ends, however, the rate of inflation is known, and people can calculate the *ex post* real interest rate—that is, the actual real interest rate during the year. The *ex post* real interest rate is equal to $i - \pi$, where π is equal to the actual rate of inflation. From this information, one can see that the *ex ante* real interest rate will equal the *ex post* real interest rate only if _____ = _____.

b. Use the information in Part a to complete Table 5-6.

Table 5-6

(1) Nominal Interest Rate (%)	(2) Expected Inflation (%)	(3) *Ex Ante* Real Interest Rate (%)	(4) Actual Inflation (%)	(5) *Ex Post* Real Interest Rate (%)
8	3	_____	3	_____
8	3	_____	5	_____
8	3	_____	1	_____
2	−1	_____	1	_____

c. Loan contracts are almost always written in terms of the nominal interest rate. The real cost of borrowing and lending, however, is the real interest rate. Unexpected inflation may change the real cost of the loan from what was expected by causing the *ex ante* real interest rate to differ from the *ex post* real interest rate. In Table 5-6, it is easy to see the following:

   i. When actual inflation is equal to expected inflation, the *ex post* real interest rate is equal to/higher than/lower than the *ex ante* real interest rate.

   ii. When actual inflation exceeds expected inflation (when there is unexpected inflation), the *ex post* real interest rate is equal to/higher than/lower than the *ex ante* real interest rate. Consequently, the real borrowing cost is equal to/higher than/lower than what was originally expected when the loan was made. Thus, unexpected inflation tends to help borrowers/lenders and hurt borrowers/lenders.

   iii. When actual inflation is less than expected inflation, the *ex post* real interest rate is equal to/higher than/lower than the *ex ante* real interest rate. Consequently, the real borrowing cost is equal to/higher than/lower than what was originally expected when the loan was made. This tends to help borrowers/lenders and hurt borrowers/lenders.

5. **The Real Cost of Borrowing and the Real Interest Rate** *In this exercise, we see why the real cost of borrowing is equal to the real interest rate.*

   a. Since a borrower's actual dollar payments are based on the nominal interest rate, it is sometimes difficult to see why the real cost of borrowing is equal to the real interest rate. Consider a family that buys a house for $300,000 and takes a mortgage loan equal to the full amount at 7 percent annual interest. The annual interest cost of the mortgage will equal $_____. Since the home is a real commodity, its nominal value will probably increase at the rate of inflation. If the expected rate of inflation is 4 percent, the home is expected to increase in value by about $_____ each year. Consequently, the expected real cost of the mortgage is equal to the difference between the annual mortgage payments and the expected appreciation of the home. This amount equals $_____ each year. Expressed as a percentage of the initial loan, this amount equals _____ percent. Thus, the expected real cost of the loan is equal to the *ex ante* real interest rate $i - E\pi =$ _____ percent.

   b. Suppose that there is unexpected inflation and the actual rate of inflation during the year is 6 percent. Since the mortgage loan was written in terms of the nominal interest rate prevailing at the time that the loan was made, the annual mortgage interest payment remains equal to $_____. The nominal value of the home, however, now increases by the actual rate of inflation, that is, by _____ percent, or by about $_____. Consequently, the real cost of the mortgage is equal to $_____ each year, or _____ percent of the initial loan. Thus, the actual real cost of the loan is equal to the *ex post* real interest rate, $i - \pi$, which equals _____ percent.

6. **The Money Demand Function** *In this exercise, we use the money demand function to derive the money demand curve.*

   a. The general money demand function can be written as

   $$(M/P)^d = L(i, Y). \tag{5-8}$$

   One specific money demand function that fits U.S. data fairly well is

   $$(M/P)^d = i^{-0.1} \times Y. \tag{5-9}$$

   Note that this equation may be written as

   $$(M/P)^d = (1/i)^{1/10} \times Y. \tag{5-10}$$

Use a calculator to complete Table 5-7.

Table 5-7

(1) Nominal Interest Rate i	(2) $i^{-0.1}$	(3) Real Output Y	(4) Real Money Demand $(M/P)^d$
0.12 (= 12%)	_____	100	_____
0.08	_____	100	_____
0.05	_____	100	_____
0.03	_____	100	_____
0.01	_____	100	_____

The numbers in Column 4 of Table 5-7 indicate that the quantity of real money demanded <u>increases/decreases</u> when the nominal interest rate decreases, holding real output constant.

b. Plot the preceding points on Graph 5-1 and draw a curve connecting these points. Label your money demand curve L_1 $(Y = 100)$.

Graph 5-1

c. Now suppose the real output Y increases to 150. Use a calculator to complete Table 5-8.

Table 5-8

(1) Nominal Interest Rate i	(2) $i^{-0.1}$	(3) Real Output Y	(4) Real Money Demand $(M/P)^d$
0.12 (= 12%)	_____	150	_____
0.08	_____	150	_____
0.05	_____	150	_____
0.03	_____	150	_____
0.01	_____	150	_____

d. Plot the points from Columns 1 and 4 of Table 5-8 on Graph 5-1 and draw a curve connecting these points. Label your curve L_2 ($Y = 150$). Note that when real output Y increases, the money demand curve shifts to the <u>right/left</u>.

e. Conversely, if real output Y decreases, the money demand curve shifts to the <u>right/left</u>.

7. **Current Price Levels and Expected Future Money Growth** *In this exercise, we use the money demand function from Exercise 6 to illustrate how the current price level depends on the expected future money growth.*

a. Assume that the money demand function is the same as in Exercise 6—that is, $(M/P)^d = i^{-0.1} \times Y$. Also assume that real output and the nominal interest rate are initially equal to 100 and 3 percent, respectively. The quantity of real money demanded will then equal _____.

b. Assume further that expected inflation is initially 0 percent and the price level P is initially equal to 1.0. Consequently, the money market will be in equilibrium (money supply equals money demand) when the Fed sets the nominal money supply equal to _____.

c. Now assume that people believe that the Fed will soon increase the nominal money supply by 5 percent per year. This will increase inflationary expectations to 5 percent per year. According to the Fisher equation, the nominal interest rate will rise immediately to _____ percent. If real output remains constant, the quantity of real money demanded will fall to

_____.

d. Since the nominal money supply has not yet changed, the money market will remain in equilibrium only if the price level immediately changes to _____. Consequently, higher expected money growth in the future leads to <u>an increase/no change/a decrease</u> in the price level today.

8. **Inflation and the Real Return to Saving and Investment** *In this exercise, we illustrate how the taxation of nominal capital gains and nominal interest payments reduces the real return to saving and investment when there is inflation.*

a. In the United States, people pay federal income taxes on nominal interest income and nominal capital gains. Because these taxes are not indexed, inflation can affect the real return on saving and investment.

  i. If the real interest rate is equal to 2 percent and inflation is equal to 4 percent, according to the Fisher equation the nominal interest rate will equal _____ percent.

  ii. If inflation rises to 7 percent, the nominal interest rate will be _____ percent and the real interest rate will equal _____ percent.

b. The preceding formulation does not take into account taxation. In the United States, most upper-middle-income families pay a marginal federal income tax rate of about one-third, or about 33.33 percent on nominal interest income. Thus, in Part a(i) of this exercise, these families pay one-third of the _____ percent nominal interest rate in taxes, leaving an after-tax nominal interest rate of _____ percent. The after-tax *real* interest rate will equal the after-tax nominal interest rate minus the rate of inflation. Thus, the after-tax real interest rate can be computed as _____ percent – _____ percent = _____ percent.

c. In Part a(ii), the (before-tax) nominal interest rate increases/stays constant/decreases, while the before-tax real interest rate increases/stays constant/decreases. Families, however, pay one-third of the _____ percent nominal interest rate in taxes, leaving an after-tax nominal interest rate of _____ percent. The after-tax real interest rate will equal the after-tax nominal interest rate minus the rate of inflation, or _____ percent – _____ percent = _____ percent.

d. Consequently, because the U.S. tax code is *not* indexed (that is, it taxes nominal interest income rather than real interest income), inflation tends to increase/decrease the real return to savings even if the Fisher effect holds.

e. Similarly, consider an individual named Alice who purchased 100 shares of Walt Disney stock in July 1997 for $2,800, or $28 per share. In July 2011, Alice sold her stock for $3,700, or $37 per share. Her nominal capital gain is equal to the nominal value of the sale minus the nominal value of the purchase, or $_____ – $_____ = $_____. This gain represents _____ percent of the original purchase. With a tax rate of 15 percent on nominal capital gains, Alice would pay $_____ in taxes, resulting in an after-tax nominal gain of $_____, or _____ percent of the original purchase.

f. Between 1997 and 2011, however, the GDP deflator rose from 84.6 (or 0.846) to 113.3 (or 1.133). Consequently, the real value of Alice's Disney stock was $_____ in 1997 and $_____ in 2011. These amounts represented a *real before-tax* gain/loss of $_____, or _____ percent of the original real value of the purchase. Since taxes are paid on nominal gains, however, Alice's taxes on the sale of the stock remain equal to $_____. Thus, the real after-tax value of the stock sale was equal to the total receipts from the stock sale minus total taxes paid, divided by the GDP deflator, or $_____. Compared with the real value of the purchase in 1997, this amount represents a real after-tax gain/loss of $_____, or _____ percent of the original real value of the purchase. As a result of these distortions, many economists have recommended that the capital gains tax be indexed so that only real gains are taxed. (These calculations exclude the value of dividends that were paid between 1997 and 2011.)

Problems

Answer the following problems on a separate sheet of paper.

1. Consider a country with a long-run rate of growth of real GDP of 4 percent per year. Because of innovations in its finance industry, suppose the velocity of money is rising at about 2 percent per year. Use the quantity equation to calculate this country's noninflationary (i.e., zero inflation) long-run rate of growth of the money supply.

2. The official rate of inflation in Zimbabwe between 2005 and 2006 (just before the surge) was 1,281 percent. If a typical item in the Zimbabwean GDP cost 100 Zimbabwean dollars (the Zimbabwe currency) in 2005, how much did the same item cost in 2006?

3. Suppose that money demand is represented by the equation $(M/P)^d = 0.25Y$. Use the quantity equation to calculate the income velocity of money.

4. **a.** What is the inflation tax?

   b. In what ways is the inflation tax a tax, and in what ways is it not a tax?

   c. Who pays for the inflation tax?

5. **a.** Take the (natural) logarithm of the quantity equation $MV = PY$.

   b. Now, totally differentiate this logarithmic version and derive the percentage change rule—% Change in M + % Change in V = % Change in P + % Change in Y—for small percentage changes.

   c. Use the percentage change rule to show that the quantity theory holds (approximately) if V is constant.

6. Suppose that money demand is represented by the equation $(M/P)^d = i^{-0.1}Y$.

    C

    a. Use calculus to compute the income elasticity of money demand, which is the elasticity of the quantity of money demanded with respect to output Y.

    b. Use calculus to compute the interest elasticity of money demand, which is the elasticity of the quantity of money demanded with respect to the interest rate i.

7. Recall that the exact formula for calculating the real interest rate is:

    $$1 + r = (1 + i)/(1 + \pi)$$

    Multiplying both sides by $(1 + \pi)$ and rearranging yields:

    $r = i - \pi - r\pi$, which is approximately $r = i - \pi$ when π is small.

    To understand this, suppose you start with $1 and earn an interest rate of 200 percent per year.

    a. How much money would you have at the end of the year?

    b. If inflation were 100 percent per year, and the initial price level were 1.0, what would the price level be at the end of the year?

    c. Calculate the real value of your wealth at the beginning and at the end of the year.

    d. Use these real values to calculate the real interest rate and use the equation at the beginning of this problem to verify your result.

8. Congress has occasionally debated a bill that would require the Federal Reserve to "establish an explicit numerical definition of 'price stability,' and maintain a monetary policy that effectively promotes long-term price stability." For the purposes of this problem, define price stability as zero inflation.

    ○

    a. Ignoring (for now) the treatment of inflation within the current U.S. tax code, what are the costs of expected inflation?

    b. These congressmen claim that zero inflation would increase both saving and investment by raising the real return on each activity. Discuss how the way in which inflation is treated within the current U.S. tax laws on capital gains and interest income might lead to higher saving and investment if both actual and expected inflation were 0 percent rather than 2 percent. Briefly explain.

    c. If the long-run annual rate of growth of output is 3 percent, use the quantity equation (and any appropriate assumptions) to calculate the approximate eventual long-run growth rate of the money supply if the congressmen's resolution were adopted.

    d. Suppose we ignore the effects of inflation on taxes described in part b. If the Fed changed the growth rate of the money supply to this long-run growth rate immediately and people believed that it would persist, what would the immediate

       CH impact be on:

       i. expected inflation?

       ii. the nominal interest rate?

       iii. real money demand?

       iv. the price level? (Assume the nominal quantity of money M does not change.)

    e. Explain how eliminating all inflation also eliminates the "grease" for the wheels of the labor market that is mentioned in Chapter 5.

Data Questions

Locate the necessary economic data and apply them to answer the following data questions. All of the relevant data may be found in the Economic Report of the President (http://www.gpoaccess.gov/eop/).

1. a. Complete Table 5-9 with data about the various consumer price indices (CPI).

Table 5-9

(1) Year	(2) CPI All Items	(3) % Change	(4) CPI Medical Care	(5) % Change	(6) CPI Energy	(7) % Change
1969	_____		_____		_____	
		_____		_____		_____
1983	_____		_____		_____	
		_____		_____		_____
1997	_____		_____		_____	
		_____		_____		_____
2011	_____		_____		_____	

   b. If a unit of medical care (for example, a visit to the physician) cost $50 in 2011, how much did it cost in 1969?

   c. During which of the three intervals in Table 5-9 (1969–1983, 1983–1997, 1997–2011) was the rate of inflation for all items the highest?

   d. During which of the three intervals in Table 5-9 was the rate of inflation for all items the lowest?

   e. Which events might account for the unusual behavior of the energy CPI index relative to the overall index?

2. **a.** Complete Columns 2, 5, 6, 7, and 8 in Table 5-10.

Table 5-10

(1) Year	(2) Nominal GDP ($ in billions)	(3) GDP Deflator	(4) % Change in GDP Deflator	(5) M1 (Dec.) ($ in billions)	(6) % Change in M1	(7) M2 (Dec.) ($ in billions)	(8) % Change in M2
1978	_____	_____		_____		_____	
			_____		_____		_____
1988	_____	_____		_____		_____	
			_____		_____		_____
1998	_____	_____		_____		_____	
			_____		_____		_____
2008	_____	_____		_____		_____	

b. The simple quantity theory suggests that during any period of time the percentage change in the price level will be equal to the percentage change in the money supply minus the long-run growth rate of real GDP. Assume that the long-run growth rate of real GDP is about 3 percent per year, or about 34 percent per decade. Use this formula to estimate the percentage change in the GDP deflator in each of the past three decades if $M1$ is used as the measure of the money supply.

c. Now complete Columns 3 and 4 in Table 5-10 and compare the exact percentage changes with your calculations in Part b. How well does the quantity theory predict the rate of inflation during these three decades?

    d. Finally, redo your estimations in Part b using *M2* as the measure of the money supply. If one uses *M2*, how well does the simple quantity theory predict the inflation rate during these three decades?

3.   **a.** Use the data in Table 5-10 to calculate the income velocity of *M2* for 1978 and 2008. Do these figures confirm the assumption of the simple quantity theory that the velocity is relatively constant?

    b. Use the data in Table 5-10 to calculate the income velocity of *M1* for 1978 and 2008. Do these figures confirm the assumption of the simple quantity theory that the velocity is relatively constant?

    c. Show how the quantity theory can easily accommodate an income velocity that is not constant but changes steadily over time, just as it can accommodate a long-run increase in real GDP.

d. Now complete Table 5-11

Table 5-11

(1) Year	(2) Real GDP ($ in billions)	(3) % Change in Real GDP	(4) M1 (Dec.) $ in billions	(5) % Change in M1	(6) M2 (Dec.) $ in billions)	(7) % Change in M2
2008	_____		_____		_____	
		_____		_____		_____
2011	_____		_____		_____	

e. Suppose the velocity of money had not changed between 2008 and 2011. Use the actual changes in M1 and real GDP in Table 5-11 to calculate the percentage change in the GDP deflator that would have occurred between 2008 and 2011.

f. Repeat part e using the actual changes in M2 and a constant velocity of money.

g. Get the values of the GDP deflator for both 2008 and 2011 and calculate the actual percentage change.

h. What do your answers to parts e, f, and g indicate must have happened to the income velocities of both M1 and M2 during this three-year period?

Questions to Think About

1.   Many economists believe that a reduction in inflation might reduce GDP, at least temporarily. Each percentage point of GDP in the United States now represents about $150 billion per year.

   a. How much would you be willing to pay in terms of percentage points of GDP in order to reduce the long-run rate of inflation from about 2.5 percent to 1.5 percent? Explain your answer.

   b. For how many years would you be willing to pay this price? Explain your answer.

2.   According to Professor Shiller's survey, the public fears moderate rates of inflation much more than most economists do. Why do you think this is the case?

3.   Ask a parent or friend what happened to her nominal wage (or earnings) in each of the last three years. Then ask what she thinks happened to her real wage (or earnings) during the same three years. Find data on the consumer price index to see if she is right about the latter.

CHAPTER 6

The Open Economy

Fill-in Questions

Use the key terms below to fill in the blanks in the following statements. Each term may be used more than once.

balanced trade

net exports

net capital outflow

nominal exchange rate

purchasing-power parity

real exchange rate

small open economy

trade balance

trade deficit

trade surplus

world interest rate

1. The total expenditure on domestic output is the sum of consumption, investment, government purchases, and _____.

2. _____ indicates the amount domestic residents are lending abroad minus the amount foreigners are lending to us. It is equal to domestic saving minus domestic investment.

3. National income accounting tells us that $S - I$, or _____ must equal _____, where the latter is called the _____.

4. A _____ is a small part of the world market and thus, by itself, can have only a negligible effect on the world interest rate.

5. If there is free access to world financial markets, investment in all small open economies will depend on the _____.

6. The _____ is the relative price of the currency of two countries, such as 0.8 euros per U.S. dollar.

7. The _____ is the rate at which one can trade the goods of one country for the goods of another. More specifically, it measures the number of foreign goods one can exchange for one comparable domestic good. It incorporates the relative price levels of the two countries as well as the _____.

8. According to the doctrine of _____, a dollar (or any other currency) must have the same purchasing power in every country.

9. If a country's exports exceed its imports, it will have a _____. If its imports exceed its exports, it will have a _____. Finally, if its exports and imports are equal, it will have _____.

Multiple-Choice Questions

1. According to the national income accounts identity, total expenditure on domestic output is the sum of:

    a. consumption of domestic goods and services, investment in domestic goods and services, government purchases of domestic goods and services, and exports of domestic goods and services.

    b. consumption, investment, government purchases, and net exports.

    c. both a and b.

    d. domestic spending on foreign goods and expenditures on imports.

2. If national output $Y = 1,000$ and domestic spending on all domestic and foreign goods and services equals 900, net exports NX will equal:

    a. 100.   c. 1,900.

    b. −100.   d. 0.

3. The FALSE statement below is:

    a. net capital outflow is the excess of domestic saving over domestic investment.

    b. the trade surplus and net capital outflow must both equal zero.

    c. according to the national income accounts identity, net capital outflow must equal net exports.

    d. according to the national income accounts identity, net capital outflow must equal the trade surplus (or the trade balance).

4. If domestic investment exceeds domestic saving, one would observe:

    a. borrowing from abroad.   c. a trade deficit.

    b. a government budget deficit.   d. both a and c.

5. If the United States has a bilateral trade deficit with China,

    a. China must have a bilateral surplus with each of its other trading partners.

    b. the United States must have a trade surplus with all the rest of its trading partners.

    c. the United States cannot have an overall trade surplus.

    d. None of the statements is true.

6. With a constant world interest rate, full employment, and an initial trade surplus of zero, a tax cut in a small open economy will result in:

    a. a trade deficit.   c. negative net capital outflow.

    b. a reduction in national saving. d. All of the answers are correct.

7. Suppose that several large foreign countries decrease government spending, leading to a decrease in the world interest rate. In a small open economy, which of the following is most likely to happen?

    a. a decrease in saving

    b. a decrease in investment

    c. an increase in the trade deficit (or a reduction in the trade surplus)

    d. an increase in net capital outflow

8.   All the following statements may explain why capital is flowing to the United States from many poorer countries EXCEPT:

   a.   property rights are enforced more fully in the United States.
   b.   according to the Cobb–Douglas production function, additional capital will be more productive in countries with more capital per worker.
   c.   the United States may have better access to advanced technology.
   d.   corruption is less prevalent in the United States.

9.   If an iMac computer costs $2,000 in the United States, how much will it cost in Germany if the nominal exchange rate is 0.8 euros per U.S. dollar?

   a.   2,008 euros   c.   1,600 euros
   b.   2,500 euros   d.   1,800 euros

10.   Suppose a comparable computer (or any other commodity) costs $5,000 in the United States and 3,000 euros in Germany. If the nominal exchange rate is 0.8 euros per U.S. dollar, then the real exchange rate of the U.S. dollar (that is, the number of German computers that can be traded for one U.S. computer) is equal to:

   a.   0.6.   c.   1.25.
   b.   0.8.   d.   1.33.

11.   As the real exchange rate of the U.S. dollar increases:

   a.   foreign goods become cheaper to U.S. citizens.
   b.   U.S. net exports fall.
   c.   the U.S. trade surplus decreases or the U.S. trade deficit increases.
   d.   All of the answers occur.

12.   The correct relationship among net exports NX, the excess of saving over investment $S - I$, and the real exchange rate ε occurs in graph:

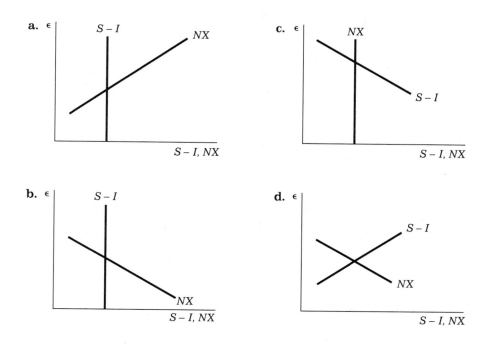

13. If the government of a small open economy increases personal income taxes, that country's:

    a. net exports increase.
    b. investment increases.
    c. equilibrium real exchange rate rises.
    d. consumption rises.

14. If the governments of several large foreign countries raise taxes:

    a. the world interest rate will rise.
    b. the domestic trade surplus will rise.
    c. the real exchange rate of the dollar will rise.
    d. domestic net exports will increase.

15. If investment demand decreases in a small open economy:

    a. the equilibrium real exchange rate rises.
    b. net exports increase.
    c. national saving increases.
    d. net capital outflow decreases.

16. In the long run, if the German government places high tariffs on all imports:

    a. Germany's net exports rise.
    b. Germany's real foreign exchange rate increases.
    c. net capital outflow in Germany decreases.
    d. All of the answers are correct.

17. Slower growth in the Japanese money supply will lead to:

    a. an increase in inflation in Japan.
    b. a decrease in inflation in the United States.
    c. a depreciation of the dollar relative to the Japanese yen.
    d. All of the answers are correct.

18. According to purchasing-power parity, if a television set sells for $500 in the United States and 2,000 yuan in China, the nominal exchange rate, expressed in yuan per dollar, is:

    a. 2.5.   c. 4.
    b. 10.   d. 1.

19. In a large open economy, an increase in government purchases or a reduction in
    Ⓐ taxes causes:

    a. an increase in the real interest rate.
    b. a reduction in net capital outflow.
    c. an increase in the real exchange rate.
    d. All of the answers are correct.

20. In a large open economy, an increase in the investment tax credit, which increases
A investment demand, will:

a. increase the real interest rate.
b. reduce net capital outflow.

c. decrease net exports.
d. do all of the above.

Exercises

1. **National Income Accounting in an Open Economy** *In this exercise, we incorporate international trade into the national income accounting identities in two alternative ways.*

a. Total purchases by U.S. households, businesses, and governments are equal to purchases of goods and services produced in the United States plus purchases of goods and services produced in other countries. Using this knowledge, complete Table 6-1.

Table 6-1

(1) Group	(2) Purchases of Goods and Services Produced in the U.S. ($ in billions)	(3) Purchases of Goods and Services Produced Elsewhere ($ in billions)	(4) Total Purchases ($ in billions)
U.S. households	$C^d = \$3{,}100$	$C^f = \$400$	$C = \$$_____
U.S. businesses	$I^d = \$\ \ 600$	$I^f = \$$_____	$I = \$\ \ 800$
U.S. governments	$G^d = \$$_____	$G^f = \$100$	$G = \$1{,}000$
Total	$$_____	$$_____	$$_____

b. Now examine the total of Column 2 of Table 6-1. $C^d + I^d + G^d$ is total domestic spending on domestic goods and services. It represents total purchases by U.S. households, businesses, and governments of goods and services that are produced in the United States. In this example, total domestic spending on domestic goods is equal to $_____ billion.

c. The total of $C^f + I^f + G^f$ (Column 3 of Table 6-1) represents total purchases by U.S. households, businesses, and governments of goods and services that are produced in foreign countries. It is more commonly called total _____. In this example, this total is equal to $_____ billion.

d. The total of $C + I + G$ (Column 4 of Table 6-1) represents total purchases by U.S. households, businesses, and governments of all goods and services, both foreign and domestic. This is sometimes called total domestic spending. In this example, it is equal to $_____ billion.

e. Recall from Chapter 2 of the textbook that Y is equal to total national output (that is, the value of the goods and services produced in the economy). In the closed economy with no foreign trade, $Y = C + I + G$. In an open economy, however, national output is not merely equal to $C + I + G$ because C, I, and G do not include foreign purchases of goods and services that are produced in the United States. These foreign purchases of U.S. goods and services represent additional expenditures on U.S. output. On the other hand, $C + I + G$ includes purchases by U.S. households, businesses, and governments of foreign production, which should not be included in U.S. output and, therefore, must be subtracted. In Table 6-1, total imports into the United States equaled $_____ billion. If total exports equal $900 billion, U.S. output can be calculated as

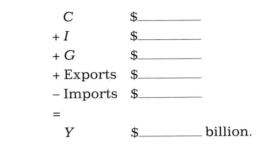

$$
\begin{array}{ll}
C & \$_____ \\
+ I & \$_____ \\
+ G & \$_____ \\
+ \text{Exports} & \$_____ \\
- \text{Imports} & \$_____ \\
= & \\
Y & \$_____ \text{ billion.}
\end{array}
$$

f. In the national income accounts, exports minus imports is often called net exports NX. In this example, $NX = \$_____$ billion.

g. There is another way to calculate Y. Total U.S. production will equal total domestic spending on domestic goods and services plus U.S. exports:

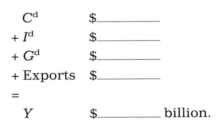

$$
\begin{array}{ll}
C^d & \$_____ \\
+ I^d & \$_____ \\
+ G^d & \$_____ \\
+ \text{Exports} & \$_____ \\
= & \\
Y & \$_____ \text{ billion.}
\end{array}
$$

2. **Net Capital Outflow and the Trade Balance** *In this exercise, we introduce net capital outflow and the trade balance, and we show how they must equal each other.*

a. According to the national income accounts, net capital outflow, or $S - I$, must equal the trade balance NX. Thus, $S - I = NX$. Recall that S represents national saving, which is the sum of private saving $Y - T - C$ and public saving $T - G$. Germany's huge exports have led to a large German trade surplus/deficit. Hence, in Germany, NX is positive/negative. Consequently, in Germany, $S - I$ is positive/negative. Therefore, the Germans will borrow/lend the difference abroad, and we say that in Germany net capital outflow will be positive/negative. Note that net capital outflow is also domestic purchases of foreign assets minus foreign purchases of domestic assets. Thus, German purchases of foreign assets are greater/less than foreign purchases of German assets.

b. For the past several years, the United States has had a trade deficit, implying that NX has been positive/negative. Consequently, in the United States, net capital outflow has been positive/negative. Thus, the United States is borrowing/lending abroad.

c. Now, complete Table 6-2:

Table 6–2

					($ in billions)				
(1)	(2)	(3)	(4)	(5)	(6)	(7)	(8) Private Saving	(9) Public Saving	(10) National Saving
Case	Y	C	I	G	NX	T			
1.	5,000	3,000	700	1,000	_____	900	_____	_____	_____
2.	5,000	3,200	900	1,000	_____	900	_____	_____	_____
3.	5,000	3,200	900	900	_____	1,000	_____	_____	_____

d. For each of the three preceding cases, calculate the trade balance and net capital outflow:

Case 1: Trade balance = $_____ billion.

Net Capital Outflow = $S – I$ = $ _____ billion.

Case 2: Trade balance = $_____ billion.

Net Capital Outflow = $S – I$ = $ _____ billion.

Case 3: Trade balance = $_____ billion.

Net Capital Outflow = $S – I$ = $ _____ billion.

e. Note in Case 2 above that a trade balance of $_____ billion can also be expressed as a trade deficit of $_____ billion.

3. **National Saving and Investment in a Small Open Economy** *In this exercise, we discuss the effects of changes in national saving and investment in a small open economy if output is fixed at full employment.*

a. Suppose that the economy is described by the following set of equations. These equations are identical to those in Exercise 6 of Chapter 3, except for the inclusion of international trade:

$$Y = \bar{Y} = F(\bar{K}, \bar{L}) = 1{,}200$$
$$Y = C + I + G + NX$$
$$C = 125 + 0.75(Y - T)$$
$$I = I(r) = 200 - 10r$$
$$G = \bar{G} = 150$$
$$T = \bar{T} = 100.$$

If the real interest rate were equal to 10 percent, then $r = 10$ and:

$C =$ _____

$I =$ _____

$G =$ _____

and, thus,

$NX =$ _____ .

Consequently, the trade balance would equal _____ .

b. Conversely,

disposable income = _____

private saving = _____

public saving = _____

national saving $S =$ _____

$S - I =$ _____

and, thus, net capital outflow would equal _____ .

c. Draw the investment and saving curves on Graph 6-1, label them I_1 and S_1, and label the initial equilibrium Point A.

Graph 6-1

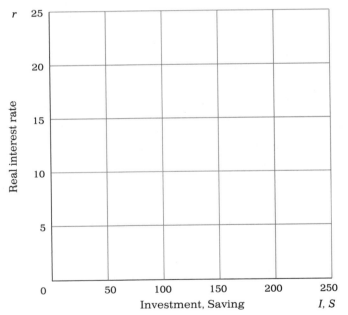

d. Now suppose that government purchases rose by 100 to 250. If Y remained equal to 1,200, this would shift the national saving curve to the <u>left/right</u> by _____ . The investment curve would <u>shift left/not shift/shift right</u>. Draw the new curve(s) on Graph 6-1 and label them I_2 and S_2.

e. If this economy were a closed economy, investment would always have to equal saving. Thus, when saving fell to _____ in Part d, investment would also fall to _____. This would be accomplished by an increase in r to _____ percent. Label the new equilibrium for this closed economy Point B.

f. Now, however, suppose this is a small open economy and the world real interest rate r^* remains equal to 10 percent both before and after the increase of 100 in government purchases. Thus, investment remains equal to _____. Following the increase in domestic government purchases, net capital outflow $S - I$ changes to _____. Consequently, the trade balance NX will change to _____. The change in net capital outflow indicates that domestic purchases of foreign assets minus foreign purchases of domestic assets will <u>rise/fall</u> by _____.

g. In the closed economy described in Chapter 3 of the textbook, a reduction in national saving leads to a(n) <u>increase/decrease</u> in the real interest rate and a(n) <u>increase/decrease</u> in investment. In a small open economy, however, a reduction in national saving <u>raises/does not change/lowers</u> the real interest rate. Consequently, investment <u>increases/does not change/decreases</u>. Instead, policies that decrease saving push net capital outflow <u>up/down</u> and the trade account toward a trade <u>surplus/deficit</u>.

h. Now suppose that we start again at $G = 150$, $I = I_1$, $S = S_1$ and the world real interest rate $r^* = 10$ percent. If domestic investment in this small open economy rose by 50 at every level of the real interest rate, the investment curve would shift to the <u>right/left</u> by 50, while the national saving curve would <u>shift to the right/not shift/shift to the left</u>. Draw the new curve(s) on Graph 6-2 and label them I_3 and S_3.

Graph 6-2

As a result of the autonomous increase in domestic investment, net capital out-flow would now equal _____, while the trade balance would now equal _____.

i.   Finally, suppose we start again at Point A and the world real interest rate rises to 15 percent. This may have occurred as a result of a decline in world saving, which, in turn, may have resulted from changes in the fiscal policies of one or more large foreign countries. These changes in foreign fiscal policy that raise the world interest rate could include a(n) increase/decrease in foreign govern-ment purchases or a(n) increase/decrease in foreign government taxes. According to Equations 6-1 to 6-6, investment I would now equal _____. (Note that this represents a movement along I_1 rather than a shift in the curve.) National saving S would increase/not change/decrease. Consequently, net capital outflow $S - I$ would now equal _____, while the trade balance NX (and the trade surplus) would equal _____. Illustrate the extent of the new level of net capital outflow on Graph 6-2 and label it $CF(r^* = 15)$.

4.   **The Nominal Exchange Rate** *In this exercise, we introduce the nominal exchange rate. We show why net exports fall as the nominal exchange rate increases when we hold the domestic and foreign price levels constant.*

Consider the trade of two mainframe computers between the United States and Germany. The IBM computer made in the United States sells for $10,000. A compa-rable computer made by Siemens in Germany sells for 15,000 euros. Although it is important to understand that net exports depend on the real exchange rate, in this exercise we assume that the price levels in both the United States and Germany remain constant. In this case, changes in the real exchange rate are reflected by changes in the nominal exchange rate.

a.   Complete Table 6-3.

Table 6-3

(1) Nominal Foreign Exchange Rate (euros per dollar)	(2) Price of IBM Computer in the U.S.	(3) Price of IBM Computer in Germany	(4) Price of Siemens Computer in Germany	(5) Price of Siemens Computer in the U.S.
1.0	$10,000	_____	15,000 euros	_____
1.5	$10,000	_____	15,000 euros	_____
2.0	$10,000	_____	15,000 euros	_____

b. Examining the numbers in Table 6-3, note that, as the nominal foreign exchange rate increases, the price of the IBM computer in Germany increases/decreases, while the price of the Siemens computer in Germany remains constant. Consequently, as the U.S. foreign exchange rate increases, U.S. exports of IBM computers will increase/decrease, assuming the price levels in both countries remain constant.

c. Similarly, as the nominal foreign exchange rate increases, the price of the IBM computer in the United States increases/remains constant/decreases, while the price of the Siemens computer in the United States increases/remains constant/decreases. Consequently, as the U.S. foreign exchange rate increases, U.S. imports of Siemens computers will increase/decrease.

d. Recall that net exports are calculated as exports/imports minus exports/imports. From Parts a–c we see that as the U.S. nominal foreign exchange rate increases, U.S. net exports increase/decrease, assuming the price levels in both countries remain constant.

e. As the nominal exchange rate of the dollar increases, it is said that the dollar has appreciated relative to the euro. Consequently, as the dollar appreciates, U.S. net exports increase/decrease. (Note: While the number of euros per dollar was less than 1.0 in 2012, it was greater than 1.0 from 2000 to 2002.)

5. **The Real Exchange Rate** *In this exercise, we allow the price levels in different countries to grow at different rates. We then show how these changes, along with changes in the nominal foreign exchange rate, are incorporated into the real exchange rate, and we illustrate its effects on net exports.*

a. Suppose that the United States now experiences 20 percent inflation while Germany's price level remains constant. As a result, the price of IBM computers in the United States rises to $12,000 while the price of Siemens computers remains equal to 15,000 euros. Complete Table 6-4.

Table 6-4

(1) Nominal Foreign Exchange Rate (euros per dollar)	(2) Price of IBM Computer in the U.S.	(3) Price of IBM Computer in Germany	(4) Price of Siemens Computer in Germany	(5) Price of Siemens Computer in the U.S.
1.5	$10,000	_____	15,000 euros	_____
1.5	$12,000	_____	15,000 euros	_____

b. Before U.S. inflation, at an initial nominal foreign exchange rate of 1.5 euros per dollar, the price of the IBM computer was greater than/equal to/less than than the price of the Siemens computer in both Germany and the United States. After the U.S. price level rises by 20 percent, however, the price of the IBM computer becomes greater than/equal to/less than the price of the Siemens computer in both countries. Consequently, U.S. net exports would increase/not change/decrease.

c. Now suppose that at the same time the nominal exchange rate falls to 1.25 euros per dollar. Complete Table 6-5.

Table 6-5

(1) Nominal Foreign Exchange Rate (euros per dollar)	(2) Price of IBM Computer in the U.S.	(3) Price of IBM Computer in Germany	(4) Price of Siemens Computer in Germany	(5) Price of Siemens Computer in the U.S.
1.50	$10,000	_____	15,000 euros	_____
1.25	$12,000	_____	15,000 euros	_____

Note that the percentage change from 1.25 euros to 1.50 euros is _____ percent while the percentage change from $10,000 to $12,000 is _____ percent. Therefore, if the nominal foreign exchange rate decreases by the same proportion as the domestic price level increases (holding the foreign price level constant), the price of the IBM computer will increase above/remain equal to/decrease below the price of the Siemens computer in both countries. Hence, net exports would increase/not change/decrease.

d. Whereas the nominal exchange rate indicates the amount of foreign currency a domestic resident gets (or a foreigner gives up) for one unit of domestic currency, the real exchange rate indicates the amount of foreign goods and services a domestic resident gets (or a foreigner gives up) for one equivalent domestic good or service. If you sell one American good, you get P, where P is the domestic (American) price level. To buy German goods you must trade these P into euros at the nominal foreign exchange rate of e, for example, 1.5 euros/$1. These $1.5 \times P$ euros will then buy $1.5P/P^*$ foreign (German) goods, where P^* equals the foreign (German) price level. The real exchange rate ε is the number of foreign goods one can buy with one domestic good. Thus,

$$\varepsilon = 1.5P/P^* = e \times (P/P^*).\qquad\text{(6-1)}$$

Use this formula to complete Table 6-6.

Table 6-6

(1) Nominal Foreign Exchange Rate (euros per dollar)	(2) U.S. Price Level	(3) German Price Level	(4) Real Foreign Exchange Rate
1.0	$10,000	15,000 euros	_____
1.5	$10,000	15,000 euros	_____
1.25	$12,000	15,000 euros	_____
1.5	$12,000	15,000 euros	_____
2.0	$10,000	15,000 euros	_____

e. Reexamining Parts a–d, we can see how net exports depend on the real foreign exchange rate. As the real foreign exchange rate rises, U.S. exports will increase/decrease, U.S. imports will increase/decrease, and U.S. net exports will increase/decrease. Remember that the real foreign exchange rate increases whenever the nominal exchange rate increases/decreases, the domestic price level increases/decreases, or the foreign price level increases/decreases.

6. **Determinants of the Real Exchange Rate in a Small Open Economy** *In this exercise, we discuss how the real exchange rate in a small open economy adjusts to equate net capital outflow and the trade surplus.*

a. The real exchange rate adjusts so that the trade surplus is equal to net capital outflow, $S - I$. Net capital outflow does not depend on the real exchange rate if the world real interest rate is constant and output remains equal to its full employment level. We have already seen, however, that the trade surplus NX increases/decreases as the real exchange rate increases.

b. Suppose that $S - I = 150$ and $NX = 250 - 100\varepsilon$. Draw these two curves on Graph 6-3 and label them $(S - I)_1$ and NX_1.

Graph 6-3

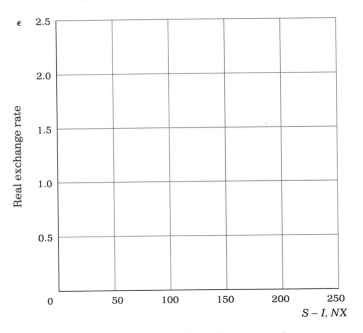

c. On Graph 6-3, net capital outflow equals _____.
Consequently, the trade surplus must equal _____, which
will occur when ε equals _____. Label this initial equilibrium Point A on Graph 6-3.

d. Now suppose that the domestic government increases government purchases by
50. This will increase/decrease national saving by _____,
while investment increases/remains the same/decreases, since the interest
rate remains equal to the world real interest rate. Consequently, net capital
outflow $S - I$ will increase/decrease by _____ to
_____. This will shift the $S - I$ curve to the left/right by
_____. Draw the new curve on Graph 6-3, label it $(S - I)_2$,
and label the new equilibrium Point B. This implies that domestic purchases of
foreign assets minus foreign purchases of domestic assets will increase/
decrease as the domestic country increases its borrowing/lending abroad.
Given the change in net capital outflow, the trade surplus must also
increase/decrease by _____ to
_____. This occurs at a new equilibrium real exchange
rate of _____. Consequently, domestic fiscal expansion, via
an increase in government purchases or a reduction in taxes, leads to a(n)
increase/decrease in the equilibrium real exchange rate.

e. Let's start again at the initial equilibrium. Redraw NX_1, $(S - I)_1$, and Point A on Graph 6-4.

Graph 6-4

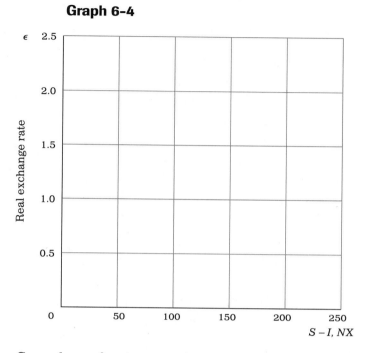

Some large foreign country now raises its taxes. This leads to a(n) increase/decrease in world saving and a(n) increase/decrease in the world real interest rate. Consequently, domestic investment would increase/decrease, $(S - I)$ would increase/decrease, and the $(S - I)$ curve would shift to the left/right. Draw the directional shift on Graph 6-4, label your new curve $(S - I)_3$, and label the new equilibrium Point B. This change would indicate a(n) increase/decrease in net capital outflow and a(n) increase/decrease in the trade surplus. To obtain this change in the trade surplus, the real exchange rate would have to rise/fall.

7. **The Nominal Foreign Exchange Rate and Purchasing-Power Parity** *In this exercise, we discuss the determinants of the nominal foreign exchange rate and purchasing-power parity.*

a. Recall that the equation for the real exchange rate is

$$\varepsilon = e \times (P/P^*).$$ (6-2)

If we multiply both sides of Equation 6-2 by P^*, we obtain

$$P^* \times \varepsilon = e \times P.$$ (6-3)

Using the percentage change rule from Chapter 2 of the textbook, we obtain

$$\% \text{ Change in } P^* + \% \text{ Change in } \varepsilon = \% \text{ Change in } e + \% \text{ Change in } P, \qquad \textbf{(6-4)}$$

or, by rearranging,

$$\% \text{ Change in } e = \% \text{ Change in } \varepsilon + \% \text{ Change in } P^* - \% \text{ Change in } P. \qquad \textbf{(6-5)}$$

Recall that the percentage change in the domestic price level is merely equal to the domestic rate of inflation π, while the percentage change in the foreign price level P^* is equal to the foreign rate of inflation π^*. Making these substitutions in Equation 6-5, complete the following equation:

$$\% \text{ Change in } e = \underline{\hspace{6cm}}. \qquad \textbf{(6-6)}$$

Assuming that changes in the real exchange rate are relatively small, this equation implies that when the domestic rate of inflation exceeds the foreign rate of inflation, the nominal exchange rate will <u>increase/decrease</u> and the U.S. dollar will <u>appreciate/depreciate</u>. Conversely, when inflation is higher abroad, the nominal exchange rate tends to <u>increase/decrease</u> and the U.S. dollar will <u>appreciate/depreciate</u>.

b. Suppose that two countries, Poland and the United States, produce only one commodity, high-quality vodka. Suppose that the Polish vodka sells in Poland for 100 zlotys per liter while the U.S. vodka sells in the United States for $20 per liter. If both countries trade on the world market and the vodkas are comparable, then their world prices must be comparable. In the United States, for example, Polish vodka must sell for $\underline{\hspace{4cm}}$ per liter, while U.S. vodka must sell for $\underline{\hspace{4cm}}$ zlotys per liter in Poland. Consequently, for each country to continue producing vodka in the long run, the exchange rate must equal $\underline{\hspace{4cm}}$ zlotys per dollar. This illustrates the concept of purchasing-power parity, which states that a dollar (or any other currency) must have the same purchasing power in every country. In this example, purchasing power is defined in terms of buying a liter of vodka. Many economists believe that purchasing-power parity is a reasonable approximation of the real-world movements in exchange rates, especially in the long run.

c. Now suppose that the U.S. money supply doubles, leading to a doubling of the U.S. price level. Consequently, a liter of American vodka will now sell for $\underline{\hspace{4cm}}$ in the United States. In Poland, on the other hand, the price level remains constant so that the price of vodka remains equal to $\underline{\hspace{4cm}}$ zlotys. For trade to persist in the long run between the two countries, the foreign exchange rate must <u>rise/fall</u> to $\underline{\hspace{4cm}}$ zlotys per dollar.

d. Let's start over and now assume that the Polish price level doubles while U.S. prices remain constant. Consequently, a liter of vodka will sell for $20 per liter in the United States and _____ zlotys per liter in Poland. For trade to persist in the long run between the two countries, the foreign exchange rate must <u>increase/decrease</u> to _____ zlotys per dollar.

e. Use the data from Parts b–d to complete Table 6-7.

Table 6-7

(1) Long-Run Nominal Foreign Exchange Rate (zlotys per dollar)	(2) U.S. Price Level	(3) Polish Price Level	(4) Long-Run Real Foreign Exchange Rate
_____	20	100	_____
_____	40	100	_____
_____	20	200	_____

Note that purchasing-power parity implies that the real foreign exchange rate is _____. For this to be true, the net export curve must be <u>vertical/horizontal</u>.

f. In the case of purchasing-power parity, ε always equals _____, so the percentage change in ε equals _____, and, from Part a, the % Change in e = _____. Thus, in this special case, <u>all/some/none</u> of the changes in the nominal exchange rate will reflect international differences in inflation rates.

8. Net Capital Outflow in a Large Open Economy *In this exercise, we examine the determinants of net capital outflow in a large open economy using the model presented in the appendix to Chapter 6 of the textbook.*

A

a. In a large open economy like the United States, the world real interest rate will change in response to that country's domestic policies. This occurs because the large country is borrowing (or lending) more than just a tiny portion of world saving, so changes in U.S. saving will have a significant effect on the international capital market. In addition, foreigners may not be willing to lend to us in unlimited amounts because of capital immobility, and the U.S. interest rate may differ from interest rates abroad. As the U.S. real interest rate rises (relative to interest rates abroad), U.S. investors will want to lend <u>more/less</u> domestically and <u>more/less</u> abroad. Similarly, foreigners will want to lend <u>more/less</u> to the United States and <u>more/less</u> to borrowers in their own countries. Recall that net capital outflow represents the amount U.S. investors lend abroad minus the amount foreigners lend to us. Consequently, as the U.S. interest rate rises, net capital outflow will <u>rise/fall</u>.

b.   Alternately, U.S. net capital outflow also reflects U.S. purchases of foreign assets, including bonds, minus foreign purchases of U.S. assets. As the U.S. interest rate rises, U.S. residents will want to purchase <u>more/fewer</u> foreign bonds and foreigners will want to purchase <u>more/fewer</u> U.S. bonds. Consequently, as U.S. interest rates rise, net capital outflow will <u>rise/fall</u>.

9.   **Equilibrium in a Large Open Economy**   *In this exercise, we illustrate the equilibrium*
Ⓐ   *conditions for a large open economy.*

Suppose that the economy is initially described by the following equations:

$$I_1 = 200 - 10r \qquad\qquad \textbf{(6-7)}$$
$$S_1 = 150 \qquad\qquad \textbf{(6-8)}$$
$$CF_1 = 100 - 5r. \qquad\qquad \textbf{(6-9)}$$

a.   Equation 6-9 represents the fact that as the domestic real interest rate in a large open economy rises, net capital outflow will <u>rise/fall</u>. To draw this curve, it is helpful to rewrite Equation 6-9 with r on the left-hand side:

$$r = \underline{\hspace{2cm}} - \underline{\hspace{2cm}} CF_1.$$

Now draw this net capital outflow curve on Graph 6-5 and label it *CF*.

Graph 6-5

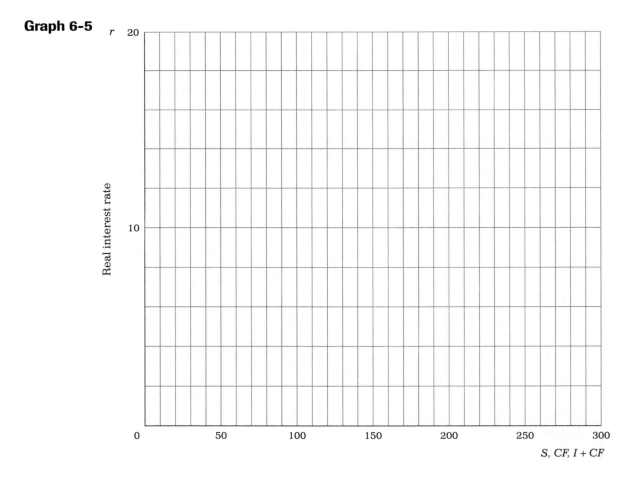

b. Recall that net capital outflow $CF = S - I$. Adding I to both sides of this equation and rearranging yields

$$S = I + CF. \qquad \text{(6-10)}$$

We write Equation 6-10 this way because both I and CF respond to changes in r, whereas S does not. Draw the S curve on Graph 6-5 and label it S. Since saving is independent of the real interest rate, the S curve is <u>vertical/negatively sloped</u>.

c. Now add Equations 6-7 and 6-9 together to derive the equation for $I + CF$:

$$I + CF = \underline{\hspace{2cm}} - \underline{\hspace{2cm}} r. \qquad \text{(6-11)}$$

Rewriting Equation 6-11 with r on the left-hand side yields

$r = \underline{\hspace{2cm}} - \underline{\hspace{2cm}} (I + CF).$

Draw this curve on Graph 6-5 and label it $I + CF$. Note that the $I + CF$ curve is <u>flatter/steeper</u> than either the I or CF curve because as the interest rate rises both I and CF will fall. Locate the initial equilibrium point at which $S = I + CF$ and label it Point A.

d. At Point A, $S = \underline{\hspace{2cm}}$ and $I + CF = \underline{\hspace{2cm}}$. Substitute this value into Equation 6-11 and solve for the equilibrium real interest rate:

$r = \underline{\hspace{4cm}}$. Now substitute this value of r into Equations 6-7 and 6-9 to obtain the equilibrium levels of I and CF:

$I = \underline{\hspace{2cm}}$ and $CF = \underline{\hspace{2cm}}$.

e. Since we also know that net capital outflow $S - I$ must equal the trade surplus NX, net exports must equal $\underline{\hspace{4cm}}$.

10. Policy Changes in a Large Open Economy *In this exercise, we use the model pre-*
A *sented in the preceding question to examine the effects of policy changes in a large*
open economy.

a. Let us now use the model presented in Exercise 9 to examine the effects of various policy changes. The three equations in that model are

$$I_1 = 200 - 10r \qquad \text{(6-12)}$$
$$S_1 = 150 \qquad \text{(6-13)}$$
$$CF_1 = 100 - 5r. \qquad \text{(6-14)}$$

Following the presentation in the textbook, draw the vertical S curve in Panel A
of Graph 6-6 and label it S_1. Now draw the CF curve in Panel B of Graph 6-6 and
label it CF. Finally, add Equations 6-12 and 6-14, derive the equation for the $I + CF$
curve, draw it in Panel A of Graph 6-6, and label it $I + CF$.

Graph 6-6

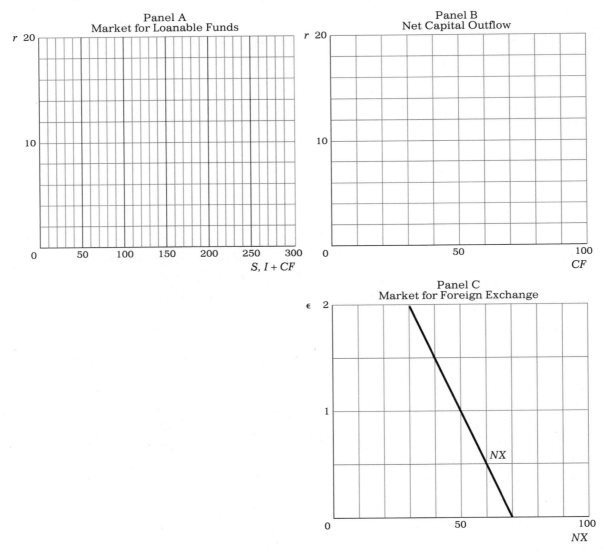

b. At the initial equilibrium, $S =$ _____ , $I + CF =$ _____ , $r =$ _____ , and $CF =$ _____ .

c. Recall that net capital outflow is assumed to be independent of the real exchange rate, whereas the trade surplus (net exports) will fall as the real exchange rate rises, as depicted in Panel C of Graph 6-6. Draw the equilibrium level of net capital outflow as a vertical line in Panel C and label it $CF\ (r = r_1)$. Since net capital outflow must equal the trade surplus, locate the original equilibrium in Panel C and label it Point A. From the graph, note that the original equilibrium value of the real exchange rate is _____ .

d. Suppose domestic government purchases rise by 30. As in earlier exercises, national saving <u>rises/falls</u> by _____ to _____, which shifts the S curve to the <u>left/right</u> by _____. Draw the new S_2 curve in Panel A of Graph 6-6 and label the new equilibrium at which $S_2 = I + CF$ Point B.

e. Since $S_2 = I + CF$, use the equations for $I + CF$, I, and CF to solve for the new levels of the equilibrium interest rate, investment, and net capital outflow:

$r =$ _____; $I =$ _____; $CF =$ _____. Locate the new value of CF in Panel B of Graph 6-6 and also label it Point B.

f. Now draw the final level of net capital outflow as a vertical line in Panel C and label it $CF\ (r = r_2)$. Label the new equilibrium Point B. As a result of the increase in government purchases, the real exchange rate <u>rises/falls</u> to

_____ .

g. In this exercise, we found that an increase in government purchases by a large open economy will <u>increase/decrease</u> national saving, <u>increase/decrease</u> the domestic real interest rate, <u>increase/decrease</u> investment, and <u>increase/decrease</u> net capital outflow. Consequently, the trade surplus NX must <u>increase/decrease</u>. For this to happen, the real exchange rate ε must <u>increase/decrease</u>.

h. If, on the other hand, an investment tax credit were enacted that increased investment at any real interest rate, the $I + CF$ curve would <u>shift right/shift left/not shift</u>, whereas the S curve would <u>shift right/shift left/not shift</u>. Consequently, the domestic real interest rate would <u>rise/fall</u>. This would <u>increase/decrease</u> net capital outflow and the trade surplus, and, consequently, the real exchange rate would <u>rise/fall</u>.

Problems

Answer the following problems on a separate sheet of paper.

1. **a.** The saving rate in the United States is low compared with many of the countries with which the United States trades. If the United States were a closed economy, how would this affect U.S. investment relative to investment in our trading partners? Explain why.

   b. The United States, of course, is not a closed economy. Consequently, our low saving rate has resulted in national saving being substantially less than investment. What effects has this had on U.S. borrowing from abroad, U.S. net capital outflow, and the U.S. trade balance?

2. **a.** During the past decade, the United States cut tax rates and increased defense spending, resulting in record budget deficits. State and explain what the effects were on:

   i. the levels of investment in Europe and Japan.

   ii. European and Japanese net capital outflow.

   iii. the European and Japanese trade balances.

   iv. the European and Japanese real exchange rates.

   b. During the same period, Belgium also experienced high budget deficits. What were the effects of the Belgian deficits on:

   i. the levels of investment elsewhere in Europe and Japan?

   ii. net capital outflow elsewhere in Europe and Japan?

   iii. the trade balances elsewhere in Europe and Japan?

   iv. the real exchange rates elsewhere in Europe and Japan?

   c. Explain why your answers to Parts a and b are different.

3. What does purchasing-power parity imply about:

   a. the nominal exchange rate between any two countries?

   b. the real exchange rate between any two countries?

   c. Explain your answers to both Parts a and b.

4. In Problem 8 of Chapter 5 in this workbook, you analyzed a congressional proposal to reduce the growth rate of the U.S. money supply. If this proposal were enacted and money growth in the United States fell substantially relative to money growth rates abroad, what would the *long-run* effect be on the:

    a. real U.S. foreign exchange rate? Use the appropriate theory to explain your answer.

    b. nominal U.S. foreign exchange rate? Use the appropriate equations and theories to illustrate and explain your answer.

5. Imagine that you are the chairman of the Federal Reserve. Assume, further, that the money supply has been growing at 3 percent per year. You have been called before Congress to testify about the long-run effects of increasing the growth of the money supply to 10 percent per year. State and then *explain* the long-run effects of this change on each of the following (give numerical estimates when possible):

    a. the annual rate of inflation

    b. the real interest rate

    c. the nominal interest rate

    d. the real exchange rate

    e. the nominal exchange rate

    f. investment (ignore both taxes and uncertainty)

    g. real GDP

6. In January, 2012 the price of a Big Mac hamburger was $4.20 in the United States and 15.42 yuan in China. Furthermore, the nominal foreign exchange rate was 6.32 yuan per dollar.

    a. Calculate the real exchange rate.

    b. If the nominal prices of Big Macs remain unchanged in both countries, what would the purchasing-power parity theory predict would eventually be:

    i. the real exchange rate. Explain.

    ii. the nominal exchange rate.

7. According to *The Economist*, Italy's past exchange rate has increased relative to Germany's real exchange rate during the past five years. How can this be true if both Italy and Germany use the euro as their currency? Explain your answer using the formula for the real exchange rate and the percentage change rule.

8. Many Americans are concerned about China's large trade surplus with the United States. They have urged the Chinese government to allow its currency, the yuan, to appreciate by acting to raise the Chinese nominal exchange rate relative to the U.S. dollar. By February, 2012, the Chinese had gradually raised their nominal exchange rate but not fast enough to satisfy many Americans.

    a. Write the formula for China's real exchange rate and identify each term.

    b. Now use the percentage change rule presented in Chapter 2 of the textbook to explain how a continued inflation in China of 4 percent will result in a lower Chinese trade surplus if U.S. inflation is 1.5 percent, even if China makes no further changes in its nominal exchange rate.

9.   **a.** Many people think that the reunification of Germany created substantial investment opportunities in what was formerly East Germany. If this is true, what would the effects be on German net capital outflow, the German trade balance, and the German foreign exchange rate?

     b. At the same time, Germany had to increase its government spending dramatically to pay for the costs of reunification. How did this development affect your answers to Part a?

10. In 2011 Congressional Democrats proposed tax increases and cuts in government spending in order to reduce the budget deficit. Throughout this problem assume (incorrectly) that the tax increases were equal to the cuts in government spending.

     a. Explain the long-run impact of this program on private saving, public saving, and national saving.

     b. Suppose the United States were a closed economy. Use the I,S diagram to illustrate what the long-run impact of this program would be on national saving, investment, and the real interest rate.

     c. Obviously, the United States is not a closed economy. Furthermore, the United States had a trade deficit (and negative net capital outflow). In 2011, the world real interest rate was about 1 percent. Illustrate this initial situation graphically using the I,S diagram.

     d. Treating the United States as a small open economy, use your graph from Part b to illustrate the long-run impact of these tax increases and (equal) cuts in government spending on national saving, investment, the real interest rate, and the trade deficit.

     e. On the appropriate graph, illustrate the effect of this program on the U.S. real exchange rate and net exports if the United States were a small open economy.

11. What does economic theory suggest is the long-run relationship between changes in a country's level of saving and its level of investment? Explain how your answer depends on whether the country is a closed economy, a small open economy, or a large open economy.

12. Suppose a presidential candidate promised to cut both taxes and government spending if elected. Suppose, too, that he promised to cut government spending by more than his proposed cut in taxes, so as to eliminate the federal budget deficit.

     a. What would the long-run effect of this plan be on public saving, private saving, and national saving?

     b. Assume the United States is a closed economy. Use a graph to compare the effects of this plan on investment and the real interest rate.

     c. Obviously, the United States is not a closed economy. Furthermore, the United States has a trade deficit (and negative net capital outflow). If the world real interest rate were about 2 percent, illustrate this initial situation graphically using the I,S diagram.

     d. Treating the United States as a small open economy, redraw your graph from Part c and illustrate the long-run impact of this plan on national saving, investment, and the real interest rate. Consequently, what happens to $S - I$?

     e. On the appropriate graph, illustrate the effect of this program on the U.S. real exchange rate and net exports if the United States were a small open economy.

13. Suppose the Republicans and Democrats in Congress proposed separate programs
that would balance the federal budget (i.e., *eliminate the existing budget deficit entirely*) within 10 years. The Republican plan would cut personal (income) taxes and dramatically reduce government expenditures (by much more than the cut in taxes). By contrast, the Democratic plan would make smaller cuts in government expenditures and practically no tax cuts. For the purposes of this problem, assume that both plans would eliminate the deficit by the same amount (i.e., entirely) at the same time.

    a. Suppose that, in the absence of these plans, budget deficits are projected to rise substantially. Relative to these projections, compare the long-run effect of *each* of the two plans on public saving, private saving, and national saving. Distinguish between (and explain) the effects of each plan when they differ, *even if the difference is in size rather than direction.*

    b. Assume the United States is a closed economy. Use a graph to compare the effects of each of the two plans on investment and the real interest rate. Label the current curves with the subscript C, the Democratic curves with the subscript D, and the Republican curves with the subscript R.

    c. Obviously, the United States does not have a closed economy. Furthermore, the United States had a trade deficit (and negative net capital outflow). Suppose the world real interest rate is about 1 percent. Illustrate this initial situation graphically using the I, S diagram.

    d. Treating the United States as a small open economy, redraw your graph from Part c and illustrate the long-run impact of *both* the Democratic and Republican plans on national saving, investment, and the real interest rate. (As before, label the current curves C, the Democratic curves D, and the Republican curves R.)

    e. On the appropriate graph, illustrate the effect of these two programs on the U.S. real exchange rate and net exports if the United States were a small open economy.

14. Consider the *small open economy* of Chile. Assume Chile has a trade surplus and the real world interest rate is 1 percent.

    a. Indicate this initial situation on an appropriately labled I, S graph and then on an appropriately labeled $(S - I), NX$ graph.

Now, suppose foreigners develop a craving for Chilean wines. Consequently, the demand for Chilean exports increases.

    b. On the same graph you drew for Part a, illustrate the effect of this change in tastes on Chile's NX curve and its real exchange rate. As a result, what happens to Chile's trade surplus?

    c. In order to assist its other industries, the Chilean government wants to adjust taxes in order to maintain the real exchange rate at its initial level.

        i. In which direction should it change taxes? (First, read Part (ii) below.)

        ii. Use a second set of graphs for a small open economy to illustrate *and state* the effects on the amounts of saving, investment, net capital outflow, net exports, and the real interest rate if foreigners develop a craving for Chilean wine and the Chilean government responds as you indicated in Part (i) to keep the real exchange rate unchanged.

15. Soon after he was elected, President Obama proposed *increases in* government spending and *decreases* in taxes. The amount of the spending increase was *not* equal to the amount of the tax decrease.

    a. Explain or show (don't just state) what the *exact* long-run impact of this program would be on:

       i. real GDP

       ii. public saving

       iii. private saving

       iv. national saving

    b. Treating the United States as a small open economy with an initial trade deficit, illustrate *and state* the long-run impact of these tax cuts and increases in government spending on national saving, investment, and the real interest rate.

    c. On the appropriate graph, illustrate *and state* the effects of this program on the United States real exchange rate and net exports if the United States were a small open economy.

    d. Obviously, the United States is a large open economy. Use the appropriate
    🅐 graphs to illustrate *and state* how President Obama's proposals to increase government spending and reduce taxes would affect national saving, investment, the domestic real interest rate, net capital outflow, net exports, and the real exchange rate.

16. In February 2012, the interest rate on 10-year bonds was 0.6 percent (per year) on Switzerland's government bonds and 1.8 percent on U.S. government bonds. Suppose the bonds for both countries were completely safe, the expected real interest rates were equal in both countries, and purchasing-power parity holds at every moment in the past, present, and future. Be as precise as you can and explain exactly what this difference in nominal interest rates (and these assumptions) implied about:

    a. expected changes in the U.S. real exchange rate vis-à-vis Switzerland.

    b. expected rates of inflation in the U.S. and Switzerland.

    c. expected changes in the U.S. nominal exchange rate vis-à-vis Switzerland.

17. Assume the United States is a large open economy. Use the appropriate graphs to
🅐 show how Congressional Democrats' 2011 proposals to increase taxes and reduce government spending would have affected national saving, investment, the real interest rate, net capital outflow, net exports, and the real exchange rate. Assume (again, incorrectly) that the tax increases were equal to the cuts in government spending.

18. Assume the United States is a large open economy. Show how the plan described in
🅐 Problem 12 to reduce taxes and government spending and eliminate the budget
🅞 deficit would affect national saving, investment, the real interest rate, net capital outflow, net exports, and the real exchange rate.

19. Suppose U.S. businesses discover that the marginal product of capital that uses the
A latest technologies is lower than they had hoped. As a result, investment demand
may decline. The United States is a large open economy with a trade deficit. Use the
appropriate graphs for a large open economy to illustrate *and state* the effects of a
decline in investment demand on each of the following: the domestic real interest
rate, national saving, the amount of investment, net capital outflow, the real
exchange rate, and net exports.

20. Many people believe that Congress will eventually have to reduce Social Security
benefits in order to reduce the budget deficit. Although most of the changes would
not take place until later, assume for the purposes of this problem that Social
Security benefits were cut today by $100 billion per year.

    a. If the marginal propensity to consume is 0.8, explain what the long-run effects
    would be on real GDP, public saving, private saving, and national saving.

    b. The United States is a large open economy with a trade deficit. Use the appro-
    A priate graphs to illustrate *and state* what the reduction in Social Security bene-
    fits would do to each of the following in the long run: national saving, investment,
    the U.S. real interest rate, net capital outflows, the real exchange rate, and the
    trade deficit.

    c. Now, consider the small open economy of Norway, which has a trade surplus. If
    the United States, a large open economy, were to reduce its Social Security ben-
    efits, use the appropriate graphs to illustrate and state what would happen in
    the long run to Norway's national saving, investment, interest rate, real
    exchange rate, and trade surplus.

21. Although the world financial crisis of 2008–2009 began in the U.S. sub-prime mort-
A gage market, it quickly spead around the world. Ironically, foreign assets became
viewed as riskier than U.S. assets. As a result, investors around the world viewed
the U.S. as a "safe haven" and increased their purchases of U.S. assets. Use the
appropriate graphs for a large open economy to illustrate and explain the theoretical long-run effects on each of the following: the U.S. real interest rate, national
saving, investment, net capital outflow, the U.S. real exchange rate, and the U.S. net
exports.

Data Questions

Locate the necessary economic data and apply them to answer the following data questions. All of the relevant data may be found in the Economic Report of the President (http://www.gpoaccess.gov/eop/).

1. **a.** Obtain the appropriate data for the United States and complete Table 6-8.

Table 6-8

(1) Year	(2) Nominal GDP ($ in billions)	(3) Exports of Goods and Services ($ in billions)	(4) Exports as a % of Nominal GDP	(5) Imports of Goods and Services ($ in billions)	(6) Imports as a % of Nominal GDP
1971	_____	_____	_____	_____	_____
1991	_____	_____	_____	_____	_____
2011	_____	_____	_____	_____	_____

b. From Table 6-8, it is clear that U.S. foreign trade has increased/decreased relative to GDP during the past 40 years. Consequently, the U.S. economy has become a more/less open economy during this period.

c. Use the data from Table 6-8 to complete Table 6-9.

Table 6-9

(1) Year	(2) Net Exports of Goods and Services ($ in billions)	(3) Net Exports as a % of Nominal GDP
1971	_____	_____
1991	_____	_____
2011	_____	_____

d. In 1971, the United States had a trade balance of $_____ billion. Ignoring official reserve transactions, which measure the purchase and sale of foreign currency by the central bank, this implies that net capital outflow in 1971 was $_____ billion.

e. In 2011, the United States had a trade balance of $_____ billion. Ignoring official reserve transactions, this implies that net capital outflow in 2011 was $_____ billion.

Unemployment

Fill-in Questions

Use the key terms below to fill in the blanks in the following statements. Each term may be used more than once.

discouraged workers
efficiency wage
frictional unemployment
insiders
labor force
natural rate of unemployment
outsiders

sectoral shift
steady state
structural unemployment
unemployment insurance
unemployment rate
wage rigidity

1. The unemployment rate is calculated as the percentage of the _____ that is unemployed.

2. The labor market reaches a(n) _____ when the _____ is constant and the flows into and out of unemployment are equal. This average rate of unemployment around which the economy fluctuates is called the _____.

3. One cause of unemployment is the change in the composition of demand among firms, industries, or regions. Economists call this change a _____.

4. The unemployment caused by the time it takes workers to search for a job is called _____. Some government policies can increase this type of unemployment. One example is _____, a government program in which unemployed workers can collect a fraction of their former wages for a certain period of time after losing their jobs.

5. _____ occurs when the real wage fails to adjust to the level at which labor supply equals labor demand. The resulting unemployment is called _____.

6. The unemployment caused by unions and by the threat of unionization is an instance of conflict between two different groups of workers—_____, such as senior union members, and _____, such as unemployed workers who would like a job in the unionized industry.

7. Some _____ theories, another cause of wage rigidity, suggest that high wages make workers more productive.

8. The official number of unemployed may underestimate the number of people who would like to work because it does not include those individuals, called _____, who may want a job but who, after an unsuccessful search, have given up looking.

Multiple-Choice Questions

1. Zero percent unemployment is an unrealistic and perhaps undesirable policy goal for all of the following reasons EXCEPT:
    a. it takes time to match jobs and workers.
    b. it would be inhumane to force the elderly to work.
    c. minimum wage laws restrict employment opportunities.
    d. some of the unemployed are unwilling to work at jobs that are available to them.

2. The main determinants of the natural rate of unemployment are the:
    a. rates of job separation and job finding.
    b. average duration of unemployment and employment.
    c. size and composition of the labor force.
    d. size and average age of the population.

3. Let L equal the size of the labor force, E the number of employed workers, and U the number of unemployed workers. The unemployment rate is equal to:
    a. $(L - E)/L$.
    c. $1 - (E/L)$.
    b. U/L.
    d. All of the answers are correct.

4. Let s denote the rate of job separation and f the rate of job finding. If the labor market is in a steady state, the natural rate of unemployment is equal to:
    a. $1/s$.
    c. $s/(s + f)$.
    b. $1/(s + f)$.
    d. $f/(s + f)$.

5. One government policy that will increase frictional unemployment is a(n):
    a. extension of job training programs.
    b. increase in unemployment insurance benefits.
    c. reduction in the minimum wage.
    d. dissemination of information about job vacancies.

6. Frictional unemployment occurs in each of the following cases EXCEPT when:

   a. there is a sectoral shift in the economy.

   b. certain firms go bankrupt.

   c. workers quit their current jobs to look for new ones in a different occupation.

   d. workers quit their current jobs and stop looking for work altogether.

7. Structural unemployment occurs when:

   a. wages are perfectly flexible.

   b. jobs are rationed.

   c. labor demand exceeds labor supply at the going wage.

   d. the labor market is perfectly competitive.

8. Economists believe that wage rigidity can be caused by:

   a. unions.

   b. minimum wage laws.

   c. efficiency wages.

   d. All of the answers are correct.

9. All of the following statements about workers who are paid the minimum wage are true EXCEPT:

   a. minimum-wage workers are more likely to be women than men.

   b. full-time workers are less likely to be paid at or below the minimum wage than part-time workers.

   c. over half of all minimum-wage workers are in the leisure and hospitality industry.

   d. minimum-wage workers are more likely to be young.

10. According to various efficiency wage theories, higher wages make workers more productive for all of the following reasons EXCEPT that higher wages:

    a. allow workers to afford more nutritious diets.

    b. attract higher-quality workers.

    c. may improve worker effort by increasing the cost of losing one's job.

    d. move people into higher tax brackets, so they have to work harder to have the same after-tax income.

11. Data on the duration of unemployment indicate that for most of the past decade:

    a. most people who become unemployed are unemployed for fewer than two months.

    b. most of the total weeks of unemployment are experienced by people who will be unemployed for more than two months.

    c. unemployed workers in Europe tend to be unemployed for longer periods of time than unemployed workers in the United States.

    d. All of the answers are correct.

12. All of the following statements about unemployment are true EXCEPT:

    a. younger workers have higher unemployment rates than older workers.

    b. unemployment rates are higher for blacks than whites.

    c. unemployment rates are higher for women than for men.

    d. groups with high rates of unemployment tend to have much higher rates of job separation than groups with low rates of unemployment rather than much lower rates of finding a job.

13. Compared with workers in the United States, Europeans typically:

    a. work fewer hours per year.

    b. are more likely to belong to a union.

    c. have higher tax rates.

    d. All of the answers are correct.

Exercises

1. **Labor-Force Movements and the Natural Rate of Unemployment** *In this exercise, we examine labor-force movements when the economy has reached its natural rate of unemployment.*

    a. The natural rate of unemployment is also the steady-state unemployment rate, the unemployment rate toward which the economy moves. Once the economy reaches this steady state, the unemployment rate tends to remain the same. Now, consider the following example: Suppose that there are 2,300 employed people in the economy and 200 unemployed people. Suppose, further, that 23 percent, or 0.23, of the unemployed find jobs each month and that 2 percent, or 0.02, of the employed lose their jobs each month.

        i. During the next month, 23 percent of the 200 currently unemployed people, or $0.23 \times 200 =$ _____ people, will find a job.

        ii. During the next month, 2 percent of the 2,300 people now employed, or $0.02 \times 2,300 =$ _____ people, will lose their jobs and become unemployed.

        iii. Consequently, at the beginning of the next month, the total number of unemployed people U will equal 200 – _____ + _____ = _____, and the total number of employed people E will equal 2,300 + _____ – _____ = _____.

        iv. Why is this situation an example of a steady-state unemployment rate?

    b. The labor force L in this example is the sum of the number of people employed plus the number unemployed, or _____.

    c. Calculate the unemployment rate u in Part a. (Remember that the unemployment rate u expressed as a percent is equal to 100 multiplied by the number of unemployed people U divided by the labor force L or $100 \times U/L$.)

d. The number of people moving out of unemployment, fU, must equal the number of people moving into unemployment, sE, at the steady state. Since employment $E = L - U$:

$$fU = sE = s(L - U) \text{ or} \tag{7-1}$$

$$fU = sL - sU. \tag{7-2}$$

Bringing all terms involving U to the left-hand side of Equation 7-2 yields:

$$(s + f)U = sL. \tag{7-3}$$

Dividing both sides of Equation 7-3 by $(s + f)L$ yields the formula for the steady-state unemployment rate:

$$\frac{U}{L} = \frac{s}{(s+f)}. \tag{7-4}$$

Perform the necessary calculations to show that the steady-state unemployment rate derived using this formula (which is the same equation used in the text-book) is identical to the unemployment rate you calculated in Part a.

2. **The Transition to a New Natural Rate of Unemployment** *In this exercise, we examine the transition to a new natural rate of unemployment when the rates of job finding and job separation change.*

   a. We use the same numbers as in Exercise 1: There are 2,300 employed people and 200 unemployed people. Suppose that the government now increases the amount of unemployment benefits paid to unemployment insurance recipients. As the textbook suggests, an increase in unemployment insurance tends to decrease the probability of the unemployed finding a job and to increase the probability of job separation. Suppose that the rate of job finding falls to 20 percent per month, while the rate of job separation rises to 3 percent per month.

   i. Use calculations similar to the ones you performed in Exercise 1a to calculate how many of the 200 currently unemployed people will find a job during the first month following the change in unemployment benefits.

ii. How many of the 2,300 people now employed will lose their jobs and become unemployed during the month?

iii. Consequently, at the beginning of the next month, the total number of unemployed U will equal _____, and the total number of employed E will equal _____.

iv. The unemployment rate at the beginning of the next month will equal $u =$ $(U/L) \times 100 =$ _____ percent.

b. Suppose that the rates of job finding and job separation remain equal to 20 percent and 3 percent, respectively.

i. During the second month following the change in unemployment benefits, how many unemployed people will find a job? (Use your answer from Exercise 2a(iii) as the initial number of unemployed and round off your answer to the nearest whole person.)

ii. How many employed people will lose their jobs and become unemployed during the second month? (Again, use your answer from Exercise 2a(iii) as the initial number of employed and round off to the nearest whole person.)

iii. Consequently, at the beginning of the third month, the total number of unemployed people U will equal _____ – _____ + _____ = _____, and the total number of employed people E will equal _____ + _____ – _____ = _____.

iv. The unemployment rate at the beginning of the third month will equal $u =$ $(U/L) \times 100 =$ _____ percent.

c. Use the formula $u = U/L = s/(s + f)$ to calculate the new steady-state natural rate of unemployment.

Problems

Answer the following problems on a separate sheet of paper.

1. a. In which two ways does unemployment insurance affect the natural rate of unemployment? Explain how each way changes the rate of unemployment.

   b. Despite its impact on the unemployment rate, the unemployment insurance program does have some beneficial effects.

      i. In which ways is the program perceived to increase overall equity (fairness)?

      ii. In which ways might the program increase overall efficiency (that is, increase real GDP)?

2. a. Explain how the elasticity of demand for low-wage workers determines the change in total wage income accruing to those workers following an increase in the minimum wage.

   b. Would policymakers be more or less likely to support higher minimum wages if economists found that the demand for low-wage workers was very inelastic? Explain.

   c. Congress has occasionally passed a subminimum wage proposal whereby young workers could be paid less than the adult minimum wage for a limited period of time. Why are minimum wage laws thought to be more onerous and less essential for teenagers than for adults?

   d. Several economists and politicians have argued that subminimum wage laws for
   CH teenagers might reduce total adult employment.

      i. Explain why these economists take this position.

      ii. Why would the effect of subminimum wage laws for teenagers and adult unemployment depend on whether adults and teenagers are substitutes or complements in production?

3. During the 1960s, most of the countries in Western Europe maintained very low rates of unemployment. In comparing the labor markets of North America and Western Europe, several economists discovered that there was considerably less mobility from employment to unemployment in Western Europe. This situation was partially the result of numerous laws in Western Europe that restricted companies' ability to lay off workers quickly.

   a. In the example given in Chapter 7 of the textbook, the probability of job finding each month was 0.20, or 20 percent, and the probability of job separation was 0.01, or 1 percent. The resulting unemployment rate was 4.76 percent. Suppose that these probabilities in Western Europe during the 1960s were 23.4 percent and 0.6 percent, respectively. Calculate the Western European natural rate of unemployment in the 1960s and compare it to the natural rate calculated in the textbook.

b. Starting in the 1970s, several changes in Western Europe altered the rates of job finding and job separation considerably, and critics claimed that these countries suffered from a "disease" they called "Eurosclerosis." Calculate the new natural rate of unemployment in Europe if the probability of job finding decreases to 9.2 percent while the probability of job separation rises to 0.8 percent.

4. **a.** Differentiate the equation for the natural rate of unemployment with respect to **C** *f*. Then show how an increase in *f* will affect that rate. Explain your answer.

   b. Now differentiate the equation for the natural rate of unemployment with respect to *s*. Then show how an increase in *s* will affect that rate. Explain your answer.

5. While it is very difficult to measure the natural rate of unemployment, the U.S. government publishes exact data every month on the overall rate of unemployment. Why do we care about the natural rate of unemployment if we have a much more precise estimate of the overall rate of unemployment?

6. The employment/population ratio is defined as the ratio of total employment to total **◻** population, expressed as a percentage, or $(E/P) \times 100$.

   a. Show the algebraic relationship among the employment/population ratio, the labor-force participation rate L/P, and the employment rate. The employment rate is equal to E/L, or 1 minus the unemployment rate u.

   b. Some economists believe that the employment/population ratio is a better measure of the economy's health than the unemployment rate. Give some reasons for supporting this position.

   c. On the other hand, many economists still believe that the unemployment rate is a better measure of the economy's health than the employment/population ratio. Give some reasons for supporting this position.

7. Explain how the elasticity of labor supply affects the reduction in the quantity of labor supplied when income tax rates increase.

8. The strength of organized labor (unions) in the United States is declining. The percentage of the labor force that is unionized has fallen below 15 percent. Since wages for a large majority of workers are determined in competitive, nonunion markets, how can it still be said that unions increase the natural rate of unemployment?

9. In January, 2012 the federal minimum wage was $7.25 per hour. Many states and several cities, however, had minimum wages in excess of the federal minimum. In San Francisco, for example, the minimum wage was $10.24 per hour.

   a. Use the graph in Figure 7-3 to explain what an economist might expect to happen to unemployment in San Francisco relative to the rest of the country.

b. In 2011, the actual unemployment rate in San Francisco was slightly below the national unemployment rate. The price level in San Francisco, however, was estimated to be about 60 percent higher in San Francisco, mainly because of higher housing costs. How do these facts affect your answer to part a?

Data Questions

Locate the necessary economic data and apply them to answer the following data questions. All of the relevant data may be found in the Economic Report of the President (http://www.gpoaccess.gov/eop/).

1. **a.** Using the appropriate data, complete Table 7-1.

Table 7-1

	Labor-Force Participation Rates (in percent)		
(1)	(2)	(3)	(4)
Year	Male and Female Civilians	Civilian Males	Civilian Females
1971	_____	_____	_____
1991	_____	_____	_____
2011	_____	_____	_____

b. How can the changes in Columns 3 and 4 during the past 40 years be explained?

c. As more women enter the labor force, the amount of household production formerly performed by housewives falls slightly. Recalling from Chapter 2 the way in which household production is treated in the national income accounts, what does this fall in household production suggest about the relationship between real GDP growth from 1971 to 2011 and the actual increase in total production? Explain your answer.

2. **a.** Define the difference between the *median* and *mean* (or average) of a group of numbers.

    b. Complete the first row of Table 7-2.

Table 7-2

(1)	(2)	(3)	(4)
Year	Unemployment Rate	Mean (Average) Duration of Unemployment (weeks)	Median Duration of Unemployment (weeks)
2006	_____	_____	_____
2011	_____	_____	_____

    c. Explain how the durations in 2006 support the typical patterns of unemployment described in Chapter 7 of the textbook.

    d. Now complete the second row of Table 7-2. According to the textbook, what does Robert Barro believe is the main cause of the dramatic increase in the duration of unemployment and the unemployment rate? What are some other possible reasons?

3. **a.** Collect the unemployment rate and rate of inflation (according to the consumer price index) and complete the first three columns of Table 7-3.

Table 7-3

(1) Year	(2) Unemployment Rate	(3) Inflation Rate	(4) Conventional Misery Index	(5) New Misery Index
2008				
2010				
2011				

b. The conventional misery index is calculated as the sum of the inflation rate plus the unemployment rate. Calculate the conventional misery index and complete Column 4 in Table 7-3.

c. As your textbook indicates, people are more concerned about unemployment than about inflation. Surveys indicate that a more accurate misery index is the sum of the inflation rate plus 1.7 times the unemployment rate. Calculate this new misery index and complete Column 5 in Table 7-3.

d. How does the use of the new misery index affect your interpretation of the changes in economic suffering during the past few years?

Questions to Think About

1. In what ways would you reform the unemployment insurance program to better achieve the dual goals of equity and efficiency?

2. Many economists favor the abolition of minimum wage laws. Do you? Why or why not?

CHAPTER 8

Economic Growth I

Fill-in Questions

Use the key terms below to fill in the blanks in the following statements. Each term may be used more than once.

Golden Rule level of capital   Solow growth model
growth effect   steady state
level effect

1. The _____ shows how saving, population growth, and technological progress affect the level of output and its growth over time.

2. In the absence of population growth, the _____ represents the long-run equilibrium of the economy, where the amount of investment equals the amount of depreciation, and the capital stock neither increases nor decreases.

3. A higher saving rate has a _____ because it affects the steady-state level of income per person but not its steady-state growth rate.

4. Polices that affect the steady-state growth rate of income per person are described as having a _____.

5. The steady-state level of capital with the highest consumption is called the

    _____.

Multiple-Choice Questions

1. The production function $Y = F(K, L)$ has constant returns to scale if:
    a. $F(zK, zL) = zY$.
    c. $zF(K, L) = Y$.
    b. $F(zK, zL) = Y$.
    d. $F(K + 1, L + 1) - F(K, L) = 1$.

2. If the production function $Y = F(K, L)$ has constant returns to scale, then:

   a. $F(zK, zL) = zY$.

   b. $F(K/L, 1) = Y/L$.

   c. $y = f(k)$, where y is output per worker and k is capital per worker.

   d. All of the answers are correct.

3. All of the following statements about the marginal product of capital MPK are true EXCEPT:

   a. $MPK = f(k + 1) - f(k)$.

   b. MPK tends to decline as k increases.

   c. when there is only a little capital, MPK is very small.

   d. MPK is equal to the slope of the production function $y = f(k)$.

4. The change in the capital stock is equal to:

   a. investment + depreciation.   **c.** investment × depreciation.

   b. investment – depreciation.   **d.** investment ÷ depreciation.

5. If capital lasts for an average of 50 years, the depreciation rate is:

   a. 50 percent, or 0.5 per year.   **c.** 0.50 percent, or 0.005 per year.

   b. 2 percent, or 0.02 per year.   **d.** 0.02 percent, or 0.0002 per year.

6. In a steady state with no population growth:

   a. the amount of capital per worker remains constant over time.

   b. investment per worker equals depreciation per worker.

   c. saving per worker equals depreciation per worker.

   d. All of the answers are correct.

7. With no population growth, the steady-state level of capital per worker will increase whenever:

   a. the amount of investment per worker decreases.

   b. the depreciation rate increases.

   c. the saving rate increases.

   d. All of the answers are correct.

8. If $y = k^{1/2}$, $s = 0.4$, and the depreciation rate $\delta = 20$ percent (or 0.20), the steady-state level of the capital stock per worker is:

   a. 4.   **c.** 2.

   b. 8.   **d.** 16.

9. At the steady state described in Question 8, the amount of saving and investment per worker is:

   a. 0.8.   **c.** 10.

   b. 1.6.   **d.** 2.

10. Suppose that a country in a steady state implements policies to increase its saving rate. After the new steady state is reached:

    a. output per worker will grow more rapidly than before.
    b. the level of output per worker will be higher than before.
    c. the amount of capital per worker will be the same as before.
    d. All of the answers are correct.

11. The Golden Rule level of capital k^*_{gold} denotes the steady state with the highest:

    a. level of consumption per worker.
    b. level of output per worker.
    c. growth rate of consumption per worker.
    d. growth rate of output per worker.

12. Excluding population growth, at the Golden Rule level of capital k^*_{gold}:

    a. $f(k^*_{gold}) = \delta k^*_{gold}$.   c. $f(k)$ reaches a maximum.
    b. $MPK = \delta$.   d. All of the answers are correct.

13. If $y = k^{1/2}$, $\delta = 5$ percent $= 0.05$, and the Golden Rule level of capital $k^*_{gold} = 100$, then the saving rate associated with the Golden Rule level of capital is:

    a. 5 percent, or 0.05.   c. 20 percent, or 0.20.
    b. 10 percent, or 0.10.   d. 50 percent, or 0.50.

14. If the current steady-state level of capital per worker is less than the Golden Rule level and the government implements policies that increase the saving rate, consumption per worker will:

    a. initially fall below the original level but will eventually rise above it.
    b. continuously rise above the original level.
    c. initially rise far above the original level and then gradually fall back toward it.
    d. continuously fall below the original level.

15. If the current steady-state level of capital per worker is greater than the Golden Rule level and the saving rate falls, consumption per worker will:

    a. initially fall below its original level but will eventually rise above it.
    b. continuously rise above its original level until the level of capital per worker reaches the Golden Rule level.
    c. initially rise far above its original level and then gradually fall until the level of capital per worker reaches the Golden Rule level.
    d. continuously fall below its original level.

16. "Break-even" investment is the amount of investment:

    a. at which economic profits are maximized.
    b. required to keep the capital stock per worker constant.
    c. at which economic profits are zero.
    d. at which the marginal product of capital is equal to its price.

17. In the Solow growth model with population growth n, the change in capital per worker is equal to:

    a. $sf(k) + (\delta + n)k$.

    c. $sf(k) - (\delta + n)k$.

    b. $sf(k) + (\delta - n)k$.

    d. $sf(k) - (\delta - n)k$.

18. An increase in the rate of population growth n will:

    a. increase the steady-state level of capital per worker.

    b. decrease the steady-state level of capital per worker.

    c. have no effect on the steady-state level of capital per worker.

    d. decrease the steady-state level of capital per worker if $\delta < n$ and increase the steady-state level if $\delta > n$.

19. The Solow growth model predicts that countries with higher population growth rates will have:

    a. lower steady-state levels of output per worker.

    b. lower steady-state growth rates of output per worker.

    c. both a and b.

    d. higher steady-state growth rates of output per worker.

20. A decrease in the rate of population growth n, like an increase in the saving rate:

    a. increases the steady-state growth rate of income per person.

    b. increases the steady-state level of income per person.

    c. decreases the steady-state growth rate of income per person.

    d. decreases the steady-state level of income per person.

21. At the Golden Rule level of capital per person with population growth:

    a. the marginal product of capital is equal to the rate of population growth.

    b. the marginal product of capital is equal to the rate of depreciation minus the rate of population growth.

    c. the marginal product of capital is equal to the rate of depreciation plus the rate of population growth.

    d. the marginal product of capital is equal to the saving rate.

22. Malthus's prediction that mankind would forever live in poverty turned out to be wrong because:

    a. Malthus did not foresee the massive technological advances in farming.

    b. Malthus did not foresee how birth control could allow people to satisfy their sexual desires without increasing the population.

    c. Malthus did not foresee that people might want to reduce the size of their families.

    d. All of the answers are correct.

23. According to Michael Kremer:

    a. Malthus will turn out to be correct after all.

    b. rapid population growth may increase economic growth.

    c. rapidly growing civilizations will eliminate each other in wars.

    d. All of the answers are correct.

Exercises

1. **The Accumulation of Capital** *In this exercise, we use a Cobb–Douglas production function to introduce the Solow growth model. You will need a calculator with a square-root key.*

    a. Consider the simple production function:

$$Y = K^{1/2} L^{1/2}. \tag{8-1}$$

For numerical simplicity, the same production function as in Chapter 8 of the textbook is used, although most of the other parameters are different. Recall from Chapter 3 of the textbook that this production function displays constant returns to scale because when all inputs double, output <u>doubles/falls by half/ remains constant</u>.

    b. Now divide Equation 8-1 by L and complete Equation 8-2, where y represents output per worker:

$$y = \frac{Y}{L} = K^{1/2}\left(\frac{L^{1/2}}{L}\right) = K^{1/2}(L)^{\underline{}} = \left(\frac{K}{L}\right)^{\overline{}} = k^{\underline{}}, \tag{8-2}$$

where $k = K/L =$ the amount of capital per worker.

    c. Use Equation 8-2 to complete Column 2 in Table 8-1.

Table 8-1

(1) Capital per Worker k	(2) Output per Worker $y = k^{1/2}$	(3) Consumption per Worker c	(4) Investment per Worker i	(5) Depreciation per Worker δk	(6) Change in Capital per Worker Δk
0	_____	_____	_____	_____	_____
4	_____	_____	_____	_____	_____
12	_____	_____	_____	_____	_____
16	_____	_____	_____	_____	_____
20	_____	_____	_____	_____	_____
36	_____	_____	_____	_____	_____

d. Plot and graph the data from Table 8-1, Columns 1 and 2, on Graph 8-1 and label the curve $f(k)$.

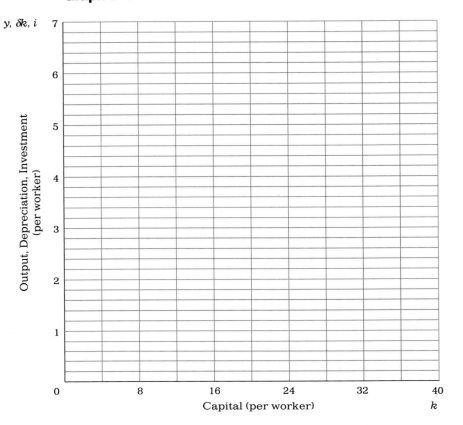

Graph 8-1

Note that the slope of this production function indicates how much extra output per worker is obtained from an extra unit of capital per worker. This amount is called the _____.

e. As in Chapter 8 of the textbook, assume that output per worker is divided between consumption per worker c and investment per worker i:

$$y = c + i. \tag{8-3}$$

Assume also that consumption per worker is a constant fraction of output per worker:

$$c = (1 - s)y, \tag{8-4}$$

where s = the saving rate. If $s = 0.20$, households save _____ percent of their income. Alternatively, if $s = 0.20$, $c = ($_____$)y$ and households consume _____ percent of their income. Use this value of s to complete Column 3 of Table 8-1.

f.   Substitute Equation 8-4 in Equation 8-3 to obtain:

$$y = (1 - s)y + i. \qquad \text{(8-5)}$$

Now solve Equation 8-5 for i.

$i =$ _____.

If $s = 0.20$, $i =$ _____ y. Use Equation 8-5 to complete Column 4 of Table 8-1. Plot and graph these points on Graph 8-1 and label the curve $sf(k)$.

g.   Although investment creates new capital per worker, part of the existing capital stock is used up or becomes obsolete each year as a result of depreciation. Let δ represent the fraction of the capital stock that wears out each year. If capital lasts for an average of 25 years, $\delta = 1/25 = 0.04$. Assume that capital lasts for an average of 20 years, so that $\delta = 1/$ _____ $=$ _____. The amount of depreciation per worker will then equal the rate of depreciation multiplied by the amount of capital per worker, or δk. Use this second value of δ to complete Column 5 of Table 8-1. Plot and graph these points on Graph 8-1, and label the curve δk.

h.   The total change in the capital stock will be equal to the additions resulting from investment minus the amount worn out because of depreciation:

$$\Delta k = i - \delta k = sf(k) - \delta k, \qquad \text{(8-6)}$$

if $s = 0.20$, $sf(k) = 0.20k^{1/2}$. If capital lasts for an average of 20 years so that $\delta =$ _____, use Equation 8-6 to solve for the change in the capital stock.

$\Delta k =$ _____ $-$ _____.

Use this expression for Δk to complete Column 6 of Table 8-1.

i. In the steady state, the amounts of capital per worker, output per worker, and consumption per worker remain constant from one year to the next. The amount of capital per worker remains constant when $\Delta k =$ _____, which occurs when $i = sf(k) = \delta k$. Locate this point on the horizontal axis of Graph 8-1 and label it k^*. At the steady-state level of capital per worker, $k^* =$ _____. Consequently, output per worker $= (k^*)^{1/2} =$ _____, consumption per worker $=$ _____, and saving per worker $=$ _____. To the right of k^* (that is, when $k > k^*$), investment is greater than/less than depreciation, so the amount of capital per worker rises/falls until it equals k^*. To the left of k^*, investment is greater than/less than depreciation, so the amount of capital per worker rises/falls until it equals k^*.

j. We can also solve for k^* algebraically, as in Chapter 8 of the textbook. In the steady state, $\Delta k = 0$, so $0 = sf(k^*) - \delta k^*$. Substitute the production function from Part b and the values for s and δ from Part h and solve for k^*.

$k^* =$ _____.

k. If households began to save a greater fraction of their incomes, s would rise. If s rises, the saving (and investment) curve on Graph 8-1 would shift upward/downward. At the old steady-state level of k^*, investment would then be greater than/less than depreciation. As a result, the amount of capital per worker would rise/fall, and the steady-state level of k^* would rise/fall. This change in k^* would increase/decrease the amount of output per worker in the steady state. Thus, a higher saving and investment rate will lead to a higher/lower steady-state level of output per worker. Once the economy reaches this new steady state, however, output per worker will increase/decrease/remain constant. Therefore, in the long run, an increase in the saving rate will increase/decrease/have no effect on an economy's growth rate. Conversely, a lower saving and investment rate will lead to a higher/lower steady-state level of output per worker but will increase/decrease/have no effect on the long-run growth rate.

2. **Moving to the Steady State** *Table 8-2 in the textbook illustrates how an economy approaches the steady state when the initial level of capital is smaller than the steady-state level. In this exercise, we illustrate how it approaches the steady state if the initial level of capital is larger than the steady-state level.*

a. Suppose the production function and relevant parameters are the same as in Exercise 1, i.e., $y = f(k) = k^{1/2}$; $c = (1-s)y = 0.8y$; $i = sy = 0.2y$; and $\delta = 0.05$. For simplicity, assume that the population growth rate $n = 0$. Suppose, furthermore, that the initial level of k is 25. Recall that the change in k, $\Delta k = i - \delta k$. Use these data to complete the first row of Table 8-2.

Table 8-2

(1) Year	(2) Capital per Worker k	(3) Output per Worker y	(4) Consumption per Worker c	(5) Investment per Worker i	(6) Depreciation per Worker δk	(7) Change in k Δk
1	25	_____	_____	_____	_____	_____
2	_____	_____	_____	_____	_____	_____
3	_____	_____	_____	_____	_____	_____
.						
.						
.						
30	_____	_____	_____	_____	_____	_____
31	_____	_____	_____	_____	_____	_____
.						
.						
.						
100	_____	_____	_____	_____	_____	_____
101	_____	_____	_____	_____	_____	_____
.						
.						
.						
∞	_____	_____	_____	_____	_____	_____

b. The amount of capital per worker in year 2 will be equal to the amount of capital per worker in year 1 plus the change in capital per worker in year 1. Using the data from Columns 2 and 7 in Table 8-2, the amount of capital per worker in year 2 will equal _____ − _____ = _____. Use this number and the information in part a to complete the second and third rows of Table 8-2. Round off to three decimal places.

c. Obviously, the amount of capital per worker will fall as long as depreciation per worker exceeds investment per worker. Using these data, the amount of capital per worker in year 30 will equal 20.063. Enter this number in Table 8-2 and complete the rows corresponding to years 30 and 31.

d. Similarly, the amount of capital per worker in year 100 will equal 16.657. Enter this number in Table 8-2 and complete the rows for years 100 and 101.

e. Eventually we reach the steady-state level of $k^* = 16$. Enter this in the last row of Table 8-2 and complete the row. When we reach the steady state, $i = \delta k$ so that Δk =_____, which is the definition of the steady state.

f. Recall that we can calculate the steady-state level of k directly since $sf(k^*) = \delta k^*$. Thus, $k^*/f(k^*) = s/\delta$. Use $f(k) = k^{1/2}$, $s = 0.2$, and $\delta = 0.05$ to solve for k^*.

$k^* =$ _____.

3. **The Golden Rule Level of Capital** *In this exercise, we use the production function and parameters from Exercise 1 to derive and illustrate the conditions for the Golden Rule level of capital.*

a. One logical goal among policymakers might be to choose the steady-state capital stock with the highest level of consumption per worker, denoted by k^*_{gold}. Although the rate of depreciation δ is typically assumed to be exogenous (fixed by external technological factors), policymakers may be able to affect the saving rate s in order to change k^*. As we saw in Exercise 1, as s increases, the steady-state level of capital per worker increases/decreases. If only steady states are considered, recall that:

$$c = y - i = f(k^*) - i = f(k^*) - \delta k^*. \tag{8-7}$$

In Equation 8-7, the condition $\Delta k = 0$ in the steady state is used so that investment equals depreciation and $i = \delta k^*$. As in Exercise 1, assume that $Y = K^{1/2}L^{1/2}$, divide Y by L, and derive the exponent on k in the equation for $y = f(k)$.

$y = f(k) = (k)^{\overline{}}$.

If k^* merely denotes certain values of k, then $f(k^*) = (k^*)^{1/2}$.

b. If it again is assumed that capital lasts an average of 20 years, $\delta = 1/20 = $ _____. Use the information from Parts a and b to complete Columns 1–4 in Table 8-3.

Table 8-3

(1) Capital per Worker k^*	(2) Output per Worker $f(k^*) = k^{*1/2}$	(3) Depreciation per Worker δk^*	(4) Consumption per Worker $c^* = f(k^*) - \delta k^*$	(5) Saving per Worker $sf(k^*) = sk^{*1/2}$
0	_____	_____	_____	_____
4	_____	_____	_____	_____
16	_____	_____	_____	_____
36	_____	_____	_____	_____
64	_____	_____	_____	_____
100	_____	_____	_____	_____
121	_____	_____	_____	_____
144	_____	_____	_____	_____

c. Plot and graph the points in Column 2 on Graph 8-2 and label the curve $f(k^*)$. Plot and graph the points in Column 3 on Graph 8-2 and label the curve δk^*. Finally, plot and graph the points in Column 4 on Graph 8-2 and label the curve c^*. Note from Graph 8-2 that consumption per worker c^* is maximized when $k^* =$ _____. Thus, the Golden Rule level of the capital stock per worker $k^*_{\text{gold}} =$ _____.

Graph 8-2

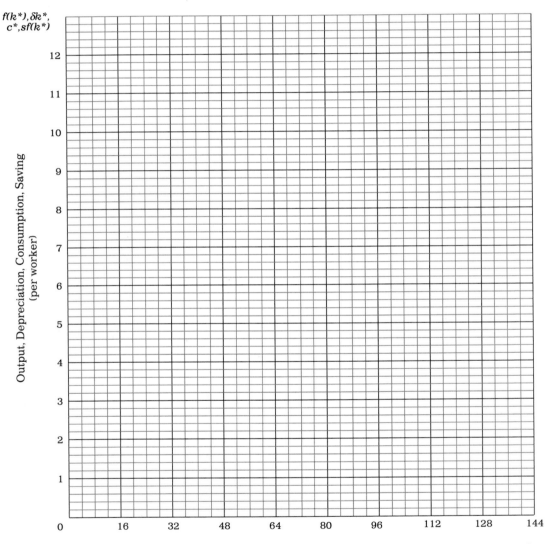

d. At this level of k^*_{gold}, depreciation equals $\delta k^*_{gold} =$ _____ and output per worker $f(k^*_{gold}) = (k^*_{gold})^{1/2} =$ _____. Since this is a steady state, $\Delta k = 0$ and investment and saving must both equal depreciation. Consequently:

$$i = sy = sf(k^*_{gold}) = \delta k^*_{gold}.$$

Substitute the values of k^*_{gold}, $f(k^*_{gold})$, and δ and calculate the Golden Rule level of s:

$s =$ _____.

Compared with the saving rate in Exercise 1 of 0.20, policymakers would have to increase/decrease the saving rate in order to achieve the Golden Rule level of capital.

e. Note that, at the Golden Rule level of k^*_{gold}, neither capital per worker nor output per worker typically is maximized. From Graph 8-2, we can see that at any levels of k^* above k^*_{gold}, the amount of depreciation δk^* is higher/lower than at k^*_{gold}. Hence, in these steady states, investment is higher/lower than at k^*_{gold}. Although output at these points is greater/less than at k^*_{gold}, there is more/less output remaining for consumption.

f. As Chapter 8 of the textbook suggests, there is an alternative way of calculating k^*_{gold}, which is easier if one knows calculus (see Problem 6 for an example). Examining Graph 8-2, consumption per worker is equal to the difference between $f(k^*)$ and δk^*. Consequently, c^* will be maximized when this difference is maximized. When k^* increases by 1 unit, δk^* increases by δ units, or by _____. When k^* increases by 1 unit, $f(k^*)$ increases by MPK units, where MPK is the marginal product of capital. At small values of k^* the slope of the $f(k^*)$ curve, which is equal to MPK, is obviously greater/less than the slope of the δk^* curve. Consequently, at small values of k^*, c^* increases/decreases as k^* is increased. At large values of k^*, the slope of the $f(k^*)$ curve is greater/less than the slope of the δk^* curve. Consequently, for large values of k^*, c^* increases/decreases as k^* is increased. Starting again at a small value of k^*, consumption per worker continues to increase as long as the slope of the $f(k^*)$ curve is greater/less than the slope of the δk^* curve. Consequently, c^* reaches a maximum when the slopes of the two curves are equal. This point occurs when $MPK = \delta$. Since $\delta =$ _____, when $k = k^*_{gold}$, $MPK =$ _____.

g. Let us verify the preceding result that $MPK =$ _____ when $k = k^*_{gold} =$
_____. MPK is defined as the change in output per worker when k increases
by 1 unit. When $k = k^*_{gold} =$ _____, $y = (k^*_{gold})^{1/2} =$ _____. When k increases by 1 unit to _____, $y = (k)^{1/2} =$ _____, so $MPK =$ _____.
Hence, the values of MPK and δ are close. The small difference is the result of
our taking a discrete (whole-unit) change in k.

h. As you discovered in Part d, the saving rate s that yielded the Golden Rule level
of capital and consumption per worker in this model was
_____. Use this value of s to complete Column 5 in Table
8-3, graph these points in Graph 8-2, and label your curve $sf(k^*)$. Note that, at
k^*_{gold}, saving per worker (which is equal to investment per worker) is <u>greater</u>
<u>than/equal to/less than</u> the amount of depreciation per worker. Thus, k^*_{gold} rep-
resents a steady-state level of the capital stock.

i. If the saving rate were higher than the rate in Part h, the $sf(k^*)$ curve would shift
<u>up/down</u> and the steady-state capital stock would be too <u>high/low</u>. If the saving
rate were lower than the rate in Part h, the $sf(k^*)$ curve would shift <u>up/down</u> and
the steady-state capital stock would be too <u>high/low</u>.

4. **Changing the Saving Rate to Reach the Golden Rule Level of Consumption** *We use*
the results of Exercises 1 and 3 to illustrate what happens when an economy changes
its saving rate to reach the Golden Rule level of consumption.

a. As in Exercises 1 and 3, suppose the production function is $y = k^{1/2}$. If the rate of
depreciation $\delta = 0.05$, we showed in Exercise 3 that the Golden Rule level of the
saving rate $s =$ _____, the Golden Rule level of the capital stock per worker
$k^*_{gold} =$ _____, the Golden Rule level of output per worker $y = (k^*_{gold})^{1/2} =$ _____
and the Golden Rule level of consumption per worker $c = (1 - s)y =$ _____.

b. In Exercise 1, we used the same production function and rate of depreciation
and found that when the saving rate was 0.2, the steady-state level of capital
per worker $k^* =$ _____ and the steady-state level of output per worker
$y = (k^*)^{1/2} =$ _____. Consequently, the level of consumption per worker at this
steady state would be $c = (1 - s)y = (1 - 0.2)$ _____ = _____. In order to
increase consumption per worker to the Golden Rule level, policymakers would
therefore have to <u>increase/decrease</u> the saving rate.

c. Suppose we begin at the steady state in Exercise 1 (and Part b above), and policymakers suddenly increase the saving rate from 0.2 to 0.5. Consumption per
worker will eventually rise from its initial steady-state level of _____ to the
Golden Rule level of _____.

d. The transition to the Golden Rule level, however, will be uncomfortable. If output per worker y initially equals 4.0 and policymakers increase the saving rate s
to 0.5, the amount of consumption per worker $c = (1 - s)y$ will immediately
change from 3.2 to $(1 - 0.5)4 =$ _____. Thus, immediately after the increase in
s, consumption per worker will <u>rise/fall</u>.

e. After the immediate increase/decrease in consumption, however, the higher saving rate will increase both k and y. In the period in which the saving rate rises to 0.5, for example, both investment and saving per worker will increase from $i = sy = 0.2(4) =$ _____ to $0.5(4) =$ _____. Since depreciation per worker $\delta k = 0.05(16) =$ _____, capital per worker will increase in the next period from its initial value of 16 to $16 + i - \delta k = 16 +$ _____ $-$ _____ $=$ _____. Consequently, in the following period, output per worker $y = k^{1/2}$ will equal _____ and consumption per worker $(1 - s)y$ will increase from 2 to $(1 - 0.5)$_____ $=$ _____. As k and y continue to increase in subsequent periods, consumption per worker will also increase until it reaches its Golden Rule level.

f. Parts c–e illustrate that when the saving rate is initially below the Golden Rule saving rate and policymakers increase it to its Golden Rule value, consumption per worker will initially rise/fall because the saving rate has risen but the amount of capital per worker has not yet increased by enough to raise consumption. Over time, however, the higher saving rate will increase/decrease the amounts of capital and output per worker, and the level of consumption per worker will gradually rise/fall until it reaches the higher Golden Rule level of consumption, as shown in Figure 8-10 in the textbook.

g. If, on the other hand, the saving rate is initially above its Golden Rule value, the transition to the Golden Rule level of consumption is more comfortable. In that case, a reduction in the saving rate to its Golden Rule level of 0.5 will immediately increase/decrease the level of consumption per worker. Since the initial levels of capital per worker and output per worker are greater than the Golden Rule levels, the level of consumption immediately after the decrease in s will also be greater/less than the Golden Rule level. The economy, however, is no longer in a steady state. Over time, the levels of capital per worker and output per worker will rise/fall to their Golden Rule levels, along with consumption.

h. As an extreme example, suppose the saving rate is initially 1.0. In the steady state, $sf(k^*) = \delta k^*$, so that

$$1.0(k^*)^{1/2} = 0.05k^*.$$

Squaring both sides of this equation yields

$$k^* = 0.0025(k^*)^2$$

Calculate the initial steady-state value of k^*:

$k^* = $ _____. Thus, the initial value of output per worker $y = (k^*)^{1/2} = $ _____, the initial level of saving per worker $sy = 1.0y = $ _____, and the initial level of consumption per worker $c = (1 - s)y = $ _____. Because society is saving (and investing) all of its output, there is nothing left over to consume. (This also illustrates how the saving rate can be too high.) If policymakers reduce the saving rate from 1.0 to the Golden Rule level of 0.5, consumption per worker at the initial level of output will immediately jump to $(1 - 0.5)y = $ _____. Note that this value is higher/lower than both the initial level of consumption and the Golden Rule level. It is not, however, a steady state. Over time, the reduction in s will lead to a higher/lower level of capital and output per worker. Consequently, after the initial increase/decrease in consumption, consumption per worker will rise/fall toward its Golden Rule level.

i. Thus, if the saving rate is initially above the Golden Rule saving rate and policymakers reduce it to the Golden Rule value, consumption will immediately rise/fall. Thereafter, however, consumption per worker will gradually rise/fall until it reaches the Golden Rule level. At all times during the transition to the Golden Rule level, however, consumption will be higher/lower than its initial level, as shown in Figure 8-9 in the textbook.

5. **Population Growth** *In this exercise, we add population growth to the Solow growth model and derive the new conditions for the steady state.*

a. Recall that k is the ratio K/L. Furthermore, recall from Exercise 5 in Chapter 2 that the percentage change of a ratio is approximately equal to the percentage change in the numerator minus the percentage change in the denominator. Suppose the amount of capital K remains constant over time (so that its percentage change equals 0), but the number of workers L grows at $n = 0.02 = 2$ percent per year. Using the ratio rule for percentage changes, the percentage change in k will then be about $0 - $ _____ $ = $ _____ percent. Consequently, k will fall by about _____ percent per year because the same amount of capital must now be spread over an increasing number of workers. If investment i is added and it is assumed, as before, that the rate of depreciation $\delta = 0.05$, the change in the capital stock per worker will now be:

$$\Delta k = i - \delta k - nk = i - 0.05k - 0.02k. \tag{8-8}$$

Note in Equation 8-8 that if i and δ both equal 0, k falls by _____ percent per year.

b. Recall that investment per worker is assumed to be a constant fraction s of output per worker. As in Exercise 1, assume that $s = 0.2$. Substituting s into Equation 8-8 yields

$$\Delta k = sf(k) - \delta k - nk = sf(k) - (\delta + n)k = 0.2f(k) - 0.07k. \tag{8-9}$$

Assume that $f(k) = (k)^{1/2}$. Use these values for s, δ, and n to complete Table 8-4.

Table 8-4

(1) Capital per Worker k	(2) Output per Worker $f(k) = k^{1/2}$	(3) Investment per Worker $sf(k)$	(4) Break-even Investment per Worker $(\delta + n)k$	(5) Change in Capital per Worker $sf(k) - (\delta + n)k$
0	_____	_____	_____	_____
4	_____	_____	_____	_____
8	_____	_____	_____	_____
16	_____	_____	_____	_____
36	_____	_____	_____	_____

c. Plot and graph Columns 2, 3, and 4 of Table 8-4 on Graph 8-3 and label the curves $f(k)$, $sf(k)$, and $(\delta + n)k$, respectively.

Graph 8-3

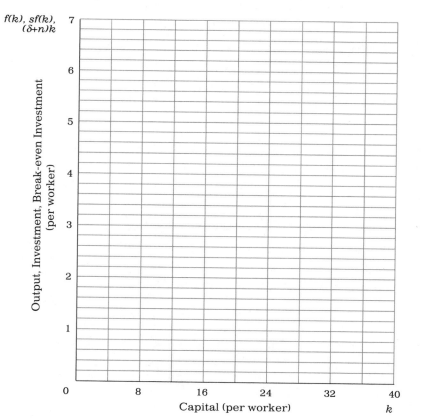

d. In the steady state, the change in the capital stock per worker equals
_____. Consequently, rearranging Equation 8-9, in the
steady state, $sf(k) =$ _____. Locate the steady-state level of
k^* on Graph 8-3 and label it Point A. Use the preceding values of s, δ, and n to
calculate k^* to within two decimal places:

$k^* =$ _____.

e. If the population growth rate increased to 3 percent per year, the $(\delta + n)k$ curve
on Graph 8-3 would <u>shift up/shift down/not shift</u>, while the $sf(k)$ curve would
<u>shift up/shift down/not shift</u>. Consequently, the steady-state capital stock per
worker would <u>increase/decrease/remain constant</u>. Thus, the Solow growth
model predicts that economies with higher population growth rates have
<u>higher/lower</u> levels of capital per worker and therefore <u>higher/lower</u> levels
of output per worker.

f. Population growth also affects the Golden Rule level of capital. Recall that
consumption per worker can be computed as

$$c = y - i. \tag{8-10}$$

Output per worker is equal to $f(k)$, and in the steady state, $\Delta k = 0$, so $i = (\delta + n)k$.
Substituting $f(k)$ and $(\delta + n)k$ into Equation 8-10 yields

$$c = f(k) - (\delta + n)k. \tag{8-11}$$

As in Exercise 3, consumption per worker is maximized when the slope of the
$f(k)$ curve, which is equal to MPK, is equal to the slope of the $(\delta + n)k$ curve, which
is equal to _____. Consequently, the Golden Rule level of
k^*_{gold} is the level of k at which the following occurs:

$MPK =$ _____ $+$ _____.   **(8-12)**

As n increases, the MPK at which the Golden Rule level is achieved
<u>increases/decreases</u>. Since MPK <u>increases/decreases</u> as k falls, this relationship
implies that an increase in n will <u>increase/decrease</u> the Golden Rule level of
capital per worker.

Problems

Answer the following problems on a separate sheet of paper.

1. Suppose that the production function is $Y = 10(K)^{1/4}(L)^{3/4}$ and capital lasts for an average of 50 years so that 2 percent of capital wears out every year. Assume that the rate of growth of population equals 0. If the saving rate $s = 0.128$, calculate the steady-state level of capital per worker, output per worker, consumption per worker, saving and investment per worker, and depreciation per worker.

2. Consider an economy in a steady state with population growth rate n and a rate of capital depreciation δ.

    a. At the steady state, $\Delta k = 0$. What condition must be met for this to hold?

    b. What is maximized at the Golden Rule level of k?

    c. What other condition must be met at the Golden Rule level of k?

3. Assume that an economy is initially in a steady state, that population growth and the rate of technological change are both zero, but that capital depreciates at rate δ. Use the appropriate graphs to illustrate <u>and explain</u> how an increase in the saving rate would affect all of the following:

    a. the steady-state capital stock per worker

    b. the steady-state level of output per worker

    c. the steady-state rate of growth of output per worker

    d. the Golden Rule capital stock per worker

    e. the rate of growth of output per worker during the transition from the initial steady state to the final steady state

4. Assume that the rate of growth of population equals 0. Suppose that there is a sudden increase in the rate at which capital depreciates. The production function remains unchanged.

    a. On a graph, illustrate the effects of this change on the steady-state level of capital per worker if the saving rate remains unchanged.

    b. Describe the effect of this change on the Golden Rule level of capital per worker, and explain your answer.

5. Consider an economy in which the rate of depreciation on capital is δ and there is no population growth. Starting from an initial steady state, suppose it experienced a long-run decline in both its saving rate and rate of depreciation.

    a. Use the appropriate graphs to illustrate what would happen to the steady-state level of capital per worker.

    b. What would happen to the Golden Rule level of capital accumulation k^*_{gold}? Illustrate and explain.

6. **C** In Chapter 3 of the text, the marginal product of capital was defined as the amount by which total output changes when capital rises by 1 unit, or $MPK = dY/dK$. In Chapter 8 of the text, MPK is equal to amount by which output per worker rises when capital per worker rises by 1 unit, or $MPK = df(k)/dk = f'(k)$, where $k = K/L$. Use calculus and the chain rule to show that the two definitions are the same.

7. Suppose that the production function is $Y = 10(K)^{1/4}(L)^{3/4}$ and that capital lasts for an
C average of 50 years. Assume that the rate of growth of population equals 0.

    a. As Chapter 8 of the textbook states, in the steady state $c = f(k^*) - \delta k^*$. Use calculus to find the Golden Rule level of capital per worker.

    b. Now, calculate the level of output per worker at this Golden Rule level, the amount of depreciation per worker, the level of investment per worker, the rate of saving per worker, and the level of consumption per worker.

8. Totally differentiate the capital–labor ratio K/L to prove that the change in the ratio,
C dk, is equal to $i - \delta k - nk$ (where i, δ, and n represent investment per worker, the rate of depreciation, and the population growth rate, respectively).

9. Assume that the current steady-state level of capital per worker is less than the Golden Rule level.

    a. What must happen to the saving rate in order to achieve the Golden Rule level?

    b. If the indicated change in the saving rate in Part a is achieved, what will happen to consumption per worker in both the short run and the long run?

    c. What kind of policies might be implemented in order to achieve this change in the saving rate?

10. Suppose a country that is initially at a steady-state level of capital per worker introduces a successful birth-control campaign that permanently reduces the growth rate of the population.

    a. Compare the initial steady state and the final steady state in terms of their:

      i. levels of capital per worker and output per worker.

      ii. growth rates of capital per worker and output per worker.

    b. What can you say about the growth rates of capital per worker and output per worker during the transition between the original and the final steady states?

11. Suppose a country has a production function that exhibits constant returns to scale. Starting from an initial steady state with population growth rate n and a rate of capital depreciation δ, the country is devastated by an epidemic (like AIDS or the Black Plague) that quickly kills half of its population without affecting its capital stock.

    a. According to the Solow growth model, what would be the immediate impact of this epidemic on total output? Explain.

    b. Explain what the Solow model implies would be the immediate impact of this epidemic on output per worker.

    c. If the saving rate is unchanged and the population regains its pre-epidemic growth rate, the economy will eventually return to its initial steady-state level of k^*. Draw three graphs with time on the horizontal axis (like the one on the next page) to illustrate the time paths of capital per worker k, consumption per worker c, and output per worker y in the initial steady state (to the left of t_0), after the epidemic strikes but before the new steady state is reached (between t_0 and t_1), and after the final steady state is reached (to the right of t_1).

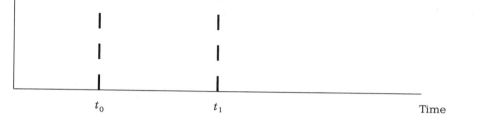

12. China's output per worker has grown very rapidly for three decades. Many people attribute this to China's high saving rate and low population growth rate. The latter is largely due to the Chinese government's policy of allowing most families to have only one child.

    a. Many observers believe that the Chinese government will enact policies to reduce China's saving rate in order to spur consumption. At the same time, China is allowing parents who both come from single-child families to have two children. Graphically illustrate how these two changes would affect China's steady-state levels of capital per worker and output per worker.

    b. Use a second graph to illustrate how these two changes would affect China's Golden Rule capital stock per worker.

Data Questions

Locate the necessary economic data and apply them to answer the following data questions. All of the relevant data may be found in the back of the Economic Report of the President *or at* (http://www.gpoaccess.gov/eop/).

1.   **a.** Calculate the *average annual* growth rate of real GDP for the United States, Germany, Japan, China, India, and sub-Saharan Africa for the following periods (for the most recent period, calculate the arithmetic average):

    1993–2002.

    2002–2011.

b. According to Table 8-1 in the textbook, GDP per capita was $47,140 in the United
CH States in 2010 and $4,260 in China. If real GDP per capita grows by 3 percent per
year in the United States and 8 percent per year in China, when will China's real
GDP per capita surpass the United States?

Economic Growth II

Fill-in Questions

Use the key terms below to fill in the blanks in the following statements. Each term may be used more than once.

creative destruction

efficiency of labor

effective workers

endogenous growth theory

human capital

labor-augmenting technological progress

technological externality

1. To introduce technological change, the Solow growth model assumes
   _____, which causes the _____ to grow
   over time.

2. The variable measuring the _____ in the production function
   depends on the health, education, skill, and knowledge of the labor force.

3. The number of _____ takes into account the number of workers
   and the efficiency of each worker. It is equal to the number of workers multiplied
   by the _____.

4. According to the Solow growth model, in the steady state, output per effective
   worker grows at the same rate as _____.

5. _____ is the knowledge and skills that workers acquire through
   education and training.

6. Although the capital variable in the Solow growth model measures only physical
   capital and the rate of _____ is usually taken as exogenous,
   research indicates that differences in _____ are at least as
   important as differences in physical capital in explaining international differences
   in standards of living.

7. A _____ exists when capital accumulation by one firm results in techno-logical advances that other firms can freely use to benefit themselves and society.

8. According to _____, the rate of technological progress is not exogenous. Many of its adherents believe that the economy can exhibit constant returns to capital, as long as capital is broadly defined to include knowledge.

9. The process of capitalist innovation by which companies with better and/or cheaper products displace existing companies is called _____.

Multiple-Choice Questions

1. The Solow growth model predicts that countries with higher population growth rates will have:
   a. lower steady-state levels of output per worker.
   b. lower steady-state growth rates of output per worker.
   c. both a and b.
   d. higher steady-state growth rates of output per worker.

2. In the Solow growth model with population growth n and labor-augmenting techno-logical progress g, the change in capital per effective worker is equal to:
   a. $sf(k) + (\delta + n + g)k$.
   b. $sf(k) + (\delta - n - g)k$.
   c. $sf(k) - (\delta + n + g)k$.
   d. $sf(k) - (\delta - n - g)k$.

3. In the Solow growth model with population growth and technological progress, the steady-state growth rate in output per *effective* worker is equal to:
   a. zero.
   b. the rate of technological progress g.
   c. the growth rate of population n plus the rate of technological progress g.
   d. the saving rate s.

4. In the Solow growth model with population growth and technological progress, the steady-state growth rate in output per worker is equal to:
   a. zero.
   b. the rate of technological progress g.
   c. the growth rate of population n plus the rate of technological progress g.
   d. the saving rate s.

5. In the Solow growth model, persistent increases in standards of living are due to:

   a. technological progress, which leads to sustained growth in output per worker.
   b. a high saving rate, which leads to sustained high rates of growth.
   c. a high rate of population growth, which leads to a larger labor force.
   d. All of the answers are correct.

6. The capital stock in the U.S. economy is well below the Golden Rule level because the net marginal product of capital, $MPK - \delta$, is:

   a. greater than zero.
   b. greater than the sum of the long-run rates of population growth and technological progress.
   c. both a and b.
   d. None of the answers are correct.

7. If the capital stock in a country is initially below the Golden Rule level of capital, the country can move toward the Golden Rule steady state by:

   a. increasing the rate of saving.
   b. reducing government expenditures on noninvestment items.
   c. Both a and b are correct.
   d. None of the answers are correct.

8. Technological progress is encouraged by:

   a. the patent system.
   b. tax incentives for research and development.
   c. government subsidies for research.
   d. All of the answers are correct.

9. Evidence concerning convergence among different countries' standards of living indicates that:

   a. unadjusted incomes per capita are not converging.
   b. incomes per capita among countries with similar cultures and policies are converging.
   c. countries with different saving rates, population growth rates, and education levels appear to be converging to different steady states.
   d. All of the answers are correct.

10. When the steady state has been reached:

    a. real wages grow at the rate of technological progress.
    b. the real rental cost of capital grows at the rate of technological progress.
    c. the number of effective workers grows at the rate of technological progress.
    d. All of the answers are correct.

11. Researchers have found that countries that permit free international trade tend to:

    a. grow more rapidly.
    b. grow more slowly.
    c. have more severe business cycles.
    d. be located near the equator.

12. Institutions that economists believe foster economic growth include:

    a. courts that uphold legal protections for shareholders and creditors.
    b. developed capital markets that facilitate borrowing and lending.
    c. governments that do not tolerate corruption.
    d. All of the answers are correct.

13. Countries that lie closer to the equator tend to:

    a. discourage free international trade.
    b. grow less rapidly than other countries.
    c. have more severe business cycles than other countries.
    d. have higher inflation rates than other countries.

14. Which of the following reasons would theoretically justify a government technology policy that encouraged investment in certain areas:

    a. a decline in the rate of investment.
    b. the identification and measurement of technological externalities in capital accumulation.
    c. a decline in the real interest rate.
    d. All of the answers are correct.

15. The worldwide slowdown in economic growth from 1972 until 1995 may be explained by:

    a. the entrance of the "baby boomers" into the workforce, which lowered the average level of experience.
    b. the depletion of the planet's natural resources.
    c. the decline in oil prices in the 1990s.
    d. All of the answers are correct.

16. Since 1995, the economic growth rate in the United States:

    a. continued the downward spiral that began in 1972.
    b. has been greater than at any other time since World War II.
    c. rebounded from the slowdown that occurred between 1972 and 1995, and then fell during the financial crisis and subsequent recession.
    d. has been close to zero.

17. In the Solow growth model, the rate of technological progress is:

    a. exogenous.
    b. endogenous.
    c. 3 percent.
    d. 0 percent.

18. Acceptance of endogenous growth theory implies:

    a. additional saving and investment can lead to persistent growth.

    b. capital may not be subject to diminishing returns if knowledge is viewed as a type of capital.

    c. the rate of technical change is endogenous.

    d. All of the answers are correct.

19. Empirical research indicates that the social rate of return to investment in research is:

    a. less than the private rate of return to investment in physical capital.

    b. about equal to the private rate of return to investment in physical capital.

    c. greater than the private rate of return to investment in physical capital.

    d. equal to the private rate of return to investment in human capital.

20. Which of the following is an example of creative destruction?

    a. Technological and design improvements in the iPhone and Android smart phones drive RIMM (the company that makes Blackberries) toward bankruptcy.

    b. Digital cameras reduce the demand for film, leading Kodak into bankruptcy.

    c. Widespread adoption of electronic readers, like the Kindle, threaten the existence of independent book stores.

    d. All of the above are examples.

21. The Solow residual is:

    A a. the change in total factor productivity.

    b. the change in output that cannot be explained by changes in inputs.

    c. an often-used measure of technological progress.

    d. All of the answers are correct.

22. Empirical studies indicate that the unusually high growth rates in Hong Kong,
    A Singapore, South Korea, and Taiwan from 1966 to 1990 were due to unusually large increases in all of the following EXCEPT:

    a. labor force participation.   c. total factor productivity.

    b. the capital stock.   d. educational attainment.

Exercises

1. **Technological Progress** *In this exercise, we incorporate technological progress into the Solow growth model.*

    a. Now, assume that each worker becomes more productive over time. To do this, we now measure the number of effective workers $L \times E$, where E grows at some constant rate g. Thus,

    $$Y = F(K, L \times E).$$ (9-1)

E measures the productive abilities of labor, which depend on health, experience, and knowledge. Recall from Exercise 5 in Chapter 2 that the percentage change of a product of two variables is approximately equal to the sum of the percentage changes in each of the variables. Thus, if the percentage change (i.e., the growth rate) in L is n and the percentage change (i.e., the growth rate) in E is g, then the percentage change in $L \times E$ (and hence the growth in the number of effective workers) is approximately equal to _____ + _____.

b. We now analyze the economy in terms of quantities per effective worker. Let $k = K/(L \times E)$ stand for capital per effective worker and $y = Y/(L \times E)$ represent output per effective worker. Thus, we can again write $y = f(k)$. Note that we can also write k as $k = (K/L)/E$. Suppose the amount of capital per worker K/L (as opposed to capital per effective worker) remains constant over time and the efficiency of labor grows by 1 percent per year. According to the percentage change approximation for a ratio, the percentage change in $k = (K/L)/E$ will then equal _____ − _____ = _____. Thus, the amount of capital per effective worker k will fall by about _____ percent per year because the same amount of capital per worker must now be spread over an increasing number of effective workers. If investment per effective worker i is added and it is assumed, as before, that the rate of depreciation $\delta = 0.05$ and the rate of population growth $n = 0.02$, the change in the capital stock per effective worker will now be:

$$\Delta k = i - \delta k - nk - gk = i - 0.05k - 0.02k - 0.01k. \tag{9-2}$$

Note in Equation 9-2 that, if i, δ, and n all equal 0 and $g = 1$ percent, k falls by _____ percent per year.

c. Investment per effective worker is assumed to be a constant fraction s of output per worker. Assume that $s = 0.2$. Substituting $sf(k)$ for i in Equation 9-2 yields:

$$\Delta k = sf(k) - \delta k - nk - gk = sf(k) - (\delta + n + g)k = 0.2f(k) - 0.08k. \tag{9-3}$$

Assume that $f(k) = (k)^{1/2}$. Use these values for s, δ, and n to complete Table 9-1.

Table 9-1

(1) Capital per Effective Worker k	(2) Output per Effective Worker $f(k) = k^{1/2}$	(3) Investment per Effective Worker $sf(k)$	(4) Break-even Investment per Effective Worker $(\delta + n + g)k$	(5) Change in Capital per Effective Worker $sf(k) - (\delta + n + g)k$
0	_____	_____	_____	_____
4	_____	_____	_____	_____
6	_____	_____	_____	_____
8	_____	_____	_____	_____
16	_____	_____	_____	_____
36	_____	_____	_____	_____

d. Plot and graph Columns 1, 2, 3, and 4 of Table 9-1 on Graph 9-1 and label the curves $f(k)$, $sf(k)$, and $(\delta + n + g)k$, respectively.

Graph 9-1

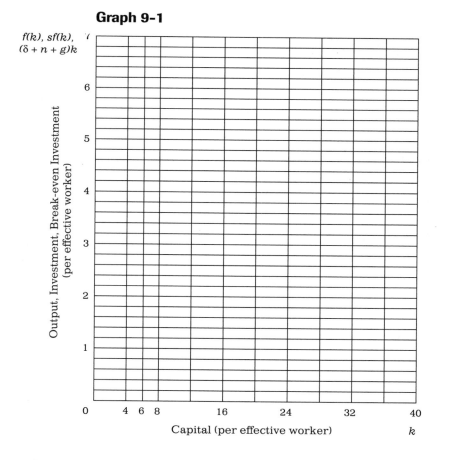

e. In the steady state, the change in the capital stock per effective worker equals
_____. Consequently, rearranging Equation 9-3, in the steady state, $sf(k)$

= _____. Locate the steady-state level of k^* in Graph 9-1 and label it Point A. Use the preceding values of s, δ, n, and g to calculate k^* to within two decimal places.

$$k^* = \underline{\hspace{3cm}}.$$

f. In the steady state, capital per effective worker is constant—that is, $\Delta k = 0$, and $sf(k) = (\delta + n + g)k$. Similarly, output per effective worker is constant. Since the number of effective workers per worker is growing at rate g, however, output per worker will grow at rate _____. Thus, in the Solow growth model, steady-state growth in output per worker depends solely on the rate of saving/depreciation/technological change.

g. Since the number of workers is growing at rate n, total output will grow at the rate of _____ + _____ .

2. **The Golden Rule with Technological Change.** *In this exercise, we see how technological change affects the Golden Rule level of capital.*

a. Technological change also affects the Golden Rule level of capital. In a world with technological progress, population growth, and capital depreciation, the Golden Rule level of capital is defined as the steady-state level of capital per effective worker that maximizes consumption per effective worker. Recall that consumption per effective worker can be computed as:

$$c = y - i \tag{9-4}$$

Output per effective worker is equal to $f(k)$, and, in the steady state, $\Delta k = 0$, so $i = sf(k) = (\delta + n + g)k$. Substituting $f(k)$ and $(\delta + n + g)k$ into Equation 9-4 yields:

$$c = f(k) - (\delta + n + g)k \tag{9-5}$$

As in Chapter 8, consumption per effective worker is maximized when the slope of the $f(k)$ curve, which is equal to MPK, is equal to the slope of the $(\delta + n + g)k$ curve, which is equal to _____. Consequently, the Golden Rule level of k^*_{gold} is the level of k at which the following occurs:

$$MPK = \underline{\hspace{2cm}} + \underline{\hspace{2cm}} + \underline{\hspace{2cm}} \tag{9-6}$$

b. Equation 9-6 can also be written as:

$$MPK - \delta = \underline{\hspace{2cm}} + \underline{\hspace{2cm}} \tag{9-7}$$

Recall that the term on the left-hand side of Equation 9-7 is called the net marginal product of capital, and the sum of the two terms on the right-hand side is equal to the growth rate of total output in the steady state.

c. Suppose the economy reaches a steady state in which the net marginal product of capital exceeds the growth rate of total output. Recall that the marginal product of capital increases/decreases as we add capital. Thus, in order to decrease the net marginal product of capital and attain the Golden Rule level of consumption, we must increase/decrease the steady-state amount of capital per effective worker by increasing/decreasing the saving rate.

d. Similarly, if the economy reaches a steady-state in which the net marginal product of capital is less than the growth rate of total output, we can attain the Golden Rule level of consumption by increasing/decreasing the steady-state amount of capital per effective worker. This can be accomplished by increasing/decreasing the saving rate.

3. **Endogenous Growth** *In this exercise, we examine a simple one-sector model to illustrate the idea of endogenous growth.*

a. Consider the simple production function:

$$Y = AK \qquad \text{(9-8)}$$

where Y is total output, K is the total capital stock, and A is a constant. Dividing both sides of Equation 9-8 by K indicates that A is equal to _____, or the amount of output produced for each unit of capital.

b. Recall that the percentage change in the product of two variables is approximately equal to the sum of the percentage changes in each of the variables. Applying this rule to Equation 9-8 yields:

$$\% \text{ Change in } Y = \% \text{ Change in } A + \% \text{ Change in } K. \qquad \text{(9-9)}$$

Since A is a constant,

$$\% \text{ Change in } Y = \text{_____} . \qquad \text{(9-10)}$$

Insofar as the percentage change in any variable X is calculated as $\Delta X/X$, we can rewrite Equation 9-10 as:

$$\text{_____} = \text{_____} . \qquad \text{(9-11)}$$

c. As before, let s be the fraction of total income that is saved and invested and let δ be the rate at which capital depreciates. Consequently, the change in the capital stock

$$\Delta K = sY - \delta K. \qquad \text{(9-12)}$$

Making this substitution for the numerator of the right-hand side of Equation 9-11 yields:

$$\Delta Y/Y = (sY - \delta K)/K = \text{_____} - \text{_____} . \qquad \text{(9-13)}$$

d. Recall from rearranging Equation 9-8 that $Y/K =$ _____ . Making this substitution in Equation 9-13 yields:

$$\Delta Y/Y = sA - \delta. \tag{9-14}$$

e. Equation 9-14 can be used to illustrate the idea behind endogenous growth theory. Note that the growth rate of output $\Delta Y/Y$ will be positive and output will grow indefinitely, even without exogenous technological progress, as long as _____ is greater than _____ . This occurs because the production function in Equation 9-8 exhibits constant, rather than diminishing, returns to capital. Advocates of endogenous growth theory believe that this assumption is reasonable if the capital stock is interpreted more broadly to include knowledge as a type of capital because knowledge may not be subject to diminishing returns. Consequently, economies that are more successful in producing knowledge may be able to sustain higher rates of economic growth, even in the long run.

4. **A Two-Sector Endogenous Growth Model** *In this exercise, we develop a simple two-sector model with endogenous growth.*

a. Consider the following Cobb–Douglas production function:

$$Y = F(K, (1 - u)LE) = K^{1/2}[1 - u)LE]^{1/2} \tag{9-15}$$

where

$Y =$ output in manufacturing

$K =$ the physical capital stock

$(1 - u) =$ the fraction of the labor force employed in manufacturing

$L =$ the labor force, and

$E =$ the efficiency of labor

If $u = 0.10$, then $(1 - u) =$ _____.

If, in addition, $K = 4$, $L = 8$, and $E = 2$, then

$Y = K^{1/2}[(1 - u)LE]^{1/2} =$ _____$^{1/2}[$_____ $\times$ _____ $\times$ _____$]^{1/2}$

Solve for manufacturing output Y.

$Y =$ _____.

b. Now, suppose that knowledge is the output of a second sector, called the university sector. Changes in the efficiency of labor E are determined by changes in the level of knowledge, which are determined by the fraction of the labor force that is employed in universities and the existing stock of knowledge;

$$\Delta E = g(u)E = uE. \tag{9-16}$$

If, for example, $u = 0.10$, then $\Delta E =$ _____ E and the growth rate of knowledge $\Delta E/E =$ _____ $=$ _____. percent per year. In this model, the growth rate of the efficiency of labor is therefore endogenously determined by the fraction of the labor force employed in universities.

c. In Part a, the number of effective workers in manufacturing is equal to $(1 - u)EL =$ _____. Suppose both the number of effective workers in manufacturing $(1 - u)EL$ and the physical capital stock double to _____ and _____, respectively. Calculate the new level of manufacturing output:

$Y =$ _____.

d. Compare your results in Parts a and c. Since the production in Equation 9-15 exhibits constant returns to scale, when both the amount of physical capital and the number of effective workers in manufacturing doubled, output quadrupled/doubled/remained constant.

e. Note that the number of effective workers in manufacturing $(1 - u)EL$ will double whenever we quadruple/triple/double any *one* of the following: the fraction of workers in manufacturing $(1 - u)$, knowledge E, or the labor force L.

f. If we interpret capital broadly to include both physical capital K and knowledge E, then when we double all capital (i.e., both K and E) output in both the manufacturing and university sectors will quadruple/double/remain constant. Consequently, this economy exhibits increasing/constant/diminishing returns to capital, broadly defined.

g. As in the Solow model, the steady-state growth of output per worker will be equal to the rate of change of the efficiency of labor, which, in this model, is the rate at which knowledge accumulates. In Part b, we found that the growth rate of E is equal to the fraction of the labor force employed in universities, or $u =$ _____ percent. Consequently, technological growth is determined endogenously in this model. Persistent growth in output per worker occurs because the creation of knowledge in universities never slows down. Furthermore, if u increases and a greater fraction of the labor force becomes employed in universities, the rate at which knowledge accumulates will increase/decrease/remain constant, and the steady-state growth of output per worker will increase/decrease/remain constant.

5. **Growth Accounting** *In this exercise, we use a Cobb–Douglas production function and*
Ⓐ *an extension of the percentage change rule that is discussed in Chapter 2 of the textbook to derive the formula for the growth in total factor productivity.*

a. Consider the following Cobb–Douglas production function:

$$Y = AK^{\alpha}\, L^{1-\alpha} = AK^{0.3}\, L^{0.7}. \qquad \textbf{(9-17)}$$

An extension of the percentage change rule presented in Chapter 2 of the textbook can be used to derive an equation for the approximate percentage change in Y:

$$\% \text{ Change in } Y = \% \text{ Change in } A + \alpha \times (\% \text{ Change in } K) +$$
$$(1 - \alpha) \times (\% \text{ Change in } L) =$$
$$\% \text{ Change in } A + \underline{\hspace{1.5in}} \times (\% \text{ Change in } K) + \qquad \textbf{(9-18)}$$
$$\underline{\hspace{1.5in}} \times (\% \text{ Change in } L).$$

The first term on the right-hand side of Equation 9-18, % Change in A, is commonly called the *percentage change in total factor productivity*. It measures increases in Y that occur over time even if the amounts of capital and labor remain constant. Equation 9-18 states that the percentage change in output over time is equal to the percentage change in total factor productivity plus 0.3 times the percentage change in capital plus 0.7 times the percentage change in labor. The coefficients on the changes in capital and labor are precisely equal to their exponents in the Cobb–Douglas production function.

b. Use Equation 9-18 to solve for total factor productivity growth if $\alpha = 0.3$:

% Change in $A = \underline{\hspace{2.5in}}.$

c. Now, use these results along with the data from Table 9-3 of the textbook to confirm the estimate of annual total factor productivity growth for the United States between 1948 and 2010. In this period, the annual growth rates of output, capital, and labor were 3.4, 3.3, and 1.7 percent, respectively. Consequently, the estimated annual growth rate of total factor productivity during this period was %

Change in $A =$ _____ − _____ − _____ = _____ percent.

Problems

Answer the following problems on a separate sheet of paper.

1. Suppose that the production function is $Y = 10(K)^{1/4}(EL)^{3/4}$ and capital lasts an average of 10 years so that 10 percent of capital wears out every year. Assume that the rate of growth of population is 4 percent, the rate of technological growth is 2 percent, and the saving rate $s = 0.128$.

    a. Derive the equation for output per effective worker $y = Y/EL = f(k)$, where k equals the amount of capital per effective worker.

    b. Calculate the steady-state levels for each of the following: capital per effective worker, output per effective worker, consumption per effective worker, saving and investment per effective worker, and depreciation per effective worker.

    c. Now, calculate the steady-state growth rates of capital per worker, output per worker, saving and investment per worker, and consumption per worker.

    d. Finally, calculate the steady-state growth rates of capital, output, saving and investment, and consumption.

2. Suppose that output per effective worker assumed the following values:

    Period 1:   100

    Period 2:   100

    Period 3:   100

    Period 4:   120

    Period 5:   132

    Period 6:   138.8

    Period 7:   138.8

    Period 8:   138.8

    a. Draw a graph with Periods 1–8 on the horizontal axis and the value of output per effective worker in each period on the vertical axis.

    b. Assume that the data refer to the value of output per worker at the beginning of that period. Draw a second graph with Periods 1–7 on the horizontal axis and the growth rate of output per effective worker during each period on the vertical axis.

3. Consider an economy in a steady state with population growth rate n, a rate of capital depreciation δ, and a rate of labor-augmenting technological progress g.

    a. At the steady state, $\Delta k = 0$, where k equals capital per effective worker. What condition must be met for this to hold? Describe the condition in words as well as symbols.

    b. Describe in words what is maximized at the Golden Rule level of k.

    c. What other condition must be met at the Golden Rule level of k?

4. Suppose the production function is $Y = 10(K)^{1/4}(EL)^{3/4}$ and capital lasts an average of 10 years. Assume that the rate of growth of population is 4 percent and the rate of technological growth is 2 percent. The marginal product of capital can be expressed as $MPK = 2.5\,(k)^{-3/4}$, where k is the level of capital per effective worker.

    a. Derive the equation for output per effective worker $y = Y/EL = f(k)$, where k equals the amount of capital per effective worker.

    b. Calculate the Golden Rule level of capital per effective worker and the saving rate associated with this steady state.

    c. Calculate all of the following at their Golden Rule levels: output per effective worker, saving and investment per effective worker, and consumption per effective worker.

5. In Chapter 3 of the textbook, the marginal product of capital was defined as the amount by which total output changes when capital rises by 1 unit, or $MPK = dY/dK$. In Chapter 9 of the text, MPK is equal to the amount by which output per effective worker rises when capital per effective worker rises by 1 unit, or $MPK = df(k)/dk = f'(k)$, where $k = K/EL$. Use calculus and the chain rule to show that the two definitions are the same.

6. As in Problems 1 and 4, suppose the production function is $Y = 10(K)^{1/4}(EL)^{3/4}$ and capital lasts an average of 10 years. Assume once more that the rate of growth of population is 4 percent and the rate of technological growth is 2 percent.

    a. Derive the equation for output per effective worker $y = Y/EL = f(k)$, where k equals the amount of capital per effective worker.

    b. Use calculus to derive the marginal product of capital $MPK = f'(k)$.

    c. In the steady state, consumption per effective worker,

       $c = f(k) - (\delta + n + g)k.$

    Use calculus to derive the condition for the Golden Rule level of k and solve.

7. Totally differentiate the ratio of capital to effective labor $k = K/(E \times L)$ to prove that the change in the ratio dk is equal to $i - \delta k - nk - gk$, where i, δ, n, and g represent investment per effective worker, the rate of depreciation, the population growth rate, and the rate of technological progress, respectively.

8. Consider an economy in a steady state with population growth rate n, a rate of capital depreciation δ, and a rate of labor-augmenting technological progress g.

   a. Use the appropriate graphs to illustrate and explain how an increase in the saving rate would affect the steady-state capital stock per effective worker.

   b. Draw three graphs with time on the horizontal axis (like the one below) to illustrate the time paths of capital per effective worker k, output per effective worker y, and output per worker in the initial steady state (to the left of t_0), after the saving rate is increased but before the new steady state is reached (between t_0 and t_1), and after the final steady state is reached (to the right of t_1).

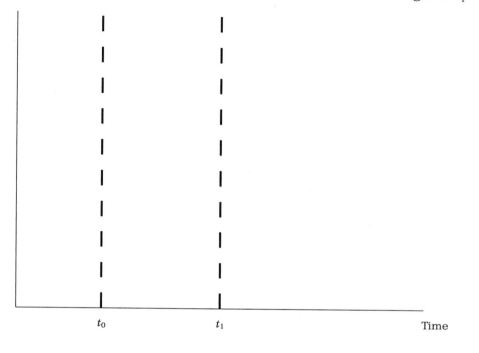

9. Suppose that a country is initially operating at a steady-state level of capital per worker and is able to double its rate of labor-augmenting technological progress.

   a. What will happen to its steady-state level of capital per effective worker?

   b. Consequently, what can one say about the growth rates of capital per effective worker and output per effective worker on the path to the new steady state?

   c. At the new steady state, what can we say about the growth rates of capital per effective worker, consumption per effective worker, and output per effective worker?

   d. Comparing the initial and final steady states, what happens to the growth rates of capital, output, and consumption *per worker*?

10. Consider an economy in which the rate of depreciation on capital is δ, population growth is n, and the rate of technological change is g.

    a. Use the appropriate graph to illustrate the initial steady-state level of capital per effective worker k_1^*.

b. At this steady state, what are the growth rates of capital per effective worker, output per effective worker, output per worker, and total output?

c. Now use the same graph to illustrate and then state what would happen to the steady-state level of capital per effective worker if both the saving rate and the rate of technological change increased.

d. Draw another graph to illustrate the initial golden-rule level of capital accumulation per effective worker k^*_{gold}.

e. On the graph you drew for part d illustrate and state what the increase in the saving rate and the rate of technological change would do to the golden-rule level of capital accumulation per effective worker k^*_{gold}.

11. In each of the following cases, determine whether the level of the capital stock per effective worker is above, below, or at the Golden Rule steady state:

a. The country of Fertilia has a population growth rate of 4 percent and a rate of technological progress of 3 percent. Capital income is 30 percent of GDP, the depreciation of capital is 12 percent of GDP, and the capital stock is 3 times one year's GDP.

b. The country of Begonia has a steady-state growth rate of real GDP of 4 percent per year. Capital typically lasts for 20 years, and the marginal product of capital is 9 percent of the value of each unit of capital.

12. Suppose that the production function is $Y = AK^{0.3}L^{0.7}$.

A a. If total factor productivity grows at 2 percent per year and both the capital stock and the number of workers grow at 1 percent per year each, calculate the growth rate of output.

b. If the rate of capital accumulation doubles to 2 percent per year, calculate the new growth rate of output.

Questions to Think About

1. Can countries differ in their rates of technological progress over long periods of time? Why can't lagging countries simply adopt the more advanced technologies?

2. In the Solow growth model with technological progress, the Golden Rule criterion maximizes the level of consumption per efficiency unit. Is this the ethically correct criterion for policymakers? If the capital stock is now below the Golden Rule steady state, reaching the Golden Rule requires a sacrifice by current generations for the benefit of future generations. Technological progress, however, will automatically make future generations richer because each person will be born with more efficiency units. Should policymakers ask current generations to sacrifice some of their consumption to benefit their richer descendants?

3. How would one measure the "stepping on toes" and "standing on shoulders" effects?

CHAPTER 10

Introduction to Economic Fluctuations

Fill-in Questions

Use the key terms below to fill in the blanks in the following statements. Each term may be used more than once.

aggregate demand

aggregate supply

demand shock

index of leading economic indicators

Okun's law

recession

stabilization policy

stagflation

sticky wages and prices

supply shock

1. If real GDP is falling and unemployment is rising, the economy is likely to be in a

   _____ .

2. _____ depicts a negative relationship between the percentage change in GDP and the change in the unemployment rate.

3. The _____ is composed of 10 data series that signal future changes in real output. If it is falling, it may signal a future _____ .

4. According to the classical model, in the long run, wages and prices are perfectly flexible and monetary policy affects only nominal variables, not real variables. In the short run, however, monetary policy appears to have a potent effect on output and employment because of _____ .

5. The _____ curve depicts a relationship between the quantity of output demanded and the aggregate price level.

6. In the long run, output is determined by technology and the amount of capital and labor. Consequently, in the long run, the _____ curve is vertical, and shifts in _____ affect the price level but do not affect output or employment.

7. _____ occurs when output falls and prices rise simultaneously.

8. When the Federal Reserve changes the money supply to offset an adverse supply or demand shock and to keep output and employment at their natural levels, this is an example of a _____.

9. A sharp, sudden increase in the price of oil is an example of a _____. The expanded availability of credit cards may be viewed as a _____.

Multiple-Choice Questions

1. The FALSE statement about economic fluctuations is:
   a. real GDP in the United States has generally increased over time, but it fluctuates around its average rate of growth.
   b. economists sometimes call the fluctuations in output and employment the *business cycle*.
   c. the fluctuations in output and employment are regular and predictable.
   d. during the recession of 1982, real GDP fell and the unemployment rate rose.

2. A recession occurs whenever:
   a. the Business Cycle Dating Committee declares a recession.
   b. the unemployment rate increases.
   c. real GDP falls for two successive quarters.
   d. real GDP falls from one year to the next.

3. Which of the following components of GDP is the most volatile over the business cycle?
   a. consumption
   b. investment
   c. government spending
   d. net exports

4. Okun's law depicts a relationship between the:
   a. percentage change in real GDP and the change in the unemployment rate.
   b. percentage change in nominal GDP and the change in the labor force.
   c. absolute change in real GDP and the percentage change in the unemployment rate.
   d. absolute change in real GDP and the percentage change in the GDP deflator.

5. Suppose the unemployment rate at the beginning of the year is 5 percent. According to Okun's law, all of the following will happen EXCEPT:
   a. if the unemployment rate is unchanged during the year, real GDP tends to rise by 3 percent.
   b. if the average unemployment rate for the year rises to 7 percent, real GDP tends to fall by 1 percent in that year.
   c. if the average unemployment rate for the year falls to 3 percent, real GDP tends to rise by 7 percent in that year.
   d. if the average unemployment rate for the year stays at 5 percent, real GDP remains constant.

6. Suppose the index of leading economic indicators falls. Economic forecasters will expect all of the following to occur EXCEPT:

   a. the unemployment rate will rise.

   b. the growth rate of real output will decrease.

   c. inflation will increase.

   d. the growth rate of tax revenue will decrease.

7. Economists generally believe that:

   a. wages and prices are flexible in the long run.

   b. wages and prices are sticky in the short run.

   c. output moves toward its full employment level in the long run.

   d. All of the answers are correct.

8. The FALSE statement about the aggregate demand curve is:

   a. for a fixed money supply, the quantity equation yields a negative relationship between the price level P and output Y.

   b. the aggregate demand curve has a negative slope.

   c. when the Federal Reserve increases the money supply, the economy moves along a stationary aggregate demand curve, real output increases, and the price level decreases.

   d. the money supply is held constant as the economy moves along a stationary aggregate demand curve.

9. The graph that shows the effect of a decrease in the money supply is:

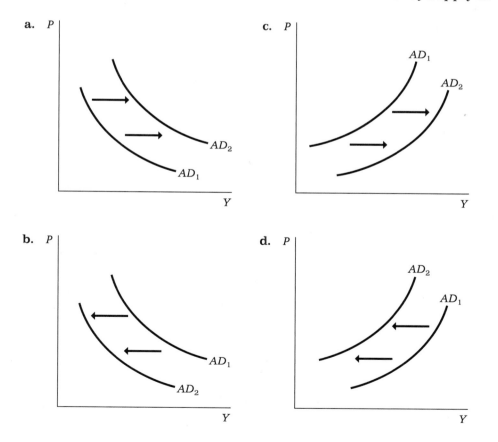

10. The long-run effects of an increase in the money supply include:

    a. an increase in the price level but no change in output.

    b. an increase in output but no change in the price level.

    c. an increase in both the price level and output.

    d. no change in either the price level or output.

11. If prices are fixed in the short run but perfectly flexible in the long run, then:

    a. the long-run aggregate supply curve will be vertical.

    b. the short-run aggregate supply curve will be horizontal.

    c. changes in the money supply will affect output in the short run but not in the long run.

    d. All of the answers are correct.

12. In the short run, suppose that *all* prices are stuck at some predetermined level. The effect of a reduction in the money supply in the short run can be seen in graph:

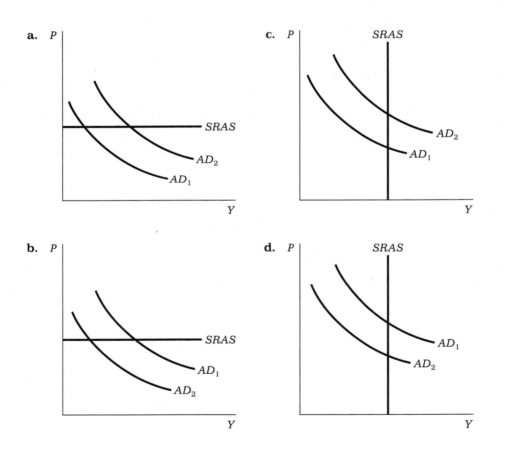

13. If the economy is originally at its long-run equilibrium level and then its aggregate demand curve shifts to the left, the path of the economy is shown in graph:

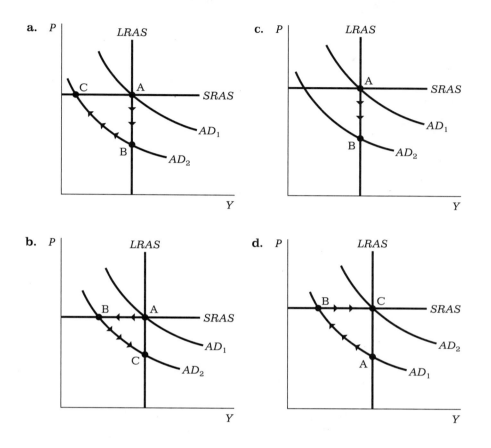

14. The introduction of credit cards results in all of the following EXCEPT a(n):

    a. increase in money demand.
    b. increase in the velocity of money.
    c. shift to the right in the aggregate demand curve.
    d. increase in output in the short run.

15. If there is an unusually good harvest and food prices fall, we will experience a(n):

    a. adverse supply shock.
    b. upward shift in the short-run aggregate supply curve.
    c. downward shift in the short-run aggregate supply curve.
    d. shift in the aggregate demand curve.

16. When the Fed uses stabilization policy to offset the decline in output following an adverse supply shock, the point on the following graph at which the economy will stabilize is:

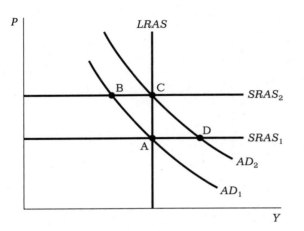

   a. A
   b. B
   c. C
   d. D

Exercises

1. **Okun's Law** *In this section, we introduce and use Okun's law.*

   Okun's law depicts a pattern between real GDP and unemployment that has been observed over a long period of time. If the unemployment rate stays constant from one year to the next, real GDP tends to increase by 3 percent because of normal increases in the labor force, capital stock, and improvements in technology. Furthermore, for every percentage point increase in the unemployment rate, real GDP growth falls by 2 percent. In equation form,

   Percentage change in real GDP = 3% − 2 × (percentage point increase in unemployment). **(10-1)**

   a. Suppose that the unemployment rate is initially 5 percent. If it doesn't change during the year, real GDP growth will equal 3% − 2 ×
   _____ = _____ percent.

b. If the unemployment rate increases to 6 percent, it will have increased by
_____ percentage point. Consequently, real GDP will rise
by 3% – 2 × _____ = _____ percent. If,
on the other hand, the unemployment rate increases from 5 percent to 7 percent, real GDP will rise by 3% – 2 × _____ =
_____ percent; that is, real GDP will fall by
_____ percent.

c. Finally, suppose that the unemployment rate starts at 5 percent and decreases
by 2 percentage points to _____ percent. This is equivalent
to an increase of _____ percentage points. Consequently,
real GDP will rise by 3% – 2 × _____ = 3% +
_____ = _____ percent.

2. **The Quantity Equation and the Aggregate Demand Curve** *In this exercise, we use the
quantity equation to derive the aggregate demand curve. We then illustrate how
changes in the money supply and the velocity of money affect the aggregate demand
curve.*

   a. The quantity equation is $MV = PY$, where M equals the money supply, V equals
   the velocity of money, P is the aggregate price level, and Y is real GDP. Assume
   the money supply is fixed at $M = 1{,}000$ and the velocity of money is fixed at
   $V = 2.0$ and complete Table 10-1.

Table 10-1

(1) M	(2) V	(3) PY	(4) P	(5) Y
1,000	2.0	_____	2.0	_____
1,000	2.0	_____	1.5	_____
1,000	2.0	_____	_____	2,000
1,000	2.0	_____	0.8	_____
1,000	2.0	_____	_____	4,000

   b. Plot on Graph 10-1 the data in Columns 4 and 5 of Table 10-1. Draw the aggregate demand curve that results when $M = 1{,}000$ and $V = 2.0$ and label your curve
   AD_1.

Graph 10-1

c. The aggregate demand curve depicts the relationship between the quantity of output demanded and the aggregate price level. As the price level falls, the quantity of output demanded <u>rises/falls</u>, holding the quantity of money and the velocity of money constant.

d. Suppose that the money supply increases to 1,500, while velocity remains equal to 2.0. Complete Table 10-2.

Table 10-2

(1) M	(2) V	(3) P	(4) Y
1,500	2.0	2.0	_____
1,500	2.0	1.5	_____
1,500	2.0	1.0	_____
1,500	2.0	0.8	_____
1,500	2.0	0.5	_____

e. Plot the data in Columns 3 and 4 of Table 10-2 on Graph 10-1. Draw the aggregate demand curve that results when $M = 1,500$ and $V = 2.0$ and label your curve AD_2.

f. Suppose that the money supply remained at its original level of 1,000, but the velocity of money increased to 3.0. The numbers in Columns 3 and 4 of Table 10-2 would then be <u>greater/the same/smaller</u>. Thus, either an increase in the money supply or a(n) <u>increase/decrease</u> in the velocity of money shifts the aggregate demand curve to the <u>right/left</u>.

g. Suppose that the money supply fell to 500 while velocity remained equal to 2.0. Complete Table 10-3.

Table 10-3

(1) M	(2) V	(3) P	(4) Y
500	2.0	2.0	_____
500	2.0	1.5	_____
500	2.0	1.0	_____
500	2.0	0.8	_____
500	2.0	0.5	_____

h. Plot on Graph 10-1 the data in Columns 3 and 4 of Table 10-3. Draw the aggregate demand curve that results when $M = 500$ and $V = 2.0$ and label your curve AD_3.

i. Suppose that the money supply remained at its original level of 1,000, but the velocity of money decreased to 1.0. The numbers in Columns 3 and 4 of Table 10-3 would be <u>greater/the same/smaller</u>. Thus, either a decrease in the money supply or a(n) <u>increase/decrease</u> in the velocity of money shifts the aggregate demand curve to the <u>right/left</u>.

3. **The Long-Run Aggregate Supply Curve** *In this exercise, we introduce the long-run aggregate supply curve and discuss the long-run effects of shifts in aggregate demand.*

a. Suppose that the economy is operating at its natural level (that is, at full employment) when $Y = 2,000$. In the long run, wages and prices are completely flexible and the economy achieves its natural level of output. Consequently, in the long run, we know that $Y =$ _____ but that the aggregate price level can take on any value, depending on monetary policy. Plot this relationship on Graph 10-2 and label it *LRAS*.

Graph 10-2

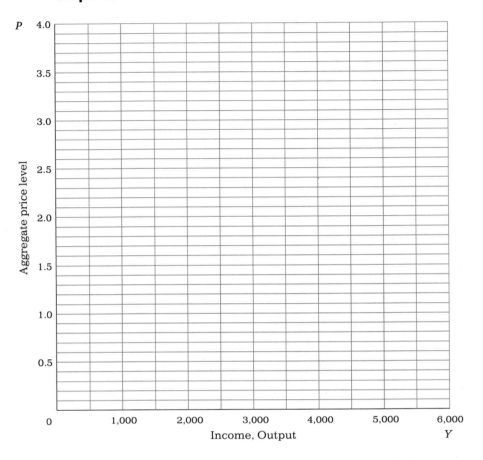

b. Redraw the aggregate demand curve AD_1 from Exercises 2a and 2b on Graph 10-2, and label the initial equilibrium levels of output and prices Y_1 and P_1, respectively.

c. Suppose that the money supply increases to 1,500, as in Exercise 2d. This will shift the aggregate demand curve to the <u>right/left</u>. Draw AD_2 from Exercise 2d on Graph 10-2 and label the new long-run equilibrium levels of output and prices Y_2 and P_2, respectively.

d. The long-run aggregate supply curve is <u>horizontal/upward sloping/vertical</u>. Consequently, increases in the money supply or in the velocity of money will <u>increase/not change/decrease</u> the aggregate price level in the long run, while they will <u>increase/not change/decrease</u> real GDP in the long run. This occurs because, in the long run, wages and prices increase or decrease in order to maintain output at its natural level. In Exercise 2d, the increase in the money supply to $M = 1,500$ would <u>increase/decrease</u> the price level to $P =$ _____ in the long run.

e. Now suppose that the money supply decreases to 500, as in Exercise 2g. This will shift the aggregate demand curve to the <u>right/left</u>. Draw AD_3 from Exercise 2g on Graph 10-2 and label the new long-run equilibrium levels of output and prices Y_3 and P_3, respectively.

f. A decrease in the money supply or a(n) <u>increase/decrease</u> in the velocity of money will <u>increase/not change/decrease</u> the aggregate price level in the long run, while it will <u>increase/not change/decrease</u> real GDP in the long run. Once again, this occurs because, in the long run, wages and prices increase or decrease in order to maintain output at its natural level.

4. **The Short-Run Aggregate Supply Curve and the Transition to the Long Run** *In this exercise, we introduce the short-run aggregate supply curve and discuss both the short-run and long-run effects of shifts in aggregate demand.*

a. Suppose that the economy is operating at its natural level when $Y = 2,000$, as in Exercise 3. In the long run, wages and prices are completely flexible, and $Y =$ _____. Redraw the long-run aggregate supply curve on Graph 10-3.

Graph 10-3

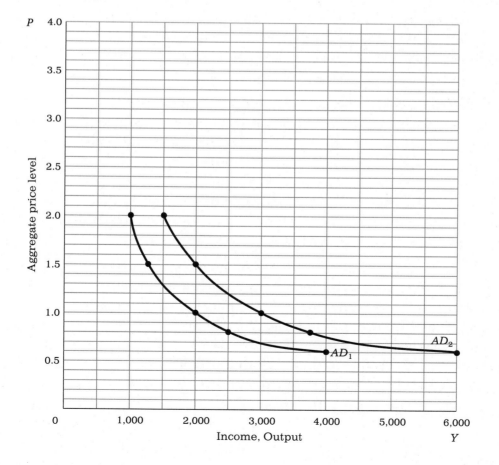

b. In the short run, output may deviate from its natural level because short-run wages and prices are sticky/flexible. Chapter 10 of the textbook describes the extreme example in which all prices are completely rigid in the short run. For simplicity, assume that the price level is fixed in the short run at $P = 1.0$, regardless of the level of output. This means that firms will supply whatever amount of output is demanded at a constant price in the short run. Draw this short-run aggregate supply curve on Graph 10-3 and label it $SRAS_1$.

c. In Graph 10-3 we have also drawn AD_1 and AD_2 from Exercises 2 and 3. (We have smoothed the edges of these curves to make them more accurate.) Locate the initial equilibrium on AD_1 and label it Point A.

d. Now suppose that the money supply increases to $M = 1,500$ while V remains equal to 2.0. As before, the aggregate demand curve shifts right/left to AD_2.

e. In the short run, the price level is fixed at $P = 1.0$ and the economy moves along $SRAS_1$. Consequently, in the short run, an increase in the money supply will increase/not change/decrease output and increase/not change/decrease the price level. Label this first short-run equilibrium following the increase in the money supply Point B. At Point B, $Y =$ _____ and $P =$ _____.

f. At Point B, output exceeds/is equal to/is less than its natural level. Consequently, over time, wages and prices will increase/not change/decrease. Suppose that the price level then rises to 1.2, regardless of the level of output. Draw this new short-run aggregate supply curve on the graph, label it $SRAS_2$, and label this second short-run equilibrium Point C. At Point C, $Y =$ _____ and $P =$ _____.

g. At point C, output exceeds/is equal to/is less than its natural level. Consequently, over time, wages and prices will increase/not change/decrease. As this occurs, the short-run aggregate supply curve will shift upward/not shift/shift downward. The price level will continue to rise until $Y =$ _____. This occurs when $P =$ _____. Draw the final short-run aggregate supply curve on Graph 10-3, label it $SRAS_F$ (for final), and label the final equilibrium Point F. Note that, like Point A, Point F represents both a short-run and a long-run equilibrium.

h. If we started again at Point A and decreased the money supply, output would increase/not change/decrease in the short run and the aggregate price level would increase/not change/decrease. Over time, however, the price level would increase/decrease as long as output remained greater than/equal to/less than its natural level. This would gradually shift the $SRAS$ curve upward/downward until the economy reached long-run equilibrium at $Y =$ _____. The initial shift in the aggregate demand curve would also occur if velocity increased/decreased.

i. Thus, in the short run, a shift in the aggregate demand curve will primarily affect output/the price level. In the long run, a shift in the aggregate demand curve will primarily affect output/the price level.

5. **Supply Shocks** *In this exercise, we introduce supply shocks and analyze the short-run effects of stabilization policy.*

a. As stated in the textbook, events that change costs and prices irrespective of demand are called *supply shocks*. Droughts and OPEC oil price increases are examples of adverse supply shocks. Starting from the initial equilibrium depicted below, an adverse supply shock would shift the short-run aggregate supply curve upward/downward. Draw this new curve on Graph 10-4 and label it $SRAS_2$. Locate the new short-run levels of output and prices if no change in economic policy is enacted, and label them Y' and P', respectively.

Graph 10-4

b. If no change in economic policy is enacted, an adverse supply shock will increase/not change/decrease output and increase/not change/decrease the aggregate price level in the short run, a phenomenon that is sometimes called

_____.

c. If, on the other hand, the Federal Reserve wishes to keep output from changing, it can increase/decrease the money supply and shift the aggregate demand curve to the right/left. This is called *accommodating policy*. Illustrate this option on Graph 10-4 by drawing the appropriate aggregate demand curve and labeling it AD_2.

d. The advantage of this option is that output will be <u>higher/lower</u> than it would have been if the Federal Reserve had done nothing. The drawback is that the price level will be permanently <u>higher/lower</u> than it would have been if the Federal Reserve had done nothing.

e. In the event of a beneficial supply shock such as a(n) <u>increase/decrease</u> in oil prices or a good harvest, we have the best of both worlds in the short run even if the Federal Reserve doesn't respond: a(n) <u>higher/unchanged/lower</u> price level and a(n) <u>higher/unchanged/lower</u> level of output.

Problems

Answer the following problems on a separate sheet of paper.

1. **a.** During the Depression, the Federal Reserve enacted policies that reduced the money supply. Sketch a graph and on it indicate what this would do to the aggregate demand and aggregate supply curves in the short run if output were originally at its natural level. What would happen to output and the aggregate price level in the short run?

b. On the same graph, indicate what would happen to the short-run aggregate supply and aggregate demand curves over time if there were no further reductions in the money supply. Consequently, what would happen to output and the price level over time?

c. What is the effect of this policy on output and the price level in the long run?

2. Totally differentiate the quantity equation and derive the slope of the aggregate demand curve.

3. Almost all economists agree that wages and prices are flexible in the long run and that real GDP moves toward its natural level. The speed with which this occurs, however, is a subject of considerable debate. Some economists believe that sticky wages and prices make the movement back to the natural level a long, protracted process, while others believe that wages and prices are sufficiently flexible to move the economy rapidly to its natural level. What do you suppose economists who believe that the natural level is achieved very slowly think about the importance of stabilization policies? Why? What do you suppose economists who believe that the natural level is achieved rapidly think about stabilization policies? Why?

4. Suppose OPEC suddenly collapsed and oil prices plummeted. Indicate what would happen to the short-run aggregate supply and aggregate demand curves, output, and the aggregate price level in the short run.

5. **a.** Suppose velocity is stable. What would the Federal Reserve need to know in order to keep output at its natural level following a supply shock?

b. Assume that velocity is unstable and unpredictable. How would this complicate the Federal Reserve's ability to stabilize the economy following a supply shock?

Data Questions

Locate the necessary economic data and apply them to answer the following data questions. All of the relevant data may be found in the Economic Report of the President (http://www.gpoaccess.gov/eop/).

1. Between 2007 and 2010, the civilian unemployment rate in the United States rose from 4.6 percent to 9.6 percent. In this question, we examine the overall anatomy of that recession.

   a. Complete Table 10-4.

   Table 9–4

	(1) 2007 (in 1,000s)	(2) 2010 (in 1,000s)	(3) % Change 2007–2010
Civilian (noninstitutional) population	_____	_____	_____
Civilian labor force	_____	_____	_____
Civilian employment	_____	_____	_____
Civilian unemployment	_____	_____	_____

   b. What happened to the relative growth rates of these four variables during this severe recession?

   c. If the natural rate of unemployment in 2010 was about 6 percent and it did not change, what eventually would happen to the actual unemployment rate?

2. **a.** Complete Columns (2), (3), (5), and (6) in Table 10-5.

Table 10-5

(1) Year	(2) Unemployment Rate (%)	(3) Change in Unemployment Rate	(4) Predicted % Change in Real GDP	(5) Real GDP ($ in billions)	(6) Actual % Change in Real GDP
2008	_____			_____	
		_____	_____		_____
2009	_____			_____	
		_____	_____		_____
2010	_____			_____	
		_____	_____		_____
2011	_____			_____	

b. Now use Okun's law and the data in Column (3) to calculate the predicted percentage change in real GDP in each year and complete Column (4). Compare your predictions in Column (4) with the actual percentage changes in real GDP in Column (6). How well did Okun's law "work" during this period?

3. Go to the Conference Board's Web site at: http://www.conferenceboard.org/data/ bcicountry.cfm?cid=1 and find the change in its index of leading indicators for the most recent two months. What do these numbers imply about the future path of real GDP?

Questions to Think About

1. **a.** In what kinds of markets and for what kinds of commodities do you think prices are very sticky in the short run?

b. In what kinds of markets and for what kinds of commodities do you think prices are fairly flexible in the short run?

2. Who benefits from wage and price stickiness? Who is harmed? Why?

Aggregate Demand 1

Fill-in Questions

Use the key terms below to fill in the blanks in the following statements. Each term may be used more than once.

actual expenditure

IS curve

Keynesian cross

liquidity preference theory

LM curve

multiplier

planned expenditure

1. _____ is the amount households, firms, and the government spend on goods and services. _____ is the amount households, firms, and the government would like to spend on goods and services. In equilibrium, the two are equal.

2. In the _____ model, the equilibrium level of income is determined by the intersection of the planned expenditure curve and the actual expenditure curve.

3. In the _____ model, every $1 increase in government purchases increases equilibrium income by $1 times the government-purchases _____.

4. The _____ shows the relationship between the interest rate and the level of income at which planned expenditure is equal to actual expenditure.

5. The _____ illustrates the combinations of income and interest rates at which real money supply is equal to real money demand.

6. A change in fiscal policy will shift the _____; a change in monetary policy will shift the _____.

7. According to the _____, people wish to hold a smaller quantity of real money balances when the interest rate increases.

Multiple-Choice Questions

1. If investment, taxes, and government purchases are held constant, the planned expenditure curve:
   a. slopes upward and its slope is equal to the *MPC*.
   b. slopes downward and its slope is equal to the *MPC*.
   c. is a 45-degree line.
   d. is a vertical line.

2. In the Keynesian cross model, the 45-degree line indicates that:
   a. GDP rises whenever consumption rises.
   b. actual expenditure is always equal to income.
   c. the equilibrium level of income increases whenever actual income increases.
   d. All of these statements are correct.

3. At the equilibrium level of income:
   a. unintended inventory accumulation is equal to zero.
   b. planned expenditure is equal to actual expenditure.
   c. there is no tendency for GDP to change.
   d. All of the answers are correct.

4. If income exceeds planned expenditure, firms will cut back production because unplanned inventory accumulation will be:
   a. positive.
   b. negative.
   c. zero.
   d. indeterminate.

5. If the consumption function is $C = 100 + 0.8(Y - T)$, the government-purchases multiplier is:
   a. 0.8.
   b. 1.25.
   c. 4.
   d. 5.

6. If the consumption function is $C = 100 + 0.8(Y - T)$ and taxes decrease by \$1, the equilibrium level of income will:
   a. decrease by \$5.
   b. decrease by \$4.
   c. increase by \$5.
   d. increase by \$4.

7. If the consumption function is $C = 100 + 0.8(Y - T)$ and both taxes and government purchases increase by \$1, the equilibrium level of income will:
   a. remain constant.
   b. increase by \$3.
   c. increase by \$1.
   d. decrease by \$4.

8.   Tax cuts do all of the following EXCEPT:

   a. stimulate aggregate demand by raising households' disposable income.
   b. reduce the government budget deficit.
   c. stimulate aggregate supply by improving workers' incentives.
   d. increase output in the short run.

9.   *Contrary* to the Keynesian model, some economists have found that:

   a. tax cuts decrease output.
   b. tax cuts increase output by more than equal increases in government spending.
   c. equal increases in taxes and government spending increase consumption.
   d. both b and c are true.

10.   As of February, 2012, the U.S. economy was recovering from a recession but much more slowly than Obama administration economists had initially forecast. This implies that:

   a. the 2009 fiscal stimulus may not have worked, since the administration's projections of the economy with the fiscal stimulus were much too optimistic.
   b. the 2009 fiscal stimulus may have worked as planned, but the economy was sicker in 2009 than people recognized.
   c. the 2009 fiscal stimulus had no effect on the economy.
   d. both a and b are correct.

11.   The FALSE statement below is:

   a. a decrease in the interest rate increases planned investment.
   b. a decrease in the interest rate shifts the planned expenditure curve upward.
   c. a decrease in the interest rate shifts the *IS* curve to the right.
   d. as the interest rate falls, planned expenditure is equal to actual expenditure at a higher level of income.

12.   An increase of $1 in government purchases will:

   a. shift the planned expenditure curve upward by $1.
   b. shift the *IS* curve to the right by $1/(1 − *MPC*).
   c. not shift the *LM* curve.
   d. All of the answers are correct.

13.   A decrease in taxes will shift the planned expenditure curve _____ and the *IS* curve to the _____.

   a. upward; left
   b. upward; right
   c. downward; left
   d. downward; right

14. The TRUE statement about the *LM* curve is:

    a. the *LM* curve slopes upward and it is drawn for a given level of income.

    b. the *LM* curve slopes downward, and an increase in price shifts it upward.

    c. the *LM* curve slopes upward and it is drawn for a given supply of real money balances.

    d. along the *LM* curve, actual expenditure is equal to planned expenditure.

15. An increase in the money supply shifts the:

    a. *LM* curve upward (to the left).

    b. *LM* curve downward (to the right).

    c. *IS* curve to the right.

    d. *IS* curve to the left.

16. Chapters 5 and 11 indicate that an increase in the money supply:

    a. reduces the nominal interest rate in the short run.

    b. increases the price level in the long run.

    c. does not affect the real interest rate in the long run.

    d. All of the answers are correct.

17. At the intersection of the *IS* and *LM* curves:

    a. actual expenditure is equal to planned expenditure.

    b. real money supply is equal to real money demand.

    c. the levels of *Y* and *r* satisfy both the goods market equilibrium condition and the money market equilibrium condition.

    d. All of the answers are correct.

Exercises

1. **The Keynesian Cross** *In this exercise, we illustrate the Keynesian cross using a simple model of a closed economy.*

    a. Consider the following model of the economy (in billions of dollars):

    $$Y = C + I + G \qquad \text{(11-1)}$$
    $$C = C(Y - T) = 125 + 0.75(Y - T) \qquad \text{(11-2)}$$
    $$I = \bar{I} = 100 \qquad \text{(11-3)}$$
    $$G = \overline{G} = 150 \qquad \text{(11-4)}$$
    $$T = \overline{T} = 100. \qquad \text{(11-5)}$$

    The *MPC* is defined as _____.

    The value of the *MPC* in this model = _____. If consumption were graphed as a function of disposable income $(Y - T)$, as is done in Chapter 3 of the textbook, the *y* intercept, which is the value of the variable depicted on the vertical axis when the value of the variable depicted on the horizontal axis is 0, would equal _____. The slope of the curve would equal _____.

b. Now, however, consumption will be graphed as a function of Y, rather than of $(Y - T)$. Substituting $T = 100$ into the equation, we obtain

$$C = 125 + 0.75\,(Y - 100), \text{ or}$$
$$C = \text{_____} + \text{_____}\,Y.$$

Use this information to plot and draw the consumption expenditure curve on Graph 11-1 and label it C.

Graph 11-1

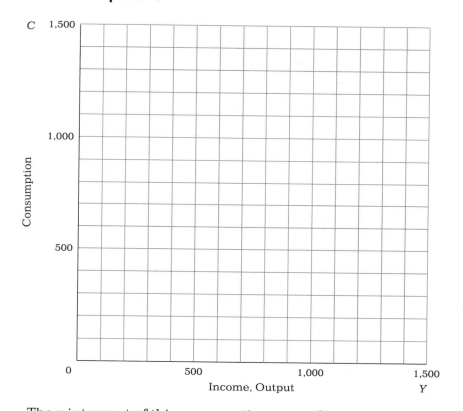

The y intercept of this consumption expenditure curve, which is the value of consumption when income $Y = 0$, is _____, and the slope is _____. When we draw consumption as a function of income Y, note that the y intercept differs from when we draw consumption as a function of disposable income $Y - T$, as you can see by comparing your answers to those in Parts a and b. When $Y = 0$ and $T = 100$, $(Y - T) =$ _____, which is greater than/less than/equal to zero.

c. In this simple model, both planned investment and government purchases are constant and independent of the level of Y, that is, they are exogenous. Use the information from Part a to draw the relationship between planned investment and Y on Graph 11-2, and label it I. Draw the relationship between government purchases and Y on Graph 11-3 and label it G.

Graph 11-2

Graph 11-3

d. Recall that total planned expenditure *PE* is equal to $C + I + G$. Use the information from Graphs 11-1, 11-2, and 11-3 to draw the planned expenditure curve on Graph 11-4. Label your curve *PE*.

Graph 11-4

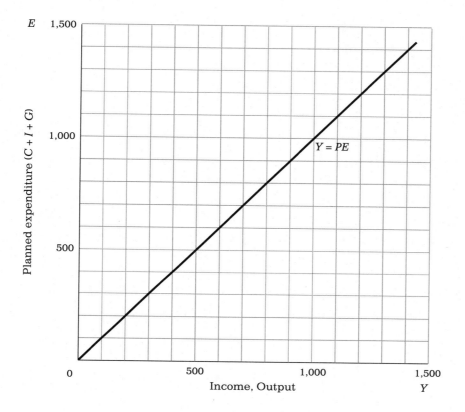

e. The value of the *y* intercept on Graph 11-4 is equal to the level of planned expenditure when $Y = 0$. This value is equal to the level of consumption when $Y = 0$, plus the level of planned investment when $Y = 0$, plus the level of government purchases when $Y = 0$. This value is equal to _____ + _____ + _____ = _____. Similarly, the numerical value of the slope of the planned expenditure curve on Graph 11-4 is equal to the slope of the consumption function curve, plus the slope of the planned investment curve, plus the slope of the government-purchases curve, or _____ + _____ + _____ = _____.

f. Since $PE = C + I + G$, the equation for the planned expenditure curve can be derived by adding together the equations for C, I, and G. Thus,

$$PE = 125 + 0.75(Y - T) + I + G. \qquad \text{(11-6)}$$

Substituting the exogenous values of T, I, and G into this equation, we get

$$PE = 125 + 0.75(Y - 100) + 100 + 150.$$

This equation can be simplified to

$$PE = \underline{\hspace{1.5cm}} + \underline{\hspace{1.5cm}} Y. \qquad \text{(11-7)}$$

g. Equation 11-7 will yield values of planned expenditure PE for any value of Y. The equilibrium, however, occurs only along the 45-degree line labeled $Y = PE$ on Graph 11-4. Only along this curve will income (or output) equal planned expenditure. The slope of this 45-degree line is \underline{\hspace{4cm}}. Solve for the equilibrium level of income in this model by setting $Y = PE = 300 + 0.75Y$ and solving for Y.

$Y = \underline{\hspace{5cm}}$.

On Graph 11-4, label this initial equilibrium Y_1.

h. If income (output) exceeds planned expenditure, there will be unplanned investment in the form of unplanned inventory accumulation. For example, if $Y = 1{,}600$, planned expenditure PE will equal $300 + 0.75(1{,}600) =$ \underline{\hspace{4cm}}. Consequently, the level of unplanned inventory accumulation will equal $Y - PE = 1{,}600 - $ \underline{\hspace{4cm}} $=$ \underline{\hspace{4cm}}. As inventories increase, firms will <u>hire/lay off</u> workers and <u>increase/decrease</u> production. As a result, Y will <u>rise/fall</u> until equilibrium is reached at $Y = $ \underline{\hspace{3cm}}. When this equilibrium is reached, unplanned inventory investment will equal \underline{\hspace{4cm}}.

i. Conversely, when Y is less than planned expenditure, inventories will fall. For example, if $Y = 1,000$, planned expenditure PE will equal $300 + 0.75(1,000) =$ _____. Consequently, the level of unplanned inventory accumulation will equal $Y - PE = 1,000 -$ _____ $=$ _____. As inventories decrease, firms will <u>hire more/lay off</u> workers and <u>increase/decrease</u> production. As a result, Y will <u>rise/fall</u> until an equilibrium is reached at $Y =$ _____. When this equilibrium is reached, unplanned inventory investment will equal _____.

2. **The Government-Purchases Multiplier** *In this exercise, we derive and graphically illustrate the government-purchases multiplier.*

   Assume the same information as in Exercise 1 (again, in billions of dollars):

$$Y = C + I + G \tag{11-8}$$
$$C = C(Y - T) = 125 + 0.75(Y - T) \tag{11-9}$$
$$I = \bar{I} = 100 \tag{11-10}$$
$$G = \overline{G} = 150 \tag{11-11}$$
$$T = \overline{T} = 100. \tag{11-12}$$

The initial equilibrium is depicted on Graph 11-5.

Graph 11-5

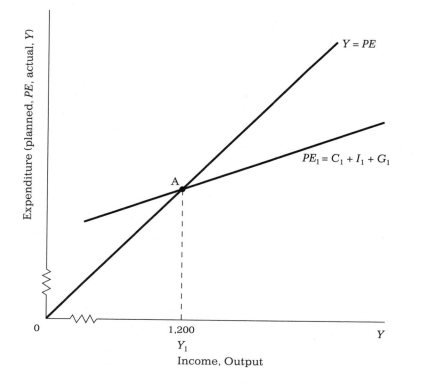

a. The initial level of government purchases is _____. This is illustrated by the curve G_1 on Graph 11-6.

Graph 11-6

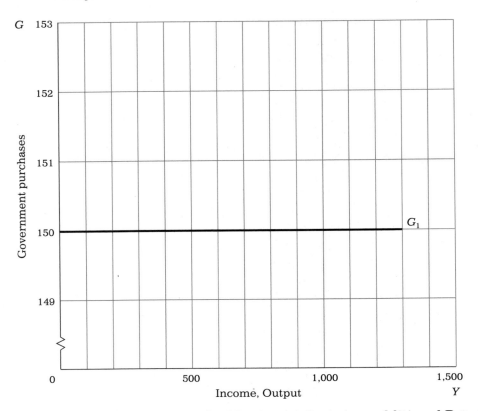

Suppose that the government decides to purchase two additional B-2 stealth bombers at a total cost of $1 (billion). Consequently, government purchases G will rise at all levels of Y to _____. This will shift the whole government purchases curve on Graph 11-6 upward by _____. Plot and draw this new curve on Graph 11-6 and label it G_2.

b. Since taxes T and planned investment I have not changed, the consumption and investment functions on Graphs 11-1 and 11-2 in Exercise 1 will not shift. Consequently, the planned expenditure curve $PE = C + I + G$ will shift upward by _____. Plot and draw the new planned expenditure curve on Graph 11-5 and label it PE_2.

c. As in Exercise 1f, the equation for the new planned expenditure curve PE_2 can be derived by adding together the equations for C, I, and G. Thus,

$$PE_2 = 125 + 0.75(Y - T) + I + G_2.$$

Substituting the same values of T and I but the new value of G into this equation, we get

$$PE_2 = 125 + 0.75(Y - 100) + 100 + 151.$$

This can be simplified to

$PE_2 =$ _____ + _____ Y.

d. It is tempting to say that the \$1 billion increase in government purchases will increase the equilibrium level of income by \$1 billion, but this would be incorrect. As government purchases increase, Y increases. This, in turn, increases disposable income and the level of consumption. Consequently, Y will increase by more than \$1 billion. Recall that in equilibrium, planned expenditure is equal to income (that is, $PE = Y$). Calculate the new equilibrium level of income by setting the equation for PE_2 in Part c equal to Y and solving for Y.

$PE_2 =$ _____ + _____ $Y = Y$.

$Y =$ _____.

On Graph 11-5, label the equilibrium Point B and label the new equilibrium level of output Y_2.

e. From Part d, we see that an increase in government purchases of $1 billion leads to a $_____ billion increase in national income and output. This value is equal to the increase in government purchases multiplied by the government-purchases multiplier, where the latter is defined as $\Delta Y/\Delta G$. In this model, the multiplier equals $1/(1 - MPC)$.

f. The theory behind the government-purchases multiplier can be seen by completing Table 11-1 (sometimes called the *round-by-round story*).

Table 11-1

	Change in $Y = C + I + G$
Round 1 G rises by $1 billion as the government purchases two new stealth bombers. Y rises immediately by . . .	+ $1 billion
Round 2 The total disposable income of workers, suppliers, and owners at Northrop Corporation (a major producer of the stealth bomber) rises by $1 billion. Consequently, their total consumption rises by $MPC \times$ ($1 billion). As new goods (Chevrolet automobiles, for example) are produced to meet this increase in consumption demand, Y rises by . . .	+ $$MPC$ billion
Round 3 The total disposable income of workers, suppliers, and owners at General Motors Corporation rises by $$MPC$ billion. Thus, their total consumption rises by $MPC(MPC \times$ $1 billion$) = $$_____ billion. As new goods (for example, Levi's jeans) are produced, Y rises by . . .	+ $ _____ billion
Round 4 The total disposable income of workers, suppliers, and owners at Levi Strauss & Co. rises by $$MPC^2$ billion. Consequently, their total consumption rises by $MPC($$MPC^2 \times$ $1 billion$) = $$_____ billion. As new goods are produced, Y rises by . . .	+ $_____ billion

The total change in Y is equal to the sum of all the changes resulting from each round. Since $MPC < 1$, the increase in Y from each successive round becomes smaller and smaller and eventually approaches zero. The sum of all of these increments is equal to $1 + MPC + MPC^2 + MPC^3 + MPC^4 + MPC^5 + . . . = 1/(1 - MPC)$. Since the MPC in our model = _____, the government-purchases multiplier = $1/(1 - $ _____ $) = $ _____.

3. **The Tax Multiplier** *In this exercise, we derive and graphically illustrate the tax multiplier and, in Part g, the balanced-budget multiplier.*

Assume the same information as in Exercise 2 (again in billions of dollars):

$$Y = C + I + G \tag{11-13}$$
$$C = C(Y - T) = 125 + 0.75(Y - T) \tag{11-14}$$
$$I = \bar{I} = 100 \tag{11-15}$$
$$G = \overline{G} = 150 \tag{11-16}$$
$$T = \overline{T} = 100. \tag{11-17}$$

The initial equilibrium is illustrated on Graph 11-7.

Graph 11-7

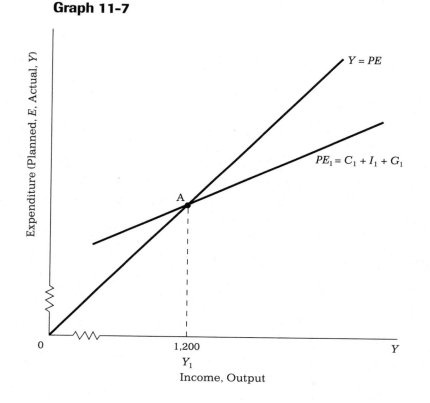

a. Suppose that the government decides to decrease (net) taxes by $1 billion by decreasing tax revenues or by increasing transfer payments. Since disposable income equals $Y - T$, this tax decrease will increase the level of disposable income at every level of Y by $1 billion. Consequently, consumption will increase by $MPC \times \$1$ billion at each level of Y. (Reread the last two sentences carefully.) As a result, the consumption expenditure curve on Graph 11-8 will shift upward from C_1 to C_3 by $MPC billion. Since $MPC =$ _____, the consumption expenditure curve will shift up by $_____ billion.

Graph 11-8

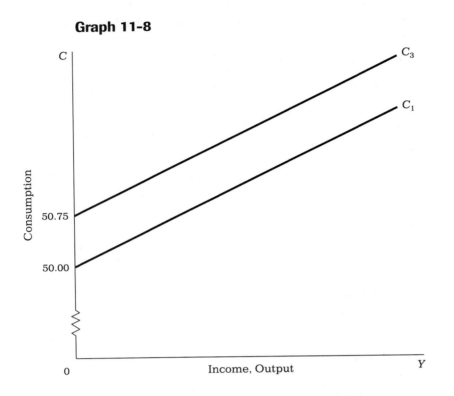

Neither government purchases nor planned investment has changed, so the I and G curves will be the same as in Graphs 11-2 and 11-3. Since $PE = C + I + G$ and $MPC = 0.75$, the \$1 billion tax reduction will shift the planned expenditure curve upward by \$ _____ billion. Plot and draw the new planned expenditure curve on Graph 11-7 and label it PE_3.

b. Once again, the equation for the new planned expenditure curve PE_3 can be derived by adding together the equations for C, I, and G. Thus,

$$PE_3 = 125 + 0.75(Y - T) + I + G.$$

Substituting the same values of I and G but the new value of T into this equation, we get

$$PE_3 = 125 + 0.75(Y - 99) + 100 + 150.$$

This can be simplified to

$$PE_3 = \underline{\hspace{4cm}} + \underline{\hspace{4cm}} Y.$$

c. Calculate the new equilibrium level of income by setting the equation for PE_3 in Part b equal to Y and then solving for Y.

$PE_3 = $ _____ + _____ $Y = Y$.

$Y = $ _____. On Graph 11-7, label the new equilibrium Point C and label the new equilibrium level of output Y_3.

d. From Part c, we see that a \$1 billion reduction in taxes leads to a \$_____ billion increase in national income and output. This is equal to the decrease in taxes (\$1 billion) multiplied by the tax multiplier, where the latter is equal to $MPC/(1 - MPC)$.

e. Complete Table 11-2 to see the rationale behind the tax multiplier.

Table 11-2

	Change in $Y = C + I + G$
Round 1 T falls by \$1 billion. Disposable income rises by \$1 billion and consumption rises by $MPC \times$ \$1 billion. As new goods (Chevrolet automobiles) are produced, Y rises by . . .	$+ \$MPC$ billion
Round 2 The total disposable income of workers, suppliers, and owners at General Motors Corporation rises by \$$MPC$ billion. Thus, their total consumption rises by $MPC(MPC \times \$1\text{ billion}) = \$$_____ billion. As new goods (Levi's jeans) are produced, Y rises by . . .	$+ \$$_____ billion
Round 3 The total disposable income of workers, suppliers, and owners at Levi Strauss & Co. rises by \$$MPC^2$ billion. Consequently, their total consumption rises by $MPC(\$MPC^2\text{ billion}) = \$$_____ billion. As new goods are produced, Y rises by . . .	$+ \$$_____ billion

The total change in Y is equal to the sum of all the changes resulting from each round. As Chapter 11 of the textbook illustrates, the sum of all these increments is equal to $MPC + MPC^2 + MPC^3 + MPC^4 + MPC^5 + . . . = MPC/(1 - MPC)$. Since the MPC in our model = _____, $MPC/(1 - MPC) = $ _____ $/(1 - $ _____ $) = $ _____.

f. Compare the algebraic expression for the tax multiplier in Part e with the algebraic expression for the government-purchases multiplier in Exercise 2f. Note that the tax multiplier is equal to the government-purchases multiplier minus 1, which equals

$$[1/(1 - MPC)] - 1 = [1 - (1 - MPC)]/(1 - MPC) = \underline{\hspace{3cm}}.$$

Examine the two round-by-round stories in Tables 11-1 and 11-2. Note that the only difference between the effects of an increase in government purchases and the effects of an equal decrease in taxes on Y is that the (direct) Round 1 effect of the increase in government purchases does not occur when taxes are reduced.

g. Now suppose that both government purchases and taxes were simultaneously increased by $1 billion. Since the government budget surplus would remain unchanged, this policy is sometimes called a *balanced-budget change* in G and T. The $1 billion increase in G would shift the planned expenditure curve upward/downward by $_____ billion, while the $1 billion increase in T would shift the planned expenditure upward/downward by $_____ billion. Consequently, the combined policy changes would shift the planned expenditure curve upward/downward by $_____ billion, and the equilibrium level of Y would rise/fall/remain constant. This occurs because an increase in G has a larger/smaller effect on Y than an equal reduction in taxes, just as Tables 11-1 and 11-2 indicated. In Exercise 2, an increase in government expenditures of $1 billion increased the equilibrium level of Y by $_____ billion. In Exercise 3, a reduction in taxes of $1 billion increased the equilibrium level of Y by $_____ billion. Reversing this second result, a $1 billion increase in taxes would increase/decrease the equilibrium level of Y by $_____ billion. Thus, a simultaneous increase in both G and T by $1 billion will increase/decrease the equilibrium level of Y by $_____ billion.

4. **The *IS* Curve** *In this exercise, we use a simple model of the economy to derive the* IS *curve and we discuss the parameters that affect its slope.*

Consider the following model of the economy (in billions of dollars):

$$Y = C + I + G \tag{11-18}$$
$$C = C(Y - T) = 125 + 0.75(Y - T) \tag{11-19}$$
$$I = 200 - 10r \tag{11-20}$$
$$G = \overline{G} = 150 \tag{11-21}$$
$$T = \overline{T} = 100. \tag{11-22}$$

a. Note that this model is identical to the one used in Exercises 1–3, except that planned investment now depends on the interest rate. For each percentage point increase in the real interest rate r, planned investment falls by _____. Now use the new investment equation to complete Column 2 in Table 11-3. Plot the data from Columns 1 and 2 on Graph 11-9, draw this investment curve, and label it I.

Table 11-3

(1) Interest Rate (%)	(2) Planned Investment	(3) Equilibrium Level of Income
0	_____	_____
5	_____	_____
10	100	1,200
15	_____	_____
20	_____	_____

Graph 11-9

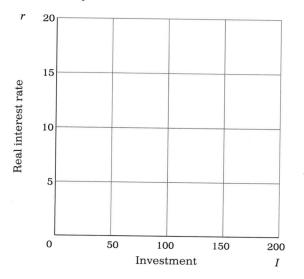

b. From Table 11-3, note that when $r = 10$, $I = 100$, and the equilibrium level of Y is the same as in Exercise 1. The equilibrium level of Y can be computed for other values of the interest rate in two ways. First, recall that total planned expenditure PE is equal to $C + I + G$. Now use the new equation for investment, along with the initial levels of T and G (which have not changed), and solve for PE in terms of Y and r:

$$PE = 125 + 0.75(Y - 100) + (200 - 10r) + 150.$$

$PE = $ _____ $+$ _____ $Y - $

_____ $r.$

c. Next, recall that the equilibrium level of Y is defined as the level of Y at which income Y is equal to total planned expenditure PE. Calculate the new equilibrium level of income by setting the equation for PE in Part b equal to Y and solving for Y. Note that the equilibrium Y will be a function of r:

$PE = $ _____ $+$ _____ $Y - $

_____ $r = Y.$

$Y = $ _____ $-$ _____ $r.$

Use this equation to complete Column 3 of Table 11-3.

d. Alternatively, the remaining equilibrium values of Y can be computed using the multiplier analysis derived in Exercise 2. The initial equilibrium is illustrated on Graph 11-10. When $r = 10$ percent, $I =$ _____, the planned expenditure curve is PE_1, and $Y =$ _____.

Graph 11-10

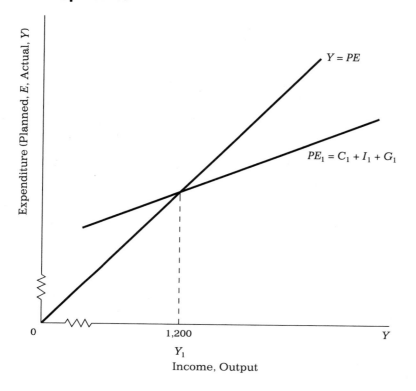

e. If r falls by 5 percentage points to 5 percent, I increases by $5(10) =$ _____. As a result, the planned expenditure curve PE would shift upward by _____. Draw the new planned expenditure curve on Graph 11-10 and label it PE_2. Since this shift is the same as one that would follow an increase in government purchases of _____, the multiplier effects on consumption will be the same, and the government-purchases multiplier can be used to calculate the change in Y. Thus, the change in Y will equal the increase in investment multiplied by the government-purchases multiplier, or

$$\text{Change in } Y = \underline{\hspace{1.5cm}} \times 1/(1 - MPC).$$

Since $MPC =$ _____, the numerical value for the

$$\text{Change in } Y = \underline{\hspace{1cm}} \times 1/(1 - \underline{\hspace{1cm}}) = \underline{\hspace{1cm}}.$$

This should be the same as the change indicated in Table 11-3.

f. The *IS* curve depicts the relationship between the interest rate *r* and the equilibrium value of income from the investment function and the Keynesian cross. (This is sometimes called the equilibrium in the goods market.) Reexamine Table 11-3 and note that as the interest rate falls, the level of planned investment falls/rises/remains the same. This shifts the planned expenditure curve upward/downward by the same amount as the increase in planned investment. Finally, the equilibrium level of income *Y* rises by the increase in planned investment multiplied by the government-purchases multiplier. This shift occurs because *Y* rises by the initial increase in investment plus the multiplier effects on consumption.

g. Use the data in Columns 1 and 3 of Table 11-3 to plot and draw the *IS* curve on Graph 11-11 (label the curve *IS*). Reread Part f to make sure that you understand how the *IS* curve is derived.

Graph 11-11

5. **Fiscal Policy and the *IS* Curve** *In this exercise, we show how changes in fiscal policy shift the* IS *curve.*

a. Consider the same model of the economy as in Exercise 4 (in billions of dollars), in which planned investment depends on the interest rate:

$$Y = C + I + G \tag{11-23}$$
$$C = C(Y - T) = 125 + 0.75(Y - T) \tag{11-24}$$
$$I = 200 - 10r \tag{11-25}$$
$$G = \overline{G} = 150 \tag{11-26}$$
$$T = \overline{T} = 100. \tag{11-27}$$

As we saw in Exercise 4, when $r = 10$, $I =$ _____ and $Y =$ _____. This original equilibrium is illustrated on Graphs 11-12 and 11-13.

Suppose that government purchases now increase by $1 billion to $151 billion, as in Exercise 2. If the interest rate remains equal to 10 percent, then investment is unchanged, the planned expenditure curve shifts upward by $1 billion, and the equilibrium level of Y rises by $1 billion multiplied by the government-purchases multiplier, which equals $1 billion $\times 1/(1 - MPC)$.

Thus, if the interest rate remains equal to 10 percent and $MPC = 0.75$, the equilibrium level of Y rises by $1 billion $\times 1/(1 -$ _____ $) =$ $ _____ billion. The new equilibrium level of Y = _____.

b. Draw the new planned expenditure curve on Graph 11-12, label it $PE_2(r = 10)$, and illustrate the change in Y if r remains constant. Note that the scales of the x and y axes have been broken so that a small shift in the expenditure curve and a small change in Y will be noticeable.

c. This change can also be depicted on Graph 11-13 by a shift in the *IS* curve to the right/left. The amount of the horizontal shift measures the change in Y if r remains constant. Given the answer to Part b, the horizontal shift in the *IS* curve must equal $1 billion $\times 1/(1 - MPC) =$ $_____ billion. Draw the new *IS* curve on Graph 11-13, and label it IS_2.

d. Thus, an increase in government purchases will shift the *IS* curve to the right/left by the change in government purchases multiplied by the government-purchases multiplier. Conversely, a decrease in government purchases will shift the *IS* curve to the right/left by the change in government purchases multiplied by the _____.

Graph 11-12

Graph 11-13

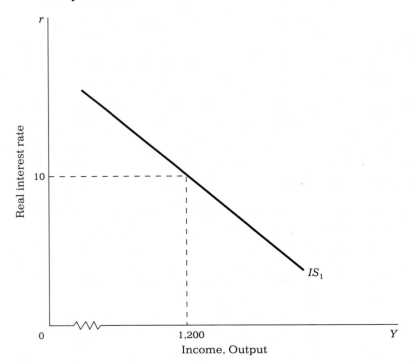

e. The government-purchases multiplier equals $1/(1 - MPC)$. As the MPC gets larger, the denominator gets larger/smaller and the value of the multiplier gets larger/smaller. Consequently, as the MPC gets larger, the horizontal shift in the *IS* curve following a change in government purchases gets larger/smaller. Therefore, as the MPC gets larger, the round-by-round multiplier effects depicted in Table 11-1 become larger/smaller, and the change in the equilibrium level of Y becomes larger/smaller.

f. Now assume that $G = 150$ and that taxes fall by \$1 billion. In Exercises 3a and d, it was shown that the planned expenditure curve would shift upward by \$$MPC$ billion and Y would increase by the reduction in taxes (\$1 billion) multiplied by the tax multiplier $MPC/(1 - MPC)$, or by \$$MPC/(1 - MPC)$ billion. Thus, if the interest rate remains equal to 10 percent and $MPC = 0.75$, the equilibrium level of Y rises by \$_____ billion × _____/(1 − _____) = \$_____ billion. The new equilibrium level of $Y =$ _____.

   Draw the new planned expenditure curve on Graph 11-14, label it PE_3 ($r = 10$), and indicate the change in Y if r remains constant.

g. This change can be depicted on Graph 11-15 by a shift in the *IS* curve to the right/left. The amount of the horizontal shift measures the change in Y if r remains constant. Given your answer to Part f, the horizontal shift in the *IS* curve must equal \$1 billion × $MPC/(1 - MPC)$. If $MPC = 0.75$, this is equal to \$_____ billion. Draw the new *IS* curve on Graph 11-15 and label it IS_3.

h. Thus, a decrease in taxes (resulting from either a reduction in taxes or an increase in government transfers) will shift the *IS* curve to the right/left by the decrease in taxes multiplied by the tax multiplier. Conversely, an increase in taxes will shift the *IS* curve to the right/left by the change in taxes multiplied by the _____.

i. The tax multiplier equals $MPC/(1 - MPC)$. As the MPC gets larger, the numerator gets larger/smaller and the denominator gets larger/smaller. Consequently, the tax multiplier gets larger/smaller. Thus, as the MPC gets larger, the horizontal shift in the *IS* curve following a change in taxes would get larger/smaller. As the MPC gets larger, the round-by-round multiplier effects depicted in Table 11-2 become larger/smaller, and the change in the equilibrium level of Y becomes larger/smaller. Consequently, a larger MPC implies a flatter/steeper *IS* curve.

Graph 11-14

Graph 11-15

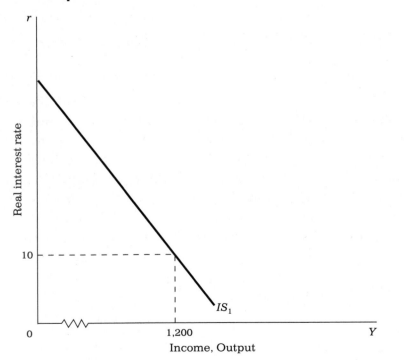

6. **The *LM* Curve** *In this exercise, we use the money supply/money demand diagram to derive the* LM *curve.*

   a. Suppose that the following equation (in billions of dollars) describes the supply of real money balances:

   $$(M^s / P) = \overline{M} / \overline{P} = 800 / 1.0 = 800. \tag{11-28}$$

   This equation states that the Fed has fixed the nominal money supply at $\overline{M} = 800$ and the price level is fixed at $\overline{P} = 1.0$. Since the supply of real money balances is independent of the interest rate, it will be depicted as a vertical line. Draw this line on Graph 11-16 and label it $\overline{M}/\overline{P}$.

   Graph 11-16

   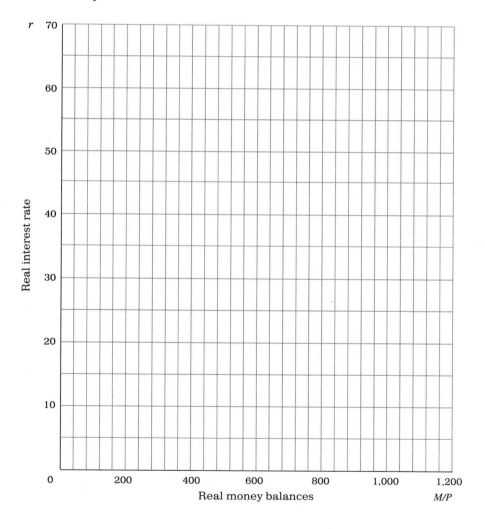

   b. Suppose that the following equation describes the demand for real money balances:

$$(M/P)^d = L(r, Y) = 0.8Y - 16r. \qquad \text{(11-29)}$$

This equation states that the demand for real money balances depends on the level of real income Y and the interest rate r. (In Chapter 11 of the textbook, footnote 6 notes that money demand actually depends on the nominal interest rate i, rather than on the real interest rate r, and that this difference will be explored more fully in Chapter 12.) Using Equation 11-29, complete Table 11-4.

Table 11-4

(1) Real Income Y	(2) Interest Rate r (%)	(3) Real Money Demand $(M/P)^d = 0.8Y - 16r$
1,100	55	_____
1,100	25	_____
1,100	10	_____
1,100	5	_____
1,100	0	_____

Plot these points on Graph 11-16, draw the resulting money demand curve, and label it $L(r, Y = 1,100)$.

c. From Graph 11-16 and Table 11-4, it can be seen that if real income $Y = 1,100$, the supply of real money balances is equal to the demand for real money balances when $r =$ _____ percent.

d. Now suppose that real income increases to $Y = 1,200$. Complete Table 11-5.

Table 11-5

(1) Real Income Y	(2) Interest Rate r (%)	(3) Real Money Demand $(M/P)^d = 0.8Y - 16r$
1,200	60	_____
1,200	50	_____
1,200	25	_____
1,200	10	_____
1,200	5	_____

Plot these points on Graph 11-16, draw the resulting money demand curve, and label it $L(r, Y = 1,200)$. When Y increases, the real money supply curve remains unchanged at $M/P = 800$, but the real money demand curve shifts to the left/right. Consequently, the interest rate at which the supply of real money balances is equal to the demand for real money balances rises/falls to $r =$ _____ percent.

e. Finally, suppose that real income increases to $Y = 1,400$. Complete Table 11-6.

Table 11-6

(1) Real Income Y	(2) Interest Rate r (%)	(3) Real Money Demand $(M/P)^d = 0.8Y - 16r$
1,400	70	_____
1,400	50	_____
1,400	25	_____
1,400	10	_____
1,400	0	_____

Plot these points on Graph 11-16, draw the resulting money demand curve, and label it $L(r, Y = 1,400)$. When Y increases again, the real money supply curve remains unchanged at $M/P = 800$, but the real money demand curve again shifts to the left/right. Consequently, the interest rate at which the supply of real money balances is equal to the demand for real money balances rises/falls to $r = $ _____.

f. The LM curve depicts the combinations of r and Y for which a given supply of real money balances is equal to real money demand. Throughout Exercise 6, the supply of real money balances has been fixed at $M/P = $

_____. From Table 11-4, we learned that when $Y = 1,100$, real money supply equals real money demand at $r = $ _____.
From Table 11-5, we learned that when $Y = 1,200$, real money supply equals real money demand at $r = $ _____. And from Table 11-6 and Graph 11-16, we learned that when $Y = 1,400$, real money supply equals real money demand at $r = $ _____. Plot and draw a curve for these three points on Graph 11-17 and label it LM_1.

g. Along each LM curve, a constant real money supply is equal to real money demand. As Y increases, real money demand will increase/decrease if the interest rate remains constant. Since the real money supply has remained unchanged, the interest rate must rise/fall to keep real money demand equal to the unchanged real money supply.

Graph 11-17

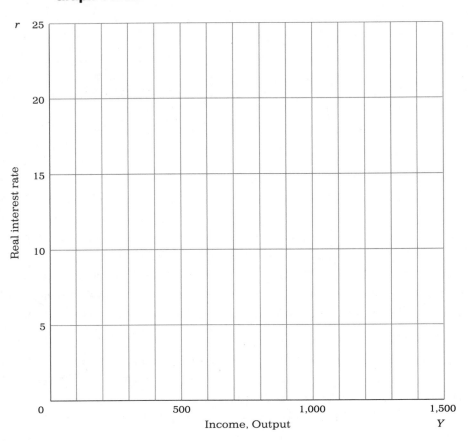

h. Now let us derive the equation for our *LM* curve. Along the LM_1 curve, the real money supply equals _____ and this value is equal to real money demand. Thus, along the LM_1 curve,

$$\overline{M} / \overline{P} = \underline{\quad\quad} = 0.8Y - 16r.$$

Since *r* appears on the vertical axis on Graph 11-17, it is useful to rearrange this equation and solve for *r*.

$r = $ _____ $+$ _____ $Y.$

The *y* intercept of this *LM* curve is _____, and the slope of the *LM* curve is _____.

7. **Monetary Policy and the *LM* Curve** *In this exercise, we show how changes in monetary policy shift the LM curve.*

a. Refer to the initial money supply and money demand equations:

$$(M^s/P) = \overline{M}/\overline{P} = 800/1.0 = 800 \tag{11-30}$$

$$(M/P)^d = 0.8Y - 16r. \tag{11-31}$$

By setting money supply equal to money demand and solving for r, the equation for the *LM* curve in Exercise 6h can be derived:

$r = $ _____ $+$ _____ Y.

Draw the curve for this equation on Graph 11-18 and label it LM_1.

Graph 11-18

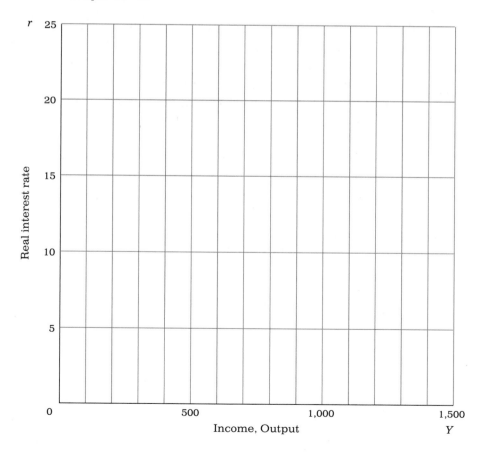

b. Following the example given in Chapter 11 of the textbook, suppose that the Fed decreased the money supply to $(M^s/P) = 640$. Set this new money supply equal to the money demand equation, Equation 11-31, and solve for r to derive the equation for the new LM curve.

$r =$ _____ $+$ _____Y.

Plot and draw the new LM curve from this equation on Graph 11-18 and label it LM_2. The slope of LM_2 is greater than/less than/equal to the slope of LM_1. The y intercept of LM_2 is greater than/less than the y intercept of LM_1. (Be careful about your signs.) Consequently, a reduction in the real money supply will shift the LM curve to the right (downward)/left (upward).

c. For the money market to remain in equilibrium, a reduction in the real money supply must be matched by an equal reduction in money demand. This match can be accomplished by a(n) increase/decrease in r at each level of Y and/or a(n) increase/decrease in Y at each level of r. Consequently, a decrease in the real money supply will shift the LM curve to the right (downward)/left (upward). Conversely, an increase in the real money supply will shift the LM curve to the right (downward)/left (upward).

8. **Short-Run Equilibrium** *In this exercise, we use the models developed in the preceding exercises to illustrate the short-run IS-LM equilibrium.*

a. Consider the model of the economy from Exercise 4, in which planned investment depends on the interest rate:

$$Y = C + I + G \tag{11-32}$$
$$C = C(Y - T) = 125 + 0.75(Y - T) \tag{11-33}$$
$$I = 200 - 10r \tag{11-34}$$
$$G = \overline{G} = 150 \tag{11-35}$$
$$T = \overline{T} = 100. \tag{11-36}$$

As we saw in Exercise 4, the equation for the *IS* curve can be derived by setting total planned expenditure, *PE = C + I + G*, equal to *Y* and solving for *r*:

$$PE = 125 + 0.75(Y - 100) + (200 - 10r) + 150 = Y. \tag{11-37}$$

$r = $ _____ $-$ _____ $Y.$

Plot and draw the *IS* curve from this equation on Graph 11-19 and label it IS_1.

Graph 11-19

b. In Exercise 6, we derived the equation for the *LM* curve by setting the money supply equation equal to the money demand equation and solving for *r*:

$$(\overline{M} / \overline{P}) = 800 = (M / P)^d = 0.8Y - 16r$$
$$800 = 0.8Y - 16r.$$

(11-38)

$r = $ _____ + _____ Y.

Plot and draw the *LM* curve for this equation on Graph 11-19 and label it LM_1.

c. The equilibrium of the economy occurs at the intersection of the *IS* curve and the *LM* curve. This point gives the interest rate *r* and the level of income *Y* at which actual expenditure equals planned expenditure, and the supply of real money balances equals the demand for real money balances. Compute the equilibrium values of *Y* and *r* by setting the equation for the *IS* curve equal to the equation for the *LM* curve and solving for *Y* and *r*.

The equilibrium value of *Y* = _____, and the equilibrium value of *r* = _____ percent. Locate these values on Graph 11-19 and label them Y_1 and r_1, respectively.

Problems

Answer the following problems on a separate sheet of paper.

1. Assume the following model of the economy:

$$C = 180 + 0.8(Y - T)$$
$$I = 190$$
$$G = 250$$
$$T = 150.$$

a. What is the value of the *MPC* in this model?

b. Draw the planned expenditure curve and indicate its slope and *y* intercept.

c. Compute the equilibrium level of income.

d. Calculate the level of unplanned inventory accumulation when *Y* = 3,000.

2. Consider the same model as in Problem 1:

$$C = 180 + 0.8(Y - T)$$
$$I = 190$$
$$G = 250$$
$$T = 150.$$

a. Compute the initial equilibrium level of income.

b. If government purchases were to increase by 10 to 260, what would happen to each of the following? State the amount as well as the direction of the changes.

    i.   the planned expenditure curve
    ii.   the equilibrium level of income
    iii. the level of consumption
    iv. the government budget deficit

c. Starting over again at $G = 250$, suppose that taxes increased by 10 to 160. What would happen to each of the following? State the amount as well as the direction of the changes.

    i.   the planned expenditure curve
    ii.   the equilibrium level of income
    iii. the level of consumption
    iv. the government budget deficit

d. Starting over one last time at $G = 250$ and $T = 150$, suppose that government expenditures and taxes were both increased by 10 to 260 and 160, respectively. What would happen to each of the following? This time, draw the consumption, government purchases, and planned expenditure graphs to indicate the amount as well as the direction of the changes.

    i.   the planned expenditure curve
    ii.   the equilibrium level of income
    iii. the level of consumption
    iv. the government budget deficit

3. Consider the following model of the economy:

$$C = 170 + 0.6(Y - T)$$
$$I = 250$$
$$G = 300$$
$$T = 200.$$

a. What is the value of the marginal propensity to consume?

b. What is the value of the government budget *deficit*?

c. Calculate the equilibrium level of GDP.

d. What is the value of the government-purchases multiplier?

e. Use your answer to Part d to calculate the amount by which government purchases of goods and services would have to rise in order to increase the equilibrium level of GDP by 50.

4. Consider the following model of the economy:

$$C = 20 + 0.75(Y - T)$$
$$I = 380$$
$$G = 400$$
$$T = 0.20Y$$
$$Y = C + I + G$$

a. What is the value of the *MPC* in this model?

b. The equation for taxes indicates that when *Y* rises by $100, taxes rise by $20. Consequently, when *Y* rises by $100, disposable income *Y* – *T* rises by $80 and consumption rises by 0.75(80) = $60. Draw the consumption and planned expenditure curves as a function of *Y* and label their slopes and *y* intercepts.

c. Compute the equilibrium level of income.

d. At the equilibrium level of income, what is the value of the government budget surplus?

e. Increase *G* by 10 to 410, calculate the government-purchases multiplier, and explain why it no longer equals $1/(1 - MPC)$.

5. Suppose that the following equations describe an economy (*C, I, G, T,* and *Y* are measured in billions of dollars, and *r* is measured as a percent; for example, $r = 10 = 10\%$):

$$C = 170 + 0.6(Y - T)$$
$$T = 200$$
$$I = 100 - 4r$$
$$G = 350$$
$$(M/P)^d = L = 0.75Y - 6r$$
$$M^S/P = \overline{M/P} = 735.$$

a. Derive the equation for the *IS* curve. (*Hint:* It is easier to solve for *Y* here.)

b. Derive the equation for the *LM* curve. (*Hint:* Again, it is easier to solve for *Y*.)

c. Now express both the *IS* and *LM* equations in terms of *r*. Graph both curves and calculate their slopes.

d. Use the equations from Parts a and b to calculate the equilibrium levels of real output, the interest rate, planned investment, and consumption.

e. At the equilibrium level of real output, calculate the value of the government budget surplus.

6. **a.** Rather than being independent of changes in Y, suppose that planned investment increases as real income Y rises and decreases as Y falls. Briefly explain why this situation might occur. Then draw the planned investment curve.

   b. Compared to the case in which investment is independent of Y, how would the situation in Part a affect each of the following?

       i. the slope of the planned expenditure curve
       ii. the government-purchases multiplier
       iii. the shapes of the IS and/or LM curves

7. Suppose that there is a sudden increase in the demand for money—that is, at the same levels of r and Y people want to hold more money. What would happen to the money demand curve and the LM curve?

8. How would each of the following changes affect the shape of the IS curve?

   a. the MPC gets bigger

   b. investment becomes more sensitive to changes in the interest rate (for example, investment now rises by a bigger amount whenever the interest rate falls by one percentage point)

9. In 2009, President Obama increased government spending on infrastructure, increased unemployment insurance benefits, and decreased Social Security taxes.

   a. What were the short-run effects on the planned expenditure curve and the equilibrium level of GDP?

   b. What were the effects on the IS and/or LM curves? Be as precise as you can about the exact shifts.

Data Questions

Locate the necessary economic data and apply them to answer the following data questions. All of the relevant data may be found in the Economic Report of the President (http://www.gpoaccess.gov/eop/).

1. **a.** Complete Table 11-7.

Table 11-7

(1) Year	(2) December Nominal *M2* ($ in billions)	(3) % Change in *M2*	(4) GDP Deflator (2005 = 100)	(5) Real *M2* *M2/P*	(6) % Change in *M2/P*
1979	————		————	————	
		————			————
1980	————		————	————	
		————			————
1981	————		————	————	
		————			————
1982	————		————	————	
		————			————
1983	————		————	————	

b. Given your calculations, would you characterize monetary policy in *each* of these five periods as expansionary, neutral, or contractionary? Which is the most appropriate measure of changes in monetary conditions: changes in the real or nominal money supply? (*Hint*: What happened to the economy in this period?)

Questions to Think About

1. Which definition of the money supply, *M*1 or *M*2, is more appropriate to use to derive the *LM* curve?

2. Banks now pay interest on checking deposits, although the interest rates they pay are usually less than those paid on government bonds. Given this, does the liquidity preference theory of money still make sense? If so, what variable should appear on the vertical axis of the money demand and *LM* curves?

3. Many companies do not need to borrow in order to invest because they have ample retained earnings from past profits. Why will their investment decisions still depend on the interest rate?

Aggregate Demand II

Fill-in Questions

Use the key terms below to fill in the blanks in the following statements. Each term may be used more than once.

debt-deflation theory
federal funds rate
liquidity trap
monetary transmission mechanism

Pigou effect
shocks to the *IS* curve
shocks to the *LM* curve
zero lower bound

1. The process by which an increase in the money supply induces greater spending is called the _____.

2. Exogenous changes in the demand for goods and services are called _____. Exogenous changes in the demand for money lead to _____.

3. The interest rate that banks charge one another for overnight loans is called the _____. It is also the Fed's short-term policy instrument.

4. A lower price level implies higher real money balances. According to the _____, consumers then feel wealthier and, therefore, spend more.

5. According to the _____, unexpected deflation hurts debtors and benefits creditors. Consequently, national income will fall if debtors have a higher propensity to spend than creditors.

6. Some economists believe that U.S. interest rates fell so low in the 1930s and again in 2008 that the United States may have been in a _____, also known as the problem of the _____. In this situation expansionary monetary policy may be unable to stimulate the economy.

Multiple-Choice Questions

1. An increase in government purchases will shift the:

   a. *IS* curve to the left and decrease both the interest rate and the level of income.
   b. *IS* curve to the right and increase both the interest rate and the level of income.
   c. *IS* curve to the right and increase the level of income but decrease the interest rate.
   d. *LM* curve downward (to the right) and increase the level of income but decrease the interest rate.

2. An increase in taxes will shift the:

   a. *IS* curve to the left and decrease both the interest rate and the level of income.
   b. *IS* curve to the right and increase both the interest rate and the level of income.
   c. *IS* curve to the right and increase the level of income but decrease the interest rate.
   d. *LM* curve downward (to the right) and increase the level of income but decrease the interest rate.

3. An increase in the money supply will shift the:

   a. *IS* curve to the left and decrease both the interest rate and the level of income.
   b. *LM* curve downward (to the right) and increase both the interest rate and the level of income.
   c. *IS* curve to the right and increase the level of income but decrease the interest rate.
   d. *LM* curve downward (to the right) and increase the level of income but decrease the interest rate.

4. If real income rose and the interest rate fell following an increase in government purchases, the:

   a. *IS* curve must be vertical.
   b. *LM* curve must be vertical.
   c. Fed must have increased the money supply at the same time.
   d. Fed must have decreased the money supply at the same time.

5. If the Fed decreases the money supply at the same time as taxes increase, the:

   a. interest rate will definitely rise.
   b. interest rate will definitely fall.
   c. equilibrium level of income will definitely rise.
   d. equilibrium level of income will definitely fall.

6. The *IS* curve will shift to the right if:

   a. consumer confidence in the economy improves.
   b. firms become more optimistic about the economy and decide to invest more at each interest rate.
   c. the government increases transfer payments.
   d. All of the answers are correct.

7. If people suddenly wish to hold more money at each interest rate:

   a. the money demand curve will shift to the right.

   b. the *LM* curve will shift upward (to the left).

   c. real income will fall.

   d. All of the answers are correct.

8. In judging the accuracy of a macroeconometric model computer simulation, one should consider:

   a. the appropriateness of the assumptions used in formulating the model.

   b. the reliability of the data used in the simulation.

   c. the appropriateness of the statistical techniques used to estimate the parameters of the model.

   d. all of the above.

9. Each of the following shocks was a contributing factor in the 2001 recession in the United States EXCEPT the:

   a. decline in the stock market in 2000.

   b. terrorist attack on the World Trade Center on September 11, 2001.

   c. drought in the Midwest farmlands.

   d. accounting scandals at Enron and WorldCom.

10. When the Fed wants to spur the economy, it:

    a. acts to increase the money supply.

    b. acts to reduce the federal funds rate.

    c. acts to shift the *LM* curve downward (to the right).

    d. All of the answers occur.

11. Which of the following statements explains why the aggregate demand curve is downward-sloping?

    a. A lower price level increases real money balances. Consequently, the *LM* curve shifts downward (to the right) and the level of income increases.

    b. A lower price level forces the Fed to increase the money supply. Consequently, the *LM* curve shifts down (to the right) and the level of income increases.

    c. A lower price level induces the government to reduce taxes. Consequently, the *IS* curve shifts to the right and the level of income increases.

    d. All of the answers are correct.

12. As we move along a stationary aggregate demand curve, one factor that is held constant is:

    a. real income.

    b. the aggregate price level.

    c. the (nominal) money supply.

    d. real money balances.

13. All of the following will shift the aggregate demand curve to the right EXCEPT a(n):

    a. increase in government purchases.

    b. reduction in transfer payments.

    c. increase in the (nominal) money supply.

    d. reduction in taxes.

14. The FALSE statement below is:
    a. the classical assumption that output reaches its natural level is best used to describe the long run.
    b. in the short run, output may deviate from its natural level.
    c. in the *IS-LM* model, the price level is assumed to be sticky in the short run.
    d. in the *IS-LM* model, aggregate demand is never equal to the natural level of output even in the long run.

15. If income is initially less than the natural level of output, the price level:
    a. will gradually fall, shifting the *LM* curve downward (to the right).
    b. will gradually rise, shifting the *LM* curve upward (to the left).
    c. will fall, shifting the *IS* curve to the right.
    d. is stuck at this level even in the long run.

16. According to adherents of the money hypothesis, the Great Depression was caused by a:
    a. sharp decline in the money supply.
    b. decline in business confidence.
    c. decline in consumer confidence.
    d. sharp decline in real money balances.

17. According to adherents of the spending hypothesis, the Great Depression was caused by:
    a. a reduction in business and consumer confidence.
    b. a contractionary (leftward) shift in the *IS* curve.
    c. the stock market crash.
    d. All of the answers are correct.

18. According to the Pigou effect:
    a. for a given supply of money, a lower price level shifts the *LM* curve outward, which leads to a higher level of income.
    b. since consumers will buy more of a good as its price falls, real output will rise during a depression.
    c. as prices fall and real balances rise, consumers will feel wealthier and spend more.
    d. All of the answers are correct.

19. According to the debt-deflation theory, unexpected deflation hurts debtors and benefits creditors. Consequently, national income will fall if:
    a. both groups have the same spending propensities.
    b. debtors have a higher propensity to spend than creditors.
    c. creditors have a higher propensity to spend than debtors.
    d. the *MPC* for both groups is less than 1.

20. The following statement is FALSE:

    a. money demand depends on the nominal interest rate.

    b. investment demand depends on the real interest rate.

    c. *IS-LM* analysis is unable to incorporate changes in expected inflation.

    d. an expected deflation causes the real interest rate to rise at each level of the nominal interest rate, which leads to a contractionary (leftward) shift of the *IS* curve if the nominal interest rate is on the vertical axis.

21. Most economists believe that a Great Depression is less likely today than it was during the 1930s because:

    a. our knowledge of monetary and fiscal stabilization policies has improved.

    b. the system of federal deposit insurance makes widespread bank failures less likely.

    c. we now have more automatic stabilizers, such as the income tax.

    d. All of the answers are correct.

22. From 1996 to 2006, housing prices in the United States doubled. When prices fell by 30 percent during the next three years, however, which of the following repercussions contributed to the recession that began in 2008?

    a. a rise in mortgage defaults and home foreclosures

    b. large losses at the financial institutions that owned mortgage-backed securities

    c. a decline in consumer confidence, due partly to increased volatility in the stock market

    d. All of the answers are correct.

23. If an economy is in a liquidity trap, then:

    a. the interest rate is so low that fiscal policy cannot stimulate the economy.

    b. the interest rate is so low that monetary policy cannot stimulate the economy.

    c. the budget deficit is so high that fiscal policy cannot stimulate the economy.

    d. All of the answers are correct.

Exercises

1. **Shifts in the *IS* and *LM* Curves and Short-Run Changes in the Equilibrium Level of Income** *In this exercise, we review the policy and nonpolicy changes that shift the* IS *and* LM *curves, and we graphically illustrate the short-run changes in the equilibrium level of income. A review of Exercises 4 and 7 in Chapter 11 would be very helpful.*

   a. Examine the initial equilibrium shown at Point A on Graph 12-1.

Graph 12-1

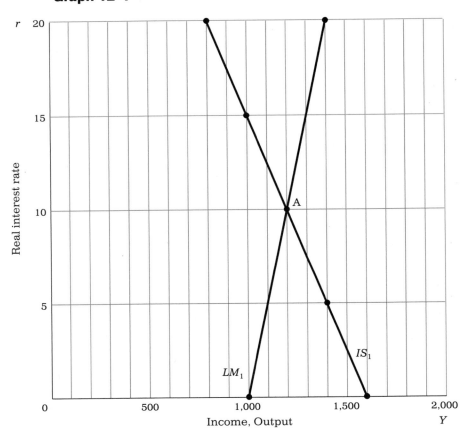

Recall that the *IS* curve depicts the relationship between the interest rate r and the equilibrium value of income that results from the investment function and the Keynesian cross. The *LM* curve depicts the combinations of r and Y for which a given supply of real money balances is equal to real money demand. At the initial situation illustrated in Graph 12-1, the initial equilibrium level of income equals _____, and the initial equilibrium interest rate equals _____ percent. This occurs at Point A.

b. Starting from the initial equilibrium illustrated on Graph 12-1, suppose that government purchases increase by $100 billion. As a result, the planned expenditure curve (which is not shown) will shift <u>upward/downward</u> by
$_____ billion. If the *MPC* equals 0.75, the *IS* curve will shift to the <u>right/left</u> by $100 billion × the government-purchases multiplier, or by
$_____ billion. Draw this *IS* curve on Graph 12-1 and label it *IS*$_2$.

c. As income rises, money demand <u>rises/falls</u>. To keep real money demand equal to a constant real money supply, any increase in income must be accompanied by a(n) <u>increase/decrease</u> in the interest rate. As a result of this change in the interest rate, firms will <u>increase/decrease</u> investment, which partially offsets the effect of the increase in government purchases. Consequently, the equilibrium level of income rises by <u>less/more</u> than the horizontal shift in the *IS* curve. Locate the new equilibrium on Graph 12-1 and label it Point B.

d. Starting again from Point A, suppose that taxes increased by $100 billion. If the *MPC* = 0.75, the expenditure curve will shift <u>upward/downward</u> by
$_____ billion, and the *IS* curve will shift to the <u>right/left</u>
by $_____ billion. Draw this curve on Graph 12-1 and label it *IS*$_3$.

e. As income falls, money demand <u>rises/falls</u>. To keep real money demand equal to a constant real money supply, any decrease in income must be accompanied by a(n) <u>increase/decrease</u> in the interest rate. This, in turn, leads to a(n) <u>increase/decrease</u> in investment, which partially offsets the effect of the increase in taxes. Consequently, the equilibrium level of income falls by <u>more/less</u> than the horizontal shift in the *IS* curve. Locate the new equilibrium on Graph 12-1 and label it Point C.

f. Now examine Graph 12-2, which again illustrates the initial equilibrium.

Graph 12-2

If the Federal Reserve were to increase the money supply, the *LM* curve would shift upward (to the left)/downward (to the right). Draw this shift on Graph 12-2. Label the new curve *LM*₂ and the new equilibrium Point D. As a result of this increase in the money supply, the equilibrium interest rate would rise/fall and the equilibrium level of income would rise/fall. When the Federal Reserve increases the money supply, at the initial interest rate people have more money than they want to hold. Consequently, they start depositing the extra money in banks or buy more bonds, which tends to raise/lower the interest rate until people want to hold all the extra money created by the Fed. This change in the interest rate increases/decreases planned investment, which increases/decreases planned expenditure and the equilibrium level of income. If, instead, the Fed reduced the money supply, the *LM* curve would shift upward (to the left)/downward (to the right), the equilibrium interest rate would rise/fall, and the equilibrium level of income would rise/fall.

g. Nonpolicy changes can also shift the *IS* and/or *LM* curves. If firms suddenly feel more optimistic about the future and decide to invest more at every interest rate, the *IS/LM* curve would shift _____, the equilibrium level of income would rise/fall, and the equilibrium interest rate would rise/fall. If households became more pessimistic about the future and decided to consume less at every level of disposable income, the *IS/LM* curve would shift _____, the equilibrium level of income would rise/fall, and the equilibrium interest rate would rise/fall. Finally, if the amount of real money demanded increases substantially at each interest rate and level of income, the money demand curve will shift to the right/left and the *IS/LM* curve would shift _____. Consequently, the equilibrium level of income would rise/fall and the equilibrium interest rate would rise/fall.

2. **The Aggregate Demand Curve** *In this exercise, we examine the changes in the* IS-LM *equilibria as the price level varies, and derive the aggregate demand curve.*

a. Graph 12-3 illustrates the initial equilibrium in the basic model presented in the exercises for Chapter 11 of this workbook.

The real money supply initially is equal to $800 billion, and the initial equilibrium is at Point A. If the real money supply increases to $1,040 billion, the *LM* curve will shift upward (to the left)/downward (to the right). Locate the appropriate curve on Graph 12-3, label it LM_2, and label the new equilibrium Point B.

b. If, on the other hand, the real money supply falls to $560 billion, the *LM* curve will shift upward (to the left)/downward (to the right). Locate this curve on Graph 12-3, label it LM_3, and label the corresponding equilibrium Point C.

c. The aggregate demand curve can now be derived using Graphs 12-3 and 12-4. As we saw in Part a, the *LM* curve will shift downward (to the right) whenever there is an increase in the real money supply. This can be accomplished if the Fed increases the nominal money supply *M*, holding the aggregate price level *P* constant. It can also be accomplished by reducing *P*, while holding *M* constant. Using this information, a more general and realistic aggregate demand curve than the one introduced in Chapter 10 can be derived. This aggregate demand curve plots the relationship between the price level and the level of income that arises from the *IS-LM* model. On Graph 12-3, Point A represents the *IS-LM* equilibrium when the real money supply equals $800 billion. If the nominal money supply *M* = $800 billion and the real money supply equals *M/P*, the aggregate price level *P* = _____. From Graph 12-3, note that real income *Y* at Point A = _____. Use this information to plot one point on what will become the aggregate demand curve on Graph 12-4 and label this Point A.

Graph 12-3

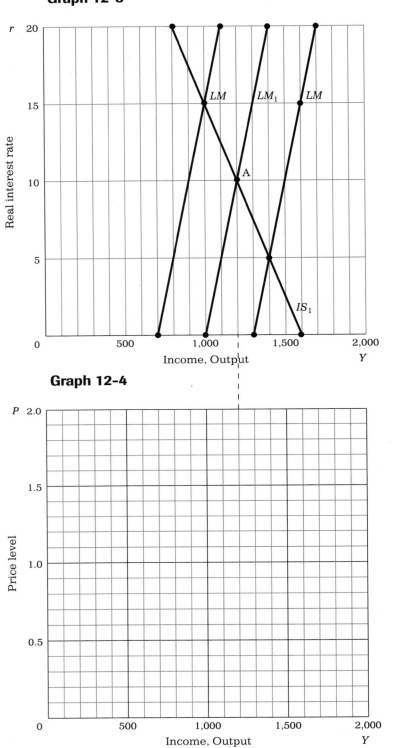

Graph 12-4

d. Similarly, Point B on Graph 12-3 represents the *IS-LM* equilibrium when the real money supply equals 1,040. If *M* remains equal to 800, this occurs as a result of a change in the price level. Thus, $M/P = 800/P = 1,040$. Calculate *P* (round off to two decimal places).

$P =$ _____.

Real income at Point B on Graph 12-3 = _____. Use this information about *P* and *Y* to plot another point on the aggregate demand curve on Graph 12-4 and label this Point B.

e. Finally, Point C on Graph 12-3 represents the *IS-LM* equilibrium when the real money supply equals 560. If, instead of a decrease in the nominal money supply, this situation occurs as a result of a change in the price level, then $M/P = 800/P = 560$. Calculate *P* (round off to two decimal places).

$P =$ _____.

Real income at Point C = _____. Use this information about *P* and *Y* to plot another point on the aggregate demand curve on Graph 12-4, and label this Point C. Now connect all three points on Graph 12-4 to draw the aggregate demand curve.

f. Summarizing Parts a–e, the aggregate demand curve slopes downward because as the aggregate price level falls, real money balances increase/decrease. This shifts the *IS/LM* curve _____, increases/decreases the interest rate, and increases/decreases planned investment. As a result, the equilibrium level of income at the intersection of the *IS* and *LM* curves increases/decreases. Note that, as we move along a stationary aggregate demand curve, government purchases, taxes, and the nominal money supply all remain constant.

3. **Fiscal Policy and the Aggregate Demand Curve** *In this exercise, we show how changes in fiscal policy shift the aggregate demand curve.*

On Graphs 12-5 and 12-6, the aggregate demand curve is derived for arbitrary *IS-LM* curves.

a. Assume that LM_A is drawn for a nominal money supply equal to 800 (billion dollars) and a price level equal to 1.0. Thus, at the initial equilibrium Point A, $P =$ _____ and $Y =$ _____. (Find Y from Graph 12-5.) Point A is also depicted on Graph 12-6. If the price level fell to 0.5, the real money supply would increase to $M/P = 800/0.5 =$ _____. This is reflected on Graph 12-5 by a shift in the *LM* curve to LM_B. The goods and money markets reach a new equilibrium at Point B, at which $Y =$ _____. This change is also reflected on Graph 12-6 by a movement along AD_1 to Point B.

b. Start again at Point A with $M/P = 800/1.0 = 800$, and let government purchases rise by 100. If the marginal propensity to consume equals 0.75 (or 3/4), the government-purchases multiplier $= 1/(1 - MPC) =$ _____. Consequently, if government purchases rise by 100, the *IS* curve shifts to the right/left by _____. Draw this new *IS* curve on Graph 12-5 and label it IS_2.

c. Because the *LM* curve has a positive slope, Y would rise by more/less than the horizontal shift in the *IS* curve. Starting at Point A on Graph 12-5, find the new equilibrium level of income if P remains equal to 1.0 and label it Point C. Find the corresponding point on Graph 12-6 and also label it Point C. (It will no longer lie on AD_1.)

d. Now start at Point B on Graph 12-5, with $M/P = 800/0.5 = 1,600$. Find the new equilibrium level of income if P remains equal to 0.5 after government purchases rise by 100 and label it Point D. Find the corresponding point on Graph 12-6 and also label it Point D. (It will no longer lie on AD_1.)

e. Connect Points C and D on Graph 12-6 to draw the new aggregate demand curve and label it AD_2. Compare Points C and A in both graphs. At Point C, real income is higher than/lower than/equal to real income at Point A, and the price

Graph 12-5

Graph 12-6

level at Point C is <u>higher than/lower than/equal to</u> the price level at Point A. Now compare Points D and B. At Point D, real income is <u>higher than/lower than/equal to</u> real income at Point B, and the price level is <u>higher than/lower than/equal to</u> the price level at Point B.

f. Consequently, an increase in government purchases will shift the *IS* curve to the <u>right/left</u> and the aggregate demand curve to the <u>right/left</u>. A reduction in taxes will shift the *IS* curve to the <u>right/left</u> and the aggregate demand curve to the <u>right/left</u>.

4. **Monetary Policy and the Aggregate Demand Curve** *In this exercise, we show how changes in monetary policy shift the aggregate demand curve.*

   On Graphs 12-7 and 12-8, the aggregate demand curve is derived for arbitrary *IS-LM* curves.

   a. Assume that LM_A is drawn for a (nominal) money supply equal to 800 (billion dollars) and a price level equal to 1.0. Thus, at the initial equilibrium Point A, $P =$ _____ and $Y =$ _____. (Find Y from Graph 12-7.) Point A is also illustrated on Graph 12-8.

   b. If the Fed were to double the nominal money supply to 1,600 and the price level remained constant, the real money supply would rise to $M/P = 1{,}600/1.0 =$ _____. This would shift the *LM* curve on Graph 12-7 <u>upward (to the left)/downward (to the right)</u>. Locate the new *LM* curve on Graph 12-7 and label it LM_E. Locate the point on Graph 12-7 at which the goods and money markets reach a new equilibrium and label it Point E. Find the corresponding point on Graph 12-8 and also label it Point E (Point E does *not* lie on AD_1).

   c. Note that, at Point E on Graph 12-8, real income is <u>higher than/lower than/equal to</u> real income at Point A, whereas the price level at Point E is <u>higher than/lower than/equal to</u> the price level at Point A. Consequently, an increase in the nominal money supply will shift the aggregate demand curve to the <u>right/left</u>. Conversely, a decrease in the nominal money supply will shift the aggregate demand curve to the <u>right/left</u>.

   d. Finally, suppose that the nominal money supply remained equal to 1,600 while the price level rose to 2.0. The real money supply would then equal $M/P = 1{,}600/2.0 =$ _____. Consequently, the *LM* curve would shift all the way back to LM_A, and Y would equal _____ (even though the price level is now 2.0). Locate the new equilibrium points on both Graphs 12-7 and 12-8 and label them Points F. Note that Point F is the same as Point A on Graph 12-7 but not the same as Point A on Graph 12-8. This situation occurs because an increase in the nominal money supply will shift the aggregate demand curve, but the *LM* curve is affected only by changes in real money balances.

Graph 12-7

Graph 12-8

5.   **The *IS-LM* Model in the Short Run and the Long Run**   *In this exercise, we start from an* IS-LM *equilibrium level of income that is lower than the long-run equilibrium level and illustrate how reductions in the aggregate price level will shift the* LM *curve toward the long-run equilibrium.*

a.   Assume the following equation for an economy's *IS* curve:

$$r = 40 - 0.025Y.$$

Plot and draw this curve on Graph 12-9 and label it IS_1.

Graph 12-9

b.   Assume the following money demand curve for this economy:

$$M/P = 0.8Y - 16r.$$

If $M = 800$ and $P = 1.0$, derive the equation for the economy's *LM* curve by setting real money balances equal to real money demand and solving for r.

$r =$ _____ $+$ _____ $Y.$

Plot and draw this curve on Graph 12-9 and label it $LM(P_1 = 1.0)$.

c. Solve the *IS* and *LM* equations simultaneously. The initial equilibrium level of income and the initial interest rate are:

$Y =$ _____; $r =$ _____.

Label the initial equilibrium Point A on Graphs 12-9 and 12-10. Remember that the initial price level is assumed to be 1.0.

Graph 12-10

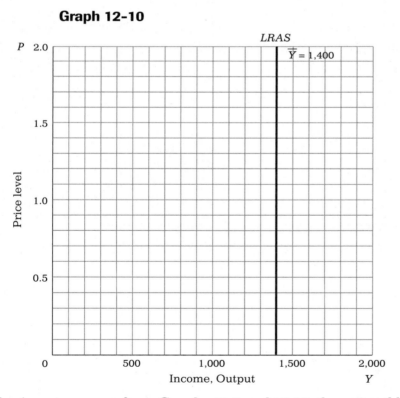

d. As you can see from Graphs 12-9 and 12-10, the natural level of output $\overline{Y}$, which is also the long-run equilibrium level of income, is assumed to equal 1,400. Consequently, the initial level of income is <u>more/less</u> than the long-run equilibrium level of income. Point A is a short-run equilibrium level because the price level is assumed to be <u>sticky/flexible</u> in the short run, leading to a <u>horizontal/vertical</u> short-run aggregate supply curve.

e. In the long run, however, prices are sticky/flexible. Thus, as time goes by, the price level will rise/fall. This change will increase/decrease the real money supply, thereby shifting the *LM* curve upward (to the left)/downward (to the right) until it intersects the *IS* curve at the natural level of output. Draw the long-run position of the *LM* curve on Graph 12-9 and label it $LM(P_2)$. Label the final equilibrium Point B on both Graphs 12-9 and 12-10.

f. The final price level can be computed in the following way. In the long run, $Y = $ **CH** 1,400, and will lie on the original *IS* curve. Substitute $Y = 1,400$ into the *IS* equation and solve for r.

$r = $ _____.

Given our long-run values for Y and r, use the money demand equation to compute real money demand.

$M/P = $ _____.

Since M is still equal to 800, this increase in M/P must come from a decrease in the price level. Solve the preceding equation for P (round off to two decimal places).

$P = $ _____.

g. Conversely, if the initial *IS–LM* equilibrium level of income were higher than the natural level of output, over time the aggregate price level would rise/fall, thereby shifting the *IS/LM* curve _____ until the *IS* and *LM* curves intersected at the long-run equilibrium.

6. **Changes in Expected Inflation in the *IS-LM* Model** *In this exercise, we illustrate how a change in expected inflation will change the* IS-LM *equilibrium.*

   a. Investment is a function of the real interest rate r, whereas money demand is a function of the nominal interest rate i. Consequently, the *IS* curve should be drawn as a function of r, and the *LM* curve should be drawn as a function of i. Assume that the equations for the *IS* and *LM* curves are:

   $$IS \text{ curve: } r = 40 - 0.025Y \text{ and}$$
   $$LM \text{ curve: } i = -50 + 0.05Y.$$

   Recall that $r = i - \pi^e$. Assume that expected inflation equals zero so that $r = i$, and it does not matter which variable we put on the vertical axis. We'll put the nominal interest rate i on the vertical axis. Draw these two curves on Graph 12-11, label them IS_1 and LM_1, and label the initial equilibrium Point A.

   Graph 12-11

   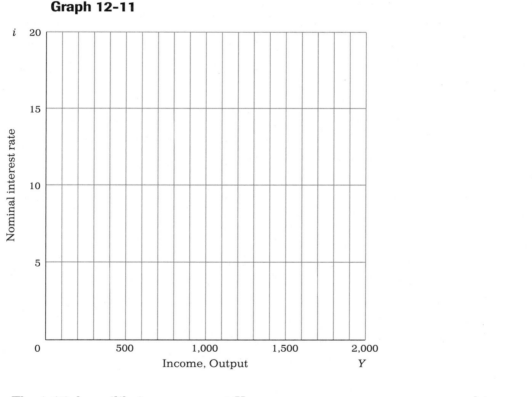

   b. The initial equilibrium occurs at $Y =$ _____ and $i =$ _____ percent. Since $\pi^e = 0$, $r =$ _____ percent.

c. Now suppose that we have deflation and expected inflation falls to –7.5 percent. As a result of this decrease in expected inflation, the real interest rate at the initial value of the nominal interest rate will rise to $r = i - \pi^e =$ _____ $- (-7.5) =$ _____ percent. Consequently, at each level of i, r will now be <u>higher/lower</u> than it was before the expected deflation. Since the LM curve is a function of the nominal interest rate, it will not shift. The IS curve, on the other hand, is a function of the real interest rate. From the IS equation, it is known that $Y = 1,200$ when $r =$ _____ percent. When $\pi^e = 0$, this value of r occurs when $i =$ _____ percent. Now that $\pi^e = -7.5$ percent, this level of r will occur when $i = r + \pi^e =$ _____ + _____ = _____ percent. Thus, the same level of investment will occur only if i falls by _____ percentage points. Consequently, the IS curve shifts <u>upward/downward</u> by _____ percentage points. Draw the new IS curve on Graph 12-11, label it IS_2, and label the new equilibrium Point B.

d. The equation for the new IS curve when $\pi^e = -7.5$ percent is $i = 32.5 - 0.025Y$. Set this equal to the equation for the LM curve, and compute the new equilibrium values of Y and i:

$Y =$ _____ ; $i =$ _____.

e. The decrease in expected inflation leads to a(n) <u>increase/decrease</u> in Y and a(n) <u>increase/decrease</u> in i. The real interest rate $r = i - \pi^e$ was initially equal to _____ – _____ = _____ percent but now equals _____ – _____ = _____ percent. Consequently, the real interest rate <u>rises/falls</u>.

7. **Determinants of the Steepness of the *IS* Curve** *In this exercise, we examine how the slope of the IS curve is affected by the marginal propensity to consume and the sensitivity of planned investment to changes in the interest rate.*

   a. Recall from Chapter 11, Exercise 4e, that when planned investment increases by 50, the planned expenditure curve shifts upward by _____, and income Y rises by the shift in the planned expenditure curve multiplied by the government-purchases multiplier, or by _____ $\times 1/(1 - MPC)$. In our example, $MPC = 0.75$, so Y rose by _____ $\times$ $1/(1 -$ _____$) =$ _____.

   b. Now suppose that the MPC were larger. If, for example, it were 0.9, the government-purchases multiplier would equal $1/(1 - MPC) = 1/(1 -$ _____$) =$ _____. This is <u>larger/smaller</u> than the multiplier in Exercise 4e in Chapter 11.

   c. If $MPC = 0.9$, the government-purchases multiplier $=$ _____, and an increase in planned investment of 50 would increase the equilibrium level of Y by $50 \times 1/(1 - MPC) =$ _____. This increase is <u>larger/smaller</u> than the increase in Y in Part a.

   d. According to our original investment equation, $I = 200 - 10r$. To increase investment by 50, as in Parts a–c, the interest rate would have to decrease by _____ percentage points. In Part a, this reduction in r increased the equilibrium level of Y by _____. In Part c, this same reduction in r increased the equilibrium level of Y by _____ because the multiplier, or round-by-round effects on consumption, were <u>larger/smaller</u>. Thus, as the MPC grows larger, the increase in Y resulting from a reduction in r becomes <u>larger/smaller</u> and the *IS* curve becomes <u>steeper/flatter</u>.

   e. Now suppose that the MPC remains equal to 0.75. Our original investment equation, $I = 200 - 10r$, implies that whenever the interest rate falls by 1 percentage point, planned investment increases by _____. This investment curve is illustrated on Graph 12-12.

Graph 12-12

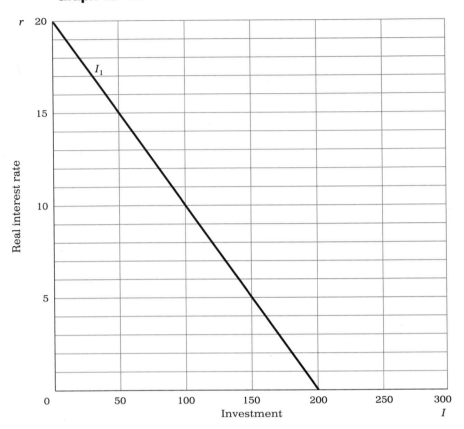

f. Suppose, instead, that $I = 300 - 20r$. According to this second equation, whenever the interest rate falls by 1 percentage point, planned investment increases by _____. Consequently, investment would be <u>more/less</u> sensitive to changes in the interest rate than in Part e. Graph this second investment equation on Graph 12-12 and label it I_2. I_2 is <u>steeper/flatter</u> than I_1.

g. Note that the two investment curves on Graph 12-12 intersect when $r = 10$ and $I =$ _____. Since all of the other parameters are the same, when $r = 10$, the equilibrium value of Y will be the same as before—that is, $Y = 1,200$.

h. Suppose that the MPC is still 0.75 and the interest rate falls by 5 percentage points. Using our original investment equation $I = 200 - 10r$, planned investment will rise by $5 \times$ _____ $= 50$, and the equilibrium level of Y will rise by $50 \times 1/(1 - MPC) = 50 \times$ _____ $=$ _____. With our new investment equation, planned investment will rise by $5 \times$ _____ $=$ _____, and the equilibrium level of Y will rise by _____ $\times 1/(1 - MPC) =$ _____. Consequently, the IS curve will be <u>steeper/flatter</u> when planned investment becomes more sensitive to changes in the interest rate.

8. **Determinants of the Steepness of the *LM* Curve** *In this exercise, we examine how the slope of the LM curve is affected by the sensitivity of money demand to changes in real income and the sensitivity of money demand to changes in the interest rate.*

   a. In Chapter 11, Exercise 6, the *LM* curve was derived from the following equations for real money supply and real money demand:

   $$\overline{M} / \overline{P} = 800 \text{ (money supply equation)} \qquad \text{(12-1)}$$
   $$(M/P)^d = 0.8Y - 16r \text{ (money demand equation)} \qquad \text{(12-2)}$$

   Now suppose that money demand were more sensitive to changes in Y, so that the coefficient on Y were equal to 1.0, rather than 0.8:

   $$(M/P)^d = 1.0Y - 16r. \qquad \text{(12-3)}$$

   If this were the case, an increase in Y would increase money demand by <u>more/less</u> than in Chapter 11, Exercise 7. To keep real money demand equal to the fixed real money supply, the interest rate would have to increase by <u>more/less</u> than in Exercise 7 of Chapter 11. This change would make the *LM* curve <u>steeper/flatter</u> than in Exercise 6.

   b. As an example, suppose that Y increased by 160. In Equation 12-2, if the interest rate were to remain constant, money demand would increase by 0.8(160) = _____. To keep real money demand equal to the fixed supply, the interest rate would have to increase by _____/16 = _____. In Equation 12-3, however, if r were to remain constant, money demand would increase by 1.0(160) = _____. To keep real money demand equal to the fixed supply, r would have to increase by _____/16 = _____. Consequently, when Y increases by 160, the interest rate rises by more when money demand is <u>more/less</u> sensitive to changes in Y, and, hence, the *LM* curve is <u>steeper/flatter</u>.

   c. Refer to the original money demand equation, Equation 12-2. According to this equation, whenever r increases by 1 (percentage point), money demand falls by _____. Now compare this equation with one in which money demand is more sensitive to changes in the interest rate:

   $$(M/P)^d = 0.8Y - 32r. \qquad \text{(12-4)}$$

   According to Equation 12-4, whenever r increases by 1 percentage point, the quantity of money demanded falls by _____.
   Consequently, money demand is now <u>more/less</u> sensitive to changes in the interest rate, and the money demand curve would be <u>steeper/flatter</u>.

d. Suppose that Y again increased by 160. In Equations 12-2 and 12-4, if the interest rate were to remain constant, money demand would increase by 0.8(160) = _____. To keep real money demand equal to the fixed supply in Equation 12-2, the interest rate would have to increase by _____/16 = _____. In Equation 12-4, however, the interest rate would have to increase by _____/32 = _____. Consequently, when Y increases by 160, the interest rate rises by more when money demand is more/less sensitive to changes in the interest rate, and the LM curve will be steeper/flatter.

Problems

Answer the following problems on a separate sheet of paper.

1. (Parts a–e of this problem are the same as Problem 5 in Chapter 11 of this work-book.) Suppose that the following equations describe an economy (C, I, G, T, and Y are measured in billions of dollars and r is measured in percent; for example, $r = 10$ means $r = 10$ percent):

$$C = 170 + 0.6(Y - T)$$
$$T = 200$$
$$I = 100 - 4r$$
$$G = 350$$
$$(M/P)^d = L = 0.75Y - 6r$$
$$M^s/P = \overline{M}/\overline{P} = 735.$$

   a. Derive the equation for the IS curve. (*Hint:* It is easier to solve for real output Y here.)

   b. Derive the equation for the LM curve. (*Hint:* Again, it is easier to solve for real output Y.)

   c. Now express both the IS and LM equations in terms of r. Plot and graph both curves and calculate their slopes.

   d. Use the equations from Parts a and b to calculate the equilibrium levels of real output Y, the interest rate r, planned investment I, and consumption C.

   e. At the equilibrium level of real output Y, calculate the value of the government budget surplus.

   f. Suppose that G increases by 36 to 386. Derive the new IS and LM equations and plot and draw these curves on the graph you drew for Part c.

   g. What is the horizontal shift in the IS curve and/or the LM curve in Part f (i.e., if r remains constant, by how much does Y increase on each curve)?

   h. Refer to the IS and LM equations you derived in Part f. With Y on the left-hand side of the equations, calculate the new equilibrium levels of real output Y, the interest rate r, planned investment I, and consumption C.

i. Instead of increasing *G*, suppose that the Fed sought to achieve the equilibrium **CH** level of real output *Y* in Part h through expansionary monetary policy alone. By how much would the Fed have to increase the money supply? (*Hint:* Start by drawing the appropriate shifts in the *IS* curve and/or the *LM* curve in Parts f and i.)

j. Compare the equilibrium levels of consumption *C*, government spending *G*, and planned investment *I* in Parts h and i. Based on this comparison, why might some economists prefer expansionary fiscal policy while others prefer expansionary monetary policy?

2. As a result of the dramatic events in Eastern Europe in the 1990s, many Americans felt less threatened by Russia and called for massive reductions in the defense budget as a "peace dividend."

a. Suppose that the defense budget had been cut by one-third, or about $100 billion. If no other policy changes are enacted, use the *IS-LM* model to analyze what would happen to real GDP and the interest rate. Illustrate the changes that would occur by graphing the *IS* and *LM* curves and indicating their shift(s).

b. Now suppose that defense spending had been cut by the same $100 billion, but government transfers were raised by the same amount ($100 billion) to alleviate poverty and subsidize education and day care. Draw the appropriate shifts in the *IS* and/or *LM* curves on your graph for Part a and predict what would happen to real GDP and the interest rate.

c. Compare the sizes of the changes in Parts a and b.

3. Many economists believe that consumption expenditures depend on household wealth in addition to disposable income.

a. If this were true, how would the U.S. stock market decline in 2007–2009 have affected the consumption expenditure curve and the planned expenditure curve?

b. Draw representative *IS* and *LM* curves on a graph and illustrate the consequent shift(s) in the *IS* curve and/or the *LM* curve. Indicate the predicted (directional) changes in real output *Y* and the interest rate *r*.

4. In 2010, the British government proposed reducing the British budget deficit by **◘** increasing net taxes and reducing government spending. Some economists claimed that this policy would reduce interest rates and increase real GDP as well as cut the deficit.

a. Draw *IS-LM* graphs to analyze the effects of this mix of fiscal policies on the deficit, interest rates, and real GDP. (Assume that taxes are lump sum, that is, taxes are an absolute amount that is unrelated to the level of income.) Are these results consistent with the economists' predictions?

b. Most economists who believed that an increase in taxes and a reduction in government spending would both increase GDP and cut the deficit implicitly assumed that the Bank of England (the British central bank) would change its monetary policy if this deficit-reduction plan were enacted. Draw *IS-LM* graphs on a separate sheet of paper to show what kind of monetary policy must accompany this mix of fiscal policy changes in order to decrease the deficit and interest rates, while increasing GDP.

c. What happens to the aggregate demand curve in Parts a and b?

5. Suppose two countries differ only in the size of their *MPC*. In Country A, the *MPC* is large, and in Country B, the *MPC* is small.

   a. Draw representative *IS* and *LM* curves for each country and label them IS^A and LM^A for Country A and IS^B and LM^B for Country B. Compare the shapes of the *IS* and *LM* curves in the two countries and explain your results.

   b. In which country will an increase in the money supply be more effective in changing real output? Illustrate using the graph you drew in Part a.

6. Suppose that private spending (for example, *C* or *I*) is volatile and unpredictable. This situation implies that the *IS* curve would frequently shift to the right and to the left.

   a. Assume that the Fed decided to keep the real money supply constant. Draw *IS-LM* curves to illustrate how real output *Y* would respond to the instability in private spending.

   b. Now suppose that the Fed tried to keep the interest rate constant at its initial level even if this required frequent changes in the real money supply. Draw a money supply and demand diagram to show what the Fed would have to do to the real money supply when *Y* increases (because of a shift in the *IS* curve to the right). What would this monetary response do to the *IS* curve and/or *LM* curve?

   c. Similarly, if the Fed tried to keep the interest rate *r* constant, what would the Fed have to do to the real money supply when the *IS* curve shifts to the left and *Y* falls? What would this response do to the *IS* curve and/or *LM* curve?

   d. Using your answers to Parts b and c, explain which of the two policies (keeping *M/P* constant or keeping *r* constant) would stabilize the economy better (by minimizing the fluctuations in real GDP) if the main source of instability in the economy were fluctuations in private spending.

7. a. In 2009, President Obama increased government spending and cut net taxes. Draw the appropriate graphs to indicate what would happen to the *IS*, *LM*, aggregate demand, and short-run aggregate supply curves, and indicate any short-run changes in the equilibrium levels of *r*, *I*, *C*, *G*, *Y*, and *P* if the Fed had not changed any of its policies.

   b. During this period, the Fed actually pursued expansionary monetary policy and kept interest rates nearly constant. Redraw your diagrams from Part a and indicate what actually happened to the *IS* curve, *LM* curve, aggregate demand curve, short-run aggregate supply curve, and the levels of *r*, *I*, *C*, *G*, *Y*, and *P*. How do they compare with the levels in Part a?

8. Suppose policymakers want to raise investment but keep real GDP constant. Use the *IS-LM* model to describe and illustrate what *mix* of monetary and fiscal policies would achieve this goal.

9. In addition to depending on disposable income, suppose household consumption were also a function of the interest rate. In particular, assume that households consume more (i.e., save less) when the interest rate falls.

   a. Explain how this situation would influence the shapes of the *IS* and/or *LM* curves relative to the case in which consumption is not a function of the interest rate.

b. Now use *IS-LM* curves to illustrate how this situation would influence the short-run effectiveness of monetary policy.

c. What, if anything, would this modification do to the shape of the aggregate demand curve?

10. **a.** Suppose the economy were initially in long-run and short-run equilibrium. Illustrate this position by drawing an *IS-LM* graph and, directly below it, the aggregate supply–aggregate demand graph.

b. Now suppose that oil prices increase dramatically. On the same graphs that you drew in Part a, illustrate what happens in both the short run and the long run to the *IS* curve, *LM* curve, short-run aggregate supply curve, long-run aggregate supply curve, and the equilibrium levels of *Y* and *P*. Explain the changes depicted in the graphs.

11. Some economists believe that the U.S. economy entered a liquidity trap in 2009 as
CH interest rates fell almost to zero. One proposed solution was an announced, long-term expansionary monetary policy that increased both the nominal money supply and inflationary expectations. Draw *IS-LM* curves using the nominal interest rate on the vertical axis and illustrate how a successful implementation of this policy would affect the equilibrium levels of *i*, *Y*, and *r*.

12. In the Case Study about the U.S. recession that began in 2001, the textbook cites the decline in the stock market and the declining perceptions of the profitability of new technologies (largely involving the Internet and telecommunications) as two causes of the slump. Use *IS-LM* curves to illustrate and explain how the preceding rise in the stock market and optimistic perceptions of the profitability of new technologies had contributed to the long economic expansion during the 1990s.

13. **a.** Draw an *IS* curve and an *LM* curve using the real interest rate *r* on the vertical axis, assuming that expected inflation is 0 percent.

b. Illustrate how the *IS* and/or *LM* curves you drew in Part a would shift if expected inflation fell to –10 percent. What happens to *Y*, *r*, and *i*? Compare your answer to the analysis presented in the textbook.

14. Several economists believe that the money supply *M* tends to increase as the interest rate increases. Draw a money-supply, money-demand graph, and, next to it, derive the *LM* curve to illustrate how this tendency would affect the slope of the *LM* curve.

15. In 2003, President George W. Bush increased government spending to finance the war on terror and the war in Iraq. He also persuaded Congress to enact substantial reductions in taxes. For the purposes of this problem, assume that taxes were reduced by a specific amount.

a. By how much would these policy changes shift the *IS* and/or *LM* curves?

b. Illustrate the shifts in the *IS* and/or *LM* curves and explain what effect these policy changes would have on output and interest rates.

c. In response to concerns about potential recession and even deflation, the Fed acted to reduce the federal funds rate from about 6.5 percent in late 2000 to 1.0 percent in June 2004. On a separate diagram, use *IS-LM* graphs to illustrate the effects of this decline, coupled with the increase in government spending and reduction in taxes.

Data Questions

Locate the necessary economic data and apply them to answer the following data questions. All of the relevant data may be found in the Economic Report of the President (http://www.gpoaccess.gov/eop/).

1. **a.** Complete Table 12-1 below (all values are in billions of dollars except for the GDP deflator).

Table 12-1

(1) Year	(2) Real GDP in billions of 2005 dollars	(3) % Change in Real GDP	(4) $M1$ (Dec.)	(5) GDP Deflator (2005 = 100)	(6) Real $M1$ (= $M1/P$)	(7) % Change in Real $M1$
1979	————		————		————	
		————				————
1980	————		————	————	————	
		————				————
1981	————		————	————	————	
		————				————
1982	————		————	————		

b. Compare the percentage changes in real GDP and real money balances during this period with those that occurred during the Great Depression. (The Depression data are presented in Table 12-2 in the textbook.)

2. **a.** Complete Table 12-2.

Table 11-2

(1) Year	(2) Real GDP in billions of 2005 dollars	(3) % Change in Real GDP	(4) Interest Rate on 10-Year U.S. Treasury Securities
1963	————		————
		————	
1965	————		————

b. Between 1963 and 1965, the government pursued expansionary fiscal policy by increasing government purchases and reducing taxes. These fiscal policies caused the *IS* curve to shift to the right. Given this information plus the data in Table 12-2, what do you conclude about the Fed's policy during this period and why? Draw an *IS-LM* diagram on a separate sheet of paper and illustrate the joint effects of the fiscal and monetary policies pursued during this period on the *IS* curve and the *LM* curve, and on the equilibrium levels of real income and the interest rate.

Questions to Think About

1. Based on the discussion presented in Chapter 12 of the textbook, do you think the Great Depression was caused primarily by a shock to the *LM* curve or a shock to the *IS* curve? What evidence do you find most convincing and why?

2. What does the experience of the Great Depression imply about the downward flexibility of prices and the speed with which the economy moves to the natural rate of output after an aggregate demand shock?

The Open Economy Revisted: The Mundell–Fleming Model and the Exchange-Rate Regime

Fill-in Questions

Use the key terms below to fill in the blanks in the following statements. Each term may be used more than once.

currency board

devaluation

dollarization

fixed exchange rate

floating exchange rate

impossible trinity

Mundell–Fleming model

revaluation

speculative attack

1. Under a _____ regime, the exchange rate is allowed to fluctuate freely in response to changing economic conditions.

2. Under a _____ regime, a central bank buys or sells the domestic currency for foreign currencies at a predetermined price.

3. Under a _____ regime, monetary policy is dedicated to the single goal of keeping the exchange rate at the announced level. Consequently, one argument in favor of a _____ regime is that it allows monetary policy to be used for other purposes.

4. In a fixed-exchange-rate regime, a reduction in the value of the currency is called a(n) _____; an increase in the value of the currency is called a(n) _____.

5. In the _____, a _____ shifts the *LM** curve to the right, whereas a _____ shifts the *LM** curve to the left.

6. Proponents of a _____ argue that this policy reduces some of the uncertainty in international business transactions.

7. A _____ occurs when there is a change in investors' perceptions that makes the maintenance of a _____ impossible.

8. A(n) _____ is an arrangement by which the central bank holds enough foreign currency to back each unit of the domestic currency.

9. _____ occurs when a foreign country adopts the U.S. dollar as its domestic currency.

10. According to the _____, a country cannot have all of the following: free capital flows, an independent monetary policy, and a _____.

Multiple-Choice Questions

1. The exchange rate is defined as the amount of foreign currency needed to buy one unit of domestic currency (for example, 80 yen per dollar). A higher exchange rate:

   a. makes domestic goods less expensive relative to foreign goods.
   b. stimulates exports and depresses imports.
   c. leads to a decrease in net exports.
   d. leads to higher income.

2. In the conventional *IS-LM* model, real income Y and the real interest rate r appear on the axes. When the exchange rate increases:

   a. investment increases and the *IS* curve shifts to the right.
   b. net exports increase and the *IS* curve shifts to the right.
   c. investment decreases and the *IS* curve shifts to the left.
   d. net exports decrease and the *IS* curve shifts to the left.

3. All of the following statements about the Mundell-Fleming model drawn with aggregate income Y and the exchange rate e on the axes are true EXCEPT:

   a. the interest rate is fixed at the world interest rate.
   b. the *LM** curve is vertical because the exchange rate does not enter the money demand or money supply equations.
   c. the *IS** curve slopes downward because a lower exchange rate stimulates investment.
   d. the intersection of the *IS** and *LM** curves determines the equilibrium exchange rate.

4. In a small open economy with a floating exchange rate, fiscal policy will be ineffective because:

   a. monetary policy will completely offset it.
   b. the exchange rate will remain constant.
   c. a fall in net exports will offset any increases in government purchases or consumption.
   d. the exchange rate will rise by the same amount as the interest rate.

5. In a small open economy with a floating exchange rate, monetary expansion does all of the following EXCEPT:

   a. lower the interest rate.
   b. increase the equilibrium income level.
   c. decrease the exchange rate.
   d. cause net exports to rise.

6. Trade restrictions have no effect on income under floating exchange rates because:

   a. net exports increase but investment decreases.
   b. the exchange rate rises to offset the initial increase in net exports.
   c. the fall in imports equals the rise in exports.
   d. All of the answers are correct.

7. If the current yen-to-dollar exchange rate (for example, 80 yen per dollar) is above the fixed exchange rate set by the Fed (for example, 50 yen per dollar), arbitragers can make profits by:

   a. buying yen in foreign exchange markets and selling them to the Fed.
   b. buying yen from the Fed and selling them in foreign exchange markets.
   c. buying dollars in foreign exchange markets and selling them to the Fed.
   d. None of the answers are correct.

8. The profit-making actions described in Question 7 will cause the money supply to:

   a. rise, thereby shifting the LM^* curve to the left.
   b. rise, thereby shifting the LM^* curve to the right.
   c. fall, thereby shifting the LM^* curve to the left.
   d. fall, thereby shifting the LM^* curve to the right.

9. If the current yen-to-dollar market exchange rate (for example, 80 yen per dollar) is below the fixed exchange rate set by the Fed (for example, 100 yen per dollar), arbitragers can make profits by:

   a. buying yen from the Fed and selling them in foreign exchange markets.
   b. buying dollars in foreign exchange markets and selling them to the Fed.
   c. buying dollars from the Fed and selling them in foreign exchange markets.
   d. both a and b.

10. The profit-making actions described in Question 9 will cause the money supply to:

    a. rise, thereby shifting the LM^* curve to the left.
    b. rise, thereby shifting the LM^* curve to the right.
    c. fall, thereby shifting the LM^* curve to the left.
    d. fall, thereby shifting the LM^* curve to the right.

11. Under a gold standard, if the Fed sells an ounce of gold for $1,000, and the Bank of England sells an ounce of gold for 500 pounds, then the exchange rate would be fixed at:

    a. 2 pounds per dollar.
    b. 0.5 pounds per dollar.
    c. 1.5 pounds per dollar.
    d. 5 pounds per dollar.

12. An expansionary fiscal policy under fixed exchange rates will:
    a. force the Fed to increase the money supply in order to prevent the exchange rate from rising.
    b. increase real income.
    c. eventually lead the *IS** and *LM** curves to shift to the right.
    d. All of the answers are correct.

13. If the Fed tries to increase the money supply under fixed exchange rates:
    a. national income will be unaffected.
    b. the initial increase in the money supply will be offset if the Fed maintains the original fixed exchange rate.
    c. the *LM** curve on a *Y – e* graph will shift first to the right and then to the left, back to its original position.
    d. All of the answers are correct.

14. If the value of the currency is reduced via a devaluation, the:
    a. *LM** curve shifts to the right, and both net exports and income rise.
    b. *LM** curve shifts to the right, net exports fall, and income rises.
    c. *LM** curve shifts to the left, and both net exports and income fall.
    d. *IS** and *LM** curves both shift to the right.

15. A restrictive trade policy under a fixed exchange rate will:
    a. have the same effect as under a floating exchange rate.
    b. raise the equilibrium level of national income.
    c. shift the *IS** curve to the right and the *LM** curve to the left on a *Y – e* graph.
    d. lead to a devaluation of the currency.

16. In the Mundell-Fleming model:
    a. both fiscal and monetary policy will have greater effects on national income if the exchange rate is fixed rather than floating.
    b. both fiscal and monetary policy will have greater effects on national income if the exchange rate is floating rather than fixed.
    c. fiscal policy will have a greater effect on national income if the exchange rate is fixed rather than floating, whereas monetary policy will be more potent if the exchange rate is floating.
    d. fiscal policy will have a greater effect on national income if the exchange rate is floating rather than fixed, whereas monetary policy will be more potent if the exchange rate is fixed.

17. The risk premium in a country's interest rate will rise if:
    a. people expect the country's exchange rate to fall.
    b. fears arise that the government may not pay all of its debt.
    c. the country's foreign exchange reserves are quickly being depleted.
    d. All of the answers are correct.

18. An increase in a country's perceived risk premium will:

    a. shift its *IS** and *LM** curves to the right, resulting in an appreciation of its exchange rate.

    b. shift its *IS** and *LM** curves to the left, resulting in a depreciation of its exchange rate.

    c. shift its *IS** curve to the left and its *LM** curve to the right, resulting in a depreciation of its exchange rate.

    d. shift its *IS** curve to the right and its *LM** curve to the left, resulting in an appreciation of its exchange rate.

19. An argument in favor of floating exchange rates is that they:

    a. reduce uncertainty and promote international trade.

    b. allow monetary policy to be used for purposes other than maintaining exchange rates.

    c. reduce the volatility of exchange rates.

    d. All of the answers are correct.

20. Countries with currency boards:

    a. typically have flexible exchange rates.

    b. restrict capital mobility.

    c. are more likely to have speculative attacks on their currency.

    d. are less likely to have speculative attacks on their currency.

21. Dollarization by a foreign country is an extreme form of maintaining:

    a. a balance of trade with the United States.

    b. a fixed exchange rate with the United States.

    c. a floating exchange rate with the United States.

    d. the impossible trinity.

22. According to the *impossible trinity,* it is impossible for a nation to have:

    a. a balanced budget, free capital flows, and a fixed exchange rate.

    b. free capital flows, a fixed exchange rate, and independent fiscal policy.

    c. free capital flows, a floating exchange rate, and independent monetary policy.

    d. free capital flows, a fixed exchange rate, and independent monetary policy.

23. Suppose the initial level of income is less than the long-run equilibrium level. Then, in the Mundell-Fleming model with a changing price level, the price level will:

    a. fall, shifting the *IS** curve to the right.

    b. rise, shifting the *IS** curve to the left.

    c. rise, shifting the *LM** curve to the left.

    d. fall, shifting the *LM** curve to the right.

24. **A** In the short-run model for a large open economy presented in the appendix to Chapter 13, a reduction in the domestic interest rate:

    a. increases net capital outflow and lowers both net exports and the exchange rate.

    b. increases net capital outflow and net exports, and reduces the exchange rate.

    c. reduces net capital outflow, net exports, and the exchange rate.

    d. reduces net capital outflow and net exports, and increases the exchange rate.

25. Fiscal policy will have the largest short-run effect on the equilibrium level of na-
A tional income in a:

    a. small open economy with a flexible exchange rate.

    b. large open economy with a flexible exchange rate.

    c. closed economy.

    d. small open economy with a fixed exchange rate.

Exercises

1. **The Effect of the Exchange Rate on the *IS* Curve** *In this exercise, we add net exports to the expenditure curve and illustrate the effects of changes in the exchange rate on the expenditure and IS curves.*

    a. Consider the following model of the economy:

$$E = C + I + G + NX \tag{13-1}$$
$$C = 125 + 0.75(Y - T) \tag{13-2}$$
$$I = 200 - 10r \tag{13-3}$$
$$G = 100 \tag{13-4}$$
$$T = 100 \tag{13-5}$$
$$NX = 150 - 50e. \tag{13-6}$$

    This model is very similar to the one presented in the Student Guide exercises for Chapters 11 and 12, except that net exports NX are now included. NX is negatively related to the nominal exchange rate e. Since both the domestic and foreign price levels are held fixed in Chapter 13 of the textbook, changes in the nominal exchange rate e are proportional to changes in the real exchange rate ε, so we can focus on changes in e.

    b. Suppose that the nominal exchange rate e is initially equal to 2.0 (for example, 2 Turkish lira per dollar). Consequently, $NX = 150 - 50($_____$) =$ _____. Substitute this value of net exports NX into Equation 13-1, along with Equations 13-2 to 13-5, and simplify to obtain the equation for aggregate expenditure E in terms of the interest rate r and aggregate income Y:

    $E=$ _____ $+$ _____ $Y -$ _____ r.

c. Recall that, in equilibrium, $E = Y$. Derive the equation for the *IS* curve by setting the preceding expenditure equation equal to Y and solving for r.

$r = $ _____ $-$ _____ Y.

Graph this equation on Graph 13-1 and label it $IS(e = 2)$.

Graph 13-1

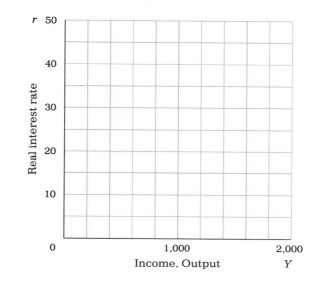

d. Now suppose that the exchange rate falls to $e = 1.0$ (for example, 1 lira per dollar). This exchange rate reflects a(n) appreciation/depreciation of the dollar relative to the lira. As a result, U.S. net exports would rise/fall to $NX = 150 - 50($_____$) = $ _____. Substitute this new value of net exports NX, along with Equations 13-2 to 13-5, into Equation 13-1, set the result equal to Y, and derive the equation for the new *IS* curve.

$r = $ _____ $-$ _____ Y.

Graph this equation on Graph 13-1 and label the curve $IS(e = 1)$.

e. Summarizing the results, we see that a reduction in the exchange rate reflects a(n) appreciation/depreciation of the dollar, which will increase/decrease net exports. This reduction shifts the aggregate expenditure curve upward/downward and thereby shifts the *IS* curve to the right/left. In this example, the reduction in the exchange rate *e* from 2 to 1 increases net exports *NX* by _____. This increase in *NX* shifts the expenditure curve upward/downward by _____ and shifts the *IS* curve to the left/right by the shift in the expenditure curve multiplied by the (government purchases) multiplier, or by _____ × _____ = _____. Conversely, an increase in the exchange rate reflects a(n) appreciation/depreciation of the dollar, which will increase/decrease net exports. This change shifts the aggregate expenditure curve upward/downward and thereby shifts the *IS* curve to the left/right.

2. **The Mundell–Fleming Model on a *Y − e* Graph** *In this exercise, we derive the Mundell–Fleming model on a graph with aggregate income Y and the exchange rate e on the axes.*

a. On Graph 13-1, each *IS* curve represents the combinations of the interest rate *r* and aggregate income *Y* for which the goods market is in equilibrium, holding the exchange rate *e* fixed. As Chapter 13 of the textbook indicates, one can also draw an *IS* curve, called *IS**, which represents the combinations of the exchange rate *e* and aggregate income *Y* for which the goods market is in equilibrium, holding the interest rate *r* fixed at the world interest rate *r**. Consider the same model utilized in Exercise 1:

$$E = C + I + G + NX \qquad \text{(13-7)}$$
$$C = 125 + 0.75(Y - T) \qquad \text{(13-8)}$$
$$I = 200 - 10r \qquad \text{(13-9)}$$
$$G = 100 \qquad \text{(13-10)}$$
$$T = 100 \qquad \text{(13-11)}$$
$$NX = 150 - 50e. \qquad \text{(13-12)}$$

Suppose that *r** = 10 percent. If *e* = 2.0, then *NX* = _____. An examination of Graph 13-1 reveals that the goods market will be in equilibrium when *Y* = _____. Locate this point on Graph 13-2 and label it Point A.

b. Now suppose that *e* falls to 1.0. Graph 13-1 shows that when *e* = 1.0 and *r* = 10, the goods market is in equilibrium when *Y* = _____. Locate this point on Graph 13-2 and label it Point B. Connect Points A and B and label the resulting curve *IS**(*r* = 10). Intuitively, as the exchange rate falls, net exports rise/fall, the aggregate expenditure curve shifts upward/downward, and the level of income increases/decreases.

Graph 13-2

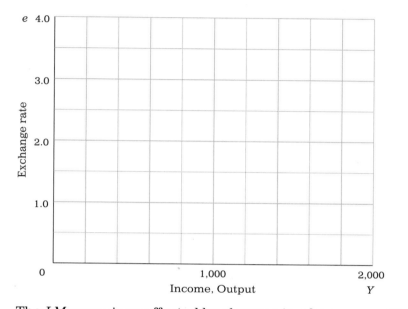

c. The *LM* curve is unaffected by changes in *e* because neither money demand nor money supply depends on the exchange rate. Alternatively, there is only one level of income for which the *LM* curve intersects the *r* = *r** curve, regardless of the level of *e*. Suppose that when *r** = 10, the money market is in equilibrium when *Y* = 1,200. Draw a vertical *LM** curve on Graph 13-2 at this level of *Y*.

d. Graph 13-2 now illustrates the combinations of *e* and *Y* for which the goods market is in equilibrium (along the *IS** curve), and the combinations of *e* and *Y* for which the money market is in equilibrium (along the *LM** curve), assuming that *r** = 10. The levels of *e* and *Y* at which both the goods and money markets are in equilibrium are at *e* = _____ and *Y* = _____. This equilibrium occurs at Point _____ on Graph 13-2.

3. **The Small Open Economy with a Floating Exchange Rate** *In this exercise, we explore the effects of fiscal and monetary policies for a small open economy with a floating exchange rate.*

a. Graph 13-3 depicts an initial equilibrium using the *IS** and *LM** curves introduced in Exercise 2.

The *IS** and *LM** curves indicate that the initial equilibrium levels of the exchange rate *e* and aggregate income *Y* are at *e* = _____ and *Y* = _____. Locate this point on Graph 13-3 and label it Point A.

Graph 13-3

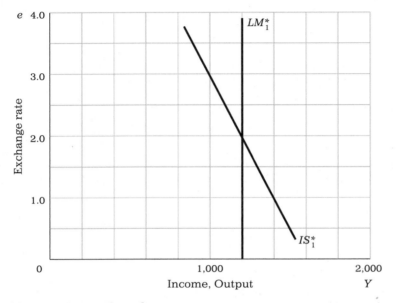

b. Now suppose that the government pursues an expansionary fiscal policy either by increasing/decreasing government purchases *G* or by increasing/decreasing taxes *T*. If the exchange rate *e* is held constant, this policy will increase/decrease aggregate income *Y*. Thus, the *IS** curve will shift to the left/right. Draw the new *IS** curve on Graph 13-3 and label it IS_2^*. Locate the point on the IS_2^* curve at which *e* = 2.0 and label it Point B.

c. At Point B on Graph 13-3, the demand for money is greater than/less than/ equal to the supply of money. Since money demand is unrelated to the exchange rate *e*, equilibrium can be achieved in the money market only if aggregate income *Y* increases/decreases/remains constant from Point B. This situation is achieved through a(n) increase/decrease in *e*. As *e* rises/falls, net exports *NX* increase/decrease, and the economy moves along the IS_2^* curve until the new equilibrium is achieved when money demand once again equals the initial money supply. Locate this point on Graph 13-3 and label it Point C. The upward pressure on *e* occurs because expansionary fiscal policy tends to increase/decrease the interest rate. Yet, whenever the domestic interest rate rises above/falls below the world interest rate, U.S. and foreign investors buy more U.S. assets, which increases/decreases the exchange rate *e*. This assumption of perfect capital mobility (from Chapter 6) results in a constant real world interest rate *r**.

d. Comparing Points A and C on Graph 13-3, note that in a small open economy with a floating exchange rate, expansionary fiscal policy increases/decreases/ has no effect on the equilibrium level of aggregate income Y and increases/ decreases/has no effect on the equilibrium exchange rate e. Consequently, net exports NX will rise/fall/remain constant. Conversely, contractionary fiscal policy increases/decreases/has no effect on the equilibrium level of Y and increases/decreases/has no effect on e.

e. The results in Part d occur because the LM* curve is vertical; only one level of income will equilibrate the money market as long as the money supply is unchanged. Now start again at Point A on Graph 13-4.

Graph 13-4

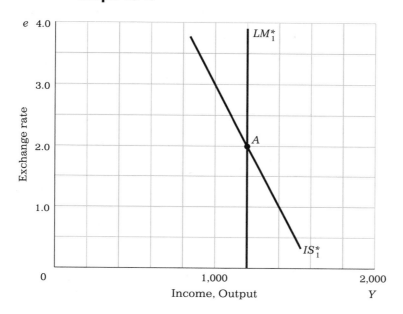

An increase in the money supply will shift the conventional LM curve drawn with r and Y on the axes to the left (upward)/right (downward). If the interest rate r is constant at the real world interest rate r*, then the level of aggregate income Y at which this higher money supply equals money demand will rise/fall. As a result, the LM* curve on Graph 13-4 will shift to the left/right. Draw a new LM* curve on Graph 13-4 and label it LM_2^*. Obviously, the equilibrium level of income increases/decreases/remains constant, and the equilibrium exchange rate e increases/decreases/remains constant. Thus, net exports NX will rise/fall/remain constant.

f. In both a closed economy and a small open economy with a floating exchange rate, expansionary monetary policy will lead to a(n) increase/decrease in the equilibrium level of national income. There are, however, some important differences. In a closed economy, an increase in the money supply increases investment (and, hence, GDP) by reducing _____. In a small open economy with a floating exchange rate, the interest rate remains fixed at the world interest rate. As soon as the domestic interest rate falls a little, capital flows into/out of the domestic economy. This causes the exchange rate to appreciate/depreciate, which increases/decreases net exports and, hence, GDP.

4. **Managing a Fixed Exchange-Rate System** *In this exercise, we illustrate how the maintenance of a fixed exchange rate requires adjustments in the money supply.*

a. Graph 13-5 depicts a hypothetical situation in which the *IS** and *LM** curves intersect at an equilibrium exchange rate of *e* = 3 at Point A. This situation implies, for example, that people could exchange 3 Turkish lira per dollar on the international currency markets.

Graph 13-5

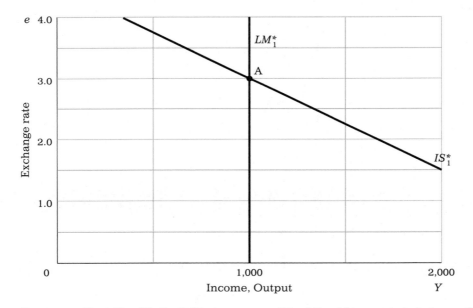

Suppose that the United States committed itself to maintaining a fixed exchange rate of *e* = 2, or _____ Turkish lira per dollar. Draw a horizontal line on Graph 13-5 to show this exchange rate, and label it *e*~Fixed~. The Fed would establish this exchange rate by holding a reserve of lira and selling them for 2 lira per dollar. It would also commit itself to buying lira for 2 lira per dollar. It is *critical* to note that whenever these transactions occurred, the Fed would be changing the U.S. money supply by buying or selling dollars.

b. In Part a, note that the initial equilibrium exchange rate is <u>greater than/less than</u> the fixed exchange rate. As Chapter 13 of the textbook indicates, this situation cannot prevail for long because it creates opportunities for arbitrage. At $e = 3$, people would profit by buying lira on the international currency markets and selling them to the Fed at its fixed exchange rate. For example, at $e = 3$, people would trade $1 for _____ lira on the international currency markets. They would then sell these _____ lira to the Fed and receive $1 for every 2 lira or

$$[\$1/(2 \text{ lira})] \times \text{_____ lira} = \$\text{_____}.$$

They would continue to profit by this kind of arbitrage as long as the equilibrium exchange rate exceeded the fixed exchange rate.

c. In Part b, the Fed buys lira with newly created dollars. This action <u>increases/decreases</u> the U.S. money supply and shifts the LM^* curve to the <u>left/right</u>. The LM^* curve will continue to shift until $e = e_{\text{Fixed}}$. Draw the final LM^* curve on Graph 13-5 and label it LM_2^*. Label the final equilibrium Point B. Consequently, under a fixed-exchange-rate regime, whenever $e > e_{\text{Fixed}}$, the domestic money supply will <u>increase/decrease</u>, and the LM^* curve will shift to the <u>left/right</u> until $e = e_{\text{Fixed}}$.

d. Now suppose that the equilibrium exchange rate is 1.0, while the Fed continues to maintain an official fixed exchange rate of 2. This initial situation is depicted on Graph 13-6 at Point C. Draw a horizontal line on Graph 13-6 at $e = 2$ and label it e_{Fixed}.

Graph 13-6

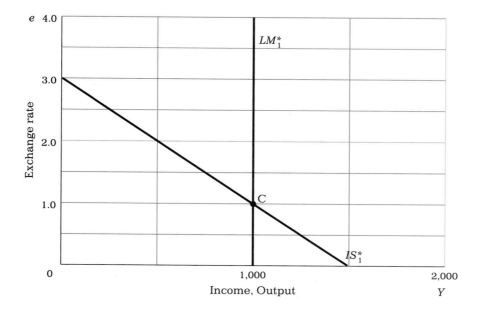

On Graph 13-6, the initial equilibrium exchange rate is <u>greater than/less than</u> the fixed exchange rate. This situation, too, creates opportunities for arbitrage. At $e = 1$, people would profit by buying dollars on the international currency markets and selling them to the Fed at its fixed exchange rate of $e_{Fixed} = 2$. For example, at $e = 1$, people would trade 1 lira for \$_____ on the international currency markets. They would then sell the \$_____ to the Fed at its fixed exchange rate and receive _____ lira. They would continue to profit by this kind of arbitrage as long as the fixed exchange rate exceeded the equilibrium exchange rate.

e. When the Fed is buying dollars in Part d, these dollars are retired from circulation and the U.S. money supply <u>increases/decreases</u>. This situation, in turn, shifts the LM^* curve to the <u>left/right</u>. The LM^* curve will continue to shift until $e = e_{Fixed}$. Draw the final LM^* curve on Graph 13-6, label it LM_3^*, and label the final equilibrium Point D. Consequently, under a fixed-exchange-rate regime, whenever $e < e_{Fixed}$, the domestic money supply will <u>increase/decrease</u> and the LM^* curve will shift to the <u>left/right</u> until $e = e_{Fixed}$.

5. **The Small Open Economy with a Fixed Exchange Rate** *In this exercise, we explore the effects of fiscal and monetary policies for a small open economy with a fixed exchange rate.*

a. Graph 13-7 depicts a situation in which the equilibrium exchange rate is equal to the fixed exchange rate of 2. Draw a horizontal line on Graph 13-7 at $e = 2$ and label it e_{Fixed}.

Graph 13-7

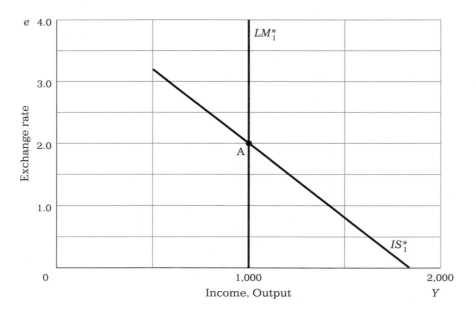

Starting from Point A, suppose that the government pursued expansionary fiscal policy. As in Exercise 3, this policy would shift the IS^* curve to the left/right. Draw the new IS^* curve on Graph 13-7 and label it IS^*_2.

b. In Exercise 3, we found that under a floating-exchange-rate regime, expansionary fiscal policy will increase/decrease/have no effect on real output Y and increase/decrease/have no effect on the exchange rate e. If, on the other hand, the exchange rate is fixed, as we saw in Exercise 4, the Fed will have to increase/decrease the money supply, shifting the LM^* curve to the left/right until $e = e_{\text{Fixed}} = $ ——————————————. Draw the new LM^* curve on Graph 13-7, label it LM^*_2, and label the new equilibrium Point B. Thus, under a fixed-exchange-rate regime, expansionary fiscal policy will increase/decrease/have no effect on real output Y and increase/decrease/have no effect on the exchange rate e. This situation occurs because the Fed will be forced to change the money supply in order to maintain the fixed exchange rate at $e = 2$.

c. Now start again at Point A on Graph 13-8 with $e = e_{\text{Fixed}}$.

Graph 13-8

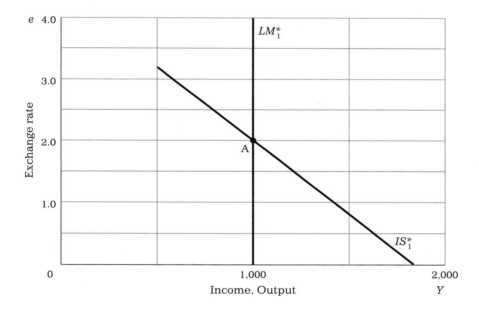

Expansionary monetary policy will initially shift the LM^* curve to the left/right. Draw this new LM^* curve on Graph 13-8 and label it LM^*_3. In Exercise 3 we found that under a floating-exchange-rate regime, expansionary monetary policy will increase/decrease/have no effect on real output Y and increase/decrease/have no effect on the exchange rate e. If, on the other hand, the exchange rate is fixed, as the equilibrium exchange rate rises above/falls below the fixed exchange rate, the Fed will find itself buying/selling Turkish lira and buying/selling dollars. This activity will increase/decrease the money supply and will shift the LM^* curve to the left/right until $e = e_{\text{Fixed}} = $ ——————————————. Draw the final LM^* curve on Graph 13-8, label it LM^*_4, and label the new equilibrium Point C. (Note the relationship between LM_1^* and LM_4^*.) Thus, under a fixed-exchange-rate regime, expansionary monetary policy will increase/decrease/have no effect on real output Y and will increase/decrease/have no effect on the exchange rate. This situation occurs because the final money supply will be greater than/less than/equal to the initial money supply. The normal power of monetary policy to change income is lost because the money supply is dedicated to maintaining the fixed exchange rate. Finally, since the exchange rate does not change, net exports NX will rise/fall/remain constant.

d. Starting over once again at Point A on Graph 13-8, suppose that the United States devalued the dollar by reducing the fixed exchange rate from 2 to 1. If the initial equilibrium exchange rate were 2, the Fed would find itself buying/selling lira and buying/selling dollars. This activity would increase/decrease/have no effect on the money supply and would shift the LM^* curve to the left/right until $e = 1$. As a result, Y would increase/decrease/remain constant. Conversely, a revaluation of the dollar to $e = 3$ would shift the LM^* curve to the left/right, and Y would increase/decrease/remain constant.

6. Incorporating Risk Premiums in the Mundell–Fleming Model *In this exercise, we use the Mundell–Fleming model to analyze the effects of changes in a country's perceived risk premium.*

a. Real interest rates may differ among countries for a variety of reasons. One reason is that assets in one country (for example, government bonds) may be viewed as riskier than similar asssets in another country if the first country is politically or economically unstable. To induce international investors to purchase their assets, the domestic interest rate in countries that are seen as more risky will be higher/lower.

Graph 13-9

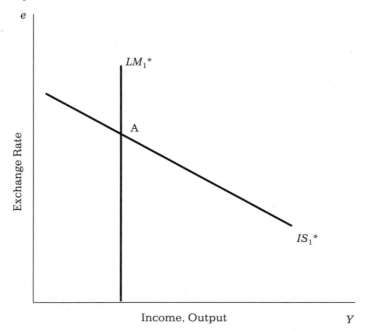

b. Point A in Graph 13-9 depicts an initial equilibrium in a small open economy. If new political turmoil raises this country's perceived risk, its domestic interest rate *r* rises/falls. This change in the interest rate would increase/decrease investment and thereby shift the *IS** curve to the left/right. Draw this new *IS** curve in Graph 13-9 and label it IS_2^*.

c. This change in the interest rate would also increase/decrease the demand for money. Because this allows a higher level of income for any given money supply, the *LM** curve would shift to the left/right. Draw the new *LM** curve in Graph 13-9, label it LM_2^*, and label the new equilibrium Point B.

d. Comparing Points A and B, we see that an increase in a country's perceived risk premium will lead to a(n) appreciation/depreciation of its exchange rate and a(n) increase/decrease in its real income.

e. Even though higher domestic interest rates reduce investment, national income rises because the change in the exchange rate increases/decreases net exports by an even greater amount. In those countries that have experienced perceived increases in risk, however, national income has often declined for one of several reasons. First, the central banks have occasionally reduced the money supply in order to counteract the exchange rate depreciation, which shifts the *IS*/LM** curve to the left/right. Second, the depreciation causes the price of imported goods to rise, which may increase the domestic price level *P*. This would increase/decrease the real money supply and shift the *IS*/LM** curve to the left/right. Finally, domestic residents may increase their demand for money because money is a liquid and relatively safe asset. This would shift the *IS*/LM** to the left/right.

7. **The Mundell–Fleming Model with a Changing Price Level** *In this exercise, we show how the long-run price adjustments that move the economy toward its long-run equilibrium operate within the Mundell–Fleming model's floating-exchange-rate regime.*

a. In Chapter 10 of the textbook, we saw how shifts in the aggregate supply curve move the economy toward its long-run equilibrium. The same phenomenon also occurs in the Mundell-Fleming model, although the aggregate demand curve is somewhat different. Points A in Graphs 13-10 and 13-11 depict an initial equilibrium at which output is greater than/equal to/less than the long-run natural level of output $\overline{Y}$.

Note that the vertical axis in Graph 13-10 now measures the real exchange rate ε. Recall that ε = e(P/P*), where *e* represents the nominal exchange rate and P/P* represents the ratio of domestic to foreign prices. It was not necessary to make this adjustment in Exercises 2–6 because the price levels there were assumed to increase/remain constant/decrease. Since ε is on the vertical axis in Graph 13-10, however, a change in *P* will not shift the *IS** curve.

b. When the short-run equilibrium level of output is less than $\overline{Y}$, the short-run aggregate supply *SRAS* curve will shift upward/downward over time, just as in a closed economy. (Although the *SRAS* curve is depicted as a horizontal line in Graph 13-11, one can derive the same results from a positively sloped *SRAS*

Graph 13-10

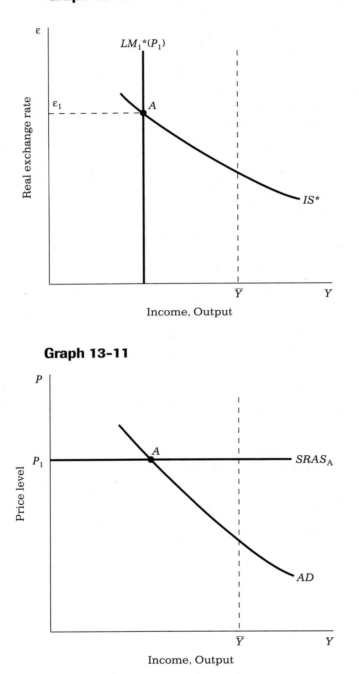

Graph 13-11

curve.) As this *SRAS* curve shifts, the domestic price level *P* will <u>rise/fall</u> and output will <u>rise/fall</u>. Draw the final *SRAS* curve in Graph 13-11, label it *SRAS*$_F$, and label the long-run equilibrium Point *F*.

c. Returning to Graph 13-10, the reduction in the domestic price level will <u>increase/decrease</u> real money <u>supply/demand</u>. This will shift the *IS**/*LM** curve to the <u>right/left</u> since the exchange rate is floating. Hence, the real exchange rate will <u>rise/fall</u> and net exports will <u>rise/fall</u>. Draw the final *LM** curve, label it

LM_{F}^*, and label the final equilibrium Point F. Comparing Points F and A, output rises/falls/remains the same and net exports rise/fall/remain the same. Investment rises/falls/remains the same because the real interest rate rises/falls/remains the same

8. **The Large Open Economy** *In this exercise, we examine the short-run model of the large open economy derived in the appendix to Chapter 13 to illustrate why the* IS *curve in a large open economy with international capital flows is flatter than the* IS *curve in a closed economy, assuming that net exports are unrelated to income.*

Graph 13-12

a. Graph 13-12 depicts a simple *IS* curve for a closed economy that is labeled IS_{CE}.

Recall that the *IS* curve for a closed economy has a negative slope because, as the real interest rate *r* falls, investment *I* increases/decreases/remains constant. This situation has both a direct and multiplier effect on *Y*. Consequently, starting at Point A, as *r* falls, *Y* increases/decreases/remains constant.

b. Recall from the appendix to Chapter 6 of the textbook that a large open economy differs from a small open economy because its domestic interest rate is not necessarily equal to a fixed world interest rate. Thus, in a large open economy, as in a closed economy, as the real interest rate falls, investment rises/falls. Furthermore, recall that net capital outflow *CF* is the amount that domestic investors lend abroad (by buying foreign assets) minus the amount foreigners lend here (by buying domestic assets). As the domestic interest rate falls, net capital outflow rises/falls. Since *CF* = *NX*, this increase/decrease in *CF* leads to a corresponding increase/decrease in the trade balance *NX*, which must be accompanied by a(n) appreciation/depreciation of the exchange rate.

c. In Part b, a reduction in the domestic real interest rate will increase/decrease investment and increase/decrease net exports. Consequently, Y will now increase by more/less than in the closed economy analyzed in Part a, and the IS curve for a large open economy will be flatter/steeper than the IS curve in a closed economy. Starting from Point A, draw the IS curve for a large open economy on Graph 13-12 and label it IS_{LOE}.

d. Recall that a flatter IS curve will make monetary policy more/less potent in changing Y and it will make fiscal policy more/less potent in changing Y.

Problems

Answer the following problems on a separate sheet of paper.

1. Explain why a monetary contraction for a small open economy under fixed exchange rates will have no effect on real income.

2. In February 2012, Greece was in a deep recession and its government debt was sky-rocketing because of lower tax revenues. The Greek government was debating whether to abandon the euro as its currency and adopt a new Greek currency. According to Chapter 13 of the textbook, what were some of the arguments for and against such a move?

3. Not all countries in Europe are currently participating in the move to a single European currency, called the euro. How has monetary unification changed the ability of each country that is currently a participant to conduct independent countercyclical monetary policy?

4. If a small open economy with a floating exchange rate is experiencing a recession, what will automatically happen over time to its trade balance, real foreign exchange rate, and national output?

5. Suppose the government in a small developing economy places restrictions on agricultural *exports* in order to increase the domestic food supply and lower food prices. Use the Mundell–Fleming model to analyze the short-run effects of this policy on the exchange rate and real GDP if the country has a:

    a. floating exchange rate.

    b. fixed exchange rate.

6. Use the Mundell–Fleming model to illustrate the short-run effects of the Mexican crisis in a small open economy with a fixed exchange rate.

7. In 1997, 1998, and 1999, the risk premiums associated with several countries in Southeast Asia rose dramatically. Since that time many of these countries have regained economic stability by reducing their foreign debt burdens and more efficiently managing their economies. Use the Mundell–Fleming model to illustrate the effects of renewed stability on these countries' domestic interest rates, exchange rates, and real GDP under a regime of floating exchange rates.

8. As the textbook states, Argentina introduced a currency board in the early 1990s. Under this arrangement the Argentine central bank held one U.S. dollar for every outstanding Argentine peso and maintained a fixed dollar–peso exchange rate of 1:1. Although the Argentine economy initially responded well to this innovation, it ran into severe difficulties by the late 1990s and was forced to abandon the currency board in 2002. One of the reasons for its difficulties was the fact that many of Argentina's major trading partners, most notably Brazil, allowed their currencies to fall in value relative to the U.S. dollar during the late 1990s. Because Argentina maintained a fixed dollar–peso exchange rate, the devaluation of Brazil's and other neighbors' currencies, essentially shifted the Argentine net export curve to the left below:

Graph 13-13

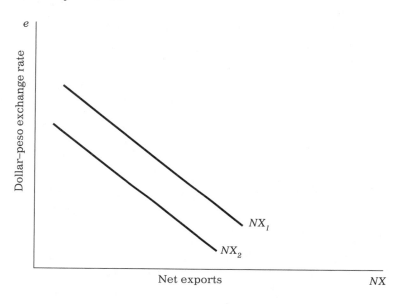

a. Treating Argentina as a small open economy, use the Mundell–Fleming model to illustrate the effects of this de-facto shift in its net export curve on Argentina's domestic interest rate and real GDP if Argentina adhered to its fixed exchange rate relative to the dollar. (This is largely what happened.)

b. Now use the appropriate graphs to show what the effects of this shift in net exports would have been on Argentina's dollar–peso exchange rate and real GDP if Argentina had allowed its dollar–peso exchange rate to float freely following Brazil's devaluation. (While many economists believe this is what Argentina should have done, others believe that earlier abandonment of the currency board would have created other difficulties by reducing the credibility of Argentina's central bank.)

9. The United States is certainly a large open economy. Suppose consumer confidence
A suddenly plummets so that consumption falls at each level of disposable income.
Use the Mundell–Fleming model for a large open economy with a floating exchange
rate to illustrate the short-run effects of this development on:

   a. the *IS* and/or *LM* curve(s).

   b. the domestic real interest rate.

   c. U.S. net capital outflow and net exports.

   d. the U.S. foreign exchange rate.

10. Suppose political stability in the United States as seen from abroad deteriorates and
A U.S. assets become less attractive to foreign investors. Assume that the United
States is a large open economy; state and show graphically what would happen in
the short run to each of the following:

   a. the U.S. net capital outflow curve.

   b. the U.S. trade balance and foreign exchange rate at the original real interest
   rate.

   c. the *IS* and *LM* curves.

   d. the domestic real interest rate.

   e. the *level* of U.S. net capital outflow and net exports after the change in the real
   interest rate.

   f. U.S. national income and output.

11. In a large open economy, suppose policymakers wanted to increase output in the
A short run without affecting the real exchange rate. What *mix* of monetary and/or fiscal policies would be required to achieve this objective? Briefly explain and use the
appropriate graphs to illustrate.

12. In 2006 the United States was close to full employment, but many observers and
A economists were worried about its trade deficit, which was over $750 billion per
year. Suppose macroeconomic policymakers wanted to maintain the level of real
GDP in the short run but change the real exchange rate to reduce the trade deficit.
Assuming the United States is a large open economy, state which specific monetary
and/or fiscal policies would be required to achieve these objectives in the short run?
Briefly explain using the appropriate graphs.

Questions to Think About

   1. Would you advise the leader of a small open economy in Africa to adopt a fixed or
   floating exchange rate? Would your answer be different if the country were in
   Europe? Why or why not?

   2. Why do policymakers in small open countries with floating exchange rates pursue
   countercyclical fiscal policies?

   3. Would the world economy be better off with just one currency? Why or why not?

4. By the time you read this question, Greece or another country may have already abandoned the euro as its currency. Did the dire predictions of those who wanted to keep the euro turn out to be true? Why or why not?

Aggregate Supply and the Short-Run Tradeoff Between Inflation and Unemployment

Fill-in Questions

Use the key terms below to fill in the blanks in the following statements. Each term may be used more than once.

adaptive expectations

cost-push inflation

demand-pull inflation

hysteresis

imperfect-information model

NAIRU

natural-rate hypothesis

Phillips curve

rational expectations

sacrifice ratio

sticky-price model

1. The _____ assumes that firms do not instantly adjust the prices they charge in response to changes in demand. It states that the slope of the short-run aggregate supply curve depends on the proportion of firms in the economy that have flexible prices.

2. The _____ assumes that all markets clear, but that short-run and long-run aggregate supply curves differ because of short-run misperceptions about prices. Therefore, when prices unexpectedly rise, suppliers infer that their relative prices have risen, which induces them to produce more output.

3. According to both the _____ and the _____ models, when aggregate output is equal to the natural level of output and there are no supply shocks, the actual price level will be equal to the expected price level.

4. The graph of the negative relationship between inflation and unemployment, holding expected inflation constant, is called the _____.

5. When the Phillips curve with adaptive expectations is written as $\pi = \pi_{-1} - \beta(u - u^n) + v$, the natural rate of unemployment is sometimes called the _____.

6. When unemployment falls below the natural rate, inflation tends to rise. This type of inflation is called _____.

7. Rising inflation due to an adverse supply shock is called _____.

8. According to the assumption of _____, people form their expectations of inflation based solely on recently observed inflation.

9. According to the assumption of _____, people form their expectations by optimally using all of the available information, including information about current policies, to forecast the future.

10. The _____ is the number of percentage points of a year's real GDP that must be foregone to reduce inflation by 1 percentage point. It will tend to be lower if people have _____ rather than _____.

11. According to the _____, the economy returns in the long run to the levels of output, employment, and unemployment described by the classical model. In the short run, however, output and unemployment are affected by fluctuations in aggregate demand.

12. _____ is the term used to describe the long-lasting influence of history on the natural rate of unemployment. For example, a recession can have permanent effects on output and unemployment if it eventually reduces the skills of those who become unemployed.

Multiple-Choice Questions

1. In the sticky-price model, prices are sticky in the short run because:
   a. some prices are set by long-term contracts and cannot be changed in the short run.
   b. once a firm has printed and distributed its catalog or price list, it is costly to change prices.
   c. firms base their prices on the costs of production, which include labor costs, and wages may be sticky because they depend on social norms that evolve slowly over time.
   d. All of the above are true.

2. In the sticky-price model:
   a. all firms adjust prices instantly in response to changes in demand.
   b. no firms adjust prices instantly in response to changes in demand.
   c. some firms adjust prices instantly in response to changes in demand while others do not.
   d. output is constant.

3.   If all firms in the economy have fixed prices in the short run:

    a.   the short-run and long-run aggregate supply curves will be identical.

    b.   the short-run aggregate supply curve will be vertical.

    c.   the short-run aggregate supply curve will be horizontal.

    d.   None of the above are true.

4.   In the sticky-price model, the equation $p = P + a(Y - \overline{Y})$ describes the behavior of:

    a.   a firm with flexible prices in the short run.

    b.   a firm with sticky prices in the short run.

    c.   all firms in the short run.

    d.   all firms in the long run but no firms in the short run.

5.   In the sticky-price model, the equation $p = EP + a(EY - E\overline{Y})$ describes the behavior of:

    a.   a firm with flexible prices in the short run.

    b.   a firm with sticky prices in the short run.

    c.   all firms in the short run.

    d.   all firms in the long run but no firms in the short run.

6.   In the sticky-price model, the equation $Y = \overline{Y} + \alpha(P - EP)$ describes the behavior of:

    a.   each and every firm in both the short run and the long run.

    b.   the overall economy in both the short run and the long run.

    c.   both a and b.

    d.   small firms but not large firms.

7.   According to the imperfect-information model, when prices unexpectedly rise, suppliers infer that their relative prices have _____, which induces them to _____ output.

    a.   increased; increase

    b.   decreased; decrease

    c.   increased; decrease

    d.   decreased; increase

8.   Recent work on imperfect information models:

    a.   stresses the increasingly limited availability of information.

    b.   stresses the limited ability of individuals to incorporate information about the economy into their decisions.

    c.   has found that people do not make forecasts about relative prices.

    d.   All of the answers are correct.

9.   Both the imperfect information and sticky-price models can explain why countries with variable aggregate demand have short-run aggregate supply curves that are:

    a.   flat.

    b.   steep.

    c.   horizontal.

    d.   vertical.

10. According to the sticky-price model, countries with higher rates of inflation will have a:

   a. steeper short-run aggregate supply curve.
   b. flatter short-run aggregate supply curve.
   c. vertical short-run aggregate supply curve.
   d. horizontal long-run aggregate supply curve.

11. Both models of aggregate supply discussed in Chapter 14 of the textbook predict:

   a. an upward-sloping short-run aggregate supply curve.
   b. a vertical long-run aggregate supply curve.
   c. that the actual level of output is equal to its natural level in the long run.
   d. All of the answers are correct.

12. According to the Phillips curve, the inflation rate depends on:

   a. expected inflation.
   b. the difference between the actual and natural rates of unemployment.
   c. supply shocks.
   d. All of the answers are correct.

13. When unemployment is below the natural rate and, as a result, inflation rises, it is characterized as:

   a. demand-pull inflation.
   b. cost-push inflation.
   c. a supply shock.
   d. stagflation.

14. Compared with the assumption of adaptive expectations, the assumption of rational expectations implies that the transition to the new long-run equilibrium following a credible change in monetary or fiscal policy will take:

   a. less time.
   b. more time.
   c. the same amount of time.
   d. Any of the answers are correct.

15. The Phillips curve immediately shifts upward whenever:

   a. inflation rises.
   b. unemployment falls.
   c. an adverse supply shock, such as an oil price increase, occurs.
   d. All of the answers are correct.

16. A typical estimate of the sacrifice ratio is about 5. Thus, if the inflation rate were to be lowered by 2 percentage points, the amount of one year's GDP we must give up is:

   a. 2 percent.
   b. 2.5 percent.
   c. 5 percent.
   d. 10 percent.

17. According to the hypothesis of unemployment hysteresis, a prolonged recession will:

    a. increase the natural rate of unemployment.
    b. decrease the natural rate of unemployment.
    c. have no effect on the natural rate of unemployment.
    d. never occur.

18. Hysteresis also:

    a. increases the sacrifice ratio.
    b. decreases the sacrifice ration.
    c. increases the sacrifice ratio when inflation is high but decreases the sacrifice ratio when inflation is low.
    d. has no effect on the sacrifice ratio.

Exercises

1. **The General Short-Run Aggregate Supply Curve** *In this exercise, we discuss the general short-run aggregate supply equation that is derived later from two different models. We graph this equation and discuss the changes that will shift the aggregate supply curve.*

    a. Both models of aggregate supply discussed in Chapter 14 of the textbook result in an aggregate supply equation of the following form:

    $$Y = \overline{Y} + \alpha(P - EP),$$

    where Y is output, $\overline{Y}$ is the natural level of output, P is the price level, and EP is the expected price level. This equation implies that output will be at its natural level when the actual price level is <u>greater than/less than/equal to</u> the expected price level. Output exceeds its natural level ($Y > \overline{Y}$) only when the actual price level is <u>greater than/less than/equal to</u> the expected price level.

    b. It is easier to graph this equation if we isolate P on the left-hand side. Subtracting $\overline{Y}$ from both sides of the equation and rearranging yields

    $$\alpha P - \alpha EP = Y - \overline{Y},$$
    $$\alpha P = \alpha EP + (Y - \overline{Y}), \text{ or}$$
    $$P = EP + \left(\frac{1}{\alpha}\right)(Y - \overline{Y}). \tag{14-1}$$

    Equation 14-1 indicates that when $Y = \overline{Y}$, $P = EP$. Graph this equation on Graph 14-1, label the curve *AS,* and label the slope of the line.

Graph 14-1

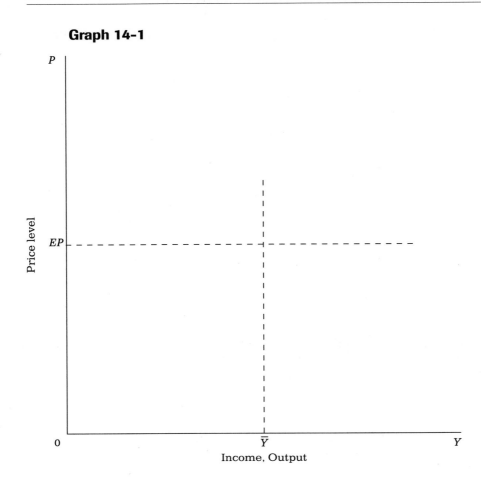

c. Equation 14-1 and Graph 14-1 indicate that an increase in the expected price level will shift the aggregate supply curve upward (to the left)/downward (to the right). An increase in the natural level of output will shift the aggregate supply curve upward (to the left)/downward (to the right) because the level of Y at which output will equal its natural level (and P will equal EP) will increase/decrease. The next two exercises illustrate how we can derive this aggregate supply curve from two different models of aggregate supply.

2. **The Sticky-Price Model** *In this exercise, we derive the aggregate supply curve using the sticky-price model.*

a. In the sticky-price model, the prices of some firms or products may be sticky because of long-term contracts or because of the way that markets are structured. The prices of other firms or products, however, will be flexible. As a result, the slope of the aggregate supply curve, reflecting the degree of price stickiness in the entire economy, will depend on the proportion of firms (or products) that have sticky prices.

b. Let us first consider a firm with flexible prices. This firm will set its price *p* so that

$$p = P + a(Y - \overline{Y}).$$

If the aggregate price level *P* rises, this firm's costs will <u>rise/fall</u>, and it will <u>raise/lower</u> its own price *p*. If aggregate income rises above its natural level, the demand curve for the firm's product will also <u>increase/decrease</u>, resulting in a(n) <u>increase/decrease</u> in price.

c. The firms with sticky prices have to set their prices before the aggregate price level and level of income become known. Therefore, they must set their prices according to their expectations of these variables:

$$p = EP + \alpha(EY - E\overline{Y}).$$

If *s* represents the fraction of all firms with sticky prices, and (1 − *s*) represents the fraction with flexible prices, then the overall price level will be a weighted average of the prices of flexible and sticky-price firms:

$$P = s[EP + a(EY - E\overline{Y})] + (1 - s)[P + a(Y - \overline{Y})].$$

Now suppose that aggregate income is expected to be at its natural level—that is, $EY = E\overline{Y}$. Consequently, $EY - E\overline{Y} =$ _____, and

$$P = sEP + (1 - s)[P + a(Y - \overline{Y})], \text{ or}$$
$$P = sEP + P - sP + [(1 - s)a(Y - \overline{Y})], \text{ or}$$
$$sP = sEP + [(1 - s)a(Y - \overline{Y})], \text{ or}$$
$$P = EP + [(1 - s)a/s](Y - \overline{Y}). \tag{14-2}$$

Equation 14-2 indicates that income will equal its natural level, that is, $Y = \overline{Y}$, whenever the aggregate price level is <u>greater than/less than/equal to</u> the expected price level. Output (income) will exceed its natural level only if the aggregate price level is <u>greater than/less than/equal to</u> the expected price level. As the proportion of firms with sticky prices rises, *s* rises. The rise in *s* <u>increases/decreases</u> the numerator of the coefficient of *Y* and <u>increases/decreases</u> the denominator. Consequently, the coefficient of *Y* <u>increases/decreases</u>. This <u>increases/decreases</u> the slope of the aggregate supply curve; hence, the aggregate supply curve becomes <u>flatter/steeper</u>. In Chapter 10 of the textbook, for example, the short-run aggregate supply curve was <u>horizontal/vertical</u>, the implicit value of *s* was _____, and <u>all/no</u> firms were assumed to have sticky prices in the short run.

3. **The Imperfect-Information Model** *In this exercise, we develop the aggregate supply curve using the imperfect-information model.*

   a. In the imperfect-information model, all markets clear, and output again deviates from its natural level whenever prices deviate from their expected levels. Following the simple example presented in Chapter 14 of the textbook, consider a wheat farmer in an imperfectly competitive wheat market. This wheat farmer will increase her production of wheat only if she thinks that the price of wheat relative to all other goods and services—that is P_{wheat}/P—has increased. Although the farmer can easily see when the price of wheat rises, she does not immediately get information about the aggregate price level. Consequently, she makes a forecast of the aggregate price level EP. As a result, the production of wheat will be positively related to P_{wheat}/EP. This relationship is graphed on Graph 14-2.

      Graph 14-2

      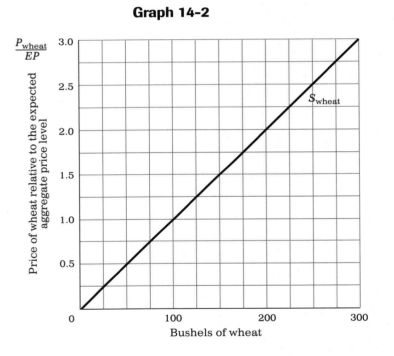

   b. Assume that the equilibrium price of wheat equals $1. If the expected aggregate price level $EP = 1.0$, and the actual price of wheat $P_{wheat} = \$1$, then the expected relative (or real) price of wheat $= P_{wheat}/EP =$

      _____/_____ = _____.

      From Graph 14-2, we see that the quantity of wheat produced will equal

      _____ bushels. Label this Point A.

c. Suppose for the moment that the expected price level remains equal to 1.0, but that the farmer suddenly finds that the price of wheat has risen to $3. As a result, the farmer thinks that the relative price of wheat has risen to $P_{\text{wheat}}/EP =$

$\$$_____/_____ = _____.

From Graph 14-2, we see that the quantity of wheat produced will rise/fall to

_____ bushels. Label this Point B.

d. In the imperfect-information model, however, farmers realize that part of the increase in the price of wheat probably reflects an increase in the aggregate price level. Thus, they respond to the increase in the price of wheat by increasing both the quantity of wheat produced and EP. On Graph 14-3, Point A reflects the situation in which $P_{\text{wheat}} = \$1$ and $EP = 1.0$. Thus, at Point A, the expected relative price of wheat $= P_{\text{wheat}}/EP =$ _____/_____ = _____.

From Graph 14-2, we see that when this occurs, the quantity of wheat supplied will equal _____ bushels.

Graph 14-3

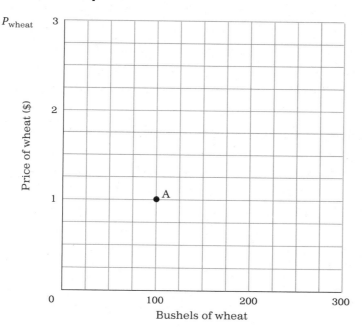

e. Starting from $1, suppose that the farmer again finds that the price of wheat has risen to $3. This represents an increase in P_{wheat} of _____ percent. Now, however, the farmer estimates that half of this percentage increase represents an increase in the aggregate price level. Consequently, her estimate of EP rises by 0.5 × _____ percent = _____ percent, that is, EP rises from 1.0 to _____. The new expected relative price of wheat is now $P_{wheat}/EP = \$3/$_____ = _____. From Graph 14-2, we see that at this expected relative price, the quantity of wheat supplied will equal _____ bushels. Label this Point C on Graph 14-2. Locate the point on Graph 14-6 that corresponds to this quantity and price of wheat ($3) and also label it Point C. Connect Points A and C on Graph 14-3 and label the curve AS_1. (In reality, of course, GDP includes more than just wheat.)

f. Extending this story to the entire economy, each producer will increase production only if she thinks that the price of the commodity she produces has risen relative to the aggregate price level. The price of all commodities taken together is merely the aggregate price level P. In long-run equilibrium, $P = EP$, so that $P/EP = $_____, and output will be at its equilibrium or natural level. If $P > EP$, output will be <u>greater/less</u> than its natural level, and if $P < EP$, output will be <u>greater/less</u> than its natural level. These conditions result in an upward-sloping short-run aggregate supply curve.

g. Now suppose that there has been a great deal of inflation in the recent past.
CH Consequently, when P_{wheat} rises from $1 to $3, or by _____ percent, our farmer assumes that 70 percent of this increase represents an increase in the aggregate price level. Thus, the farmer's EP rises by 0.70 × _____ percent = _____ percent, that is, from $EP = 1.0$ to $EP = $_____. The new expected relative price of wheat is now $P_{wheat}/EP = \$3/$_____ = _____. From Graph 14-2, we see that at this expected relative price, the quantity of wheat supplied will equal _____ bushels. Locate this quantity and this price of wheat ($3) on Graph 14-3 and label it Point D. Connect Points A and D on Graph 14-3 and label your curve AS_2. AS_2 is <u>flatter/steeper</u> than AS_1. Thus, if firms believe that most of any increase in the price of their output is the result of general inflation, the aggregate supply curve will be relatively <u>flat/steep</u>. In the extreme case in which all increases in P_{wheat} are assumed to result from general inflation, P_{wheat}/EP will always equal _____, the quantity of wheat supplied will always equal _____ bushels, and the aggregate supply curve will be <u>horizontal/vertical</u>.

4. **Short-Run and Long-Run Effects of an Increase in Aggregate Demand** *In this exercise, we link the aggregate supply and aggregate demand curves developed in Chapters 11 and 12 of the textbook with the long-run aggregate supply curve presented in Chapter 10 of the textbook.*

a. On Graph 14-4, we put the aggregate supply and aggregate demand curves together to depict an initial equilibrium at Point A.

Graph 14-4

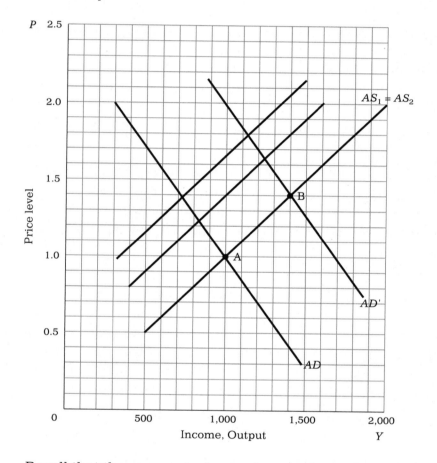

Recall that the aggregate demand curve slopes downward because as the aggregate price level falls, real money balances increase/decrease. This change in real money balances shifts the *IS/LM* curve _____. Consequently, the equilibrium level of income at the intersection of the *IS* and *LM* curves increases/decreases. The short-run aggregate supply curve slopes upward because output increases above its natural level only if the price level rises above/falls below the expected price level. Finally, the long-run aggregate supply curve is vertical because in the long run all prices and wages are sticky/flexible, and in the long run output will always be greater than/less than/equal to its natural level, regardless of the price level.

b. At Point A, output is equal to the natural level of output, which we arbitrarily set equal to 1,000. Consequently, the aggregate price level P must be greater than/less than/equal to its expected level EP. If EP does not change, it must therefore equal _____ all along the short-run aggregate supply curve AS_1.

c. Now suppose that the aggregate demand curve shifts to the right, to AD', in the second period. This shift could result from a(n) increase/decrease in government purchases, a(n) increase/decrease in net taxes, a(n) increase/decrease in the money supply, or a variety of other reasons. If the expected price level does not change (this is an important assumption), it will remain equal to _____. Consequently, in the second period, the short-run aggregate supply curve will not immediately shift (and, as on Graph 14-4, $AS_1 = AS_2$), and we will move to Point B. At Point B, output $Y =$ _____ and $P =$ _____. (These numbers must be read from the graph itself.)

d. If the policy change is a one-time, permanent change, the aggregate demand curve will not shift again. Nevertheless, the economy will not stay at Point B forever because, at Point B, the actual price level is greater than/less than/equal to the expected price level. Consequently, in the next period, the expected price level will increase/remain the same/decrease.

e. Suppose that the expected price level in any period t is equal to the last period's actual price level—that is, $EP_t = P_{t-1}$. Since the actual price level P in Period 2 = _____, the expected price level in Period 3 will equal _____. This change will shift the short-run aggregate supply curve upward/downward because, in Period 3, output will equal its natural level only if $P = EP =$ _____. Label as AS_3 the curve on Graph 14-4 that depicts the short-run aggregate supply curve in Period 3.

f. Consequently, in Period 3 the economy moves to the intersection of AD' (since AD' remains stationary) and AS_3. Label this Point C on Graph 14-7. At Point C, $Y =$ _____ and $P =$ _____. (Again, read these data from the graph; round off if necessary.) Between Periods 2 and 3, output has risen/fallen, whereas the price level has risen/fallen.

g. At Point C, the actual price level is greater than/less than/equal to the expected price level. Consequently, in the next period, the expected price level will increase/remain the same/decrease. If $EP_t = P_{t-1}$ and the actual price level in Period 3 = _____, then the expected price level in Period 4 will rise to _____. This rise in EP will shift the short-run aggregate supply curve upward/downward so that, in Period 4, output will equal its natural level only if $P = EP =$ _____. Label as AS_4 the curve on Graph 14-4 that depicts the short-run aggregate supply curve in Period 4. Label as Point D the point that represents the short-run equilibrium in Period 4.

h. At Point D on Graph 14-4, the actual price level is <u>greater than/less than/equal to</u> the expected price level. Consequently, in the next period, the expected price level will <u>increase/remain the same/decrease</u>, and this change will shift the short-run aggregate supply curve <u>upward/downward</u>. The short-run aggregate supply curve will continue to shift in each successive period as long as $P > EP$. This shift will occur as long as actual output is <u>greater than/less than</u> the natural level of output. The short-run aggregate supply curve will stop shifting when $P = EP$, which occurs when $Y = \overline{Y}$. At this point, the short-run aggregate supply curve will intersect the aggregate demand curve at a point along the long-run aggregate supply curve. Label the long-run equilibrium on Graph 14-4 Point F. At Point F, $Y =$ _____ and $P =$ _____.
Draw the short-run aggregate supply curve that corresponds to this long-run equilibrium on Graph 14-4 and label it AS_F. At Point F, the expected price level $EP =$ _____, and this is equal to the actual price level. The equilibrium level of output Y is also equal to the natural level of output $\overline{Y}$. Consequently, there are no forces pushing the economy away from Point F.

i. Comparing Points A and F, the long-run effects of the increase in aggregate demand were <u>an increase/no change/a decrease</u> in output and <u>an increase/no change/a decrease</u> in the price level.

j. Now suppose that we start again at Point A, and the aggregate demand curve once again shifts to AD'. Since this shift occurred unexpectedly, the economy would move to point B. In Period 3, however, people (particularly those who have taken an intermediate macroeconomics course) may begin to realize that prices will continue to rise. Consequently, they may try to revise their expectations of the future price level to take this into account. If they did, the expected price level would rise more rapidly than indicated in Parts e through h, and the short-run aggregate supply curve would shift upward <u>more/less</u> rapidly, provided that wages and prices could change as rapidly as price expectations. As a result, the economy would reach its long-run equilibrium <u>more/less</u> rapidly.

5. **The Phillips Curve** *In this exercise, we use the Phillips curve to analyze the short-run and long-run effects of changes in macroeconomic policies.*

a. The Phillips curve is an alternative way to analyze the interactions between aggregate supply and aggregate demand. The Phillips curve equation is

$$\pi = E\pi - \beta(u - u^n) + v, \tag{14-3}$$

where π equals the actual inflation rate, $E\pi$ equals expected inflation, u and u^n equal the actual and natural rates of unemployment, v represents the effects of supply shocks that shift the Phillips curve, and β is greater than zero. According to Equation 14-3, when the unemployment rate exceeds the natural rate of unemployment and there are no supply shocks, $\beta(u - u^n)$ is <u>positive/negative</u> Thus, actual inflation, $\pi = E\pi - \beta(u - u^n)$, will be <u>greater/less</u> than expected inflation. Conversely, when unemployment is less than its natural rate, actual inflation rises above expected inflation. When $u < u^n$, the higher inflation is called *demand-pull inflation*.

b. Suppose that the Phillips curve equation was

$$\pi = E\pi - 0.4(u - u^n) + v.$$

Suppose, in addition, that expected inflation was 8 percent, the natural rate of unemployment was 5 percent, and there were no supply shocks. Consequently, the Phillips curve equation corresponding to this situation would be

$$\pi = 8 - 0.4(u - 5).$$ **(14-4)**

Solve this equation for π.

$$\pi = \underline{\hspace{4cm}} - \underline{\hspace{4cm}} u.$$

Note that in Equation 14-4, inflation and unemployment are expressed as percentages rather than decimals. Plot and draw Equation 14-4 on Graph 14-5 and label it PC_1.

Graph 14-5

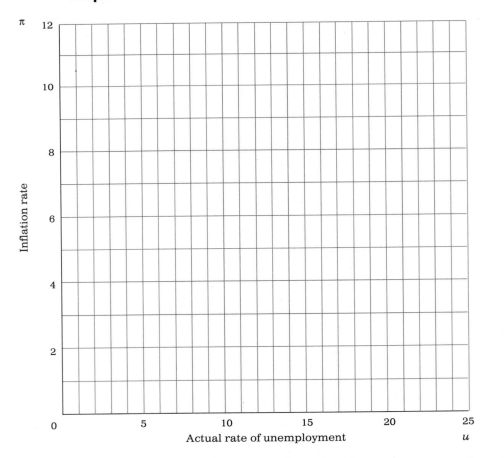

Note that on Graph 14-5, when $u = u^n$, actual inflation is greater than/ less than/equal to the expected inflation rate of 8 percent.

c. Suppose that the economy was initially at the natural rate of unemployment. Find the point along PC_1 on Graph 14-5 at which the unemployment rate is equal to the natural rate of unemployment and label it Point A. If the Fed and/or the government thought that inflation must be reduced, they could decrease aggregate demand in the second period by <u>increasing/decreasing</u> government purchases, <u>increasing/decreasing</u> taxes, and/or <u>increasing/decreasing</u> the money supply. If expected inflation does not change (this is an important assumption), it will remain equal to _____ percent. Consequently, in the second period, the Phillips curve will not shift, and we will move along PC_1 to the <u>left/right</u>. Since the Phillips curve did not shift, change the label of PC_1 on Graph 14-5 to $PC_1 = PC_2$.

d. Suppose that these policies increased the unemployment rate to 10 percent. Find this point on your Phillips curve on Graph 14-5 and label it Point B. At Point B, $u =$ _____ percent and $\pi =$ _____ percent.

e. At Point B, actual inflation is <u>greater than/less than/equal to</u> expected inflation. Consequently, in the next (third) period, expected inflation will <u>rise/fall</u> and the Phillips curve will shift <u>upward/downward</u>.

f. Suppose that expected inflation in any period t was equal to actual inflation during the preceding period, that is,

$$E\pi_t = \pi_{t-1}.$$

In Period 2, we found that $\pi =$ _____ percent. Consequently, in Period 3, $E\pi =$ _____ percent. This value will change the Phillips curve equation to

$$\pi = E\pi - 0.4(u - 5) = \underline{\hspace{3cm}} - 0.4(u - 5). \tag{14-5}$$

Solve this equation for π.

$\pi =$ _____ $-$ _____ u.

Plot and draw Equation 14-5 on Graph 14-5 and label the curve PC_3.

g. In Period 3, suppose that the government and/or the Fed continued their policies and kept the unemployment rate at 10 percent. Find this point on PC_3 on Graph 14-5 and label it Point C. At Point C, $u =$ _____ percent and $\pi =$ _____ percent.

h. At Point C, actual inflation is <u>greater than/less than/equal to</u> expected inflation. Consequently, in the next (fourth) period, expected inflation will <u>rise/fall</u> and the Phillips curve will shift <u>upward/downward</u>. Since actual inflation in Period 3 = _____ percent, expected inflation in Period 4 will equal _____ percent. Once again, this value will change the Phillips curve equation to

$$\pi = E\pi - 0.4(u - 5) = \text{_____} - 0.4(u - 5). \qquad \textbf{(14-6)}$$

Solve this equation for π.

$$\pi = \text{_____} - \text{_____} u.$$

Plot and draw Equation 14-6 on Graph 14-5 and label the curve PC_4.

i. In Period 4, suppose that the government and the Fed eased their policies and allowed the unemployment rate to resume its natural rate of 5 percent. Find this point on PC_4 on Graph 14-5 and label it Point D. At Point D, $u =$ _____ percent, $\pi =$ _____ percent, and actual inflation is <u>greater than/less than/equal to</u> expected inflation. Consequently, in the next (fifth) period, expected inflation will <u>rise/stay the same/fall</u>, and the Phillips curve will <u>shift upward/remain stationary/shift downward</u>. Thus, Point D represents a new long-run equilibrium.

j. In this exercise, it took two periods of excess unemployment to reduce inflation from 8 percent to _____ percent. If each period lasted for one year, it took two years of unemployment that exceeded the natural rate by $10 - 5 =$ _____ percentage points, or a total of $2 \times$ _____ $=$ _____ percentage-point years of cyclical unemployment, to reduce inflation by $8 -$ _____ $=$ _____ percentage points. For each percentage-point reduction in inflation, it took _____ percentage-point years of cyclical unemployment. According to Okun's law (see Chapter 10 of the textbook), each percentage-point year of cyclical unemployment represents 2 percentage points in lost GDP. Consequently, in our example, it took _____ percentage points in lost GDP to reduce inflation by 1 percentage point. This is called the _____ ratio.

k. Now suppose that we start over at Point A, and unemployment again rises to 10 percent. Since this rise occurs unexpectedly, the economy would move to Point B. In Period 3, however, people may realize that inflation will continue to fall. As a result, they may try to revise their expectations of future inflation to take this into account. If they did, expected inflation would fall more rapidly than indicated in Parts c through i, and the Phillips curve would shift downward <u>more/less</u> rapidly, provided that wages and prices could change as rapidly as inflationary expectations. As a result, the economy would reach its long-run equilibrium <u>more/less</u> rapidly and the sacrifice ratio would be <u>higher/lower</u> than in Part j.

l. The path depicted in Parts c through i is only one of several ways to reduce inflation, even if expected inflation changes slowly. On Graph 14-6, the initial Phillips curve and the initial equilibrium have been redrawn.

Graph 14-6

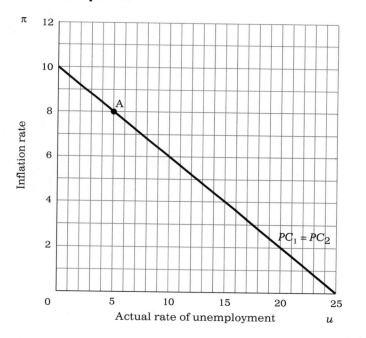

At Point A, $E\pi = 8$, $u =$ _____ percent, and $\pi =$ _____ percent. Now suppose that the Fed and/or the government thought it necessary to reduce inflation more rapidly than in Part c. Consequently, they pursued more restrictive policies and increased unemployment to 15 percent in the second period. Find this point on the Phillips curve on Graph 14-6 and label it Point B. At Point B, $u =$ _____ percent and $\pi =$ _____ percent. (Note that $E\pi$ has not yet changed.) If expected inflation in the third period is equal to actual inflation in the second period, $E\pi$ would fall to _____ percent. Consequently, the Phillips curve equation would change to

$$\pi = E\pi - 0.4(u - 5) = \underline{\hspace{4cm}} - 0.4(u - 5). \qquad \textbf{(14-7)}$$

Solve this equation for π.

$\pi = \underline{\hspace{4cm}} - \underline{\hspace{4cm}} u.$

Plot and draw Equation 14-7 on Graph 14-6 and label the curve PC_3. In Period 3, suppose that the government and the Fed eased their policies and allowed the unemployment rate to resume its natural rate of 5 percent. Find this point on PC_3 on Graph 14-6 and label it Point C. At Point C, $u =$ _____ percent, $\pi =$ _____ percent, and actual inflation is <u>greater than/less than/equal to</u> expected inflation. Consequently, Point C represents a new long-run equilibrium. This situation shows that inflation could be reduced more quickly if a more restrictive policy were enacted that increased unemployment more drastically. Note, however, that it took _____ percentage-point years of cyclical unemployment here to reduce inflation by _____ percentage points, which is <u>more than/less than/equal to</u> the amount it took in Parts c through i.

m. Finally, suppose that we start again at Point A on Graph 14-6 and that there is an adverse supply shock, such as a substantial increase in oil prices. In this case, the Phillips curve would shift <u>shift upward/remain stationary/shift downward</u> even if expected inflation did not change. Inflation caused by adverse supply shocks is called *cost-push inflation*.

Problems

Answer the following problems on a separate sheet of paper.

1. Use the sticky-price model of aggregate supply to explain how the ability of monetary and fiscal policy to change real GDP would be affected by the fraction of firms in the economy that have flexible prices.

2. Suppose that the economy is initially at the natural level of output, and the expected price level in any period is equal to the actual price level in the preceding period. If the Fed makes a credible, permanent reduction in the money supply, draw a graph to illustrate the path of the economy in both the short run and the long run, using aggregate supply and aggregate demand curves.

3. **a.** Explain how your answer to your answer to Problem 2 would be different if expectations were rational.

   b. Explain how your answer to Problem 2 would depend on the fraction of firms that have flexible prices

4. In the sticky-price model, the equation for the short-run aggregate supply curve is:

$$P = EP + [(1 - s)a/s](Y - \overline{Y})$$

where s is the fraction of firms with sticky prices and $a > 0$. The slope of this curve dP/dY is $(1 - s)a/s$. Calculate the derivative of this expression with respect to s, and discuss what this tells us about how the fraction of firms with sticky prices affects the steepness of the short-run aggregate supply curve. (You may treat both EP and $\overline{Y}$ as constants.)

5. If the economy is initially at the natural level of output and inflation rises, what additional macroeconomic data would enable one to determine whether the inflation was demand-pull or cost-push? Explain.

6. Suppose the economy has the Phillips curve:

$$\pi = E\pi - 0.25(u - 0.04)$$

   a. What is the natural rate of unemployment in this economy?

   b. Graph the short-run Phillips curve if the expected rate of inflation is 3 percent, or 0.03.

   c. What is the sacrifice ratio in this economy?

7. **a.** Draw an appropriately labeled Phillips curve and illustrate the current position of the U.S. economy. Somewhere in your graph clearly indicate each of the following: the current actual unemployment rate, the (approximate) natural rate of unemployment, the actual rate of inflation, and the (approximate) expected rate of inflation.

   b. Illustrate what will happen over time if no new macroeconomic policies are implemented.

8. What does the hysteresis theory of unemployment imply about the effects of a recession on the long-run aggregate supply curve? Briefly explain.

Data Questions

Locate the necessary economic data and apply them to answer the following data questions. All of the relevant data may be found in the Economic Report of the President (http://www.gpoaccess.gov/eop/).

1. **a.** Complete Table 14-1 with figures for the last three years for which you can find data. The average unemployment rate should be the average of the unemployment rate above the blank line, and the unemployment rate below the line. The change in the consumer price index that excludes food and energy (sometimes called "core inflation") is often used as an indicator of the ongoing inflationary trend, as discussed in Chapter 2 of the textbook.

Table 14-1

(1) Year	(2) Unemployment Rate (%)	(3) Average Unemployment Rate (%)	(4) Consumer Price Index Excluding Food and Energy	(5) Percentage Change in the CPI Excluding Food and Energy
____	_____		_____	
	_____			_____
____	_____		_____	
	_____			_____
____	_____		_____	

b. On an appropriately labeled graph, plot the average unemployment rate in Column 3 on the horizontal axis and the core inflation rate in Column 5 on the vertical axis. Draw one or two Phillips curves (whichever you think is more appropriate) that contain these two points.

c. Based on the theory of the Phillips curve, what do you think will soon happen to each of the following: the expected core inflation rate, the Phillips curve, and the actual core inflation rate? Explain your reasoning.

Question to Think About

1. Some economists have criticized the imperfect information model because the expansion of the Internet must have shortened the period of time during which suppliers are uncertain about whether an increase in the price of the product they produce represents an increase in relative prices or a general increase in all prices. As your text states, recent work on imperfect information models of aggregate supply focus on the limited ability of people to absorb and process information that is widely available. As a result, price setters may respond slowly to macroeconomic news. Consider the asparagus farmer introduced in the text and describe the difficulties he would have absorbing new price and other macroeconomic information. It might be useful to read the references cited in Footnote 3 in the textbook.

CHAPTER 15

A Dynamic Model of Aggregate Demand and Aggregate Supply

Fill-in Questions

Use the key terms below to fill in the blanks in the following statements. Each term may be used more than once.

impulse response function
natural rate of interest
predetermined variable

random variable
Taylor principle
Taylor rule

1. The _____ is the real interest rate at which, in the absence of any shock, the demand for goods and services equals the natural level of output.

2. A _____ is a variable whose values are determined by chance.

3. According to the _____, the real federal funds rate equals 2 percent when inflation is 2 percent and GDP is at its natural level.

4. A(n) _____ is a variable that was endogenous in an earlier period but is treated as essentially exogenous in the current period.

5. A(n) _____ is a graph of the time path of an endogenous variable after a shock.

6. According to the _____, the central bank must respond to an increase in inflation with an even greater increase in the nominal interest rate in order to keep inflation stable.

7. According to the _____, the central bank must respond to an increase in inflation by increasing the real interest rate in order to keep inflation stable.

Multiple-Choice Questions

1.   The dynamic aggregate demand, aggregate supply, or *DAD–DAS*, model:

   a. focuses on how output and inflation respond over time to exogenous changes in the economic environment.

   b. explicitly incorporates the response of monetary policy to economic conditions.

   c. better exemplifies the macroeconomic models used by economists at the research frontier than models in previous chapters.

   d. All of the answers are correct.

2.   In the aggregate demand equation $Y_t = \overline{Y}_t - \alpha(r_t - \rho) + \varepsilon_t$, the term ε_t:

   a. represents a random variable that fluctuates over time but equals zero, on average.

   b. can capture nonpermanent changes in fiscal policy that affect the demand for goods and services.

   c. can capture a variety of exogenous influences on the demand for goods and services.

   d. All of the answers are correct.

3.   The natural rate of interest ρ is the real interest rate at which:

   a. the inflation rate is equal to zero.

   b. the unemployment rate is equal to zero if there are no shocks.

   c. the demand for goods and services equals the natural level of output if there are no shocks.

   d. All of the answers are correct.

4.   The amount of aggregate demand falls as the real interest rate r rises because:

   a. firms engage in fewer investment projects.

   b. consumers save more and spend less.

   c. the dollar might appreciate, causing net exports to fall.

   d. All of the answers are correct.

5.   In the expression $E_t\pi_{t+1}$:

   a. $E_t\pi_{t+1}$ represents the expectation formed in period t of inflation in period $t + 1$.

   b. $E_t\pi_{t+1}$ represents the expected change in inflation between periods t and $t + 1$

   c. $E_t\pi_{t+1}$ is equal to zero when output is at its natural level.

   d. All of the answers are correct.

6.   In the Fisher equation $r_t = i_t - E_t\pi_{t+1}$, r_t represents the:

   a. natural rate of interest.

   b. *ex post* real interest rate.

   c. *ex ante* real interest rate.

   d. expected change in the real interest rate.

7. In the augmented Phillips curve equation $\pi_t = E_{t-1}\pi_t + \varphi(Y_t - \overline{Y}_t) + \upsilon_t$:

   a. inflation depends on expected inflation because some firms set prices in advance. When firms expect high inflation, they anticipate higher costs and raise their own prices.

   b. inflation rises when actual output rises because firms experience increasing marginal costs.

   c. the term υ_t is a random supply shock, such as a temporary oil price shock.

   d. All of the answers are correct.

8. In the monetary policy rule $i_t = \pi_t + \rho + \theta_\pi(\pi_t - \pi_t^*) + \theta_Y(Y_t - \overline{Y}_t)$:

   a. π_t^* is the central bank's target for the inflation rate in period t.

   b. a large value of θ_π means that the Fed will raise interest rates more vigorously when actual inflation rises.

   c. a large value of θ_Y means that the Fed will raise interest rates more vigorously when actual output rises.

   d. All of the answers are correct.

9. According to the Taylor rule, the nominal federal funds rate is:

   a. equal to 2 percent if inflation is 2 percent and real GDP is at its natural level.

   b. equal to 3 percent if inflation is 4 percent and real GDP is at its natural level.

   c. equal to 5 percent if inflation is 2 percent and real GDP exceeds its natural level by 2 percent.

   d. All of the answers are correct.

10. According to the Taylor rule, the *real* federal funds rate is:

   a. equal to 2 percent if inflation is 2 percent and real GDP is at its natural level.

   b. equal to 3 percent if inflation is 4 percent and real GDP is at its natural level.

   c. equal to 3 percent if inflation is 2 percent and real GDP exceeds its natural level by 2 percent.

   d. All of the answers are correct.

11. In long-run equilibrium:

   a. both output and the real interest rate are at their natural values.

   b. both inflation and expected inflation are at the target rate of inflation.

   c. the nominal interest rate is equal to the natural rate of interest plus the target rate of inflation.

   d. All of the answers are correct.

12. One difference between the conventional aggregate supply model developed in Chapter 14 and the dynamic aggregate supply model developed in this chapter is that:

   a. in the dynamic aggregate supply model, inflation replaces the price level as the variable measured on the vertical axis.

   b. in the dynamic aggregate supply model, the rate of growth of output replaces the level of output as the variable measured on the vertical axis.

   c. supply shocks no longer shift the dynamic aggregate supply model.

   d. All of the answers are correct.

13. The dynamic aggregate supply curve shifts when:

   a. the natural level of output changes.

   b. there is a supply shock.

   c. the rate of inflation in the preceding period changes.

   d. Any of the answers occur.

14. One difference between the conventional aggregate demand model developed in Chapters 11–13 and the dynamic aggregate demand model is that:

   a. in the dynamic aggregate demand model, inflation replaces the price level as the variable measured on the vertical axis.

   b. in the dynamic aggregate demand model, the rate of growth of output replaces the level of output as the variable measured on the vertical axis.

   c. changes in fiscal policy no longer shift the dynamic aggregate demand curve.

   d. All of the answers are correct.

15. The dynamic aggregate demand curve is downward sloping because:

   a. when inflation falls, goods and services become cheaper, so people buy more.

   b. when inflation falls, the central bank responds by decreasing the real interest rate, which increases the quantity of goods and services demanded.

   c. when inflation falls, the Fed decreases the money supply, which increases output.

   d. All of the answers are correct.

16. The dynamic aggregate demand curve shifts when:

   a. the natural level of output changes.

   b. the inflation target changes.

   c. there is a change in the demand shock ε_t.

   d. All of the answers are correct.

17. An increase in government spending or a reduction in taxes:

   a. shifts the *DAD* curve downward (to the left).

   b. results in a movement along a stationary *DAD* curve upward and to the left.

   c. shifts the *DAD* curve upward (to the right).

   d. results in a movement along a stationary *DAD* curve downward and to the right.

18. An increase in the central bank's inflation target:

   a. shifts the *DAD* curve upward (to the right).

   b. results in a movement along a stationary *DAD* curve downward and to the right.

   c. may result in either a. or b., depending on whether the money supply changes.

   d. shifts the *DAD* curve downward (to the left).

19. If the short-run equilibrium level of output lies below the natural level, the

   a. *DAD* curve will shift upward (to the right).

   b. *DAD* curve will shift downward (to the left).

   c. *DAS* curve will shift downward (to the right).

   d. *DAS* curve will shift upward (to the left).

20. If the natural level of output increases, the:

   a. *DAD* curve and the *DAS* curve both shift to the right.
   b. *DAD* curve and the *DAS* curve both shift to the left.
   c. *DAD* curve shifts to the right and the *DAS* curve shifts to the left.
   d. *DAD* curve shifts to the left and the *DAS* curve shifts to the right.

21. Starting at the natural level of output, if there is an adverse supply shock in period t such that v_t is positive for one period and subsequently returns to zero, then:

   a. in period t, the *DAS* curve shifts upward by the exact size of the shock.
   b. in period $t + 1$, the *DAS* curve starts to shift back down toward its initial position.
   c. the *DAD* curve does not shift.
   d. All of the answers are correct.

22. Starting at the natural level of output, if there is an adverse supply shock in period t such that v_t is positive for one period and subsequently returns to zero, then:

   a. output falls in period t but subsequently returns gradually to its natural level.
   b. the real interest rate rises in period t but subsequently returns gradually to its natural rate.
   c. inflation rises in period t but subsequently returns gradually to its target rate.
   d. All of the answers are correct.

23. Impulse response functions are graphs of the time paths of the:

   a. expected future shocks.
   b. economic variables before a shock.
   c. economic variables after a shock.
   d. pulse rates of the Federal Reserve Board of Governors after a shock.

24. Starting from the natural level of output, a positive shock to aggregate demand (like expansionary fiscal policy) in period t that lasts for five periods and then returns to zero will:

   a. shift the *DAD* curve to the right for five periods and then shift it back.
   b. lead to a series of upward shifts in the *DAS* curve, starting in period $t + 1$.
   c. increase both output and inflation in the short run.
   d. All of the answers are correct.

25. In the periods following a positive shock to aggregate demand, the *DAS* curve starts to shift upward because the:

   a. shock increases inflation, which, in turn, increases expected future inflation.
   b. shock leads to a series of additional supply shocks.
   c. central bank raises its target rate of inflation.
   d. central bank reduces its target rate of inflation.

26. If the central bank reduces its inflation target permanently:

    a. the *DAD* curve shifts downward by the change in the target and both output and inflation fall in the short run.

    b. the *DAD* curve shifts upward by the change in the target and both output and inflation rise in the short run.

    c. the *DAS* curve starts to shift upward in later periods.

    d. output remains permanently below its natural level.

27. If expectations are formed rationally rather than adaptively, then:

    a. inflation will always be zero.

    b. future inflation will always equal expected inflation.

    c. people may respond to announcements of new policy by altering their expectations of inflation more rapidly and output will return to its natural level more quickly.

    d. All of the answers are correct.

28. If the central bank responds strongly to inflation and weakly to output:

    a. the central bank will raise interest rates a lot in response to a supply shock.

    b. the *DAD* curve will be very flat.

    c. a supply shock will have a big effect on output and a small effect on inflation.

    d. All of the answers are correct.

29. Compared to the Federal Reserve, the European Central Bank seems to:

    a. give more weight to output stability and less weight to inflation stability.

    b. give more weight to inflation stability and less weight to output stability.

    c. lower interest rates more during recessions.

    d. allow inflation to fluctuate more than the Fed.

30. According to the Taylor principle, in order for inflation to be stable, the central bank must respond to an increase in inflation by:

    a. increasing its inflation target.

    b. increasing the nominal interest rate by more than the increase in inflation.

    c. decreasing the real interest rate.

    d. All of the answers are correct.

Exercises

1. **The Dynamic Aggregate Demand Curve** *In this exercise, we derive the dynamic aggregate demand curve and discuss the variables that make it shift.*

The dynamic aggregate demand curve (which we shall call the *DAD* curve) is the intertemporal analogue of the aggregate demand curve derived in Chapter 12 of the text. It is based on the demand for goods and services, the Fisher equation (which was introduced in Chapter 5), and a monetary policy rule set by the central bank. The demand for goods and services is given by the equation:

$$Y_t = \overline{Y}_t - \alpha(r_t - \rho) + \varepsilon_t, \tag{15-1}$$

where Y_t is the total output of goods and services in the current period, which we call period t, $\overline{Y}_t$ is the natural level of output in period t, r_t is the real interest rate in period t, and ε_t is a random variable representing a shock to demand in period t. Both α and ρ are parameters greater than zero. The parameter ρ represents the natural rate of interest. This is defined as the real interest rate at which, in the absence of any demand shocks, the demand for output equals the natural level of output.

a. Equation 15-1 indicates that the demand for output rises along with the natural level of output. As a country becomes richer over time, its demand for goods and services increases proportionately. The second term on the right-hand side of Equation 15-1 indicates that, when the real interest rate rises, the demand for output will <u>rise/fall/remain constant</u>. The reasoning is similar to that in earlier chapters. When the real interest rate rises, borrowing becomes more expensive and saving is more rewarding. Consequently, firms' investment falls and consumers save more and spend less, both of which reduce the demand for output. The larger the value of the parameter α, the <u>more/less</u> the demand for goods and services falls in response to a given increase in the real interest rate.

b. The second building block of the dynamic aggregate demand curve is the Fisher equation, according to which the (*ex ante*) real interest rate in period t is equal to the nominal interest rate in period t minus the expected rate of future inflation:

$$r_t = i_t - E_t \pi_{t+1}. \tag{15-2}$$

The last term in Equation 15-2, $E_t \pi_{t+1}$, represents the expectation of what the inflation rate will be in period _____ (the subscript on π) based on information available in period _____ (the subscript on E).

c. The third building block of the *DAD* curve is the way in which people form their expectations. The text assumes that inflation expectations are adaptive, which means that the expectation of next period's inflation is equal to the current rate of inflation. This is represented by the equation:

$$E_t\pi_{t+1} = \pi_t. \tag{15-3}$$

Thus, if the current rate of inflation is 2 percent, people expect next period's inflation rate will be _____ percent. This is an admittedly simple way of forming expectations, and we shall discuss a more sophisticated alternative in a later exercise.

d. The fourth building block is the monetary policy rule, which determines the nominal interest rate. The monetary policy rule reflects the behavior of the central bank and the way in which it responds to inflation and output gaps:

$$i_t = \pi_t + \rho + \theta_\pi(\pi_t - \pi_t^*) + \theta_Y(Y_t - \overline{Y}_t). \tag{15-4}$$

In Equation 15-4, π_t^* is the central bank's target for the inflation rate in period _____. The parameter θ_π represents the responsiveness of the central bank to high inflation. Similarly, the parameter θ_Y represents the responsiveness of the central bank to higher levels of output. Both θ_π and θ_Y are assumed to be greater than zero.

e. The monetary policy rule can also be seen as the way in which the central bank controls the real interest rate. According to Equation 15-2, the real interest rate is $r_t = i_t - E_t\pi_{t+1}$. Furthermore, if inflationary expectations are adaptive, $E_t\pi_{t+1}$ is equal to _____. Substituting this into the preceding equation yields $r_t = i_t - \pi_t$. If we subtract π_t from both sides of Equation 15-4, we obtain:

$$i_t - \pi_t = [\pi_t + \rho + \theta_\pi(\pi_t - \pi_t^*) + \theta_Y(Y_t - \overline{Y}_t)] - \pi_t, \text{ or}$$
$$r_t = \rho + \theta_\pi(\pi_t - \pi_t^*) + \theta_Y(Y_t - \overline{Y}_t). \tag{15-5}$$

Consequently, whenever inflation rises above the inflation target, the central bank responds by increasing/decreasing the real interest rate. This will tend to increase/decrease investment and consumption and push inflation back toward its target. Similarly, whenever output rises above its natural level, the central bank responds by increasing/decreasing the real interest rate. This will tend to increase/decrease investment and consumption and increase/decrease output, pushing it back toward its natural level. Equation 15-5 also indicates that, when $\pi_t = \pi_t^*$ and $Y_t = \overline{Y}_t$, the central bank will set the real interest rate equal to _____, the natural rate of interest.

f. Our final step in deriving the *DAD* curve involves the substitution of Equation 15-5 for r_t in Equation 15-1 to obtain:

$$Y_t = \overline{Y}_t - \alpha(\rho + \theta_\pi(\pi_t - \pi_t^*) + \theta_Y(Y_t - \overline{Y}_t) - \rho) + \varepsilon_t, \text{ or}$$
$$Y_t = \overline{Y}_t - \alpha[\theta_\pi(\pi_t - \pi_t^*) + \theta_Y(Y_t - \overline{Y}_t)] + \varepsilon_t. \tag{15-6}$$

Equation 15-6 indicates that, whenever inflation rises, output <u>rises/falls</u>. This occurs because the central bank responds to higher inflation by increasing the real interest rate, which <u>increases/decreases</u> investment and consumption and thereby <u>increases/decreases</u> output.

g. Now, expand the second term within the brackets of Equation 15-6 to obtain:

$$Y_t = \overline{Y}_t - \alpha\theta_\pi(\pi_t - \pi_t^*) - \alpha\theta_Y Y_t + \alpha\theta_Y \overline{Y}_t + \varepsilon_t. \tag{15-7}$$

The *DAD* equation in the text may be derived by collecting the terms involving Y_t on the right-hand side of Equation 15-7, bringing all the terms involving Y_t to the left-hand side of the equation and solving for Y_t to obtain:

$Y_t = $ _____.   (*DAD*)

(Make sure you check your answer with the equation in the text or in the answer section of the Study Guide before proceeding.)

h. When inflation is on target ($\pi_t = \pi_t^*$) and there is no demand shock ($\varepsilon_t = 0$), the *DAD* equation indicates that actual output Y_t equals the natural level of output $\overline{Y}_t$. Since all the parameters in the first bracket in the *DAD* equation are positive and the brackets are preceded by a minus sign, the equation also indicates that there is an inverse relationship between inflation and output along the *DAD* curve. Holding the other variables constant, when inflation rises, output rises/falls.

i. The story behind this inverse relationship between output demanded and inflation is important. When inflation rises, the central bank follows its rule and increases/decreases the nominal interest rate by more than/less than the change in inflation, so the real interest rate rises/falls. This increase/decrease in the real interest rate increases/reduces the quantity of goods and services demanded.

j. Assume that the inflation target is initially 2 percent. Locate the point in Graph 15-1 at which $\pi_t = \pi_t^*$ and $Y_t = \overline{Y}_t$, and label it Point A. Then draw a negatively sloped curve in Graph 15-1 through Point A and label it *DAD* ($\pi_t^* = 2\%$; $\varepsilon_t = 0$).

Graph 15-1

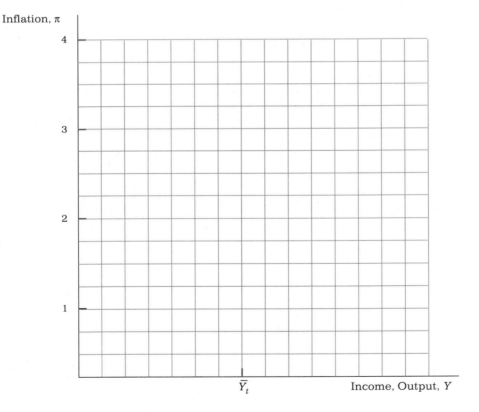

k. The *DAD* equation also indicates three exogenous events that will shift the *DAD* curve. First, suppose there is a demand shock and $\varepsilon_t > 0$. The demand shock could be caused by temporary consumer or business optimism or by an increase in government spending or a decrease in net taxes. The *DAD* equation indicates that the level of output Y_t will then rise/fall even if inflation doesn't change. This means that the entire *DAD* curve will shift upward (to the right)/downward (to the left).

l. Secondly, a change in the central bank's inflation target also shifts the *DAD* curve. Since π_t^* is preceded by two minus signs in the *DAD* equation, an increase in π_t^* will increase/decrease the level of output Y_t if inflation doesn't change. Consequently, the *DAD* curve will shift upward (to the right)/downward (to the left). When the central bank raises its inflation target, it pursues a more expansionary monetary policy by increasing/decreasing the nominal interest rate. The higher/lower nominal rate is accompanied by an increase/decrease in the real interest rate, which stimulates the demand for goods and services, so the *DAD* curve shifts to the right/left.

m. Finally, if we begin again at Point A in Graph 15-1, and both actual output and the natural level of output rise by the same amount, then $Y_t - \overline{Y}_t$ will still equal zero. If there is no demand shock, the *DAD* equation indicates that inflation will then be greater than/equal to/less than its target. In this case, the entire *DAD* curve will shift to the right/left by the amount of the increase in the natural level of output.

2. **The Taylor Rule** *We introduce the Taylor rule and illustrate how the Fed might use it to conduct monetary policy.*

Recall the monetary policy rule presented in Exercise 1:

$$i_t = \pi_t + \rho + \theta_\pi(\pi_t - \pi_t^*) + \theta_Y(Y_t - \overline{Y}_t). \tag{15-4}$$

After examining the behavior of the federal funds rate over time, John Taylor developed a modified version, which has become known as the Taylor rule:

$$\text{Nominal Federal Funds Rate} = \text{Inflation} + 2\% + \tag{15-8}$$
$$0.5(\text{Inflation} - 2\%) + 0.5(\text{GDP gap})$$

where the GDP gap is equal to the percentage by which the actual level of GDP lies above the natural level of GDP. Because the Taylor rule tracked the actual behavior of the federal funds rate so closely, Taylor suggested that the Federal Reserve may have implicitly been following it in conducting monetary policy.

a. Comparing Equations 15-8 and 15-4, the Taylor rule implies that the natural rate of interest is _____ percent and the Fed's inflation target is _____ percent.

b. When actual GDP is equal to its natural level, the GDP gap is _____ percent. Therefore, according to the Taylor rule, when actual GDP is equal to its natural level and actual inflation is 2 percent, the Fed sets the nominal federal funds rate equal to _____ + 2 + 0.5(_____ − 2) + 0.5(_____) = _____ percent. In accordance with the general monetary policy rule, the Fed increases the nominal federal funds rate whenever the actual inflation rate rises/falls.

c. If the actual level of GDP is 101 and the natural level of GDP is 100, the actual level of GDP is _____ percent above the natural level, and the GDP gap is 1 percent. Whenever actual GDP rises further above the natural level, the GDP gap rises/falls, and the Fed increases/decreases the nominal federal funds rate in order to slow down the economy.

d. Use the Taylor rule to complete Columns 4 and 5 of the following table.

Table 15-1

(1) Inflation (%)	(2) Actual GDP $ billions	(3) Natural Level of GDP $ billions	(4) GDP gap (%)	(5) Nominal Federal Funds Rate (%)	(6) Real Federal Funds Rate (%)
2	100	100	_____	_____	_____
3	100	100	_____	_____	_____
2	106	100	_____	_____	_____
2	94	100	_____	_____	_____
4	96	100	_____	_____	_____

e. Recall that the real federal funds rate is equal to the nominal federal funds rate plus/minus the actual rate of inflation and complete Column 6 in Table 15-1.

f. Finally, examine the first two rows of Table 15-1. When inflation rose by 1 percentage point, the Fed increased the nominal federal funds rate by _____ percentage points so that the real federal funds rate rose/fell by _____ percentage points.

3. **The Dynamic Aggregate Supply Curve** *In this exercise, we derive the dynamic aggregate supply curve, compute its slope, and discuss what factors shift it.*

a. The dynamic aggregate supply (*DAS*) curve is the intertemporal analogue of the short-run aggregate supply curve derived in Chapter 14 of the text. It is based on the expectations-augmented Phillips curve with exogenous supply shocks, according to the equation:

$$\pi_t = E_{t-1}\pi_t + \varphi(Y_t - \overline{Y}_t) + \upsilon_t. \tag{15-9}$$

In Equation 15-9, inflation in period t depends on $E_{t-1}\pi_t$, which is what people in period _____ expected inflation to be in period _____. This term reflects the fact that some firms set their prices in advance. When expected inflation rises, these firms expect their costs will rise, too, so they raise their own prices.

b. Inflation in period t also depends on the deviation of output from its natural level, $Y_t - \overline{Y}_t$. In Chapter 14, the Phillips curve was expressed in terms of the deviation of the unemployment rate from the natural rate of unemployment, but it was derived from Equation 15-9 using one form of Okun's law. When output rises above its natural level, the unemployment rate <u>rises above/falls below</u> its natural rate. Firms then experience increasing marginal costs and raise prices. The parameter φ reflects how quickly firms raise prices in response to the higher marginal costs. It is assumed to be greater than zero.

c. Finally, as in Chapter 14, inflation in period t depends on a supply shock v_t. This supply shock is an exogenous random variable. Although its average value is zero, it can be positive or negative in any particular period. One example is an oil shock in which oil prices rise temporarily because of a supply disruption in the Middle East. In this case, v_t would be positive during the disruption and then return to zero when the disruption ends. Supply shocks can be positive or negative. If good weather results in an abundant harvest, v_t would be <u>positive/negative</u> during the bountiful period in which food prices fell, and it would return to zero in the following period.

d. As in Exercise 1, we assume expectations are adaptive, in which case the current expectation of next period's inflation rate is merely the current rate of inflation. Similarly, last-period's expectation of this period's inflation is equal to last period's actual rate of inflation. This is represented by the equation:

$$E_{t-1}\pi_t = \pi_{t-1}.$$ (15-10)

If we substitute Equation 15-10 into Equation 15-9, we obtain the equation for the dynamic aggregate supply curve, which we shall henceforth call the *DAS* curve:

$$\pi_t = \pi_{t-1} + \varphi(Y_t - \overline{Y}_t) + v_t.$$ (*DAS*)

Use the *DAS* equation to complete Table 15-2.

Table 15-2

(1) $\pi_{t-1}(\%)$	(2) φ	(3) Y_t	(4) $\overline{Y}_t$	(5) v_t	(6) $\pi_t(\%)$
2	0.25	100	100	0	_____
2	0.25	101	100	0	_____
2	0.25	99	100	0	_____
2	0.25	100	100	1	_____
2	0.25	101	100	1	_____

e. In the first row of Table 15-2, output is equal to its natural level of 100 and there is no supply shock (i.e., $v_t = 0$). Consequently, inflation in period t will be equal to inflation in period $t - 1$, or $\pi_t = \pi_{t-1} =$ _____ percent. Find this point in Graph 15-2 and label it Point A. In the second row of Table 15-3, last period's inflation is 2 percent, there is no supply shock, and output exceeds its natural level by _____ unit(s). Thus, in the second row, which is not meant to be one period later than the first row, but a separate scenario, inflation in period t will be

_____ percent. Find this point in Graph 15-2 and label it Point B. And in the third row of Table 15-3, note that, when last period's inflation is 2 percent, there is no supply shock, and output falls below its natural level by _____, then inflation in period t will be _____ percent. Find this point in Graph 15-2, label it Point C. Now, connect Points A, B, and C in Graph 15-2 and label the curve $DAS(\pi_{t-1} = 2\%; \upsilon_t = 0)$.

f. The slope of the *DAS* curve in Graph 15-2 is _____, which we can see from the *DAS* equation is equal to the parameter _____. If marginal costs and prices rise more rapidly in response to increases in output, the value of φ will rise/fall, the slope of the *DAS* curve will become bigger/smaller, and the curve itself will become steeper/flatter.

g. In Rows 4 and 5 of Table 15-2, we see how a supply shock affects the *DAS* curve. In these rows, a temporary supply shock increases the value of υ_t to 1. If actual output remains equal to 100, inflation in period t rises to _____ percent. If, on the other hand, output rises to 101, inflation in period t rises to _____ percent. Find these points in Graph 15-2 and label them Points D and E, respectively, and draw the corresponding *DAS* curve and label it $DAS(\pi_{t-1} = 2\%; \upsilon_t = 1)$. Comparing the two *DAS* curves, note that, when there is a supply shock that increases υ_t to 1, the *DAS* curve shifts upward/downward by _____ percentage point(s).

h. Now, let's explore two other changes that will shift the *DAS* curve. Complete Table 15-3.

Table 15-3

(1) $\pi_{t-1}(\%)$	(2) φ	(3) Y_t	(4) $\overline{Y}_t$	(5) υ_t	(6) $\pi_t(\%)$
3	0.25	100	100	0	_____
3	0.25	101	100	0	_____
3	0.25	110	110	0	_____

The only difference between the first two rows of Table 15-3 and Table 15-2 is that inflation in period $t-1$ has now risen to 3 percent. As a result, if the level of output is 100, inflation in period t is _____ percent, and if output rises to 101, inflation in period t rises to _____ percent. Find these points in Graph 15-3 and label them Points F and G, respectively, and draw the corresponding dynamic aggregate supply curve and label it $DAS(\pi_{t-1} = 3\%; \upsilon_t = 0)$. Compare the new *DAS* curve with the original curve, which is already drawn in Graph 15-3. Note that, when inflation in period $t-1$ rises by 1 percentage point, the *DAS* curve shifts <u>upward/downward</u> by _____ percentage point(s). Similarly, if inflation in period $t - 1$ were to fall, the *DAS* curve would shift <u>upward (to the left)/downward (to the right)</u>.

Graph 15-2

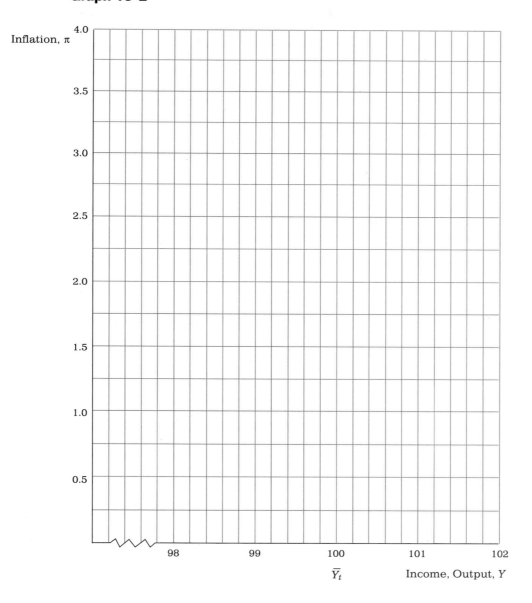

i. Finally, in the last row of Table 15-3, we illustrate what happens when there is an increase in the natural level of output to 110. Compare Rows 1 and 3 in Table 15-3. In Row 1, $Y_t = \overline{Y}_t =$ _____ so that $\varphi(Y_t - \overline{Y}_t) = 0$ and inflation in period t equals _____ percent. In Row 3, $Y_t = \overline{Y}_t =$ _____ so that $\varphi(Y_t - \overline{Y}_t) =$ _____ and inflation in period t equals _____ percent. Consequently, an increase in the natural level of output will shift the *DAS* curve to the right by the amount of the increase in $\overline{Y}_t$.

4. Long-run Equilibrium *In this exercise, we derive the long-run equilibrium conditions for the dynamic aggregate supply, aggregate demand model.*

a. In order to derive the long-run equilibrium conditions for the *DAS–DAD* model, it is useful to repeat some of the basic equations from Exercises 1 and 3:

$$Y_t = \overline{Y}_t - \alpha(r_t - \rho) + \varepsilon_t, \tag{15-1}$$

$$i_t = \pi_t + \rho + \theta_\pi(\pi_t - \pi_t^*) + \theta_Y(Y_t - \overline{Y}_t) \tag{15-4}$$

$$Y_t = \overline{Y}_t - [\alpha\theta_\pi/(1+\alpha\theta_Y)](\pi_t - \pi_t^*) + [1/(1+\alpha\theta_Y)]\varepsilon_t \tag{DAD}$$

$$\pi_t = \pi_{t-1} + \varphi(Y_t - \overline{Y}_t) + \upsilon_t. \tag{DAS}$$

b. In long-run equilibrium, there are no shocks ($\varepsilon_t = \upsilon_t = 0$) and inflation remains constant over time ($\pi_t = \pi_{t-1}$). When these two conditions are substituted into the *DAS* equation, we are left with the first long-run condition $Y_t =$ _____. Thus, like the earlier aggregate supply, aggregate demand model of Chapter 14, output returns to its natural level in the long run.

c. Equation 15-1 indicates that, at long-run equilibrium when $Y_t = \overline{Y}_t$ and $\varepsilon_t = 0$, the real interest rate $r_t =$ _____. This is a reflection of the fact that the natural interest rate is the real interest rate at which, in the absence of any shocks, output is equal to its natural level.

d. If we set output equal to its natural level in the *DAD* equation and set $\varepsilon_t = 0$, we obtain the result $\pi_t =$ _____. Thus, in the long run, inflation eventually equals the _____. Furthermore, if inflation is stable in the long run and expectations are adaptive, then $E_t\pi_{t+1} = \pi_t =$ _____. Thus, in long-run equilibrium expected inflation is also equal to the _____ rate of inflation.

e. Finally, making these substitutions in Equation 15-4 yields the long-run condition that $i_t = \pi_t + \rho$. If inflation in the long run is equal to its target, then $i_t =$ _____ + ρ, and the nominal interest rate is equal to the _____ plus the natural rate of interest.

Graph 15-3

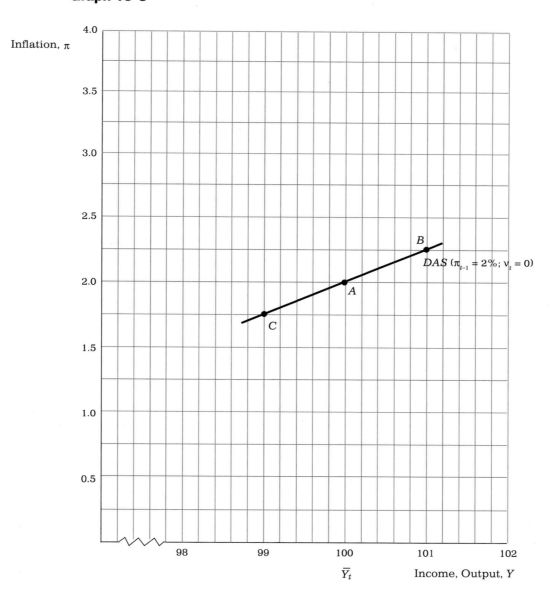

5. **Short-Run Equilibrium and Aggregate Supply Shocks** *In this exercise, we introduce the short-run DAS–DAD equilibrium and examine the short-run and long-run effects of temporary supply shocks.*

a. In Exercise 4, we examined the long-run *DAS–DAD* equilibrium conditions. In the short run, the model reaches an equilibrium when the *DAS* curve intersects the *DAD* curve. This occurs when the two endogenous variables, inflation and output, have adjusted so that both the *DAS* and the *DAD* equations are satisfied:

$$Y_t = \overline{Y}_t - [\alpha\theta_\pi/(1 + \alpha\theta_Y)](\pi_t - \pi_t^*) + [1/(1 + \alpha\theta_Y)]\varepsilon_t \qquad \textbf{(DAD)}$$

$$\pi_t = \pi_{t-1} + \varphi(Y_t - \overline{Y}_t) + \upsilon_t. \qquad \textbf{(DAS)}$$

The long-run equilibrium conditions derived in Exercise 4 do not necessarily hold in short-run equilibrium. Thus, when the *DAD* and *DAS* equations are satisfied, the inflation rate does not have to be equal to what it was in the preceding period, nor must it equal the inflation target. Similarly, output does not have to equal its _____. The economy, however, will adjust over time and converge to its long-run equilibrium, at which all of these three conditions do hold. The mechanism by which this occurs is contained in the *DAS* equation and the *DAS* curve, which will shift upward or downward whenever π_{t-1} changes until long-run equilibrium is attained.

b. Suppose, for example, that inflation has been rising so that $\pi_{t-1} > \pi_{t-2}$. When this happens, the lagged inflation term π_{t-1} in this period's *DAS* equation will be greater than the lagged inflation term π_{t-2} in last period's *DAS* equation. As we saw in Exercise 3, an increase in the preceding period's inflation rate will shift the entire *DAS* curve upward (to the left)/downward (to the right). The *DAS* curve will keep shifting until inflation no longer changes from one period to the next, that is, until inflation is greater than/equal to/less than inflation in the preceding period. From the *DAS* equation, we can see that, in the absence of any supply shocks, this will occur when output is equal to the

_____.

c. Now, consider what happens when the economy is hit by a supply shock that lasts for one period. This could result from an oil price shock or an increase in union power that pushes up wages and prices. For simplicity, let us assume we begin in period $t - 1$ in long-run equilibrium so that $Y_{t-1} =$ _____ and $\pi_{t-1} = \pi_{t-2} = \pi_{t-1}^*$. Let us also assume that the natural level of output and the inflation target do not change over time so that $\overline{Y}_{t-2} = \overline{Y}_{t-1} = \overline{Y}_t = \overline{Y}_{all}$ and $\pi_{t-2}^* = \pi_{t-1}^* = \pi_t^*$. Thus, we start at Point A in Graph 15-4. Note that Point A is located at the intersection of the DAD_{t-1} curve and the DAS_{t-1} curve.

Graph 15-4

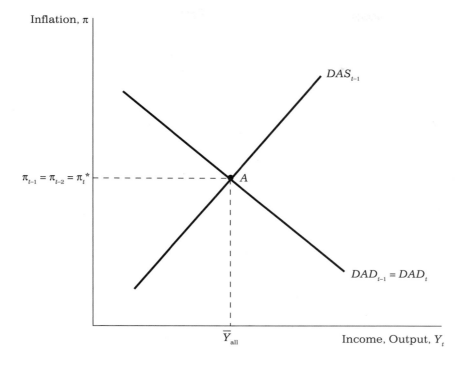

d. Recall that a supply shock represents an increase in v_t. Suppose that v_t rises from zero to 1 percent in period t. According to the *DAS* equation and Exercise 3, the *DAS* curve will shift <u>upward/downward</u> by the same amount as the shock. Draw the new *DAS* curve in Graph 15-4 and label it DAS_t. Since the *DAD* curve will not shift, we move to the intersection of the DAS_t curve and the $DAD_{t-1} = DAD_t$ curve. Locate this point in Graph 15-4, label it Point B, and label the inflation rate at Point B π_t. From Point A to Point B, output <u>increases/remains the same/decreases</u> while inflation <u>increases/remains the same/decreases</u>.

e. In period $t + 1$, two important things happen. On the one hand, the temporary supply shock disappears, so the value of v_{t+1} returns to _____. If nothing else occurred, the *DAS* curve would shift all the way back down to its original position at DAS_{t-1}. However, something else *has* happened. In period t, the supply shock led to an increase in inflation. Thus, expected inflation has risen. If the increase in expected inflation is all that happened, the *DAS* curve would shift up because of the increase in the preceding period's inflation rate. The combination of these two events will still shift the *DAS* curve down in period $t + 1$ (if the system is stable), but not all the way to DAS_{t-1}. Consequently, draw a *DAS* curve on Graph 15-4 in between DAS_{t-1} and DAS_t and label it DAS_{t+1}. Find the new short-run equilibrium in Period $t + 1$, label it Point C, and label the inflation rate at Point C π_{t+1}. From Point B to Point C, output <u>increases/remains the same/decreases</u> while inflation <u>increases/remains the same/decreases</u>.

f. In period $t + 2$ the supply shock remains equal to zero, but inflation continues to fall because inflation in the preceding period π_{t+1} is less than it was in period t. Thus, inflation expectations will rise/fall, and the *DAS* curve will continue to shift downward (to the right) until it reaches long-run equilibrium at the natural level of output. Consequently, relabel the initial *DAS* curve $DAS_{t-1} = DAS_{\text{Final}}$.

g. Thus, a supply shock that temporarily increases υ_t will lead to temporarily higher/lower output and temporarily higher/lower inflation. In the long run, however, the economy returns to its long-run equilibrium.

6. **The Dynamic Response to Aggregate Supply Shocks and Impulse Response Functions** *In this exercise, we introduce simple impulse response functions to track the dynamic response to aggregate supply shocks.*

   a. In Exercise 5, we used *DAS–DAD* graphs to illustrate the response to a temporary aggregate supply shock. In this exercise, we place values on the parameters in the *DAS* and *DAD* equations to illustrate how one can calculate the paths of both output and inflation after a supply shock.

   b. Recall our basic *DAD* and *DAS* equations:

   $$Y_t = \overline{Y}_t - [\alpha\theta_\pi/(1 + \alpha\theta_Y)](\pi_t - \pi_t^*) + [1/(1 + \alpha\theta_Y)]\varepsilon_t \qquad \textbf{(DAD)}$$

   $$\pi_t = \pi_{t-1} + \varphi(Y_t - \overline{Y}_t) + \upsilon_t. \qquad \textbf{(DAS)}$$

   In order to calculate numerical values of output and inflation, we use the numerical values of the relevant parameters suggested in the textbook, which are: $\overline{Y}_t = 100$; $\pi_t^* = 2.0$; $\alpha = 1.0$; $\varphi = 0.25$; $\theta_\pi = 0.5$; and $\theta_Y = 0.5$. Substituting these values into the *DAD* and *DAS* equations yields:

   $$Y_t = \underline{\qquad} - \underline{\qquad}(\pi_t - \underline{\qquad}) + \underline{\qquad} \varepsilon_t \qquad \textbf{(15-11)}$$

   $$\pi_t = \pi_{t-1} + \underline{\qquad}(Y_t - \underline{\qquad}) + \upsilon_t. \qquad \textbf{(15-12)}$$

   c. Assume that we begin in period $t - 2$ at long-run equilibrium. Thus, output is equal to its natural level and inflation is and has been equal to its target rate. As in Exercise 5, we make two additional assumptions. First, the natural level of output does not change over time so that $\overline{Y}_{t-2} = \overline{Y}_{t-1} = \overline{Y}_t = \overline{Y}_{t+1} = \overline{Y}_{\text{all}} = \underline{\qquad}$. Second, the inflation target π_t^* remains constant over time so that $\pi_{t-2}^* = \pi_{t-1}^* = \pi_t^* = \underline{\qquad}$ (percent). These results are shown in the first row of Table 15-4:

Table 15-4

(1) Period	(2) Supply Shock υ	(3) Demand Shock ε	(4) Inflation in Preceding Period	(5) Output Y	(6) Inflation π
$t-2$	0	0	2	100	2
$t-1$	0	0	_____	100	_____
t	1	0	_____	_____	_____
$t+1$	0	0	_____	_____	_____
$t+2$	0	0	_____	_____	_____
$t+3$	0	0	_____	_____	_____

d. We now use Equations 15-11 and 15-12 to complete the second row of Table 15-4. In period $t-1$, inflation in the preceding period (i.e., in period $t-2$) is given in the first row of Column 6. This number is _____ (percent). Enter this number in Column 4 of period $t-1$. If we are still in long-run equilibrium in period $t-1$, output will still be equal to its natural level of 100, which is entered in Column 5. Finally, if there are no supply shocks in period $t-1$, we can use Equation 15-12 to calculate inflation in period $t-1$ as $\pi_{t-1} = \pi_{t-2} + $ _____ $(Y_{t-1} - $ _____ $) + 0 = $ _____ $+ 0.25($ _____ $-$ _____ $) + 0 = $ _____. Enter this number in the second row of Column 6. Since this also becomes the preceding period's inflation rate for period t, enter it again in the third row of Column 4.

e. In period t, suppose a temporary supply shock increases υ_t from zero to 1 as shown in Column 2. The economy will no longer be in long-run equilibrium. Instead, it will move to a new intersection of the *DAS* and *DAD* curves at Point B in Graph 15-4 of Exercise 5. In order to calculate the values of output and inflation at Point B (in period t), we substitute the expression on the right-hand side of Equation 15-12 for π_t in Equation 15-11 to obtain:

$$Y_t = 100 - (1/3)[\pi_{t-1} + 0.25(Y_t - 100) + \upsilon_t - 2] + (2/3)\varepsilon_t. \tag{15-13}$$

We have one more step to derive the equation we can use to calculate the value of Y_t in all periods once we know the values π_{t-1} and the two shocks. We need to solve Equation 15-13 for Y_t by multiplying through the right-hand side, collecting terms, and solving for Y_t. You should try this yourself, but the result is:

$$Y_t = 100.6154 - (4/13)\pi_{t-1} - (4/13)\upsilon_t + (8/13)\varepsilon_t. \tag{15-14}$$

Inserting the values in Columns 2, 3, and 4 of Row 3 into Equation 15-14 gives $Y_t = 100.6154 - (4/13)$_____ $- (4/13)$_____ $+ (8/13)$_____ $= $_____. Enter this number in Column 5 of Table 15-4.

f. Finally, we can calculate inflation in period t by substituting the values of π_{t-1}, v_t, and Y_t into Equation 15-12, which yields $\pi_t =$ _____ $+ 0.25($_____ $- 100) +$ _____ $=$ _____. Enter this number in Column 6. We now have the values for output and inflation in period t, which are the values at Point B in Graph 15-4.

g. Equations 15-14 and 15-12 can now be used to calculate the values of output and inflation in all future periods. In period $t + 1$, the supply shock disappears and the value of v_t returns to 0, as shown in Column 2 of Table 15-4. The value of ε_t remains equal to 0. The value of inflation in the preceding period is the rate of inflation in period t, which we calculated to be _____. Enter this number in Column 4. Then, use Equation 15-14 to calculate $Y_{t+1} =$ $100.6154 - (4/13)$ _____ $- (4/13)$ _____ $+ (8/13)$ _____ $=$ _____ and enter this number in Column 5. Finally, use Equation 15-12 to calculate $\pi_{t+1} = \pi_t +$ $0.25(Y_{t+1} - 100) + v_{t+1} =$ _____ $-$ _____ $+$ _____ $=$ _____ and enter this number in Column 6. The numbers in Columns 5 and 6 are the values of output and inflation at Point C in Graph 15-4.

h. In period $t + 2$, the values of both shocks are again 0, and inflation in the preceding period (i.e., π_{t+1}) is equal to _____. Enter this number in Column 4 and use Equations 15-14 and 15-12 to calculate Y_{t+2} and π_{t+2} as follows: $Y_{t+2} = 100.6154$ $- (4/13)$ _____ $- (4/13)$ _____ $+ (8/13)$ _____ $=$ _____, and $\pi_{t+2} = \pi_{t+1} +$ $0.25(Y_{t+2} - 100) + v_{t+2} =$ _____ $-$ _____ $+$ _____ $=$ _____. Enter these values in Columns 5 and 6. If you feel courageous, try to complete the last row of Table 15-4 by yourself to verify that $Y_{t+3} = 99.758$ and $\pi_{t+3} = 2.726$.

i. We shall now use the numbers in Table 15-4 to derive what economists call *impulse response functions*, which are graphs of the time paths of variables after a shock. The impulse response functions for v and Y are illustrated in the top two panels of Graph 15-5. The values for periods $t - 2$ and $t - 1$ are those before the shock, when the value of $v = 0$ and the value of $Y = 100$. In period t, the value of v_t $=$ _____ and the value of Y_t rises/falls to _____. In period $t + 1$, the value of v_{t+1} returns to _____ and the value of Y_{t+1} rises/falls to _____. In period $t + 2$, $v_{t+2} =$ _____ and $Y_{t+2} =$ _____. As we noted in Exercise 5, in the period in which a supply shock occurs that increases v for one period, output rises/falls. In future periods, output starts to rise/fall until we return to the long-run equilibrium.

Graph 15-5

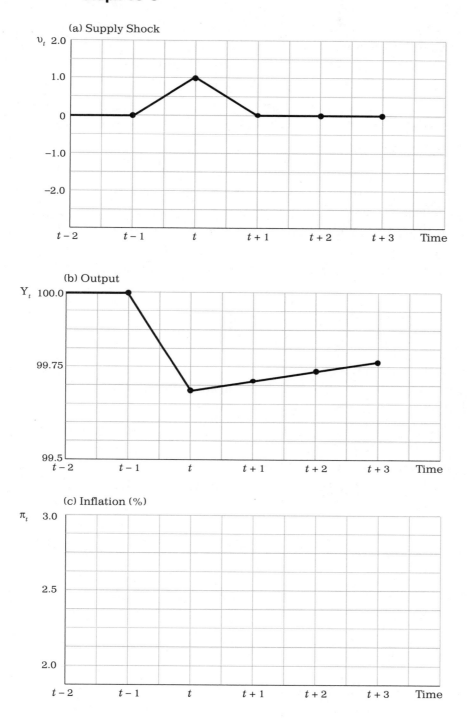

j. Use the data in Table 15-4 to draw the impulse response function for inflation in the bottom section of Graph 15-5. As we noted in Exercise 5, in the period in which a supply shock occurs that increases v_t for one period, inflation <u>rises/falls</u>. In future periods, inflation starts to <u>rise/fall</u> until we return to the long-run equilibrium. As your text illustrates, we could also use the monetary policy rule to derive impulse response functions for the nominal and real interest rates.

7. **Aggregate Demand Shocks** *In this exercise, we analyze an aggregate demand shock that lasts for two periods.*

a. Recall that the random variable ε_t in the *DAD* equation represents an aggregate demand shock. An aggregate demand shock might be caused by an increase in government purchases, a sudden change in the stock market that affects household wealth, and thereby consumption, or a change in consumer or business optimism. The text analyzes a shock that lasts for five periods, but in this exercise, we analyze one that lasts for two. Starting with our basic *DAD* and *DAS* equations,

$$Y_t = \overline{Y}_t - [\alpha\theta_\pi/(1 + \alpha\theta_Y)](\pi_t - \pi_t^*) + [1/(1 + \alpha\theta_Y)]\varepsilon_t \qquad \textbf{(DAD)}$$

$$\pi_t = \pi_{t-1} + \varphi(Y_t - \overline{Y}_t) + v_t \qquad \textbf{(DAS)}$$

we again assume that we have been in long-run equilibrium at Point A in Graph 15-6 for several periods $t - 1$, $t - 2$, etc. We also assume that both the natural level of output and the inflation target remain constant over time. Starting at Point A, suppose there is a demand shock in period t that increases the value of ε to 1.0 for two periods. According to the *DAD* equation, an increase in ε_t will <u>increase/decrease</u> the value of Y_t in the period in which it occurs. Consequently, the *DAD* curve will shift to the <u>right/left</u>. Draw the new *DAD* curve in Graph 15-6 and label it DAD_t.

Graph 15-6

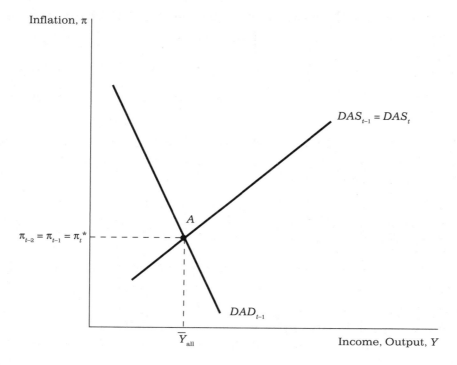

b. Because ε_t is not explicitly included in the *DAS* curve, it will not shift in period *t*. Hence, $DAS_t = DAS_{t-1}$ and the economy moves to the intersection of the DAD_t curve and the DAS_t curve. Locate this point in Graph 15-6 and label it Point B. From Point A to Point B, output has <u>increased/decreased</u> and inflation has <u>increased/decreased</u>.

c. Since the demand shock lasts for two periods, the value of ε_t will remain equal to _____ in period *t* + 1. Consequently, the *DAD* curve will not shift again, so add the label $DAD_t = DAD_{t+1}$ to your DAD_t curve in Graph 15-6. Because inflation has increased from period *t* – 1 to period *t*, expected inflation in period *t* + 1 will <u>rise/fall</u>, which will shift the *DAS* curve <u>upward (to the left)/downward (to the right)</u>. Draw a new *DAS* curve and label it DAS_{t+1}. Locate the new equilibrium at the intersection of the DAS_{t+1} and DAD_{t+1} curves and label it Point C. From Point B to Point C, output has <u>increased/decreased</u> and inflation has <u>increased/decreased</u>. These changes occur partially because the central bank has responded to the changes in output and inflation in period *t* by <u>increasing/decreasing</u> the real interest rate in period *t* + 1.

d. In period *t* + 2, the demand shock disappears and the value of ε_{t+2} falls back to zero. This will shift the *DAD* curve permanently back to DAD_{t-1}, so modify your label of this curve to $DAD_{t-1} = DAD_{t+2}$. Because inflation has increased from period *t* to period *t* + 1, expected inflation in period *t* + 2 will <u>rise/fall</u>, which will shift the *DAS* curve <u>upward (to the left)/downward (to the right)</u>. Draw the new

DAS curve, label it DAS_{t+2}, locate the new equilibrium and label it Point D. From Point C to Point D, output will definitely <u>increase/decrease</u> because both the *DAS* and *DAD* curves have shifted left. Inflation may continue to rise temporarily, depending on the parameter values in the model, but it will soon begin to fall. When it starts to fall, the *DAS* curve will shift <u>upward (to the left)/downward (to the right)</u> until the economy returns to long-run equilibrium at Point A. At Point A, inflation will again equal the _____, and output will return to the _____.

e. As in Exercise 6, we could construct the impulse response functions using the numbers suggested in the textbook, and this is left as one of the problems that follow the Exercise section of this *Study Guide*.

8. **A Change in Monetary Policy** *In this exercise, we analyze the effects of a reduction in the target for the inflation rate.*

a. In earlier exercises, the central bank used a monetary policy rule to change the real interest rate in response to deviations of inflation from its target and deviations of output from its natural level. The central bank may also change its target for inflation. Suppose we again start in long-run equilibrium in period $t-1$ at Point A in Graph 15-7. Inflation has been constant for several periods and is equal to the central bank's initial target π_1^*.

Graph 15-7

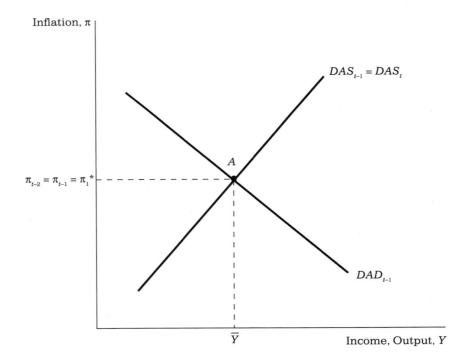

Now, suppose the central bank reduces its target for the inflation rate π_t^* to π_2^* in period t. Since π_t^* does not appear in the *DAS* equation, the *DAS* curve will not immediately be affected, so $DAS_t = DAS_{t-1}$. In the *DAD* equation, however, π_t^* does appear as an exogenous variable. As we discussed in Exercise 1, a reduction in π_t^* will shift the *DAD* curve <u>downward (to the left)</u>/upward (to the right). Draw the new *DAD* curve and label it DAD_t. Then, locate the short-run equilibrium in period t and label it Point B. From Point A to Point B, output <u>increases/decreases</u> and inflation <u>increases/decreases</u>.

b. After the initial decline in the inflation target, the *DAD* curve will not shift again. Therefore, relabel the DAD_t curve $DAD_t = DAD_{t+1...}$. When inflation starts to fall from Point A to Point B, however, inflation expectations will fall, and the *DAS* curve will start to shift <u>upward (to the left/downward (to the right)</u>. Draw the new *DAS* curve and label it DAS_{t+1}. Locate the new short-run equilibrium and label it Point C. From Point B to Point C, output <u>increases/decreases</u> and inflation <u>increases/decreases</u>.

c. In period $t + 2$ and thereafter, the *DAS* curve will continue to shift <u>upward (to the left/downward (to the right)</u> until a new long-run equilibrium has been reached at the natural level of output. Draw the final *DAS* curve in Graph 15-7 and label it DAS_{final}. Locate the final equilibrium and label it Point Z. At Point Z, inflation will be <u>greater than/equal to/less than</u> the new, lower inflation target π_2^*.

d. Throughout these exercises, we have assumed that people have adaptive expectations. If, however, people have rational expectations, they optimally use all available information in making their predictions. In this case, if the central bank's announcement of a lower inflation target is credible, the *DAS* curve will shift down more <u>quickly/slowly</u>, and the economy may move immediately to the new long-run equilibrium.

9. **The Tradeoff Between Output Variability and Inflation Variability** *In this exercise, we illustrate how the monetary policy rule can affect the variability of output and inflation.*

a. The slope of the *DAD* curve determines whether a supply shock has a big or small impact on output and inflation. Graph 15-8 has one *DAS* curve and two *DAD* curves. One *DAD* curve is flat, and the other is steep. Point A is the initial equilibrium because it is the intersection of the *DAS* curve and both *DAD* curves. Now, suppose there is a supply shock, such as an oil price increase. This will shift the *DAS* curve upward. Draw the new *DAS* curve in Graph 15-8 and label it DAS_{t+1} $(v_{t+1} > 0)$. Locate the two new equilibria, one for each *DAD* curve. Label the equilibrium along the flat *DAD* curve Point B, and label the equilibrium along the steep *DAD* curve Point C. Your graph indicates that a supply shock that shifts the *DAS* curve upward (to the left) will reduce output by more when the *DAD* curve is <u>flat/steep</u>, while inflation rises by more when the *DAD* curve is <u>flat/steep</u>.

Graph 15-8

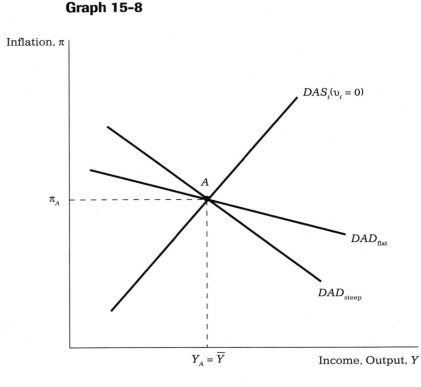

b. The central bank can influence the slope of the *DAD* curve through its monetary policy rule. Remember the equation for the monetary policy rule:

$$i_t = \pi_t + \rho + \theta_\pi(\pi_t - \pi_t^*) + \theta_Y(Y_t - \overline{Y}_t) \tag{15-4}$$

where the parameter θ_π represents the responsiveness of the central bank to inflation and the parameter θ_Y represents the responsiveness of the central bank to output. Both parameters are assumed to be greater than zero. If we then take the *DAD* equation,

$$Y_t = \overline{Y}_t - [\alpha\theta_\pi/(1 + \alpha\theta_Y)](\pi_t - \pi_t^*) + [1/(1 + \alpha\theta_Y)]\varepsilon_t, \tag{DAD}$$

after some manipulation and rearranging, we can write the *DAD* equation in terms of inflation:

$$\pi_t = \pi_t^* - [(1 + \alpha\theta_Y)/\alpha\theta_\pi](Y_t - \overline{Y}_t) + (1/\alpha\theta_\pi)\varepsilon_t. \tag{15-15}$$

If there is no demand shock (i.e., $\varepsilon_t = 0$) and output is equal to its natural level, Equation 15-15 indicates that inflation will be <u>greater than/equal to/less than</u> its target. Furthermore, for every unit that output rises above its natural level, inflation falls by _____. Since the brackets in Equation 15-15 are preceded by a minus sign, the slope of the *DAD* curve is

_____. If the term in brackets in Equation 15-15 is large, the *DAD* curve will be steep. If the term in brackets is small, the *DAD* curve will be flat.

c. If the central bank responds strongly to inflation, θ_π will be large/small. Since θ_π appears in the denominator of the term in brackets in Equation 15-15, the entire term in brackets will then be large/small, and the *DAD* curve will be flat/steep. As a result, when the central bank responds strongly to inflation, a supply shock will result in a large/small increase in inflation and a large/small decrease in output. This occurs because a central bank that responds strongly to inflation will respond to a supply shock by increasing the real interest rate a lot/a little. As a result, the variability in inflation will be relatively high/low, and the variability in output will be relatively high/low.

d. Conversely, if the central bank responds strongly to output, θ_Y will be large/small. Since θ_Y appears in the numerator of the term in brackets in Equation 15-15, the entire term in brackets will then be large/small, and the *DAD* curve will be flat/steep. As a result, when the central bank responds strongly to output, a supply shock will result in a large/small increase in inflation and a large/small decrease in output. This occurs because a central bank that responds strongly to output will respond to a supply shock by increasing the real interest rate a lot/a little. As a result, the variability in inflation will be relatively high/low, and the variability in output will be relatively high/low.

10. **The Taylor Principle.** *In this exercise we present the Taylor principle and discuss its implications for the stability of inflation.*

a. Recall the monetary policy rule from Exercise 1:

$$i_t = \pi_t + \rho + \theta_\pi(\pi_t - \pi_t^*) + \theta_Y(Y_t - \overline{Y}_t) \tag{15-4}$$

An increase in inflation prompts the Fed to increase/decrease the nominal interest rate, but this may not always result in an increase in the real interest rate. If we expand the terms in the first set of parentheses of Equation 15-4, it can be rewritten as

$$i_t = \pi_t + \rho + \theta_\pi\pi_t + \theta_\pi\pi_t + \theta_Y(Y_t - \overline{Y}_t) \tag{15-16}$$

Now collect the two inflation terms π_t to rewrite the monetary policy rule as

$$i_t = \pi_t(1 + \theta_\pi) + \rho - \theta_\pi\pi_t^* + \theta_Y(Y_t - \overline{Y}_t) \tag{15-17}$$

According to Equation 15-17, an increase in inflation will prompt the Fed to increase the nominal interest rate by $1 + \theta_\pi$ times the increase in inflation. If θ_π is positive, the nominal interest rate will rise by more than/less than the increase in inflation, and the real interest rate will increase/decrease. As a result, spending on goods and services increases/decreases, and the *DAD* curve has a positive/negative slope.

b. If, on the other hand, θ_π is negative (but less than 1 in absolute value), higher inflation will lead the central bank to increase the nominal interest rate by more than/less than the increase in inflation, resulting in an increase/decrease in the

real interest rate. As a result, spending on goods and services would
increase/decrease. Consequently, higher inflation would be accompanied by
more output demanded, and the *DAD* curve would have a positive slope. In this
case, a positive demand shock would lead to runaway inflation.

c. In order to see why, examine Graph 15-9, which depicts a *DAD* curve with a positive slope.

Graph 15-9

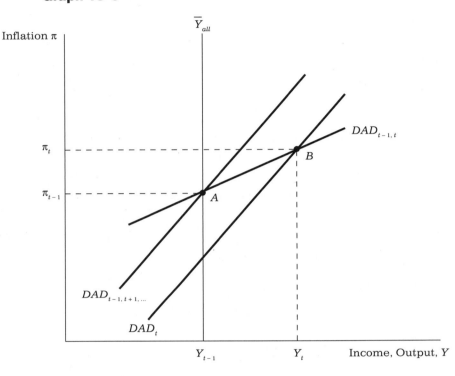

Suppose we began at Point A in period $t - 1$ and a positive demand shock shifts
the *DAD* curve to the right from DAD_{t-1} to DAD_t for one period. In period t the
economy moves to Point B. Both inflation and output increase/decrease.

d. This change in inflation would increase/decrease expected inflation.
Consequently, in the next period (period $t + 1$) the *DAS* curve shifts
upward/downward. Draw this new *DAS* curve in Figure 15-9 and label it DAS_{t+1}.
At the same time, the demand shock from the first period disappears. This shifts
the *DAD* curve back to its initial position at DAD_{t-1}. Find the new equilibrium
and label it Point C. From Point B to Point C inflation increases/decreases.

e. In the following period (period $t + 2$) the *DAD* curve will not shift, but the *DAS*
curve will. As a result of the change in inflation from Point B to Point C, expected inflation will increase/decrease. This will shift the *DAS* curve
upward/downward. Draw the new *DAS* curve in Graph 15-9, label it DAS_{t+2}, and
label the new equilibrium Point D. Between Points C and D inflation has
increased/decreased.

f. In the following period the *DAS* curve will shift <u>upward/downward</u> again and inflation will <u>rise/fall</u> again. This upward spiral in inflation will continue indefinitely.

g. Consequently, in order for inflation to be stable following a demand shock, the *DAD* curve must have a <u>positive/negative</u> slope. This requires the central bank to respond to an increase in inflation by increasing the nominal interest rate by <u>more than/less than</u> the increase in inflation, so that the real interest rate <u>rises/falls</u>. The parameter representing the central bank's responsiveness to deviations in inflation above its inflation target θ_π must therefore be <u>positive/ negative</u>. According to the textbook, this was the case after 1979 but not between 1960 and 1978.

Problems

Answer the following problems on a separate sheet of paper.

1. **a.** What determines the size of α, which appears in the equation representing the demand for goods and services?

   b. How does the size of α affect the flatness or steepness of the *DAD* curve? Briefly explain.

   c. Use the appropriate graph to illustrate and then describe how the value of α (and hence the steepness or flatness of the DAD curve) will affect the economy's short-run and long-run responses to a reduction in the central bank's target for the inflation rate.

2 According to the Taylor rule, what are the recommended nominal and real federal funds rate if:

   a. inflation is 4 percent and the GDP gap is 2 percent (i.e., GDP is 2 percent above its natural level)?

   b. inflation is 1 percent and unemployment is at its natural rate?

3. In October 2009, the U.S. unemployment rate was 10.0 percent.

   a. One can use Okun's law to determine that the GDP gap is twice the difference between the natural unemployment rate and the actual rate of unemployment. If the natural rate of unemployment was 6 percent in October 2009, calculate the GDP gap.

   b. In October 2009, the inflation rate was about 1 percent. According to the Taylor rule, what were the recommended nominal and real federal funds rates? (*Note:* Some economists prefer to use the inflation rate excluding food and energy, which was somewhat greater.)

   c. The nominal interest rate cannot fall below zero. What might the Fed do to try to achieve the optimal real interest rate you calculated in part c?

4. Suppose inflation expectations for period $t + 1$ depended on both current inflation and last period's inflation such that $E_t\pi_{t+1} = \frac{1}{2}\pi_t + \frac{1}{2}\pi_{t-1}$. How would this affect the speed with which inflation expectations would change in response to a sudden change in the inflation rate resulting from a supply shock? Consequently, how would it affect the speed with which the economy returned to its long-run equilibrium following a temporary supply shock?

5. Use the *DAD* and *DAS* equations:

$$Y_t = \overline{Y}_t - [\alpha\theta_\pi/(1 + \alpha\theta_Y)](\pi_t - \pi_t^*) + [1/(1 + \alpha\theta_Y)]\varepsilon_t \qquad \text{(DAD)}$$

$$\pi_t = \pi_{t-1} + \varphi(Y_t - \overline{Y}_t) + \upsilon_t \qquad \text{(DAS)}$$

along with the values of the parameters, inflation target, and natural level of output given in the textbook (i.e., $\overline{Y}_t = \overline{Y}_{\text{all}} = 100$; $\pi_t^* = 2.0$; $\alpha = 1.0$; $\varphi = 0.25$; $\theta_\pi = 0.5$; and $\theta_Y = 0.5$) to derive the equations we used in Exercise 6 to solve for the endogenous variables in each period:

$$Y_t = 100.6154 - (4/13)\pi_{t-1} - (4/13)\upsilon_t + (8/13)\varepsilon_t, \text{ and} \qquad \text{(15-14)}$$

$$\pi_t = \pi_{t-1} + 0.25(Y_t - 100) + \upsilon_t. \qquad \text{(15-12)}$$

6. Suppose the economy has been in long-run equilibrium and experiences a demand shock that lasts for two periods starting in period t, as in Exercise 7. Use the values of the parameters, inflation target, and natural level of output given in the textbook (i.e., $\overline{Y}_t = \overline{Y}_{\text{all}} = 100$; $\pi_t^* = 2.0$; $\alpha = 1.0$; $\varphi = 0.25$; $\theta_\pi = 0.5$; and $\theta_Y = 0.5$) and Equations 15-14 and 15-12 from Problem 5 to complete Table 15-5. Then, draw the impulse response functions for periods $t - 2$ through $t + 3$ for the demand shock, output, and inflation.

Table 15-5

(1) Period	(2) Supply Shock υ_t	(3) Demand Shock ε_t	(4) Inflation in Preceding Period	(5) Output Y_t	(6) Inflation π_t
$t - 2$	0	0	2	100	2
$t - 1$	0	0	2	100	2
t	0	1	2	___	___
$t + 1$	0	1	___	___	___
$t + 2$	0	0	___	___	___
$t + 3$	0	0	___	___	___

7. **C**

   a. Use the *DAD* equation

   $$Y_t = \overline{Y}_t - [\alpha\theta_\pi/(1 + \alpha\theta_Y)](\pi_t - \pi_t^*) + [1/(1 + \alpha\theta_Y)]\varepsilon_t, \qquad \text{(DAD)}$$

   to derive the inverted *DAD* equation introduced in Exercise 9:

   $$\pi_t = \pi_t^* - [(1 + \alpha\theta_Y)/\alpha\theta_\pi](Y_t - \overline{Y}_t) + (1/\alpha\theta_\pi)\varepsilon_t. \qquad \text{(15-15)}$$

   b. The slope of the *DAD* curve is $d\pi_t/dY_t$. Use Equation 15-15 to calculate this slope.

   c. Recall that θ_π and θ_Y measure the central bank's responses to inflation and output, respectively. Use calculus to determine whether an increase in θ_π increases or decreases the slope of the *DAD* curve. Consequently, will an increase in the central bank's responsiveness to inflation make the *DAD* curve flatter or steeper? (Be careful about the minus sign.)

d. Use calculus to determine whether an increase in θ_Y increases or decreases the slope of the *DAD* curve. Consequently, will an increase in the central bank's responsiveness to output make the *DAD* curve flatter or steeper?

e. Confirm the answer to Problem 1 mathematically by using calculus to prove that an increase in α makes the *DAD* curve flatter.

8. Use the appropriate graph to illustrate how the steepness or flatness of the *DAD* curve will affect the economy's response to an adverse demand shock, defined as $\upsilon_t < 0$, in the period in which it occurs. (*Hint:* A demand shock will shift the *DAD* curve by the same *horizontal amount* regardless of its slope.)

CHAPTER 16

Understanding Consumer Behavior

Fill-in Questions

Use the key terms below to fill in the blanks in the following statements. Each term may be used more than once.

average propensity to consume	marginal propensity to consume
behavioral economics	marginal rate of substitution
borrowing constraint	normal good
budget constraint	permanent income
discounting	permanent-income hypothesis
income effect	precautionary saving
indifference curve	random walk
intertemporal budget constraint	substitution effect
life-cycle hypothesis	transitory income

1. The amount that an individual consumes out of an additional dollar of (disposable) income is called the _____.

2. According to the Keynesian consumption function, as income rises an individual's _____ falls. Over time, however, as income per person increases, the _____ actually remains relatively constant. This phenomenon can be explained by both the _____ and the _____.

3. All consumers face a(n) _____, which is a limit on how much they can spend in the current period.

4. When consumers are deciding how much to consume today versus how much to save for future consumption, they face a(n) _____.

5. Since saving earns interest, one should compare future income with current income by _____, which reduces the value of $10,000 of income received in the future below the value of $10,000 of current income.

6. In Irving Fisher's model of consumption, a(n) _____ shows the combinations of first-period consumption and second-period consumption that make the consumer equally happy.

7. The slope of the indifference curve equals the _____, which represents the amount of second-period consumption the consumer requires to be compensated for a one-unit reduction in first-period consumption.

8. If a consumer wants to consume more of a good when his or her income rises, that good is said to be a _____.

9. When the real interest rate changes, the change in consumption can be divided into two components. The change in consumption resulting from the movement to a higher indifference curve is called the _____. The change in consumption arising from the change in the relative price of consumption between different periods is called the _____.

10. When the interest rate rises for someone who saves part of her income, the _____ tends to make consumers choose more consumption in all periods, and the _____ tends to make consumers choose less consumption in the current period and more consumption in future periods.

11. A consumer who wishes to consume more than her current income may be unable to borrow against her future income if she faces a _____.

12. The _____ suggests that people save their income in order to smooth their consumption over their entire adult lifetime. In reality, the elderly do not dissave to the extent predicted by this model, possibly because of _____, which is additional saving that arises from uncertainty.

13. The _____ distinguishes between two types of income that affect consumption. _____ is the part of income that people expect to persist in the future. The part of income that people do not expect to persist is called _____.

14. The combination of the permanent-income hypothesis and rational expectations implies that consumption follows a _____, which is a term that economists use to describe the path of a variable whose changes are unpredictable.

15. _____ is a new subfield of economics that infuses psychology into economics and often finds that human behavior is far from rational.

Multiple-Choice Questions

1. According to the Keynesian theory of consumption, when individuals experience an increase in their income their:

   a. consumption will rise by the total amount of the increase in income.
   b. consumption will rise by less than the increase in income.
   c. average propensity to consume will increase.
   d. marginal propensity to consume will increase.

2. According to the Keynesian theory of consumption, the primary determinant of consumption is the:

    a. interest rate.

    b. wealth of the consumer.

    c. consumer's ability to borrow.

    d. consumer's current income.

3. According to Fisher's model of consumption, all of the following statements about the intertemporal budget constraint are true EXCEPT:

    a. if current consumption rises, the resources available for future consumption will fall.

    b. consumption in Period 1 must be less than or equal to consumption in Period 2.

    c. in the first period, saving is equal to first-period income minus consumption.

    d. consumers take into account both current income and expected future income when making consumption choices.

4. In the Fisher model, if the real interest rate is positive:

    a. second-period consumption costs less in terms of first-period income than the same amount of first-period consumption.

    b. second-period income is worth more than an equal amount of first-period income.

    c. consumers will be unwilling to borrow money, so their consumption in Period 1 will be less than their income in Period 1.

    d. All of the answers are correct.

5. All of the following statements about indifference curves are true EXCEPT:

    a. if first-period consumption is decreased, second-period consumption must be increased in order for the consumer to remain equally satisfied.

    b. the slope is equal to the marginal rate of substitution.

    c. the greater the decrease in first-period consumption, the less second-period consumption must increase to keep the consumer's utility constant.

    d. the consumer prefers to be on a higher indifference curve than a lower one.

6. According to the Fisher model, the optimal level of consumption for a consumer occurs when the marginal rate of substitution:

    a. equals one.

    b. equals zero.

    c. equals the slope of the budget line.

    d. is maximized.

7. An increase in the real interest rate leading to an increase in consumption in all periods because of a movement to a higher indifference curve is an example of:

    a. the substitution effect.

    b. the income effect.

    c. the life-cycle hypothesis.

    d. the permanent-income hypothesis.

8. Which of the following will not always occur when the real interest rate increases?

    a. The income effect works to increase consumption in both Periods 1 and 2 for consumers who initially save part of their income in Period 1.

    b. Consumption rises in all periods.

    c. A consumer who saves part of her income in Period 1 will move to a higher indifference curve.

    d. The substitution effect works to increase second-period consumption and reduce first-period consumption.

9. If a consumer wishes to consume more than his current income in Period 1:

    a. he will be unable to consume anything in Period 2.

    b. the real interest rate must be greater than one.

    c. the decision to consume more must satisfy both his budget constraint and his borrowing constraint.

    d. None of the answers are correct.

10. If a consumer faces a borrowing constraint:

    a. she will be unable to consume anything in the second period.

    b. she may or may not be less satisified than if she was able to borrow.

    c. consumption in the first period must be less than consumption in the second period.

    d. All of the answers are correct.

11. The life-cycle consumption function takes into account all of the following EXCEPT the:

    a. amount of wealth.

    b. government budget deficit.

    c. expected number of working years.

    d. expected number of years of retirement.

12. According to the life-cycle hypothesis, a person who expects to work 40 more years before retiring and who expects to live a total of 50 more years will have the following consumption function:

    a. $C = 0.2W + 0.6Y$.

    c. $C = 0.04W + 0.8Y$.

    b. $C = 0.2W + 0.8Y$.

    d. $C = 0.02W + 0.8Y$.

13. Under the life-cycle hypothesis, the consumption function, $C = 0.025W + 0.5Y$, implies that:

    a. the individual expects to live 40 more years.

    b. half of the person's expected remaining life will be spent in retirement.

    c. for every additional dollar of wealth, consumption increases by 2.5 cents.

    d. All of the answers are correct.

14. An example of precautionary saving is when:

    a. a newly married couple saves to buy a house in 10 years.

    b. high interest rates cause a business professional to reduce investment.

    c. an individual automatically deposits a fraction of his weekly income in a Christmas Club to save for the coming holiday.

    d. an individual increases her saving in preparation for retirement because she fears that poor health may lead to added expenses.

15. According to the permanent-income hypothesis:

    a. the average propensity to consume is the ratio of transitory income to current income.

    b. consumption depends equally on permanent and transitory income.

    c. people use saving to smooth consumption in response to transitory changes in income.

    d. None of the answers are correct.

16. A change in permanent income occurs when a(n):

    a. Florida resort owner enjoys unusually good business during a particularly harsh winter.

    b. individual wins $10,000 in a lottery.

    c. injured worker receives workers' compensation benefits for six months.

    d. tenured college professor receives a $10,000 increase per year in her salary.

17. Which of the following statements is TRUE?

    a. Studies indicate that households with high incomes tend to have low average propensities to consume.

    b. Over long periods of time, the average propensity to consume is fairly constant.

    c. The life-cycle and permanent-income hypotheses can explain most of the empirical facts about the average propensity to consume.

    d. All of the answers are correct.

18. According to the permanent-income hypothesis, an artist whose income fluctuates from year to year will:

    a. have a higher average propensity to consume in years of lower income.

    b. have a higher average propensity to consume in years of high income.

    c. have a constant average propensity to consume every year.

    d. never save any of her income.

19. According to the permanent-income hypothesis, which of the following is likely to happen if Congress enacts a temporary tax cut?

    a. Consumers will view the year as a temporarily good one and will increase their saving by almost the full amount of the tax cut.

    b. Consumers will increase their consumption by the full amount of the tax cut.

    c. The tax cut will have a large effect on aggregate demand.

    d. Both b and c are true.

20. When a consumer borrows money to allow for greater consumption, he is:

    a. increasing his total income.

    b. escaping his intertemporal budget constraint.

    c. borrowing against his future income.

    d. able to increase his consumption in all periods.

21. Many economists believe that Americans should save a greater fraction of their incomes because:

    a. people would be better prepared for retirement.

    b. greater national saving and investment would increase the nation's productive capacity in the long run.

    c. less domestic investment would need to be financed by capital flows from abroad.

    d. All of the answers are correct.

22. Behavioral economics suggests that all the following measures would induce people to save more EXCEPT:

   a. forcing all workers to participate in a retirement savings plan at their place of employment.

   b. automatically enrolling workers in a retirement savings account at their place of employment, but giving them the opportunity of opting out.

   c. allowing people to borrow more on their credit cards.

   d. having people commit in advance to saving a portion of their future salary increases.

23. Recent economic research suggests that consumption is a function of:

   a. current and expected future income.

   b. wealth.

   c. interest rates.

   d. All of the answers are correct.

Exercises

1. **The Keynesian Consumption Function** *In this exercise, we use a Keynesian consumption function to illustrate the algebraic and graphical differences between the marginal and average propensities to consume.*

   a. Consider the simple consumption function

   $$C = 125 + 0.75(Y - T),$$ (16-1)

   where T = taxes and $Y - T$ = disposable income. If $T = 0$, we may write

   $$C = 125 + 0.75Y,$$ (16-2)

   where Y is both national income and disposable income. Graph this equation on Graph 16-1 and label the curve C.

Graph 16-1

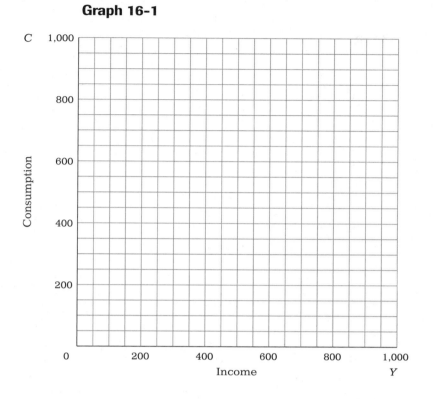

b. The marginal propensity to consume (*MPC*) is defined as:

The value of the *MPC* in this model is _____. This fraction is also equal to the slope of the consumption function in Graph 16-1. As *Y* increases in this model, the value of the *MPC* <u>increases/decreases/remains constant</u>. Furthermore, Keynes postulated that the *MPC* would always be greater than _____ but less than _____.

c. The average propensity to consume (APC) is defined as the ratio of consumption to disposable income, which, when $T = 0$ as in this model, is equal to Y. Thus, in this model, $APC = C/Y$. Substituting Equation 16-2 into the numerator of the APC and simplifying yields

$APC =$ _____ $+$ _____ $\times (1/Y)$.

When $Y = 250$, $APC =$ _____ $+$ _____ $\times (1/250) =$ _____.

When $Y = 500$, $APC =$ _____ $+$ _____ $\times (1/500) =$ _____.

When $Y = 1,000$, $APC =$ _____ $+$ _____ $\times (1/1,000) =$ _____.

This example illustrates that as Y increases, the value of the APC increases/ decreases/remains constant.

d. The value of the APC can also be illustrated on Graph 16-1. Suppose that $Y = 1,000$. According to Equation 16-2, when $Y = 1,000$, $C =$ _____. Locate this point on Graph 16-1, label it Point A, and draw a line between Point A and the origin. The slope of this line is equal to the rise over run, or _____/_____ = _____. This is equal to the MPC/APC when $Y = 1,000$. Consequently, the slope of the line connecting the origin to any point on the consumption function is equal to the MPC/APC at that level of income. Note that the slope of the line connecting the origin to the consumption function (and thus, the APC) increases/decreases/remains constant as Y increases.

2. **The Short-Run and Long-Run Consumption Functions** *In this exercise, we review the cross-section and time-series evidence concerning the average propensity to consume and discuss the resulting short-run and long-run consumption functions.*

a. Data collected from various households at any one point in time, called *cross-sectional data,* confirm the basic implications of the Keynesian consumption function. In these studies, the MPC is greater than _____ and less than _____. Furthermore, people with higher incomes tend to save a greater percentage of their income, which is another way of saying that the APC increases/decreases/remains constant as Y increases. Aggregate (economywide) data over short time periods also confirm these implications.

b. Aggregate data collected over long periods of time, called *time-series data,* however, seem to contradict some of the implications of the Keynesian consumption function. Greater amounts of inputs and improved technology lead to rising income over time. As income rises, the Keynesian consumption function predicts that the *APC* will <u>increase/decrease/remain constant</u>. Economists who have studied the data, however, find that the *APC* tends to <u>increase/decrease/remain constant</u> over long periods of time despite substantial increases in *Y*.

Graph 16-2

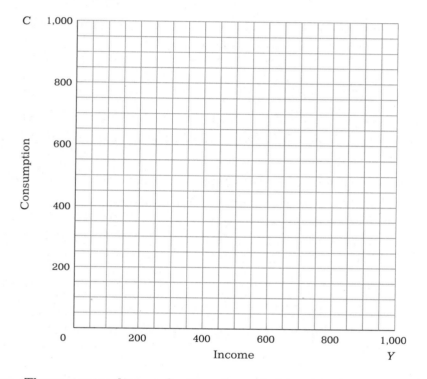

c. These contradictory findings have led economists to conclude that the aggregate short-run consumption function is different from the aggregate long-run consumption function. The short-run consumption function is very similar to the Keynesian consumption function: the *MPC* lies between _____ and _____, and the *APC* <u>increases/decreases/remains constant</u> as *Y* increases. Draw an arbitrary line on Graph 16-2 that satisfies these properties and label it *SRCF* (short-run consumption function). As stated in Part b, in the long run, the *APC* tends to <u>increase/decrease/remains constant</u> as *Y* increases. Draw an arbitrary line on Graph 16-2 that satisfies these properties and label it *LRCF* (long-run consumption function). (You may find it useful to review Part d of Exercise 1.) Note that any positively sloped straight line with a *y* intercept of _____ will satisfy the properties of the *LRCF*.

3. **Present and Future Value** *In this exercise, we present the concepts of present and future value.*

a. Suppose you have $100 and the bank interest rate is 5 percent. If you put this $100 in the bank, at the end of one year you would have $100 + 0.05 ($100) = $_____. Note that we can express this algebraically as:

$$FV_1 = PV + i(PV) = PV(1 + i) \qquad \text{(16-3)}$$

where FV_1 is the future value at the end of year 1, PV represents the present (initial) value, and i represents the annual interest rate.

b. Conversely, if you knew you could get FV_1 at the end of one year and the interest rate is i, you could calculate the "present value" of this option by solving Equation 16-3 for PV:

$$PV = FV_1/(1 + i) \qquad \text{(16-4)}$$

As you might expect, the present value of receiving $105 at the end of one year with an interest rate of 5 percent is therefore $_____ /(1 + 0.05) = $_____.

c. If you keep your original $100 in the bank, you would earn interest in the second year on the full amount of money you had at the end of the first year. Consequently, at the end of two years, you would have $105 + 0.05($105) = $_____. Note that this can be written as 1[$100(1 + i)] + i[$100(1 + i)] or (1 + i)$100(1 + i), which is also equal to $100(1 + i)^2$. Thus, we can write:

$$FV_2 = PV(1 + i)^2 \qquad \text{(16-5)}$$

d. Conversely, if you knew you could get FV_2 at the end of two years and the annual interest rate is i, you could calculate the "present value" of this option by solving Equation 16-5 for PV:

$$PV = FV_2/(1 + i)^2 \qquad \text{(16-6)}$$

As you might expect, the present value of receiving $110.25 at the end of two years with an interest rate of 5 percent is therefore $_____ / (1 + 0.05)^2 = $_____.

e. Using the results from Parts a–d, you may surmise that the formula for determining the amount you would have if you left your money in the bank for T years at annual interest rate i is _____. Conversely, if you know the future value in year T, FV_T, and the interest rate i, the formula for determining the present value is _____.

4. **The Intertemporal Budget Constraint** *In this exercise, we use a simple two-period model to derive the intertemporal budget constraint.*

a. Suppose that a typical consumer named Jennifer lives for two consumption periods. Her real income in each of Periods 1 and 2, Y_1 and Y_2, equals 12. Designate consumption during Periods 1 and 2 as C_1 and C_2, respectively. The portion of Jennifer's income in Period 1 that she does not consume in Period 1 is her saving S. Obviously,

$$S = Y_1 - C_1 = \underline{\hspace{4cm}} - C_1. \qquad \textbf{(16-7)}$$

Assume that any saving from Period 1 earns interest at a real interest rate of 50 percent, or 0.50. Since Jennifer knows she will die at the end of Period 2, she does not save in the second period. Consequently, her consumption in Period 2, C_2, is equal to her income in Period 2, $(Y_2 = 12)$, plus any saving from Period 1 plus accumulated interest:

$$C_2 = Y_2 + S + rS = Y_2 + (Y_1 - C_1) + r(Y_1 - C_1) = \qquad \textbf{(16-8)}$$

$$\underline{\hspace{2cm}} + (\underline{\hspace{2cm}} - C_1) + \underline{\hspace{2cm}} (\underline{\hspace{2cm}} - C_1), \text{ or}$$

$$C_2 = \underline{\hspace{4cm}} - \underline{\hspace{4cm}} C_1.$$

Graph this equation on Graph 16-3 and label it *ITBC* (intertemporal budget constraint).

Graph 16-3

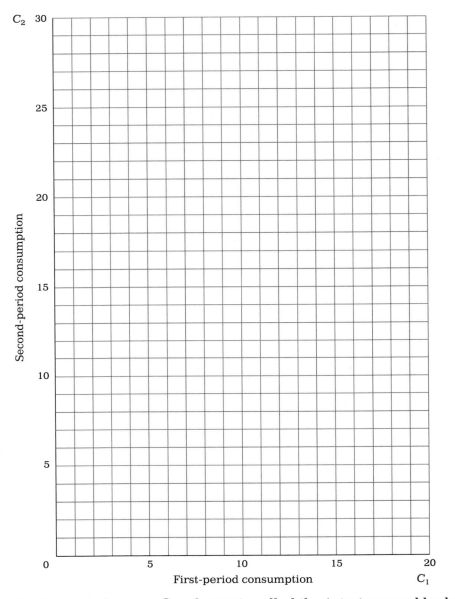

b. The line you drew on Graph 16-3 is called the *intertemporal budget constraint*. Given Jennifer's income and the real interest rate, the intertemporal budget constraint depicts the combinations of C_1 and C_2 that are available to her. The slope of this line is equal to $-(1 + r) = -(1 + \underline{\hspace{2cm}}) = -\underline{\hspace{2cm}}$. This number indicates that each unit of consumption in Period 1 can be transformed into \underline{\hspace{1.5cm}} units of consumption in Period 2 because any saving earns interest at the rate of \underline{\hspace{2cm}} percent.

c. Although Jennifer can consume at any point along her intertemporal budget constraint, three points are worth noting. Locate the point on Graph 16-3 at which Jennifer consumes all of her current income in each of the two periods and label it Point A. At Point A, $C_1 = Y_1 = $ _____. Consequently, during Period 1, saving $S = $ _____, and $C_2 = Y_2 = $ _____. Now locate the point on Graph 16-3 at which Jennifer saves all of her income in Period 1 in order to maximize C_2 and label it Point B. At Point B, $C_1 = $ _____. Consequently, during Period 1, $S = $ _____ and $C_2 = Y_2 + S + rS = $ _____ + _____ + _____ × _____ = _____. Graph 16-3 can also be used to illustrate the situation in which Jennifer borrows at the same real interest rate to finance a level of consumption during Period 1 that exceeds her income in Period 1. Locate the point on Graph 16-3 at which Jennifer maximizes C_1 by borrowing against all of her income in Period 2 and label it Point C. At Point C, $C_2 = $ _____ and $C_1 = Y_1 + [Y_2/(1 + r)] = $ _____ + [_____ / _____] = _____.

5. **The Consumer's Optimal Levels of Consumption** *In this exercise, we derive a set of indifference curves from a specific utility function and illustrate the optimal consumption pattern given the intertemporal budget constraint in Exercise 4.*

   a. Suppose that Jennifer, the same consumer from Exercise 4, lives for two periods and derives pleasure from her consumption in each of them. Assume, furthermore, that the amount of her total satisfaction is given by this utility function:

$$U = C_1 \times C_2 = C_1 C_2. \tag{16-9}$$

Given this utility function, complete Table 16-1. Round off your answers to one decimal place.

Table 16-1

	(1)	(2)	(3)	(4)	(5)	(6)	(7)	(8)
C_1		8.0	9.0	_____	_____	12.0	14.0	16.0
C_2		18.0	16.0	14.4	13.09	_____	_____	_____
$U = C_1 C_2$		_____	_____	144.0	144.00	144.0	144.0	144.0

   b. Plot the numbers from Columns 2–8 on Graph 16-4, connect them (try to make the curve smooth), and label this curve $IC_{U=144}$.

   Inasmuch as Jennifer's levels of utility at these seven combinations of C_1 and C_2 all equal _____, Jennifer is indifferent among them. Hence, $IC_{U=144}$ is called the indifference curve for a level of utility equal to 144.

   c. Now complete Table 16-2, which lists all the combinations of C_1 and C_2 for which Jennifer's level of utility would equal 150.

Graph 16-4

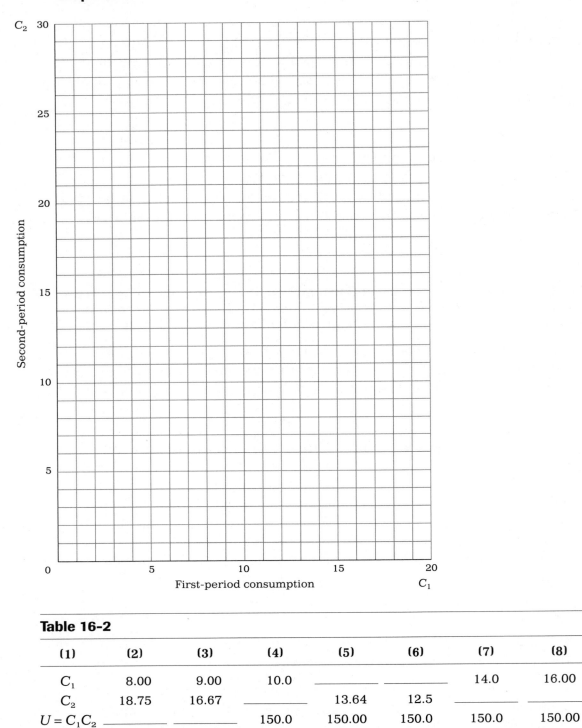

Table 16-2

(1)	(2)	(3)	(4)	(5)	(6)	(7)	(8)
C_1	8.00	9.00	10.0	_____	_____	14.0	16.00
C_2	18.75	16.67	_____	13.64	12.5	_____	_____
$U = C_1 C_2$	_____	_____	150.0	150.00	150.0	150.0	150.00

Plot the numbers from Table 16-2 on Graph 16-4, connect them (again, try to make the curve smooth), and label this curve $IC_{U=150}$.

d. Finally, complete Table 16-3, which lists the combinations of C_1 and C_2 for which Jennifer's level of utility would equal 162.

Table 16-3

	(1)	(2)	(3)	(4)	(5)	(6)	(7)	(8)
C_1		8.00	9.0	10.0	_____	_____	14.0	16.0
C_2		20.25	18.0	_____	14.73	13.5	_____	_____
$U = C_1C_2$		_____	_____	162.0	162.00	162.0	162.0	162.0

Plot the numbers on Graph 16-4, connect them (again, try to make the curve smooth), and label this curve $IC_{U=162}$.

e. Along each indifference curve, the level of utility is held constant. As the level of utility increases, the entire indifference curve shifts to the left (downward)/ right (upward) because, in order to achieve the higher level of utility, consumption in one or both periods must increase/decrease. The slope of the indifference curve at any point shows how much second-period consumption Jennifer requires to be compensated for a one-unit reduction in first-period consumption and remain equally satisfied. This slope is called the

_____ between first-period consumption and second-period consumption.

f. Suppose that Jennifer faces the same intertemporal budget constraint that she did in Exercise 4 (that is, $C_2 = 30 - 1.5C_1$). Graph this equation on Graph 16-4 and label it *ITBC*.

g. If Jennifer follows Polonius's advice to Laertes ("neither a borrower nor a lender be") and decides to consume all of her current income in each period, then $C_1 = Y_1 =$ _____ and $C_2 = Y_2 =$ _____. Locate this point on Graph 16-4 and label it Point A. Because Point A lies on the indifference curve labeled _____, Jennifer's level of utility at Point A equals _____.

h. Note, however, that Jennifer can move to a higher indifference curve and a higher level of utility by saving some of her income in Period 1 and increasing her consumption in Period 2. Indeed, she can move up to the indifference curve labeled _____ on Graph 16-4 and achieve a level of utility equal to _____ by reducing C_1 to 10 and thereby saving _____ in Period 1. If this amount of saving is put in a bank and earns interest of 50 percent, it will grow to _____ by Period 2, at which time Jennifer can add it to her income in Period 2 to obtain $C_2 = Y_2 + (1 + r)S =$ _____ + _____ = _____. Locate this point on Graph 16-4 and label it Point D. At Point D, $U = C_1C_2 =$ _____ × _____ = _____. Also note that at Point D, Jennifer's indifference curve is just tangent to her intertemporal budget constraint line, which means that the slopes of these two curves are equal. Thus, at her optimal levels of consumption, Jennifer's marginal rate of substitution is equal to $1 + r$. All indifference curves corresponding to a still higher level of utility, such as $IC_{U=162}$, lie to the left of (below)/right of (above) Jennifer's intertemporal budget constraint line and are consequently unattainable.

6. **The Effects of Changes in Income and the Real Interest Rate on the Consumer's Optimal Levels of Consumption** *In this exercise, we graphically illustrate the effects of increases in income and the real interest rate on the consumer's optimal levels of consumption and discuss the income and substitution effects.*

   a. Graph 16-5 illustrates Jennifer's initial optimal levels of consumption at Point D from Exercise 5 and the indifference curves corresponding to utility levels of 150 and 162, respectively. The real interest rate equals 50 percent. The curve labeled $ITBC_1$ represents Jennifer's initial intertemporal budget constraint. Suppose that Jennifer's income in Period 1 rises to 12.78, while Y_2 remains equal to 12. Consequently, Jennifer's intertemporal budget constraint would change to the following:

   $$C_2 = Y_2 + S + rS = Y_2 + (Y_1 - C_1) + r(Y_1 - C_1)$$
   $$= 12 + (12.78 - C_1) + 0.50(12.78 - C_1), \text{ or}$$

   $C_2 = \underline{\hspace{4cm}} - \underline{\hspace{4cm}} C_1.$

   Graph this new intertemporal budget constraint on Graph 16-5 and label it $ITBC_2$.

Graph 16-5

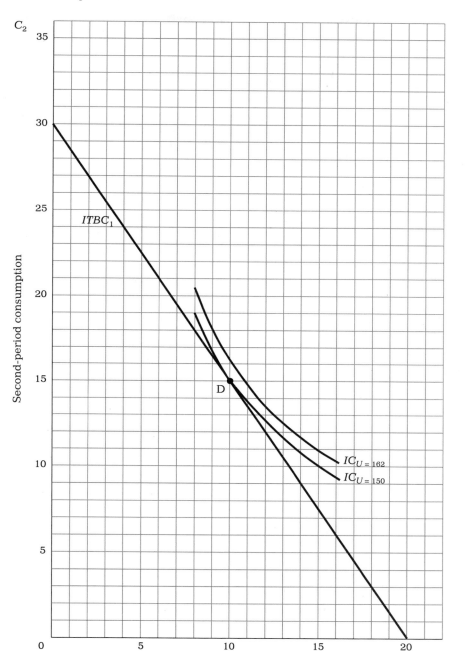

This shift of the intertemporal budget constraint curve could have also occurred from an increase in income in Period 2 or from increases in income in both periods. The slope of $ITBC_2$ is <u>greater than/less than/equal to</u> the slope of $ITBC_1$.

b. As a result of her increase in income, Jennifer is now able to move to a higher indifference curve. Indeed, the new optimum occurs at the tangency of $ITBC_2$ with $IC_{U=162}$, indicating that Jennifer is able to increase her level of utility to _____. Locate this point on Graph 16-5 and label it Point E.

At Point E, $C_1 = 10.39$. Since $U = C_1 C_2$ and $U =$ _____, $C_2 =$ $U/C_1 =$ _____. We can see that consumption during each period has increased/decreased. The changes in consumption between Points D and E are the result of the income effect, which measures the change in consumption resulting from the movement to a higher indifference curve, holding the slope of the intertemporal budget constraint (whose absolute value is equal to 1 plus the real interest rate) constant.

c. Finally, suppose that Jennifer's income in each period returns to its former level of 12 and that the real interest rate rises to 100 percent, or 1.0. Jennifer's intertemporal budget constraint becomes

$$C_2 = Y_2 + S + rS = Y_2 + (Y_1 - C_1) + r(Y_1 - C_1), \text{ or}$$
$$C_2 = \text{_____} + (\text{_____} - C_1) + 1.0(\text{_____} - C_1), \text{ or}$$

$$C_2 = \text{_____} - \text{_____} \; C_1.$$

Graph Jennifer's new intertemporal budget constraint on Graph 16-5 and label it $ITBC_3$. Once again, Jennifer is able to move to a higher indifference curve. Indeed, the new optimal levels of consumption occur at the tangency of $ITBC_3$ with $IC_{U=162}$, which is where the new intertemporal budget constraint just touches $IC_{U=162}$ and has the same slope. Thus, Jennifer is again able to increase her level of utility to _____. Plot this point on Graph 16-5 and label it Point F. At Point F, $C_1 = 9$. Since $U = C_1 C_2$ and $U =$ _____, $C_2 = U/C_1 =$ _____.

d. The changes in consumption between Points D and F resulting from the increase in the real interest rate can be decomposed into two different effects. The first reflects the change in consumption resulting from Jennifer's ability to move to a higher indifference curve while holding the real interest rate constant. This effect is called the income/substitution effect, and it is represented by a hypothetical movement from Point D to Point E (since Point E lies on the new indifference curve but would be the equilibrium only if the slope of the intertemporal budget constraint had remained unchanged, as in Part b). The change in consumption from Point E to Point F reflects the second effect, called the income/substitution effect. This represents the change in consumption arising from the change in the relative price of consumption in the two periods. As the interest rate increases from 50 percent to 100 percent, Jennifer must now give up less first-period consumption to obtain an extra unit of second-period consumption. Comparing Points E and F, Jennifer responds to this change in the relative price of consumption in the two periods by increasing/decreasing C_1 and increasing/decreasing C_2.

e. In Part d, the income effect increases/decreases C_1 and increases/decreases C_2, while the substitution effect increases/decreases C_1 and increases/decreases C_2. The combination of these two effects will always increase/decrease C_2. Depending on the specific circumstance, however, C_1 can either increase or decrease. In this example, C_1 obviously increases/decreases.

7. **The Life-Cycle Hypothesis** *In this exercise, we develop a simple life-cycle model of consumption and derive some of its implications.*

a. The life-cycle hypothesis is based on the assumption that people try to smooth their consumption over their (adult) lifetimes. Assume that a typical adult named Tanya expects to live for another T years. She intends to work for R years, earning an annual real income equal to Y, and then retire for $(T - R)$ years. If Tanya wishes to smooth her annual consumption C over her remaining lifetime, she will plan to spend her lifetime earnings $(R \times Y)$ over her remaining T years in equal amounts so that

$$C \times T = R \times Y, \qquad \text{(16-10)}$$

or $C = Y \times ($ _____ / _____ $)$. This equation implies that Tanya will consume a fraction of her income during her working years and save the remaining portion to fund her consumption during her retirement. (Although the real interest rate is implicitly assumed to equal zero here, a positive real interest rate could easily be incorporated into the model.)

b. Suppose that Tanya begins working at age 20, intends to retire at age 65 after working for 45 years, and expects to live until age 80. Thus, $T = 80 - 20 =$ _____, $R = 65 - 20 =$ _____, and $T - R =$ _____. If $Y = \$40,000$, then Tanya's annual consumption will be $C = \$$ _____ $\times ($ _____ / _____ $) =$ $\$$ _____. During each of her working years, Tanya will consume $\$$ _____, or _____ / _____ of her income, and will save $\$$ _____, or _____ / _____ of her income. During her working years, therefore, Tanya's consumption function will be $C =$ _____ Y. An extra dollar of annual income would raise consumption by _____ cents.

c. Draw a rectangle on Graph 16-6 whose height is equal to $Y = \$$ _____ and whose width is equal to $R =$ _____ years. The area of this rectangle represents Tanya's total lifetime earnings and is equal to $\$$ _____. Now draw a second rectangle whose height is equal to C and whose width is equal to T. The area of this second rectangle, representing Tanya's total lifetime consumption, is equal to $\$$ _____. Now shade in the area of a third rectangle, labeled saving, which represents Tanya's total saving during her working years and a fourth rectangle, labeled dissaving, which represents her total consumption during retirement. The size of the shaded rectangle representing Tanya's total saving is greater than/less than/equal to the size of the shaded rectangle representing her total consumption during retirement.

Graph 16-6

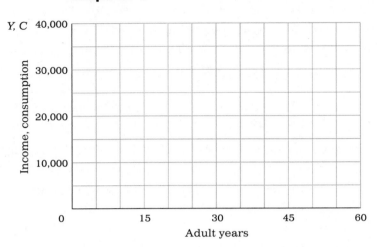

d. Now suppose that Tanya begins her adult life with an initial wealth equal to W. Consequently, the total amount that she will now have available to spend during her lifetime will equal $RY + W$. If Tanya still wishes to consume equal amounts in every year,

$$C \times T = (R \times Y) + W, \qquad \text{(16-11)}$$

or $C = [(\underline{\hspace{1.5cm}}/\underline{\hspace{1.5cm}}) \times Y] + W/\underline{\hspace{1.5cm}}$. Substituting from Part b the values for $T = \underline{\hspace{1.5cm}}$ and $R = \underline{\hspace{1.5cm}}$, we obtain Tanya's new consumption function, $C = \underline{\hspace{1.5cm}}Y + \underline{\hspace{1.5cm}}W$. An extra dollar of wealth raises annual consumption by $\underline{\hspace{1.5cm}}$ cents. Draw this consumption function on Graph 16-7 and label it C. The y intercept of this line, which is already marked in Graph 16-7, is $\underline{\hspace{1.5cm}}W$, and the slope of the line equals $\underline{\hspace{1.5cm}}$.

Graph 16-7

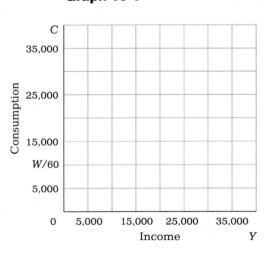

e. As Chapter 16 of the textbook states, the life-cycle model can explain the cross-sectional evidence concerning the average propensity to consume. Dividing the consumption function in Part d by Y yields $APC = C/Y =$ _____ + _____ × (W/Y). Suppose that $W = \$120,000$ and $Y = \$40,000$. Then $APC =$ _____ + _____ (_____ / _____) = _____. As Chapter 16 of the textbook explains, in the short run, wealth does not vary with income from person to person or from year to year. Consequently, if Y rises to $\$80,000$ and W remains equal to $\$120,000$, $APC =$ _____ + _____ (_____ / _____) = _____. Obviously, as income rises, APC rises/falls. Conversely, if Y falls to $\$20,000$ and W remains equal to $\$120,000$, $APC =$ _____.

f. The life-cycle model can also explain the time-series evidence concerning the relative constancy of the economy's APC in the long run. Over long periods of time, wealth and income grow together. If $W = 3Y$ in the long run, then, in this model, $APC =$ _____.

8. **The Permanent-Income Hypothesis** *In this exercise, we present the permanent-income model of consumption and discuss its implications.*

a. According to the permanent-income hypothesis, current income Y is the sum of permanent income Y^P plus transitory income Y^T, or $Y = Y^P + Y^T$. Permanent income is a measure of expected or average income. Transitory income is the random difference between current income Y and permanent income Y^P that occurs because of unexpected and temporary increases or decreases in income. On average, however, transitory income equals zero. Consumption is a function of permanent income. For example, assume the following:

$$C = aY^P = 0.75Y^P. \qquad \text{(16-12)}$$

Equation 16-12 suggests that people consume _____ percent of their permanent income; the remainder is saved, presumably for retirement.

b. Let us examine the consumption patterns of three people: a college professor having a typical year; an artist who is experiencing an especially good year, having just sold several paintings; and another artist who is having a dry spell, having sold only two paintings during the year. Assume that the average or permanent income of each of these three people equals $\$80,000$ and that $C = 0.75Y^P$. Now complete Table 16-4.

Table 16-4

(1)	(2) Y^P	(3) $C = 0.75Y^P$	(4) Y	(5) $APC = C/Y$	(6) Y^T
College professor	$80,000	_____	$ 80,000	_____	_____
Artist in a good year	$80,000	_____	$100,000	_____	_____
Artist in a bad year	$80,000	_____	$ 60,000	_____	_____

c. The data in Table 16-4 indicate that changes in transitory income will increase/decrease/not change consumption. Consequently, if a person's actual current income temporarily rises above her permanent income, then her consumption will increase/decrease/not change. This situation will increase/decrease/not change her *APC*. Conversely, if a person's actual current income temporarily falls below her permanent income, her consumption will increase/decrease/not change but her *APC* will increase/decrease/not change.

d. As stated previously, cross-sectional household data indicate that the average propensity to consume tends to increase/decrease/remain constant as income increases. If, at any one time, people who have high incomes are generally having temporarily good years and those who have low incomes are generally having temporarily bad years, data in Table 16-4 indicate that the *APC* will increase/decrease/remain constant as current income *Y* increases.

e. This theory can also be used to explain short-term variations in the average propensity to consume. If the economy slips into a recession and the majority of the population is having a bad year, the *APC* will increase/decrease/remain constant. If, on the other hand, the economy is in a temporary boom and the majority of the population is having a good year, the *APC* will increase/decrease/remain constant.

f. Alternatively, if the government enacts a temporary tax cut, everyone will experience a temporarily good year, so the *APC* will increase/decrease/remain constant and most of the tax cut will be consumed/saved. If, on the other hand, the government enacts a permanent tax cut, everyone will experience an increase in permanent/transitory income, and most of the tax cut will be consumed/saved.

g. Over time, the good and bad years will cancel out. In the long run, as the economy grows, permanent income also grows. Thus, if the economywide permanent income Y^P equals actual income Y in the long run, the *APC* will increase/decrease/remain constant, just as the time-series evidence indicates.

Problems

Answer the following problems on a separate sheet of paper.

1. Consider the Keynesian consumption function $C = 100 + 0.8(Y - T)$.

   a. If $T = 0$, calculate the value of the marginal propensity to consume (*MPC*) and the formula for the average propensity to consume (*APC*).

   b. Choose two values of *Y* and compute the directional changes in the *MPC* and *APC* when *Y* increases.

2.   Suppose someone offers you a piece of paper (a bond) that will pay you a (coupon) payment of $100 at the end of *each* of the next three years. You will also get an additional $1,000 at the end of the third year.

   a.   Calculate the present value of this bond if the prevailing interest rate is 5 percent per year.

   b.   Calculate the present value of this bond if the prevailing interest rate rises to 15 percent per year.

   c.   Consequently, what do you conclude about the relationship between the present value of a bond and the prevailing interest rate?

3.   a.   Suppose that income in each of two periods is equal to 100 and the interest rate is 10 percent per year. Draw a graph of the intertemporal budget constraint and calculate its slope.

   b.   On the same graph, draw a hypothetical indifference curve that is tangent to this intertemporal budget constraint at a point at which saving in the first period is positive, and label it IC_1. Label the initial equilibrium Point A.

   c.   Suppose that the interest rate rises to 25 percent. Draw the new budget line on your graph. Draw a new indifference curve that is tangent to this budget line and label it IC_2. Label the new equilibrium Point B.

   d.   On the same graph, illustrate both the income and substitution effects of this increase in the interest rate.

   e.   From your answer to Part d, under what circumstances might an increase in the interest rate lead to an *increase* in C_1 and hence a *reduction* in saving?

4.   Suppose that Bart has the following utility function: $U = C_1 C_2 = (C_1 C_2)^{1/2}$, where C_1
C   and C_2 are Bart's levels of consumption in Periods 1 and 2, respectively. Suppose
O   that his income is $120 in Period 1 and $100 in Period 2, and the real interest rate is 25 percent.

   a.   Calculate Bart's optimal levels of consumption in Periods 1 and 2 and his saving in Period 1. (You may wish to use a Lagrange multiplier to solve this problem, but it isn't necessary.)

   b.   Suppose that the real interest rate increases to 50 percent. Calculate Bart's new optimal levels of consumption in Periods 1 and 2 and his saving in Period 1.

5.   Consider the Keynesian consumption function, $C = a + b(Y - T)$, where a and b are
C   constants.

   a.   Let $T = 0$ and calculate the value of the marginal propensity to consume and the formula for the average propensity to consume.

   b.   Differentiate your answers to Part a with respect to income Y to calculate the directional changes in the *MPC* and *APC* when Y increases.

6.   What does the life-cycle model of consumption predict about the relative saving
O   rates between:

   a.   a country with a rapidly increasing population and a country with a steady population, all other things being equal? Explain.

   b.   a country where real GDP per capita is growing rapidly and a country with a stagnant economy, all other things being equal? Explain.

7. People who support an active role for macroeconomic policymakers occasionally argue that policy activism is necessary to buffer the economy from extreme fluctuations in private spending. What do the life-cycle and permanent-income models of consumption imply about this argument, especially as it relates to consumption, which is by far the largest component of private spending? Explain.

8. Suppose that Jan expects to live for 25 more years and work for 10 of those years.

   a. Derive Jan's consumption function in terms of her annual income Y and initial wealth W according to the life-cycle model.

   b. Suppose that Jan expects her income to be $50,000 per year until she retires. In addition, she has accumulated $250,000 in wealth. Calculate her annual level of consumption.

9. Many economists advocate a reduction in tax rates on interest and dividends to stimulate saving and investment. What does the Fisher model of consumption imply about the effects of such a tax reduction on saving?

10. In 1981, Congress passed President Reagan's proposed tax cuts. This legislation called for a permanent reduction in tax *rates* by 5 percent in 1981, another 10 percent in 1982, and an additional 10 percent in 1983. If people had rational expectations, fully expected all of the tax cuts to occur (which they did), and incorporated these expectations into their estimates of their permanent incomes, in what years would the permanent-income hypothesis predict that the greatest *change* in consumption would occur? Explain.

11. In 2001 Congress passed President Bush's proposed tax cuts. Over the following decade taxes were scheduled to be cut by $1.6–$2.0 trillion. Only a small portion of the total, however, took effect in 2001 and 2002. Critics complained that the tax cut was not well-suited to combat the recession that began in 2001 because of this "backloading."

   a. Explain how these critics used Keynesian consumption function to support their criticism.

   b. Now explain how defenders of the cuts might use the permanent income or life-cycle hypothesis to argue that the timing of the tax cuts was not critical in changing consumption in 2001–2002 as long as they were implemented within the decade.

   c. Even if one accepted the theoretical arguments presented in Part b, how might considerations of borrowing constraints weaken their argument?

   d. Finally, how would proponents of the Ricardian equivalence proposition respond to the two economists in Parts a and b?

12. As the recession deepened in late 2001, President Bush proposed that Congress speed up (or accelerate) the implementation of his income tax cuts so that they all became effective much earlier. Given that the phased-in tax cuts had already been passed by Congress in 2001, explain how the acceleration would affect consumption in the year 2002 according to:

   a. the Keynesian consumption function?

   b. the permanent income hypothesis?

13. In the Case Study in Chapter 16 of the textbook on the tax rebate of 2008, how would households have behaved according to the life-cycle hypothesis? How was their actual behavior different?

14. Suppose there is a one-time tax cut of $30,000 and a 50-year-old man spends $24,000 of his tax cut on a new car that is expected to last until his retirement. Is this behavior consistent with the Keynesian consumption function, the permanent-income (or the life-cycle) hypothesis, or both? Explain.

Data Questions

Locate the necessary economic data and apply them to answer the following data questions. All of the relevant data may be found in the Economic Report of the President (http://www.gpoaccess.gov/eop/).

1. **a.** Use the real (deflated) values of the following variables to complete Table 16-5.

Table 16-5

(1) Year	(2) Real Consumption Expenditures ($ in billions)	(3) Real Disposable Income ($ in billions)	(4) Average Propensity to Consume (APC)*
1971	_____	_____	_____
1991	_____	_____	_____
2011	_____	_____	_____

*Round off to three decimal places.

b. Calculate the total percentage changes in real disposable income and the APC between 1971 and 2011.

c. What do you conclude about the stability of the APC over long periods of time?

2. **a.** Use the nominal values of the following variables to complete Table 16-6.

Table 16-6

(1) Year	(2) Consumption Expenditures ($ in billions)	(3) Disposable Income ($ in billions)	(4) Average Propensity to Consume (APC)*
1967	_____	_____	_____
1968	_____	_____	_____
1970	_____	_____	_____

*Round off to three decimal places.

b. Use the permanent-income hypothesis and the facts about fiscal policy presented in Chapter 16 of the textbook to explain the temporary rise in the *APC* in 1968.

Questions to Think About

1. **a.** Which aspects of your family's consumption behavior are described by each of the four models of consumption presented in Chapter 16 of the textbook? Which aspects are not described by these theories?

b. Which of the four models is the most appropriate for describing your family's consumption behavior? Explain.

2. Does the life-cycle model of consumption accurately explain the consumption behavior of your grandparents? Why or why not?

3. If you won $10,000,000 in the lottery, how and when would you spend it? Which of the four models of consumption presented in Chapter 16 of the textbook would be consistent with your behavior?

4. The movie *Die Hard* is based on a novel entitled *Nothing Is Forever*. Since many economists believe that taxes must eventually be increased to solve the U.S. long-term debt problem (along with reductions in the growth of government spending), how can households determine how long a so-called "permanent" tax cut will last?

CHAPTER 17

The Theory of Investment

Fill-in Questions

Use the key terms below to fill in the blanks in the following statements. Each term may be used more than once.

business fixed investment

corporate income tax

depreciation

efficient markets hypothesis

financing constraints

inventories as a factor of production

inventory investment

investment tax credit

neoclassical model of investment

net investment

production smoothing

real cost of capital

residential investment

stock market

stock-out avoidance

subprime

Tobin's *q*

work in process

1. Economists distinguish among three types of investment spending: _____ includes the new housing that people buy to live in and that landlords buy to rent out; _____ includes the equipment and structures that businesses buy to use in production; and _____ includes materials, supplies, and finished goods that businesses put aside in storage.

2. The _____ examines the benefit and cost to firms of owning capital goods by showing how investment is related to the marginal product of capital, the interest rate, and the tax rules affecting firms.

3. As capital ages, it undergoes wear and tear, which decreases its value. This process is called _____.

4. The cost of buying and renting out a unit of capital, measured in units of the economy's output, is called the _____.

5. The change in the capital stock is called _____. Recall from Chapter 2 of the textbook that it is equal to gross investment minus _____.

6. According to the _____, firms find it profitable to add to their capital stock if the marginal product of capital exceeds the _____.

7. The _____ is a tax on corporate profits.

8. Many economists believe that the _____ may discourage investment because it does not define profit as the rental price of capital minus the cost of capital.

9. The _____ reduces a firm's taxes by a certain amount for each dollar that the firm spends on capital goods. It works as a subsidy on investment.

10. According to one theory of investment, firms base their investment decisions on the ratio of the market value of installed capital divided by the replacement cost of installed capital. This ratio is known as _____.

11. According to the q-theory of investment, net investment will be positive whenever managers can raise their firm's market value by buying more capital. More precisely, if the _____ value of capital exceeds its replacement cost, _____ will exceed 1.0, and net investment will be positive.

12. According to the _____, the price of a company's stock is the fully rational valuation of that company's value, given current information about the company's business prospects.

13. When firms are limited in the amount that they can raise in financial markets, they are said to face _____.

14. One of the causes of the recession of 2008–2009 was the rising default rate on mortgages made to households with questionable credit histories, called _____ borrowers.

15. Firms have several motives for holding inventories. One motive, called _____, exists when it is cheaper for a firm to produce goods at a steady rate when that firm experiences temporary booms and busts in sales. Firms can also view _____ when inventories increase output by improving efficiency. A third motive, called _____, exists when firms hold inventories to avoid running out of goods when sales are unexpectedly high. A final motive exists because many goods take time to produce, so they are counted as part of a firm's inventory when they are only partly completed. These inventories are called _____.

Multiple-Choice Questions

1. Investment spending is an important component of GDP because:

    a. it provides a higher standard of living in the future.

    b. it is the most volatile component of GDP.

    c. it is an important part of the mechanism by which monetary policy affects GDP.

    d. All of the answers are correct.

2. All of the following are parts of the investment spending component of GDP EXCEPT:

    a. business fixed investment.

    b. residential investment.

    c. investment in stocks and bonds.

    d. inventory investment.

3. According to the neoclassical model of investment:

    a. investment falls as the real interest rate rises.

    b. investment falls as the real interest rate falls.

    c. an increase in the marginal product of capital causes the investment function to shift to the left.

    d. both a and c are true.

4. In equilibrium, the real rental price of capital is equal to:

    a. 1.0.   **c.** the price of output.

    b. the marginal product of capital.   **d.** All of the answers are correct.

5. In a Cobb–Douglas production function, the equilibrium rental price of capital increases as:

    a. the stock of capital used by the firm falls.

    b. the amount of labor employed by the firm rises.

    c. technology improves.

    d. All of the answers are correct.

6. The cost of capital is determined by all of the following EXCEPT the:

    a. rate of depreciation.

    b. corporate profit rate.

    c. interest rate.

    d. price of capital and its rate of change.

7. Assume that the price of capital goods rises at the same rate as the price of other goods. If the price of capital is $1,500 per unit, the real interest rate is 4 percent, and the depreciation rate is 6 percent, then the cost of capital equals:

    a. $30.   **b.** $300.   **c.** $150.   **d.** $100.

8. If the price of capital goods rises at the same rate as the price of other goods, the real cost of capital may be written as:

    a. $(P_K/P)(r + \delta)$.   **b.** $(P_K/P)(r - \delta)$.   **c.** $(P/P_K)(i + \delta)$.   **d.** $(P/P_K)(r - \delta)$.

9. Firms find it profitable to add to their capital stock if the:

   a. real cost of capital exceeds the marginal product of capital.

   b. marginal product of capital exceeds the real cost of capital.

   c. marginal product of capital exceeds the real interest rate.

   d. rental price of capital exceeds the marginal product of capital.

10. Expansionary monetary policy spurs investment in the short run via:

    a. a decrease in inflation.

    b. a decrease in the cost of capital.

    c. an increase in the rental price of capital.

    d. All of the answers are correct.

11. An event that decreases the marginal product of capital will:

    a. shift the investment function to the left.

    b. shift the investment function to the right.

    c. raise the real cost of capital.

    d. raise the rate of depreciation.

12. The corporate income tax discourages investment because it:

    a. defines profit as the rental price of capital minus the cost of capital.

    b. taxes profits at an exorbitant rate of 60 percent.

    c. does not appropriately take inflation into account in calculating depreciation and profit.

    d. All of the answers are correct.

13. All of the following statements about the investment tax credit are true EXCEPT:

    a. it stimulates investment.

    b. most of the benefits go to unprofitable corporations.

    c. it reduces the after-tax cost of capital.

    d. it operates as a subsidy for investment.

14. A policy that allows firms to deduct the cost of depreciation earlier in the life of an investment project will:

    a. reduce the after-tax cost of capital.

    b. make investment more profitable.

    c. increase the amount of investment.

    d. All of the answers are correct.

15. All of the following statements about the q-theory of investment are true EXCEPT:

    a. Tobin's q is equal to the market value of installed capital divided by the replacement cost of installed capital.

    b. if Tobin's q is greater than 1.0, firms will allow their capital to wear out without replacing it.

    c. it assumes that stock prices play an influential role in investment decisions.

    d. it implies that investment depends on the current and expected future profits from installed capital.

16. According to the efficient markets hypothesis, an increase in today's stock price may reflect all of the following EXCEPT:

    a. a new invention by the company.

    b. a merger with another company that was announced last year.

    c. an announcement of a future merger with another company.

    d. a new earnings report.

17. Financing constraints that limit the amount of money firms can raise in financial markets:

    a. tend to reduce the length of recessions.

    b. induce firms to invest on the basis of their current cash flow rather than their expected profitability.

    c. make investment less sensitive to current economic conditions.

    d. All of the answers are correct.

18. Residential investment depends on:

    a. the relative price of housing P_H/P.

    b. the real interest rate.

    c. the size of the adult population.

    d. All of the answers are correct.

19. The tax treatment of interest paid on a residential mortgage:

    a. allows homeowners to deduct these interest payments from their taxable income.

    b. increases the size of the subsidy to new homeownership as inflation rises.

    c. may lead the United States to invest too much in housing compared to other forms of capital.

    d. All of the answers are correct.

20. Some firms hold inventories in order to avoid changing production frequently in response to fluctuations in sales. This motive is called:

    a. holding inventories as a factor of production.

    b. production smoothing.

    c. stock-out avoidance.

    d. holding inventories as work in process.

21. Inventory investment depends on:

    a. the real interest rate.

    b. conditions in the credit market.

    c. the level of output (and hence sales) in the economy.

    d. All of the answers are correct.

Exercises

1. **The Demand for Capital** *In this exercise, we use a numerical example to illustrate how the demand for capital is related to the real rental price of capital. Note: Students may wish to review Exercises 1–3 in Chapter 3 of this Study Guide.*

   a. The owners of Acme Car Wash must decide how many units of capital to rent. They have the data shown in Columns 1 and 2 of Table 17-1 to help them in making a decision. (All data are for a given number of workers.)

   Table 17-1

(1) Units of Capital	(2) Number of Cars Washed per Hour	(3) Marginal Product of Capital
0	0	
		_____
1	20	
		_____
2	35	
		_____
3	45	
		_____
4	50	

   Recall that the marginal product of capital *MPK* is the extra output produced when one unit of capital is added. Thus, the *MPK* for the first unit of capital is equal to 20 – 0 = _____. Use this information to complete Column 3 in Table 17-1. Then use the data from Columns 1 and 3 to plot and draw the *MPK* curve on Graph 17-1, and label it *MPK*.

Graph 17-1

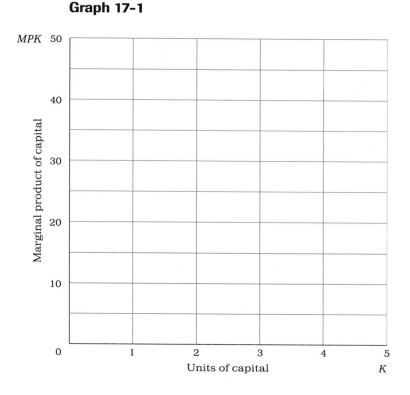

b. To maximize profits, firms rent capital until *MPK* is equal to the real rental price of capital, where the latter is defined as the rental rate of capital *R* divided by the price of the firm's output *P*, or *R/P*. Thus, in equilibrium, *R/P* = *MPK*. Using the data from Table 17-1, if *R/P* = 15, Acme will want to rent

_____ units of capital because this is the point at which *R/P* = *MPK*. Remember that this will occur if *R* = $15 and *P* = $1 or if *R* = $30 and *P* = $2. (*Note:* Review the exercises in Chapter 3 if this is not clear.) If *R/P* = 5, Acme will want to rent _____ units of capital because this is now the point at which *R/P* = *MPK*. Thus, the demand curve for capital is the same as the *MPK* curve. Consequently, add *R/P* as an additional label for the vertical axis on Graph 17-1, and add Capital demand as an additional label for the *MPK* curve. Obviously, as the real rental price of capital falls, firms will want to rent <u>more/fewer</u> units of capital.

c. You can construct an aggregate *MPK* and an aggregate capital demand curve for the entire economy in a similar way. One such curve is depicted on Graph 17-2. On this graph, *P* represents the aggregate price level, which can also be viewed as the price of output for a representative firm.

Graph 17-2

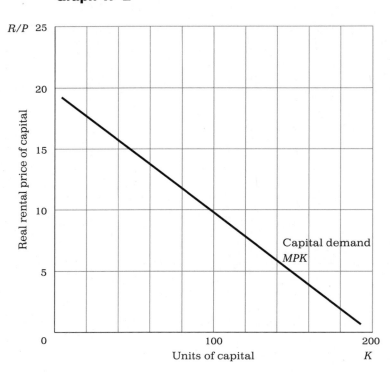

In the short run, the total amount of capital in the economy is fixed at $\overline{K}$. Suppose that $\overline{K} = 100$. Draw a vertical capital supply curve at $\overline{K} = 100$ on Graph 17-2, and label it Capital supply. In this case, the equilibrium real rental price of capital R/P will equal _____ in the short run because at this price the supply of capital equals the demand for capital.

d. Several factors can affect the equilibrium real rental price of capital R/P. Chapter 17 of the textbook illustrates some of these factors using the Cobb–Douglas production function, but one can also present them intuitively. If the capital stock were to increase suddenly, the capital supply curve would shift to the left/right and the equilibrium real rental price of capital would rise/fall. If capital and labor both became more productive, the marginal product of each unit of capital would be higher/lower, thereby shifting the capital demand curve to the left/right and increasing/decreasing the equilibrium real rental price of capital. If more workers were employed, each unit of capital would probably become more productive, thereby increasing the MPK at each level of capital, shifting the capital demand curve to the left/right, and increasing/decreasing the equilibrium real rental price of capital.

2. **The Cost of Capital** *In this exercise, we derive the cost of capital.*

a. Following the simplification introduced in Chapter 17 of the textbook, assume that the firms in Exercise 1 rent capital from other firms that own it. The nominal rent received by these other firms per unit of capital is R; the real rent is R/P, where P is the aggregate price level. As Chapter 17 of the textbook illustrates, the nominal cost of one unit of capital per period to the firm that owns it is

$$\text{(Nominal) Cost of Capital} = iP_K - \Delta P_K + \delta P_K, \qquad \textbf{(17-1)}$$

where i equals the nominal interest rate, P_K equals the purchase price of a unit of capital, ΔP_K equals the change in the price of (new) capital, and δ equals the rate of physical or technological depreciation. The first term on the right-hand side of Equation 17-1, iP_K, represents the forgone interest income the firm could have earned had it put its money in the bank or purchased bonds instead of purchasing capital. The second term, ΔP_K, represents the amount by which capital prices increase, and the third term, δP_K, reflects the amount by which the capital is reduced by depreciation. The minus sign before ΔP_K indicates that the cost of capital to firms that own it falls when capital prices increase, because the capital can then be sold to other firms that own capital for a higher price. Factoring P_K from the right-hand side of Equation 17-1 yields

$$\text{(Nominal) Cost of Capital} = P_K[i - \Delta P_K/P_K + \delta], \qquad \textbf{(17-2)}$$

where $\Delta P_K/P_K$ equals the rate at which capital prices are changing.

Now complete Table 17-2.

Table 17-2

(1) Price of Capital P_K	(2) Nominal Interest Rate i	(3) Rate of Growth of Capital Prices	(4) Rate of Depreciation δ	(5) Cost of Capital
$100	0.05	0.05	0.10	_____
$100	0.10	0.05	0.10	_____
$100	0.10	0.08	0.10	_____
$100	0.10	0.08	0.20	_____
$200	0.10	0.08	0.20	_____
$100	_____	0.08	0.20	$15

b. Equation 17-2 and the data in Table 17-2 indicate that an increase in the nominal interest rate will increase/decrease the cost of capital, and an increase in the rate of growth of capital prices will increase/decrease the cost of capital. Finally, an increase in the rate of depreciation will increase/decrease the cost of capital because the capital now wears out more quickly/slowly, thereby lasting for a longer/shorter period of time.

c. If capital prices are rising at the same rate as the aggregate price level, then $\Delta P_K/P_K = \pi$, and Equation 17-2 becomes

$$\text{(Nominal) Cost of Capital} = P_K[i - \pi + \delta] = P_K[r + \delta], \qquad \text{(17-3)}$$

where r is the real interest rate. Given this assumption, the real interest rate in the first row of Table 17-2 is _____ percent, and the real interest rate in the second row of Table 17-2 is _____ percent.

d. Finally, recall that the nominal rental cost of capital R for the firms that rent capital must be divided by the price level to obtain the real rental cost of capital R/P. Similarly, the real cost of capital to the firms that own the capital is $(P_K/P)(r + \delta)$. An increase in the real interest rate will increase/decrease the real cost of capital, and an increase in the rate of depreciation will increase/decrease the real cost of capital.

3. **The Determinants of Investment** *In this exercise, we combine the results from Exercises 1 and 2 to illustrate the determinants of investment.*

a. In Exercise 1, it was shown that firms rent additional units of capital until the marginal product of capital *MPK* is greater than/less than/equal to the real rental cost of capital R/P. In Exercise 2, it was also shown that if capital prices rise at the same rate as the aggregate price level, the real cost of capital to the firms that own it is $(P_K/P)[_____ + _____]$. Consequently, the real profit rate from owning one unit of capital and renting it is

$$\text{Profit Rate} = MPK - (P_K/P) \times (_____ + _____). \qquad \text{(17-4)}$$

If the profit rate is positive, firms that own capital will add to/subtract from their capital stock, resulting in positive/negative net investment. If the profit rate is negative, firms that own capital will add to/subtract from their capital stock, leading to positive/negative net investment. Total, or gross, business fixed investment is equal to net investment plus replacement investment, where the latter is equal to δK. Consequently, total investment may be positive even if net investment is negative.

b. In competitive long-run equilibrium, *MPK* is greater than/less than/equal to the real cost of capital $(P_K/P)(r + \delta)$, and the profit rate is positive/zero/negative. Starting from equilibrium, a reduction in the real interest rate *r* (resulting from either a(n) increase/decrease in the nominal interest rate or a(n) increase/decrease in the rate of inflation) will increase/decrease the real cost of capital and hence increase/decrease the profit rate from owning capital. As a result, firms that own capital will add to/subtract from their capital stock, resulting in a(n) increase/decrease in investment. Thus, as *r* falls, investment rises/falls. This result is similar to/different from that obtained in earlier textbook chapters. As capital is added and lent out, firms move along the aggregate *MPK* curve, and the marginal product of capital will rise/fall until it equals the new real cost of capital.

c. Starting from equilibrium again, a technological innovation that increases the marginal product of capital will increase/decrease/have no immediate effect on the real cost of capital, but it will increase/decrease the profit rate from owning capital. As a result, firms that own capital will add to/subtract from their capital stock, resulting in a(n) increase/decrease in investment. As capital is added/subtracted and lent out, firms move along the aggregate *MPK* curve, and the marginal product of capital will rise/fall until it equals the real cost of capital.

d. As Chapter 17 of the textbook indicates, many provisions of the tax code encourage or discourage the accumulation of capital by firms. Most economists believe that a reduction in the corporate income tax on accounting profits will increase/decrease investment. The investment tax credit reduces a firm's taxes by a certain amount for each dollar the firm spends on investment goods. An increase in the investment tax credit would increase/decrease the real after-tax cost of capital and thereby increase/decrease investment.

4. **Residential Investment** *In this exercise, we discuss the supply and demand for housing and residential investment.*

a. Graph 17-3 depicts an initial equilibrium in the housing market at Point A. Housing demand, labeled D_1, is negatively related to the relative price of housing P_H/P. Housing supply, labeled S_1, is fixed in the short run. If the residential construction industry is perfectly competitive, economic profits will be postive/negative/zero.

Graph 17-3

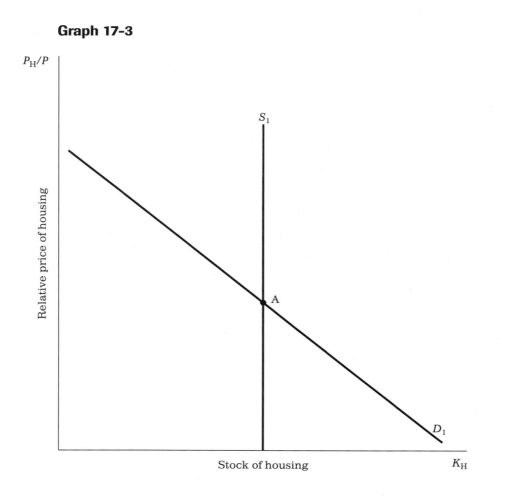

b. An economic boom that increases households' income will shift the housing demand curve to the <u>left/right</u>. Draw the new demand curve on Graph 17-3, label it D_2, and label the new short-run equilibrium Point B. Obviously, the relative price of housing will <u>increase/decrease</u>. This trend will induce the residential construction industry to <u>increase/decrease</u> the production of new houses, which will <u>increase/decrease</u> residential investment. This change in residential investment will eventually shift the housing supply curve on Graph 17-3 to the <u>left/right</u>. As it shifts, the relative price of housing will <u>rise even more/fall</u> from Point B.

c. Starting again at Point A, an increase in mortgage interest rates will shift the housing demand curve to the <u>left/right</u>. Draw the new demand curve on Graph 17-3, label it D_3, and label the new short-run equilibrium Point C. Obviously, the relative price of housing will <u>increase/decrease</u>, and residential investment will <u>increase/decrease</u>.

Problems

Answer the following problems on a separate sheet of paper.

1. In Chapters 11 and 12 of the textbook, it was assumed that investment *I* depends on the real interest rate *r* but is independent of changes in real output *Y*. Now suppose that *I* also increases as *Y* rises, and decreases as *Y* falls.

   a. Draw an investment curve that illustrates this relationship between *I* and *Y*.

   b. Explain why *I* might be an increasing function of *Y*.

   c. If *I* increases as *Y* rises and decreases as *Y* falls, what would happen to the:
      i. slope of the planned expenditure curve? Explain.
      ii. government-purchases multiplier? Explain using the round-by-round story.
      iii. slopes of the *IS* and *LM* curves?
      iv. slopes of the *AD* and *AS* curves?

2. a. Consider a harvester that costs $10,000. If harvester prices are rising at 3 percent per year, the nominal interest rate is 6 percent, and harvesters depreciate by 20 percent per year, calculate the cost of capital on this investment.

   b. Now consider a computer that costs $10,000. Once again, assume that the nominal interest rate is 6 percent and computers depreciate by 20 percent per year. Computer prices, however, *fall* by 15 percent per year. Calculate the cost of capital on this investment.

3. Suppose that there were large increases in the prices of certain basic commodities, such as oil and food. Consequently, the prices of capital goods increase by less than the overall rate of inflation. Would the use of the real interest rate in the cost-of-capital equation over- or underestimate the true cost of capital? Explain.

4. Consider the following Cobb–Douglas production function: $Y = 12(K^{1/3}L^{2/3})$. Assume that labor $L = 64$.

   C

   a. Derive the equation for the marginal product of capital *MPK*.

   b. Find the specific values for *MPK* when capital $K = 1, 8, 27,$ and 64. Plot these values of *MPK* on a graph and draw the resulting capital demand curve.

   c. Now suppose that *L* rises to 125, and repeat Parts a and b.

5. Suppose there is a reduction in personal income taxes.

   a. Use the *IS-LM* model and the relevant sections in Chapter 17 of the textbook to illustrate what happens to investment according to the neoclassical (cost of capital) model of investment.

   b. Now suppose that investment depends on real GDP (as in Problem 1) as well as the real cost of capital. Thus, if the real cost of capital does not change, an increase in real GDP will increase investment. How would this affect your answer to Part a?

6. In its first public stock market trade in August 2004, the price of one share of Google stock sold for $95. Eighteen months later, in February 2006, one share was selling for $475. What may have caused the stock price to quintuple according to each of the following theories: the efficient markets hypothesis and Keynes's "beauty contest" hypothesis about stock prices?

7. During the next decade, the enormous baby-boom generation will retire, and many of them will move to warmer climates in the South and Far West. What might one expect to be the effects of this demographic change on the demand for housing, the relative price of housing, and investment in housing in both the South and the North?

8. Mortgage interest payments are tax deductible in the United States. Many economists have argued for the elimination of this provision. What would the effects of an elimination on the tax deductibility on mortgage interest payments be on the demand for housing, the relative price of housing, investment in housing, and the profits of residential construction firms in the short run?

9. **a.** Define what is meant by an investment tax credit of 8 percent.

   b. Assume that the United States is a closed economy and Congress enacts an investment tax credit of 8 percent. If the aggregate price level is held constant, what happens to the *IS* and/or *LM* curves in the short run? Briefly explain.

   c. Now assume that the United States is a large open economy. If the price level is still held constant and Congress enacts an 8 percent investment tax credit for domestic firms only, explain what happens to each of the following in the short run:

   i. the *IS* and/or *LM* curves.
   ii. U.S. net capital outflow.
   iii. the U.S. trade surplus and the U.S. real foreign exchange rate.

Data Questions

Locate the necessary economic data and apply them to answer the following data questions. All of the relevant data may be found in the Economic Report of the President (http://www.gpoaccess.gov/eop/).

1. **a.** Complete Table 17-3 (in billions of 2005 dollars), which presents data about various forms of real private gross investment. (To locate the data in Column 5 you may have to look in tables on the components of GDP.)

Table 17-3

(1) Year	(2) Real Nonresidential Investment in Structures	(3) Real Nonresidential Investment in Equipment and Software	(4) Real Residential Investment	(5) Real Change in Business Inventories
2001	_____	_____	_____	_____
2006	_____	_____	_____	_____
2011	_____	_____	_____	_____

b. Calculate the percentage change in each category of investment between its highest and lowest values. What do you conclude about the relative volatility of the different components of investment?

2. The Standard and Poors (S&P) 500 index is an index of the stock market value of 500 of the largest companies in the United States. Complete Column 2 in Table 17-4 and calculate the percentage changes in the index in Column 3. Then obtain the data for real GDP for each quarter listed in Column 4, calculate the percentage changes, and complete Column 5.

Table 17-4

(1) Month	(2) Average Value of S&P 500 Index	(3) Percentage Change in S&P 500 Index	(4) Quarter and Year	(5) Real GDP	(6) Percentage Change in Real GDP
August, 2008	_____		2008: Q4	_____	
		_____			_____
November, 2008	_____		2008: Q1	_____	
		_____			_____
February, 2009	_____		2009: Q2	_____	
		_____			_____
May, 2009	_____		2009: Q3	_____	
		_____			_____
August, 2009	_____		2009: Q4	_____	
		_____			_____
November, 2009	_____		2010: Q1	_____	

The stock market is a leading index insofar as changes in the stock market tend to predate changes in real GDP. How well did the changes in the stock market during this period predict future changes in real GDP?

Questions to Think About

1. Many economists support the introduction of investment tax credits during recessions to spur investment. Critics argue, however, that investment may merely get crowded into recessions in anticipation of the subsidies—that is, critics suggest that firms may wait until recessions to invest in order to receive the investment subsidy. How might one control for this potential effect in an academic study?

2. Discuss the efficient markets hypothesis with your parents or grandparents. Ask them how, if at all, it has influenced their investment behavior.

Alternative Perspectives on Stabilization Policy

Fill-in Questions

Use the key terms below to fill in the blanks in the following statements. Each term may be used more than once.

automatic stabilizers
inflation targeting
inside lag
Lucas critique

monetarists
outside lag
political business cycle
time inconsistency

1. The _____ is the time between a shock to the economy and the policy action responding to that shock.

2. The _____ is the time between a policy action and its ultimate influence on the economy.

3. Fiscal policy has a relatively long _____; monetary policy has a relatively long _____.

4. _____ stimulate or depress the economy when necessary without any deliberate policy changes.

5. The _____ argues that traditional methods of policy evaluation did not adequately take into account the impact of policy on expectations.

6. The manipulation of the economy by politicians in an attempt to gain reelection is called the _____.

7. The phenomenon of _____ implies that policymakers can sometimes better achieve their own goals by having their discretion taken away from them.

8. _____ advocate that the Fed keep the money supply growing at a steady rate as a method of preventing most large fluctuations in real output.

9. _____ may be viewed as fiscal policy without any inside lag.

10. If the Fed adopted a policy of _____, it would announce a target for the rate of inflation and then adjust the money supply accordingly whenever the actual inflation rate deviated from its target.

Multiple-Choice Questions

1. The outside lag is the time between a:
   a. shock to the economy and the policy action responding to that shock.
   b. policy action and its influence on the economy.
   c. shock to the economy and the realization that some policy action needs to be taken.
   d. decision to implement a policy and the enactment of that policy.

2. The following statement is TRUE:
   a. monetary policy has an especially long outside lag.
   b. fiscal policy has an especially long inside lag.
   c. automatic stabilizers eliminate part of the inside lag in the conduct of fiscal policy.
   d. All of the answers are correct.

3. Arguments against the use of active stabilization policy include all of the following EXCEPT the:
   a. existence of long inside and outside lags.
   b. limited ability of economic forecasters to predict future economic conditions accurately.
   c. responsiveness of labor force participation rates to changes in national output.
   d. historical view that ill-advised policy choices were the cause of the Great Depression.

4. The system of unemployment insurance can be used to illustrate:
   a. the time inconsistency of policy.
   b. the way that the economy is automatically stabilized in the event of a shock.
   c. the Lucas critique.
   d. long inside lags in policy implementation.

5. Countries with more independent central banks tend to have:
   a. lower unemployment rates.
   b. lower inflation rates.
   c. higher rates of economic growth.
   d. All of the answers are correct.

6. According to the Lucas critique:

    a. traditional methods of policy evaluation do not adequately account for the impact of policy changes on expectations.

    b. traditional estimates of the sacrifice ratio are unreliable.

    c. economists cannot be completely confident when they make assessments about the effects of alternative economic policies.

    d. All of the answers are correct.

7. Comparing the time period before World War I with the period after World War II, Christina Romer found that:

    a. real GDP and unemployment have been much more stable in the later period.

    b. real GDP and unemployment have been much less stable in the later period.

    c. real GDP and unemployment have been slightly more stable in the later period.

    d. the levels of real GDP and unemployment have been approximately equal in the two periods.

8. All of the following are examples of a policy conducted by rule EXCEPT:

    a. the Fed automatically increases the money supply every year by 3 percent.

    b. the federal government is required, by a constitutional amendment, to balance the budget every year.

    c. the Fed adopts the following monetary policy for the indefinite future: % Change in M = 3% + 2 × (Actual Unemployment Rate − 5.5%).

    d. after a decline in private spending, Congress debates and then decides to stimulate aggregate demand by reducing taxes.

9. The following statement is FALSE:

    a. a policy that is active cannot be conducted by rule.

    b. the problem of time inconsistency is especially relevant to policy conducted by discretion.

    c. the conflicting interests of politicians reduce the desirability of policy conducted by discretion compared with policy conducted by rule.

    d. monetary policy currently is conducted by discretion.

10. If the Fed conducts monetary policy by setting a targeted unemployment rate of 5.5 percent, then the:

    a. unemployment rate will never rise above or fall below 5.5 percent.

    b. natural rate of unemployment will converge to the Fed's target.

    c. Fed will increase the growth rate of the money supply whenever unemployment exceeds this targeted rate.

    d. Fed will adjust its target whenever unemployment deviates from this rate.

11. Which of the following policies might lead to suboptimal results in the long run because of time inconsistencies?

    a. negotiation with terrorists who have taken hostages after a policy of nonnegotiation has been announced

    b. the enactment of a temporary "tax amnesty" for tax evaders

    c. the use of discretionary monetary policy rather than monetary rules

    d. All of the answers are correct.

12. The best argument against the monetarists' view that a steady growth in the money supply would prevent most large fluctuations in output and unemployment is that:

   a. steady growth in the money supply would prevent fluctuations in output only if the aggregate price level is constant.

   b. steady growth in the money supply need not stabilize aggregate demand because the velocity of money is not always stable.

   c. large fluctuations in the money supply do not occur because there is a limited amount of money available in the economy.

   d. fluctuations in output and unemployment are best treated by fiscal policy because the federal government has a more direct control over the economy through its use of the tax system.

Exercises

1. **Active versus Passive Macroeconomic Policies** *In this exercise, we review the arguments for active and passive policy responses to fluctuations in real output.*

   a. Suppose that the economy is initially at Point A on Graph 18-1.

Graph 18-1

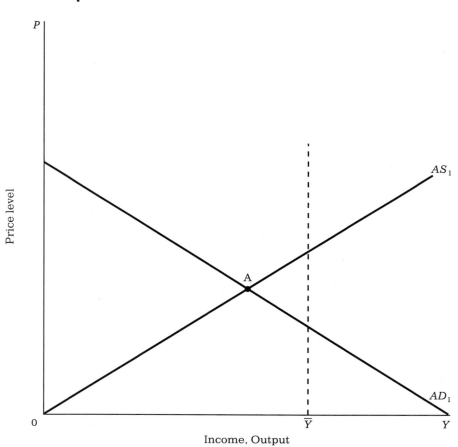

Clearly, at Point A, real output Y is greater than/equal to/less than the natural level of output $\overline{Y}$. Consequently, the actual price level P must be greater than/equal to/less than the expected price level EP.

b. In future years, therefore, EP will rise/fall/remain the same. If macroeconomic policies remain unchanged, the change in EP will shift the short-run aggregate supply curve upward/downward until eventually actual output is greater than/equal to/less than the natural level of output. Draw the final short-run aggregate supply curve on Graph 18-1 and label it AS_{final}. Label the final equilibrium Point Z. Comparing Points A and Z, one can conclude that if no policy response is taken, real output will eventually rise/fall/remain the same, and the price level will rise/fall/remain the same.

c. The initial equilibrium from Graph 18-1 is redrawn on Graph 18-2.

Graph 18-2

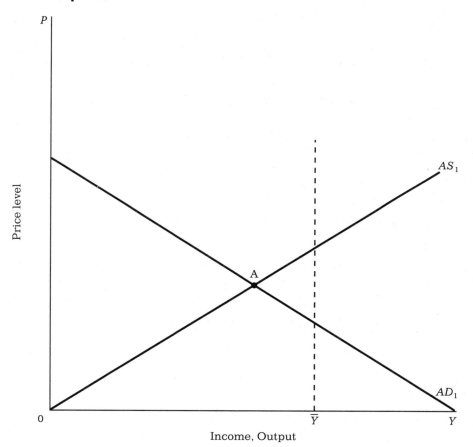

If policymakers wanted to increase output to the natural level quickly, they could increase/decrease the money supply, increase/decrease government purchases, or increase/decrease taxes. These policies would shift the aggregate demand curve to the left/right. Draw the new aggregate demand curve on Graph 18-2, label it AD_2, and label the new equilibrium Point B. Comparing Points A and B, one can conclude that if an active policy response is taken, real output will rise/fall/remain the same, and the price level will rise/fall/remain the same.

d. In Parts a and b, the economy eventually reaches the natural level of output. If an active policy response is taken, however, the eventual price level is greater than/equal to/less than the eventual price level if no policy response is taken.

The case for an active policy response to fluctuations in output relies partially on the belief that the transition back to the natural level of output will be longer/shorter if expansionary monetary and fiscal policies are pursued than if no new policies are pursued. It also relies on the belief that policymakers will be able and willing to implement the appropriate policies.

e. In Chapter 14 of the textbook, there is a discussion of some of the issues that determine the speed with which the economy approaches the natural level of output when policy is passive. Instead of assuming that expected inflation is equal to last year's actual rate of inflation, suppose that inflationary expectations are rational. Then real output will return to its natural level more/less rapidly. If prices are flexible rather than sticky, real output will return to its natural level more/less rapidly. If the duration of wage and price contracts is relatively long rather than short, real output will return to its natural level more/less rapidly.

f. In Chapter 18 of the textbook, there is a discussion of several problems that commonly arise when active policy measures are taken to stabilize output. One limitation of active policy concerns the fact that fiscal policy has a relatively long inside/outside lag, whereas monetary policy has a relatively long inside/outside lag. Another limitation is that the track record of economic forecasters has not been especially good. Finally, policymakers occasionally seem to be unwilling or unable to implement the appropriate macroeconomic policies because of political considerations.

2. **The Lucas Critique** *In this exercise, we use a simple Phillips curve example to illustrate the Lucas critique.*

   a. Suppose that the following equation represents the Phillips curve for an imaginary economy:

$$u = u^n - \beta \, (\pi - E\pi) = 6 - 0.2(\pi - E\pi). \tag{18-1}$$

According to Equation 18-1, the natural rate of unemployment is _____ percent. Furthermore, whenever the actual inflation rate exceeds the expected rate of inflation by 1 percentage point, the unemployment rate is _____ percentage points <u>above/below</u> the natural rate of unemployment.

b. During the nineteenth century, suppose that the actual rate of inflation was +5 percent half the time and –5 percent the remaining half. In the absence of any prior information, the average or expected rate of inflation for any year would be

$$EP = 0.5 \times 5\% + 0.5 \times (-5\%) = \text{_____}\%.$$

During those years in which the actual rate of inflation turned out to be +5 percent, the Phillips curve equation indicates that the actual unemployment rate was 6 – 0.2(_____ – _____) = _____ percent. On the other hand, during those years in which the actual rate of inflation was –5 percent, the actual rate of unemployment was 6 – 0.2 (_____ – _____) = _____ percent. Since each of the two rates occurred half of the time, the average unemployment rate during the entire century was _____ percent.

c. After a century of this pattern, advisers recommended policies designed to keep the inflation rate equal to +5 percent in every year. It was the advisers' hope that people's expectations of inflation would remain equal to the last century's expected inflation rate of _____ percent, so that the unemployment rate would be 6 – 0.2(_____ – _____) = _____ percent in every year.

d. Alas, after several years of these new policies and persistent 5 percent inflation, people soon increased their forecast of inflation to 5 percent. As a result, unemployment thereafter equaled 6 – 0.2(_____ – _____) = _____ percent in every year, which was <u>more than/less than/equal to</u> the average during the preceding century.

e. This example illustrates the Lucas critique, whereby an evaluation of a change in economic policy must take into account the impact of the policy change on people's expectations of the future. Several economists believe that the imaginary economy in this exercise resembles the experience of the U.S. economy during the past two centuries. Finally, the more quickly people changed their expectations in response to the more inflationary policies, the more <u>quickly/slowly</u> unemployment returned to its natural rate.

3. **Rules versus Discretion** *In this exercise, we present and evaluate several rules for the conduct of monetary policy.*

a. As stated in Exercise 1, many observers are wary about the ability and/or willingness of policymakers to implement the appropriate macroeconomic policies. Some economists believe that monetary policy should be governed by a set of rules or formulas. One example is the constant-growth-rate rule, advocated by many monetarists, in which the Fed would increase the money supply by a fixed percentage each year. Suppose, for example, that the goal of monetary policy is to fuel noninflationary long-run economic growth. Recall the quantity equation presented in Chapter 5 of the textbook.

$$MV = PY \tag{18-2}$$

The percentage change version of the quantity equation is

   % Change in M + % Change in V = % Change in P + % Change in Y.

The long-run rate of growth of output is about 3 percent per year. If velocity were constant, monetary growth that kept the price level stable would require that % Change in M = % Change in P + % Change in Y – % Change in V =

_____   +   _____   –   _____   =   _____%.

b. One frequently mentioned problem with the constant-growth-rate rule is that large fluctuations in velocity would lead to large fluctuations in aggregate demand. As a result, some economists advocate a money-growth rule that sets a target for nominal income PY. Suppose that the target growth rate for nominal income is 3 percent per year. If velocity were constant, this target growth rate would require a _____ percent annual increase in the money supply M. Suppose, however, that nominal income increases by 7 percent in one year. If the money supply continued to grow by _____ percent, then velocity must have increased/decreased by _____ percent. Following a nominal-income targeting rule, the Fed would then reduce the growth rate of the money supply to dampen aggregate demand. If, on the other hand, nominal income increased by 1 percent in one year and the money supply continued to grow at its initial rate, then velocity must have increased/decreased by _____ percent. The Fed would then increase the growth rate of the money supply to spur aggregate demand. In this way, the Fed would have the ability and the authority to offset fluctuations in the velocity of money.

c. A third group of economists believes that inflation stability should be the sole goal of monetary policy. Consequently, they advocate a money-growth rule that is based on a target inflation rate. If the actual inflation rate were to exceed the target, money growth would increase/decrease. If the actual inflation rate were less than the target, money growth would increase/decrease.

Problems

Answer the following problems on a separate sheet of paper.

1. Suppose you do not know the exact natural rate of unemployment, but you are confident that it is between 5 and 6 percent. Given the evidence cited in the textbook concerning the accuracy of economic forecasts and policy time lags, what might you reasonably conclude about the appropriate changes in monetary and fiscal policies if:

   a. the actual unemployment rate is 6.1 percent? Explain.

   b. the actual unemployment rate is 10.1 percent? Explain.

2. Explain why you agree or disagree with the following statement: The acceptance of rational expectations *totally* discredits the notion that policy activism should be pursued if output lies below its natural level.

3. Since World War II there has often been a recession in the second year of Republican presidential administrations but not in the second year of Democratic administrations.

   a. Use the aggregate supply, aggregate demand model presented in Chapters 12 and 14 of the textbook to explain what differences in the conduct of monetary and/or fiscal policy by Republicans and Democrats would explain these differences in economic growth.

   b. If people have rational expectations and the imperfect-information model of the **CH** economy is correct, how could differences in the conduct of monetary policy explain these differences in economic growth?

4. As the textbook notes, countries with more independent central banks tend to have lower average inflation rates. Nevertheless, the average unemployment rates among countries is unrelated to the degree of central bank independence. How would one explain this finding using the Phillips curve?

5. a. According to what measure has real GDP become much less variable (volatile) in the post-World War II period relative to its variability in the 40-year period prior to World War II?

   b. According to what measure has the volatility of real GDP been roughly the same in these two periods?

   c. Why is this issue important for the debate concerning the desirability of pursuing macroeconomic stabilization policies when the economy is in a boom or a recession?

6. a. Many economists advocate a reduction in the capital gains tax in order to stimulate saving and investment. (See Exercise 8 in Chapter 5 of the Student Guide for a discussion of the capital gains tax.) Briefly explain these economists' reasoning.

   b. Other economists believe that a capital gains tax reduction on past acquisitions would reduce tax revenues without stimulating additional saving and investment. Briefly explain their reasoning.

   c. Instead, this second group of economists suggests that saving and investment could be stimulated more by focusing all of the tax reduction on new acquisitions. This action would allow the tax rates on additional saving and investment to be reduced even more. Explain how the problem of time inconsistency might be used to dispute their assertion.

7. Suppose current consumption depends on current disposable income and expected future disposable income. In forming their expectations of future disposable income, households must also forecast future taxes.

    a. During his election campaign, Barack Obama promised to reduce taxes for 95% of Americans. If people believed these promises, how would his election in November 2008 affect consumption in 2008? Explain your answer.

    b. After the election, it took many months for Congress to pass some of the proposed tax cuts. Once they were finally passed, what effect would their passage have on consumption? Explain your answer.

    c. How do your answers to Parts a and b illustrate the Lucas critique?

8. Your textbook suggests that one plausible range for an inflation target might be 1 to 3 percent. There are several reasons why most economists believe that an inflation target of zero percent, resulting in absolute price stability, might not be optimal. One reason, suggested in Chapter 5, is that some small inflation rate might make labor markets work better. Another reason is that disinflation (negative inflation) can be very dangerous. A third reason is that zero-percent inflation prevents central banks from pushing real interest rates below zero, which is something they might want to do in a severe recession. Why does zero-percent inflation have this effect?

9. Suppose a central banker was concerned *only* about price stability, resulting in the
    A loss function $L(\pi) = \pi^2$.
    C

    a. Use calculus to derive the optimal level of inflation for this central banker. (The answer should not be surprising.)

    b. What will be the resulting rate of unemployment in the long run? Explain.

Data Questions

Locate the necessary economic data and apply them to answer the following data questions. All of the relevant data may be found in the Economic Report of the President (http://www.gpoaccess.gov/eop/).

1. a. Paste the following Web site address in your browser and go to the First Quarter of 2012 *Survey of Professional Forecasters*:
        http://www.philadelphiafed.org/research-and-data/real-time-center/
        survey-of-professional-forecasters/2012/survq112.cfm. Then complete Columns 2 and 4 in Table 18.1.

Table 18-1

(1) Year	(2) Real GDP Growth Forecast (%)	(3) Actual Real GDP Growth Rate (%)	(4) Unemployment Rate Forecast (%)	(5) Actual Unemployment Rate (%)
2012	_____	_____	_____	_____
2013	_____	_____	_____	_____

b. Now get the most recent data you can find for the actual growth rates of real GDP and the actual unemployment rate in the years 2012 and 2013 and complete Columns 3 and 5 in Table 18-1. (One place to try is the *Economic Report of the President* at http://www.gpoaccess.gov/eop/.) How well did the forecasters do?

Questions to Think About

1. **a.** Are inflationary expectations rational?

   b. What empirical tests would prove or disprove the hypothesis that expectations are rational?

2. As the textbook illustrates, different economists believe in different models of the economy. In what sense, then, can everyone have a rational expectation of the effects of various policies on real output?

3. If policymakers decided to conduct monetary policy by a rule, should they be allowed to change the rule? If so, under what circumstances?

4. If monetary policy is governed by a rule, but policymakers are allowed to change this rule, how can one apply the problem of time inconsistency to the debate about whether policy should be conducted by rules or by discretion?

5. How might policymakers make a commitment to a policy rule? Might the policy-makers' reputation be a form of commitment?

6. If you believe that democracy is the best form of government, how could you justify greater central bank independence from a political perspective?

Government Debt and Budget Deficits

Fill-in Questions

Use the key terms below to fill in the blanks in the following statements. Each term may be used more than once.

capital budgeting   Ricardian equivalence
cyclically adjusted budget deficit   traditional view of government debt
government debt

1. When the conventionally measured government budget deficit is positive, there is an increase in the nominal value of the _____.

2. Some economists believe that the budget deficit should measure changes in the real value of the _____.

3. A budget procedure that accounts for assets as well as liabilities is sometimes called _____.

4. The _____ measures what the budget deficit would be if the economy were operating at its natural level of output and employment.

5. According to the _____, a tax cut that is unaccompanied by current or expected future reductions in government spending stimulates current consumption.

6. According to the _____ hypothesis, a tax cut that is unaccompanied by current or expected future reductions in government spending has no effect on current consumption.

Multiple-Choice Questions

1. Compared with other industrial countries, the gross U.S. national debt as a percentage of its GDP is:

   a. very high.
   b. very low.
   c. about average.

2. The ratio of federal government debt to GDP:

   a. has never been higher than it is today.
   b. peaked during the Civil War years.
   c. has never been lower than it has been during the past 15 years.
   d. is smaller today than it was at the end of World War II.

3. If no changes are made to Social Security and Medicare, projected demographic changes will:

   a. worsen our budgetary problems in the next 50 years.
   b. alleviate our budgetary problems in the next 50 years.
   c. have little effect on our budgetary problems in the next 50 years.

4. The government budget deficit is equal to:

   a. $G - T$.
   b. $T - G$.
   c. $G + T$.
   d. $-G$.

5. The stock of government debt is equal to:

   a. the current government budget deficit.
   b. the total debt of all individuals in the nation.
   c. the outstanding debt of the government.
   d. government expenditures minus the tax revenues.

6. Most economists believe that the budget deficit should measure the change in the government's:

   a. nominal debt.
   b. real debt.
   c. tax revenues.
   d. fiscal policy.

7. During periods of inflation, the official measure of the budget deficit:

   a. overstates the change in the government's real indebtedness.
   b. understates the change in the government's real indebtedness.
   c. equals the change in the government's real indebtedness.
   d. should equal the expected rate of inflation.

8. Economists argue that the official measure of the budget deficit is an incomplete measure of the change in the government's overall indebtedness because it:

   a. measures the change in the nominal debt rather than the real debt.

   b. does not consider any changes in the value of government assets.

   c. excludes the accrual of future pension benefits that must be paid to government employees.

   d. All of the answers are correct.

9. During recessions the:

   a. actual budget deficit will be smaller than the cyclically adjusted budget deficit.

   b. actual budget deficit will be greater than the cyclically adjusted budget deficit.

   c. actual budget deficit will be equal to the cyclically adjusted budget deficit.

   d. cyclically adjusted budget deficit will always be positive.

10. According to the traditional view of government debt, a tax cut will lead to all of the following in the short run EXCEPT a(n):

    a. increase in consumption.

    b. increase in private saving.

    c. increase in investment.

    d. decrease in public saving.

11. According to the traditional view of government debt, a tax cut will lead to all of the following in the long run EXCEPT a:

    a. decrease in public saving.

    b. decrease in national saving.

    c. decrease in net exports.

    d. depreciation of the foreign exchange rate.

12. Supply-siders believe:

    a. that people will have to work more if their hourly wage falls.

    b. that the incentive effects of tax cuts are very large.

    c. that income taxes provide more incentives to save than do consumption taxes.

    d. All of the answers are correct.

13. According to the Ricardian view of government debt, consumers will treat a current tax cut as an increase in:

    a. their wealth.

    b. the sum of their current and expected future income.

    c. their current disposable income accompanied by a future tax increase.

    d. public saving.

14. According to the Ricardian view of government debt, consumers will respond to a current tax cut by:

    a. increasing their current consumption.

    b. increasing their private saving by the amount of the tax cut.

    c. increasing their future consumption.

    d. decreasing their private saving by the amount of the tax cut.

15. According to the Ricardian view of government debt, a current tax cut will:

    a. decrease public saving.

    b. increase private saving.

    c. have no effect on national saving.

    d. result in all of the above answers.

16. According to the Ricardian view of government debt, the relevant decision-making unit is the:

    a. infinitely lived family.

    b. finitely lived family.

    c. finitely lived individual.

    d. infinitely lived world community.

17. During the early 1980s, taxes were cut substantially, and national saving fell. This evidence by itself would seem to support:

    a. the traditional view of government debt.

    b. the Ricardian view of government debt.

    c. neither view of government debt.

    d. the view that government debt is neutral.

18. The events of the early 1980s, when taxes were cut and national saving fell, are consistent with the Ricardian view of government debt if:

    a. people suddenly became less optimistic about future economic growth.

    b. people expected future reductions in government spending.

    c. people expected that the tax cuts were temporary.

    d. the tax cuts were unexpected.

19. High budget deficits may:

    a. encourage excessively expansionary monetary policy.

    b. increase the risk of government default on its debt.

    c. reduce a nation's political influence throughout the world.

    d. All of the answers are correct.

20. If higher deficits raise fears of default on a country's national debt:

    a. domestic interest rates will rise.

    b. the foreign exchange rate will depreciate.

    c. capital flight may occur.

    d. All of the answers are correct.

21. Indexed government bonds:

    a. have higher interest rates than nonindexed bonds.

    b. reduce the government's incentive to produce surprise inflation.

    c. were introduced in the United States in 1946.

    d. involve all of the answers.

22. Adherence to a balanced-budget rule by the federal government results in:

    a. an inability to use monetary policy to stimulate the economy when it slips into a recession.

    b. persistent inflation.

    c. an inability to lower tax rates to stimulate the economy when it slips into a recession.

    d. All of the answers are correct.

Exercises

1. **Adjusting the Budget Deficit for Inflation** *In this exercise, we illustrate how inflation can lead to an overestimate of the correctly measured budget deficit and how the inclusion of real, rather than nominal, interest payments in government expenses overcomes this problem.*

    Consider Table 19-1.

Table 19–1

(1)	(2) Country A	(3) Country B
Initial debt (in billions of dollars)	$2,000	$2,000
Nominal government outlays (made near the end of the year), excluding interest payments (in billions of dollars)	$200	$200
Price level at the beginning of the year	1.0	1.0
Annual inflation rate	0	0.10
Nominal interest rate	0.03	0.13
Nominal taxes (in billions of dollars)	$260	$260

Countries A and B are identical, except that Country B has 10 percent more inflation. If the real interest rates are 3 percent in both economies, Country B therefore has a 10 percent higher nominal interest rate than Country A.

a. These data indicate that government (nominal) interest payments during the year in Country A = 0.03 × $2,000 = $_____ billion. In Country B, however, government (nominal) interest payments during the year = _____ × $2,000 = $_____ billion.

b. The official government deficit in each country is equal to nominal government outlays, *including* nominal interest payments minus nominal taxes. In Country A, this amount equals $200 + (0.03 × $2,000) − $260 = $_____ billion. In Country B, however, the official government budget deficit equals $_____ + (_____ × $2,000) − $_____ = $_____ billion.

c. The nominal value of outstanding government debt at the end of the fiscal year is equal to the initial value of debt plus any additional nominal budget deficits during the year. Consequently, the nominal value of outstanding government debt at the end of the fiscal year in Country A equals $2,000 + $_____ = $_____ billion, whereas in Country B it equals $_____ + $_____ = $_____ billion.

d. Given the initial price level of 1.0 in both countries and the different inflation rates in Table 19-1, the price level at the end of the fiscal year is _____ in Country A and _____ in Country B. The real value of outstanding government debt at the end of the fiscal year in Country A is equal to the nominal debt at the end of the year divided by the aggregate price level at the end of the year, or $_____/_____ = $_____ billion. The real value of outstanding government debt at the end of the fiscal year in Country B is equal to $_____/_____ = $_____ billion. The real value of government debt at the end of the year in Country A is greater than/less than/equal to the real value of government debt at the end of the year in Country B. If deficits truly measured changes in the real value of outstanding government debt, the budget deficits in both countries would equal $_____ billion. Thus, during periods of high inflation, as in Country B, official deficit measures tend to overstate/understate the true value of the deficit.

e. Suppose that one counts only *ex post* real interest payments in the deficit. The *ex post* real interest rate is _____ (or _____ percent) in Country A and _____ in Country B. Consequently, real interest payments are $_____ billion in Country A and $_____ billion in Country B. The adjusted budget deficit would then equal nominal government outlays excluding interest payments plus real interest payments minus nominal taxes. This adjusted budget deficit would equal $_____ + $_____ – $_____ = $_____ billion in both countries. Thus, one way to eliminate the distortionary effects of inflation on the deficit is to include in the budget only real interest payments on the government debt.

2. **The Traditional View of Government Debt** *In this exercise, we review the short- and long-run effects of tax cuts according to the traditional view of government debt.*

a. In a closed economy in the short run, a tax cut will shift the *IS/LM* curve to the left/right. This shift will increase/decrease real income, increase/decrease consumption, and increase/decrease the real interest rate. As a result, investment will rise/fall and the tax cut partially crowds out government purchases/investment.

b. In an open economy, the short-run effects of the tax cut will depend upon whether the country is small or large and whether its foreign exchange rate is fixed or floating. If the country is a small open economy, the real interest rate will increase/decrease/remain constant. If the foreign exchange rate is floating, a tax cut will lead to a(n) appreciation/depreciation of the domestic currency and national income will increase/decrease/remain constant. Disposable income and consumption, however, will increase/decrease/remain constant, and the tax cut will completely crowd out investment/government purchases/net exports. If the foreign exchange rate is fixed, the tax cut will increase/decrease/have no effect on real income and increase/decrease/have no effect on consumption. To maintain the fixed exchange rate, the Fed will have to increase/decrease the money supply.

c. If the country is a large open economy, the short-run effects of a tax cut **A** will be an increase/a decrease/no change in real income and an increase/a decrease/no change in consumption. Since the *IS* curve for a large open economy is flatter/steeper than the *IS* curve for a closed economy, the changes in income and consumption following a tax cut will be larger/smaller than those in a closed economy.

d. In the long run, output will be at its natural level. According to the traditional view of government debt, if the steady-state capital stock is unaffected, then in a closed economy the tax cut will increase/decrease/have no effect on national saving in the long run and increase/decrease/have no effect on consumption.

e. If the steady-state capital stock is affected and the economy starts from a position below the Golden Rule level of capital, the tax cut will increase/decrease/have no effect on the saving rate. Consequently, the steady-state level of the capital stock will increase/decrease/remain constant, and the steady-state levels of output and consumption will rise/fall/remain constant.

3. **The Ricardian View of Government Debt** *In this exercise, we present the Ricardian view that tax cuts will increase private saving and have no effect on current consumption.*

a. According to the Ricardian view of government debt, a tax cut does not stimulate consumption because it does not affect the current and expected future income of current citizens and their descendants. Let us begin by analyzing a simple two-period model. Suppose that the government cuts taxes by $1,000 in Period 1. If this tax cut represents an increase in current and expected future income, consumers will respond by increasing/decreasing/not changing consumption.

b. Now suppose that the government finances the tax cut by issuing a bond for $1,000 plus interest of 10 percent. When the government pays back its loan in Period 2, it will pay $1,000 + 0.10($1,000) = $_____. To pay this amount, it will have to increase taxes in Period 2 by $_____. If in Period 1 you had saved all of the money you received from the initial tax cut and put it into the bank at an interest rate of 10 percent, you would have $1,000 + 0.10($1,000) = $_____ in Period 2. Consequently, after you pay the tax increase in Period 2, you will be better off/worse off/equally well off compared with your situation before the initial tax cut in Period 1. As a result, the early tax cut and the later tax increase will increase/decrease/have no effect on the sum of your current and expected future income, and consumption in Period 1 will increase/decrease/remain constant.

c. Ricardians expand this simple model to include many periods in the distant future. Any tax reduction in the current period unaccompanied by current or future reductions in government spending will eventually lead to a tax increase in the future that is equal to the amount of money that will accumulate if current citizens save all of the current tax reduction. (Alternatively, the "present value" of the future tax increase is equal to the initial tax cut.) Consequently, if the indefinite future is considered, an early tax cut and a later tax increase will increase/decrease/have no effect on the sum of current and expected future income, and consumption in Period 1 will increase/decrease/remain constant.

4. **Fiscal Policy Rules** *Chapters 15 and 18 examined several policy rules for monetary policy. In this exercise we present and evaluate several rules for the conduct of fiscal policy.*

a. The most well-known rule for fiscal policy is one that requires the federal budget to be balanced in each year, that is, $G - tY = 0$ where t is the tax rate. This balanced-budget rule would reduce the ability of policymakers to use fiscal policy to offset fluctuations in real output. It might even exacerbate these fluctuations. If, for example, the economy slipped into a recession, tY would increase/remain constant/decrease. To keep the budget balanced, policymakers might then have to increase/decrease G or increase/decrease the tax rate t. Either change would shift the aggregate demand curve to the left/right and thereby magnify the reduction in output.

b. As the textbook states, policymakers should avoid large changes in tax rates in order to minimize the distortion of incentives caused by the tax system. Relatively constant tax rates, however, would lead to government surpluses/deficits during recessions and surpluses/deficits during economic booms. Finally, budget deficits may be the appropriate way to shift a portion of the burden of a current government expenditure to future generations if they, too, benefit from the expenditure.

c. To avoid the first problem mentioned in Part a, the reduction in the ability of policymakers to use fiscal policy to offset fluctuations in real output, some economists have advocated a rule that balances the "cyclically adjusted budget deficit," which is the budget deficit that would occur if $Y = \overline{Y}$. (See Problem 4 in

Chapter 19 of the textbook.) This amount is roughly equal to $G - t\overline{Y}$. Consequently, if the economy slipped into a recession, tax rates would/ would not have to be increased because the cyclically adjusted budget deficit would/would not increase.

Problems

Answer the following problems on a separate sheet of paper.

1. How does an increase in Social Security taxes, unaccompanied by any changes in Social Security benefits or changes in government spending, affect current consumption in a closed economy, according to the traditional and Ricardian views of government debt? Explain.

2. Suppose the government cuts taxes by $100 billion. According to Ricardian equivalence, indicate exactly what will happen to each of the following and briefly explain your answer.

    a. current consumption

    b. current private saving

    c. current national saving

3. Suppose that the assumptions behind the Ricardian view of government debt are true, and you are planning to emigrate to another country with your family next year. How would you respond to a tax reduction in this year? If the Ricardian view of government debt is true, how would the economy as a whole respond?

4. How does an expected future reduction in government purchases affect current ▣ consumption and current private saving, according to the traditional and Ricardian views of government debt? Explain.

5. Consider Table 19-2.

▣ **Table 19-2**

(1)	(2) Country A	(3) Country B
Initial debt (in billions of dollars)	$2,000	$2,000
Nominal government outlays (made near the end of the year), excluding interest payments (in billions of dollars)	$200	$200
Price level at the beginning of the year	1.0	1.0
Annual inflation rate	0	−0.05
Nominal interest rate	0.07	0.02
Nominal taxes (in billions of dollars)	$340	$340

Countries A and B are identical, except that Country B has 5 percent less inflation and, therefore (assuming that the real interest rate is 7 percent in both economies), a 5 percent lower nominal interest rate than Country A.

a. What is the nominal value of government interest payments in each economy?

b. What are the official government deficits in each economy?

c. Calculate the nominal value of outstanding government debt at the end of the fiscal year in each economy.

d. Show that the real value of outstanding government debt at the end of the fiscal year is the same in both economies, so that the difference in official deficits does not reflect any real difference in the governments' net debt positions.

e. Show that, if one counts only *ex post* real interest payments in the deficit, then Country A's and Country B's deficits are equal.

f. During deflationary periods, do official deficit measures tend to understate or overstate the true value of the deficit? Explain.

6. The value of the Treasury securities owned by the U.S. Social Security Trust Fund is not included in the (net) debt figures presented in Table 19-5 of the textbook.

   a. Why not?

   b. Some observers believe their exclusion underestimates the true financial liability of the U.S. government. Why?

7. At the end of January 2009, China owned about $740 billion in U.S. Treasury bonds. (Since then, China has increased its ownership of U.S. Treasury bonds to $1.1 trillion.) Along with a comparable amount of bonds issued by U.S.–government-sponsored enterprises, like Fannie Mae and Freddie Mac, and other assets, China owned an estimated $1.5–$2.5 trillion in dollar-denominated assets. In April, 2009, China's Premier Wen Jiabao expressed concern that President Obama's fiscal stimulus package and the Federal Reserve's expansionary monetary policies might adversely affect the value of China's dollar-denominated assets in two ways: They might lead to inflation and they might lead to a reduction in the foreign exchange rate of the dollar. Use the traditional view of government debt and the appropriate graphs to determine whether his concerns were justified in:

   a. the short run, and

   b. the long run.

   (*Hint:* Somewhere in your answer, consider the possible effects of an increase in the risk premium on dollar-denominated assets.)

8. Suppose a president facing budget deficits asked his economic advisers to solve the following dilemma: he would like to reassure the "financial markets" that he is serious about proposing a long-run plan that will eventually reduce the federal budget deficit further, but he is concerned that any contractionary fiscal policy might push the economy into a recession. One adviser suggests that the president propose (and Congress pass) legislation *now* that will raise taxes, *starting four years from now*. Assume throughout this problem that everyone believes that taxes will indeed rise four years from now.

   a. Why would the simple Keynesian consumption function predict that this strategy would work?

   b. Many of the president's economists argue that the legislation will affect the economy now even if taxes do not increase for another four years. Explain their reasoning and the theory (or theories) they use.

c. A small group of economists argues that the tax increase will have no effect on real GDP, regardless of when it takes effect. Why?

d. Even if the theory cited by economists in Part c is correct, other economists argue that the tax increase will still affect consumption when it takes effect if people have borrowing constraints. Explain their reasoning.

9. During the Mexican crisis of 1994–1995, the U.S. government guaranteed up to $50 billion of Mexican government debt. This guarantee helped to calm the crisis, and the Mexican government did not default. Explain what the effect of a U.S. guarantee for another country's debt (for example, Brazil) would be on the U.S. budget deficit if that country does not default.

10. Many people associate high budget deficits with high real interest rates and rising prices. Taxes in the United States are primarily linked to income. Throughout this problem assume that $T = tY$; where t is the net tax rate.

a. Use *IS–LM* and *AS–AD* graphs to illustrate and explain whether this association (that is, high budget deficits with high real interest rates and rising prices) is true in the short run if the deficits are primarily due to expansionary fiscal policies (like increases in government purchases).

b. Use *IS–LM* and *AS–AD* graphs to illustrate and explain whether this association is true in the short run if there is a sudden decline in consumer or business confidence.

Data Questions

Locate the necessary economic data and apply them to answer the following data questions. All of the relevant data may be found in the Economic Report of the President (http://www.gpoaccess.gov/eop/).

1. a. Complete Table 19-3 (the data in Columns 2–5 should be in billions of current dollars).

Table 19-3

(1) Fiscal Year	(2) Total Federal Government Receipts	(3) Total Federal Government Outlays	(4) Official Federal Budget Surplus	(5) Gross Federal Debt Held by the Public (end of year)
2006	_____	_____	_____	_____
2007	_____	_____	_____	_____
2008	_____	_____	_____	_____
2009	_____	_____	_____	_____
2010	_____	_____	_____	_____

b. Now complete Columns 2–4 of Table 19-4, noting the difference between Column 4 in Table 19-4 and Column 5 in Table 19-3.

Table 19-4

(1) Calendar Year	(2) Price Deflator for GDP (2005 = 100)	(3) Percentage Change	(4) Gross Federal Debt Held by Public (end of *preceding* fiscal year) ($ in billions)	(5) Approximate "True" Federal Budget Surplus ($ in billions)
2007	_____		_____	_____
		_____		
2008	_____		_____	_____
		_____		
2009	_____		_____	_____
		_____		
2010	_____		_____	_____
		_____		
2011	_____			

c. As the textbook states, many economists believe that one should adjust the official budget deficit or surplus to account for the reduction in the real value of government debt that results from inflation. Calculate the approximate "true" budget surplus in Column 5 by multiplying the inflation rate for each calendar year (expressed as a decimal) by the amount of outstanding federal debt held by the public at the end of the preceding fiscal year and adding this amount to the official (negative or positive) budget surplus for the current year, which is given in Column 4 of Table 19-3. For example, multiply the inflation rate for 2007–2008 by the debt held at the end of fiscal year 2006 (that is, September 30, 2006) and add this to the official budget surplus for 2007 to approximate the "true" surplus for fiscal year 2007.

2. a. Use the data in Table 19-1 in Chapter 19 of the textbook to complete Column 2 in Table 19-5

Table 19-5

(1) Country	(2) Ratio of Net Federal Debt in 2011 to GDP (%)	(3) Standard and Poor's "Local Currency" Bond Rating
Greece	_____	_____
Japan	_____	_____
Italy	_____	_____
United States	_____	_____
Germany	_____	_____
Spain	_____	_____
Switzerland	_____	_____

b. Go to the Web site at http://www.standardandpoors.com/ratings/sovereigns/ratings-list/en/us/?subSectorCode=39
Find the current "local currency" bond rating for each of the countries in Column 1, and complete Column 3.

c. What is the pattern you observe between a country's net debt/GDP ratio in 2011 and its current bond rating?

d. Go to the Web site at http://www.standardandpoors.com/ratings/definitions-and-faqs/en/us and read what the letter ratings mean. What do you think is the relationship between a country's debt rating and the real interest rate it must pay on its bonds?

Questions to Think About

1. Would your own spending change in response to a tax cut that was not linked to current or future changes in government spending? Explain.

2. Why does the government have to pay off its debt at some point in the future? Can debt continue to grow at any rate indefinitely? Examine two cases, one in which the real interest rate on government debt exceeds the economy's long-run rate of growth of real output, and a second in which the economy's long-run growth rate exceeds the real interest rate.

3. Under what circumstances do you think indexed bonds would be especially attractive?

CHAPTER 20

The Financial System: Opportunities and Dangers

Fill-in Questions

Use the key terms below to fill in the blanks in the following statements. Each term may be used more than once.

adverse selection	idiosyncratic risk
asymmetric information	lender of last resort
bond	leverage
debt finance	liquidity crisis
diversification	moral hazard
equity finance	mutual funds
financial crisis	risk averse
financial intermediary	shadow banks
financial markets	speculative bubble
financial system	stocks
fire sale	systematic risk

1. When an institution facilitates the flow of funds between savers and investors, it is acting as a _____. All such institutions, taken together, are parts of an economy's _____.

2. A _____ represents a loan from an individual or institution to a firm or government. It does not represent ownership in the firm. On the other hand, people who buy _____ do become part owners of the firm. The markets for these two assets are two of an economy's many _____.

3. Raising investment funds by issuing new bonds is called _____, while raising investment funds by issuing new stock is called _____.

4. People who would pay to avoid risk are called _____.

5. One way to avoid unnecessary risk is to own assets whose financial returns do not move together. This is called _____.

6. Financial intermediaries that sell shares to savers and use their funds to buy diversified pools of assets are called _____.

7. There are two kinds of risk. The risk that can be reduced by diversification is called _____; the risk that cannot be reduced by diversification is called _____.

8. The situation in which one party to an economic transaction knows more information about the transaction than the other is called _____.

9. The situation in which some people have more information to sort themselves in a way that disadvantages people with less information is an example of _____.

10. The risk that an imperfectly monitored agent will act in a dishonest or otherwise inappropriate manner is called _____.

11. A _____ occurs when there is a major disruption in the financial system that impedes the proper functioning of financial intermediaries.

12. One of the causes of the financial crisis of 2008–2009 was the sharp increase in the prices of houses, which turned out to be a _____.

13. The use of borrowed funds for the purposes of investment is called _____.

14. During a financial crisis, people may be forced to sell assets at prices far below normal because investors are afraid to take risks. This phenomenon is called a _____.

15. When a solvent bank has insufficient funds to pay its depositors' withdrawals, it is facing a _____.

16. When a central bank lends to a bank in the middle of a liquidity crisis, it is acting as a _____.

17. Financial institutions that serve functions similar to banks but are not technically banks are called _____.

Multiple-Choice Questions

1. When banks take deposits from savers and use these deposits to make loans to firms that have investment projects, they are acting as:
    a. mutual funds.
    b. financial intermediaries.
    c. lenders of last resort.
    d. insurance companies.

2.   Which of the following is NOT a financial intermediary?

   a. banks
   b. mutual funds
   c. credit card companies
   d. insurance companies

3.   Asset diversification can reduce:

   a. idiosyncratic risk.
   b. systematic risk.
   c. leverage.
   d. All of the answers are true.

4.   People with serious illnesses are more likely to want to buy life insurance. This is an example of:

   a. asset diversification.
   b. adverse selection.
   c. moral hazard.
   d. idiosyncratic risk.

5.   During the credit boom of 2004–2007 banks may have taken excessive risks because they expected that the government would bail them out, if necessary. This is an example of:

   a. asset diversification.
   b. adverse selection.
   c. moral hazard.
   d. systematic risk.

6.   Which of the following is a type of asymmetric information?

   a. hidden knowledge about attributes
   b. hidden knowledge about actions
   c. Both a and b are correct.
   d. Neither a nor b are correct.

7.   Banks can reduce the problem of moral hazard by:

   a. monitoring their borrowers after loans are made.
   b. including restrictions about how their loans can be spent.
   c. increasing the penalties on those who cannot repay their loans.
   d. All of the answers are correct.

8.   The leverage ratio is the ratio of:

   a. bank assets to bank capital.
   b. bank loans to bank capital.
   c. bank deposits to bank loans.
   d. bank loans to bank reserves.

9. The TED spread is the difference between the interest rates on:

    a. three-month Treasury bills and 10-year Treasury bonds.

    b. three-month interbank loans and three-month Treasury bills.

    c. 10-year bank loans and 10-year Treasury bonds.

    d. commercial loans and residential mortgage loans.

10. A sharp increase in the TED spread is an indication that:

    a. banks believe that it is unsafe to lend to homeowners.

    b. banks believe it is unsafe to lend to other banks.

    c. investors believe that interest rates will increase in the future.

    d. investors believe it is unsafe to buy stocks.

11. The people and institutions responsible for the financial crisis of 2008–2009 include:

    a. the Federal Reserve.

    b. home-buyers.

    c. mortgage brokers and investment banks.

    d. All of the answers are correct.

12. An institution responsible for the financial crisis of 2008–2009 was:

    a. the bond-rating agencies.

    b. regulators of banks and other financial institutions.

    c. government policymakers.

    d. All of the answers are correct.

13. The financial crisis of 2008–2009 was caused by:

    a. a speculative bubble in housing.

    b. insolvencies at financial institutions.

    c. declining confidence in the economy and financial institutions.

    d. All of the answers are correct.

14. During the financial crisis of 2008–2009 which of the following expansionary policies were implemented?

    a. The Federal Reserve reduced the federal funds rate.

    b. The federal government cut taxes.

    c. The federal government increased government spending.

    d. All of the answers are correct.

15. Which of the following institutions is the lender of last resort in the U.S. economy?

    a. the federal government

    b. the Bank of America

    c. the Federal Reserve

    d. the Money Store

16. CoCo bonds are bonds that:

    a. are issued by the Nestle Corporation.

    b. are converted to equity when the issuers have insufficient capital.

    c. are indexed to inflation.

    d. All of the answers are correct.

17. Which of the following has been proposed as a way to limit the size of financial firms?

    a. Restrict mergers among banks.

    b. Require higher capital requirements for larger banks.

    c. Both a and b are correct.

    d. Neither a nor b is correct.

18. Under the Volcker Rule:

    a. commercial banks are restricted from making certain speculative investments.

    b. larger banks have higher capital requirements.

    c. commercial banks are broken up if their assets exceed $250 billion.

    d. larger banks pay higher premiums to the Federal Deposit Insurance Corporation.

Exercises

1. **The Advantage of Diversification** *In this exercise, we use a simple mathematical example to illustrate how asset diversification can reduce risk.*

    a. The idea behind diversification is the same as elsewhere in life. *Don't put all your eggs into one basket.* To illustrate how asset diversification can reduce risk, suppose you had enough money to buy only two shares of stock. You have two companies to choose from: Body Beautiful Sun-Tan Cream Corp. and Rainy Day Umbrella Corp. They have the same initial price per share, but their future price increases depend on the weather during the summer. These future price increases are depicted in Table 20-1, which is called a *payoff matrix*.

Table 20-1

| | Gain in stock price (per share) | |
	Body Beautiful Sun-Tan Cream Inc.	Rainy Day Umbrella Corp.
Actual Weather		
Sunny	+2	−1
Rainy	−1	+2

If the summer is sunny, sales of suntan lotion will soar and the price of Body Beautiful will rise by $2. If the summer is rainy, Body Beautiful's sales will fall and the stock price will fall by $1.

The opposite is true of the stock price for Rainy Day Umbrella Company. If the summer is sunny, sales of umbrellas will slump and the price of Rainy Day will fall by $____. If, on the other hand, the summer is rainy, umbrella sales will sky-rocket and the stock price will rise by $____.

In parts b–e, suppose the probability of having a sunny summer is ½, and the probability of a rainy summer is also ½.

b. If you buy 2 shares of Body Beautiful, half the time you will gain 2 × $2 = $____ and half the time you will lose 2 × $1 = $____, which can also be expressed as a gain of 2 × (–$1) = ____. In statistics we say the *expected gain* is ½ (4) + ½ (–$2) = $____, which is the average amount you can expect to earn per year over the course of many summers.

c. Alternatively, suppose you buy 2 shares of Rainy Day. Recall that the payoffs are reversed for Rainy Day. If the summer is sunny, umbrella sales fall and the stock will fall by $1, but if the summer is rainy, the stock price will rise by $2. If you buy 2 shares of Rainy Day, half the time you will gain 2 × $2 = $____ and half the time you will lose 2 × $1 = $____, which is also a gain of 2 × (–$1) = ____. The expected yearly gain is ½ (____) + ½ (____) = $____, the same as your expected gain if you purchased two shares of Body Beautiful. In both cases, however, the gains can vary from year to year, and for several years you might receive above-average or below-average gains.

d. By diversifying you can reduce your risk. Suppose you buy 1 share of each company. If the summer is sunny, you will gain 1 × $2 = $2 on your Body Beautiful stock and lose 1 × $1 = $1 on your Rainy Day stock for a net gain of $____ . If, on the other hand, it is rainy, you make 1 × $2 = $2 on your Rainy Day stock and lose 1 × $1= $1 on your Body Beautiful stock for a net gain of $____.

e. Thus, by diversifying your purchases of stocks and buying companies whose profits move in opposite directions but still make money on average, you can increase/decrease your risk (and, in this example, eliminate your risk entirely) and get the same expected return.

Problems

Answer the following problems on a separate sheet of paper.

1. a. What does the Federal Deposit Insurance Corporation (FDIC) do?

   b. Describe in your own words what the problem of moral hazard is and how it applies to bank depositors and the FDIC?

   c. Only bank deposits less than $250,000 are insured by the FDIC. Why are savers with more than $250,000 of deposits in a bank treated differently? How might this different treatment mitigate the problem of moral hazard?

   d. In order to eliminate this problem of moral hazard, why don't we just abolish the FDIC?

2. People with serious illnesses are more likely to want life insurance to protect their families.

   a. How does this create a problem of adverse selection?

   b. What do life insurance companies do to mitigate this problem?

3. **a.** Why don't conventional for-profit banks make micro-loans?

   b. As noted in Chapter 20 of the textbook, microfinance clients have surprisingly high loan repayment rates. Some observers suggest that repayment is high because villagers put pressure on neighbors who have taken a microfinance loan to repay the loan. Why might it be in the villagers' economic interest to do so?

   c. How do these villagers' actions mitigate the problem of moral hazard?

4. Just before Lehman Brothers went bankrupt, it was rumored to have an effective leverage ratio of 50.

   a. What does this mean? Define each of the terms in your answer. (You might find it helpful to reread the section on leverage in Chapter 4 of the textbook.)

   b. Suppose a bank had loans and other assets worth $100 and liabilities worth $98. Calculate the value of its bank capital and its leverage ratio.

   c. Now suppose the value of its loans fell by 2 percent. Calculate the new values of its assets and bank capital. Obviously, a small change in the value of highly-leveraged institutions can result in insolvency.

5. **a.** Why are some banks considered "too big to fail"?

   b. If a bank is considered "too big to fail," how does this create a problem of moral hazard?

   c. Banks borrow from each other and also from the public (by issuing bonds). If a bank is considered too big to fail, what will happen to the interest rate it pays on its bonds and other loans? How does this affect smaller banks? Explain.

Questions to Think About

1. At what specific times in your life have you experienced or observed a situation involving adverse selection? At what times have you been involved with moral hazard?

2.   Chapter 20 of the textbook suggests that all of the following groups bear some responsibility for the financial crisis of 2008–2009: the Federal Reserve, home-buyers, mortgage brokers, investment banks, rating agencies, regulators, and government policymakers.

   a.   On which groups do Republicans tend to place most of the blame? Why?

   b.   On which groups do Democrats tend to place most of the blame? Why?

3.   By the time you read this book, the financial crisis in Greece may have been resolved. Has it been? If it has, how was it resolved and how well has the resolution worked?

Answers

CHAPTER 1

Fill-in Questions

1. Macroeconomics; Microeconomics
2. Real GDP; recession; depression
3. unemployment
4. inflation
5. models
6. exogenous; endogenous
7. price flexibility; price stickiness
8. market-clearing

Multiple-Choice Questions

1. b   2. d   3. d   4. b   5. d   6. c

Exercises

1. **a.** 20 percent   **b.** 325 percent   **c.** −20 percent
2. **a.** $Y = 3.5$; $Y = 4.0$; $Y = 4.5$
   b. Graph 1-1

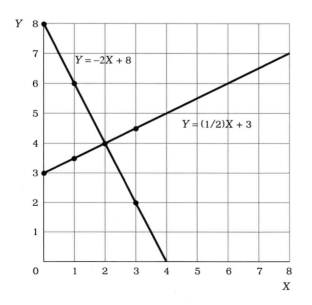

    c. Slope = 1/2, or 0.5. Every time the value of X increases by 1 unit, the value of Y increases by 1/2.

    d. Y intercept = 3. When X = 0, Y = 3.

    e. Y = 6; Y = 4; Y = 2

    f. See Graph 1-1.

    g. Slope = −2; Y intercept = 8

    h. X = 2 and Y = 4

    i. By definition, the point of intersection must lie on both lines. This means that the values of X and Y at this point must satisfy both equations, that is, Y = (1/2)X + 3, and Y = −2X + 8. Consequently, at the intersection (1/2)X + 3 = −2X + 8.

3.   **a.** 8; 9; 5

    b. 1/8; 1/3; 1/1,000

    c. 5^5 = 3,125 = 25 × 125; 6^2 = 36 = 216 × 1/6; 4^1 = 4 = 2 × 2

Problems

1.   **a.** In a controlled experiment, researchers observe changes in two or more samples in which the only conditions that are different in the two samples are the variables whose effects are being tested. All other variables are held constant.

    b. In experiments that are not controlled, it is often difficult to attribute any differences in the results from the two (or more) samples to the differences in the variables that were purposefully changed because other influencing variables may have also changed.

    c. It is extremely difficult to hold constant all of the macroeconomic variables we would ideally like to hold constant. Even if it could be done, it would be very expensive and often politically impossible.

2.   **a.** Graph for Problem 2a.

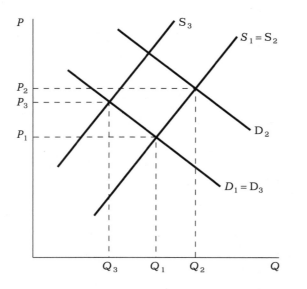

b. The demand curve for coal shifts to the right to D_2, and the supply curve does not shift. The equilibrium price of coal rises, and the equilibrium quantity of coal also rises.

c. The supply curve of coal shifts to the left to S_3, and the demand curve does not shift. The equilibrium price of coal rises and the equilibrium quantity of coal falls.

CHAPTER 2

Fill-in Questions

1. Nominal gross domestic product; Real gross domestic product
2. unemployment rate; labor force
3. value-added
4. consumer price index; Laspeyres
5. GDP deflator; nominal gross domestic product; real gross domestic product; Paasche
6. stock; flow
7. Depreciation
8. labor-force participation rate
9. disposable personal income
10. imputed value
11. Nominal gross national product; Nominal gross domestic product
12. national income accounts identity; consumption; investment; government purchases; net exports
13. Core inflation

Multiple-Choice Questions

1. c   2. b   3. c   4. c   5. c   6. c   7. a   8. d   9. b   10. b
11. a   12. c   13. c   14. a   15. d   16. d   17. c   18. d   19. b   20. d

Exercises

1. **a.** intermediate; intermediate; final; final
   b. $1,500 million

   c. **Table 2-1**

	Value-Added per Unit	Number of Units	Company Value-Added
Intel	$200	1 million	$200 million
Princeton Graphics	$300	1 million	$300 million
IBM	$700	1 million	$700 million
Anheuser-Busch	$1.50	200 million	$300 million
Total			$1,500 million

2.   **a.** Nominal GDP in 2002 = $15 billion; nominal GDP in 2012 = $40 billion
     b. $15 billion
     c. $48 billion
     d. 220 percent
     e. Real GDP in 2002 using 2012 as base year = $21 billion; real GDP in 2012 using 2012 as base year = $40 billion.
     f. 90.5 percent
     g. In 2002, computers were expensive relative to automobiles. Consequently, when 2002 is used as the base year, the dramatic increase in the quantity of computers produced between 2002 and 2012 is multiplied by a big price ($6,000), resulting in a large increase in real GDP. In 2012, however, computers were cheap relative to automobiles. Consequently, when 2012 is used as the base year, the large change in the quantity of computers produced in the period is multiplied by a relatively low price ($2,000), resulting in a much smaller increase in real GDP.

3.   **a.** $48 billion
     b. $15 billion
     c. 220%; 3.20
     d. 90.5%
     e. 1.905
     f. 2.47; 147%

4.   **a.** 140
     b. 83.3
     c. $40 billion; 0.833; $48 billion
     d. Percentage change in CPI (2002 = 100) = 40 percent; percentage change in GDP deflator (2002 = 100) = −16.7 percent.
     e. In 2002, computers comprised a small portion of the consumer market basket. Therefore, in a Laspeyres index like the CPI, the dramatic reduction in the price of computers will be outweighed by the increase in the price of automobiles. For a Paasche index like the GDP deflator, however, the weight given to computers is much greater because they comprise a much larger portion of the GDP in 2012 than in 2002. Consequently, in this index the reduction in computer prices will outweigh the increase in automobile prices.

5.   **a.** and **b.**

Table 2-4

(1) Period	(2) Nominal GDP (PY)	(3) % Change in PY	(4) P	(5) % Change in P	(6) Y	(7) % Change in Y
1	100		1.00		100	
		5		2		3
2			1.02		103	

c. 2; 3; 5

d. 1.02; 103; 105.06; 105.06; 5.06

e. 2

f. minus; 3

6. **a.** **Table 2-5**

(1) Event	(2) Included in U.S. GNP	(3) Included in U.S. GDP
1. Lady Gaga performs a rock concert in New York	Yes	Yes
2. Lady Gaga performs a rock concert in London	Yes	No
3. The Rolling Stones perform a rock concert in New York	No	Yes
4. The Rolling Stones perform a rock concert in London	No	No
5. Toyota earns profits from its car factory in California	No	Yes
6. Ford earns profits from its car factory in Germany	Yes	No

7. **a.** **Graph 2-1**

b. **Graph 2-2**

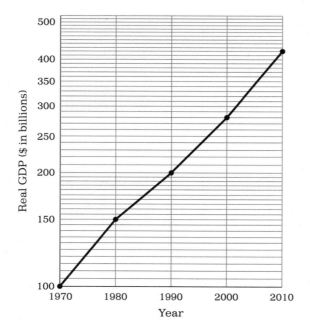

Problems

1. **a.** $13,389.4 billion
   b. $13,005.3 billion (Some additional items were included in related categories)
   c. $11,605.0

2. Prices are a better measure than weight of the (marginal) value that consumers place on various goods and services.

3. Education may be viewed as an investment because part of its value lies in its ability to increase a student's future production, just like a new piece of equipment. Economists sometimes refer to education as an investment in human capital.

4. There are at least two reasons why the ratios in GDP per capita may overstate the true differences in standards of living between the United States, on the one hand, and Bangladesh, Ethiopia, and Burundi, on the other. First, many researchers think that nonmarketed household production, which is usually not included in the official GDP statistics, may be larger relative to measured GDP in these three countries than in the United States. Second, the official GDP per capita measures generally use the market exchange rates to convert different currencies. These exchange rates are usually determined by the flows of tradable goods, services, and assets among countries. If the relative prices of nontradable and tradable goods and services are not the same in all countries, this conversion will not accurately reflect differences in standards of living. Very few people, however, would deny that the standard of living in the United States is many times that in Bangladesh, Ethiopia, and Burundi.

5. **a.** Yes. It represents consumption.

    b. No. The purchase of a used computer from a friend does not increase GDP.

    c. No. Although many people think of stock purchases as investment, this is not true in the national income accounts.

    d. Yes. It represents investment.

    e. Yes. It represents investment.

    f. No. Your grandmother's Social Security check is a transfer payment.

    g. Yes. It represents a government purchase of a good.

6. Investment rises by $300,000; consumption rises by $12,000.

7. **a.** U.S. GNP falls.

    b. U.S. GDP remains unchanged.

8. **a.** $220,000

    b. $250,000

    c. 88

CHAPTER 3

Fill-in Questions

1. Factors of production
2. Factor prices
3. marginal product of labor; marginal product of capital
4. production function
5. constant returns to scale
6. competition; marginal product of labor; real rental price of capital
7. real wage
8. Accounting profit
9. Euler's theorem; economic profit
10. Cobb–Douglas production function
11. diminishing marginal productivity
12. consumption function; marginal propensity to consume; disposable income
13. nominal interest rate; real interest rate
14. national saving
15. private saving
16. public saving; crowding out
17. loanable funds; loanable funds; loanable funds

Multiple-Choice Questions

1. c	2. d	3. b	4. c	5. a	6. a	7. a
8. b	9. b	10. a	11. c	12. d	13. d	14. a
15. c	16. d	17. c	18. b	19. b	20. c	21. c

Exercises

1. a.   **Graph 3-1**

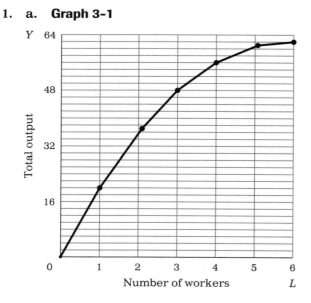

The positive slope indicates that as the number of workers employed increases, total output increases. The decreasing slope indicates that as more workers are hired, each additional worker adds less to total output.

b.   **Table 3-1**

(1) No. of Workers (L)	(2) No. of Loaves Baked per Hour	(3) Marginal Product of Labor (MPL)	(4) Price per Loaf	(5) Price per Loaf × MPL	(6) Nominal Wage Rate (W)	(7) Real Wage Rate (W/P)
0	0				$8	8
		20	$1	$20		
1	20				$8	8
		16	$1	$16		
2	36				$8	8
		12	$1	$12		
3	48				$8	8
		8	$1	$8		
4	56				$8	8
		4	$1	$4		
5	60				$8	8
		2	$1	$2		
6	62				$8	8

c. **Graph 3-2**

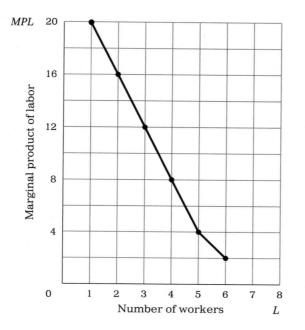

d. See Table 3-1 in Part b.

e. See Table 3-1 in Part b. The company hires four bakers.

f. **Graph 3-3**

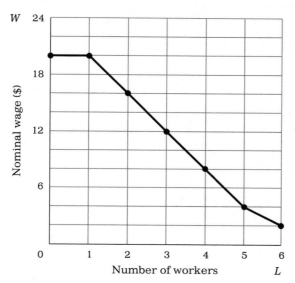

2. **a.** See Table 3-1 in the answer to Exercise 1.

b. Table 3-2

(1)	(2)	(3)	(4)	(5)	(6)	(7)
No. of Workers (L)	No. of Loaves Baked per Hour	Marginal Product of Labor (MPL)	Price per Loaf	Price per Loaf × MPL	Nominal Wage Rate (W)	Real Wage Rate (W/P)
0	0				$16	8
		20	$2	$40		
1	20				$16	8
		16	$2	$32		
2	36				$16	8
		12	$2	$24		
3	48				$16	8
		8	$2	$16		
4	56				$16	8
		4	$2	$8		
5	60				$16	8
		2	$2	$4		
6	62				$16	8

c. Four

d. $32; right

Graph 3-4

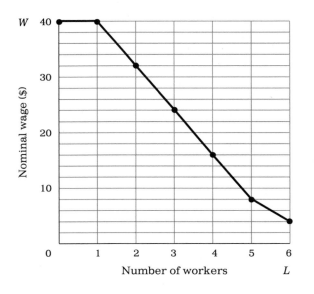

e. **Table 3-3**

(1) Nominal Wage (W)	(2) Price of Bread (P)	(3) Real Wage (W/P)	(4) Number of Bakers Hired
$20	$1	20	1
$40	$2	20	1
$16	$1	16	2
$32	$2	16	2
$12	$1	12	3
$24	$2	12	3
$ 8	$1	8	4
$16	$2	8	4
$ 4	$1	4	5
$ 8	$2	4	5

Graph 3-5

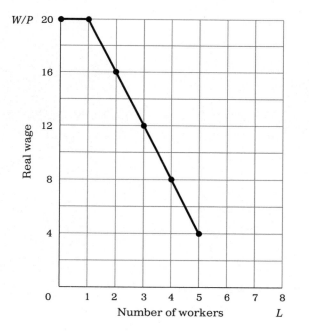

3. **a.** $Y = 50$

    b. Constant returns to scale refers to a production function in which an x percentage change in all inputs leads to the same x percentage change in output.

    Table 3-4

K	L	$Y = K^{1/2}L^{1/2}$
100	25	50
200	50	100
2,500	625	1,250

    doubled; increased 25-fold

    c. $MPL = 1$; equilibrium real wage = 1

    d. $MPK = 0.25$; equilibrium real rental price of capital = 0.25

    e. Step 1: 50

    Step 2: 1; 25

    Step 3: 1/2

    Step 4: 0.25; 25

    Step 5: 1/2

    Step 7: When $K = 100$ and $L = 625$, $Y = 250$, $MPL = W/P = 0.2$, $MPK = R/P = 1.25$, factor payments to labor = 0.2(625) = 125, factor payments to capital = 1.25(100) = 125, labor's share = capital's share = 1/2.

    f. $25 + 25 = 50$

4. **a.** **Table 3-5**

(1) Disposable Income $(Y - T)$	(2) Consumption (C)
$ 0	125
100	200
200	275
500	500
800	725
1,000	875

b. **Graph 3-6**

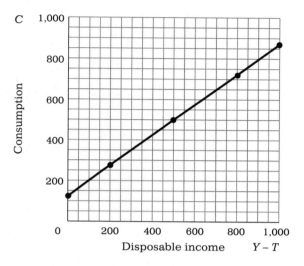

c. 125

d. 0.75; The slope is equal to the marginal propensity to consume here because it measures the change in consumption resulting from a $1 increase in disposable income.

5. a. 100; 50; −50

b. **Table 3-6**

(1) Net Taxes (T)	(2) Government Purchases (G)	(3) Budget Surplus	(4) Budget Deficit
200	100	100	−100
200	200	0	0
100	200	−100	100
−100	100	−200	200

6. **a.** 950

 b. 100; 100; $r = 10$

 c. **Graph 3-7**

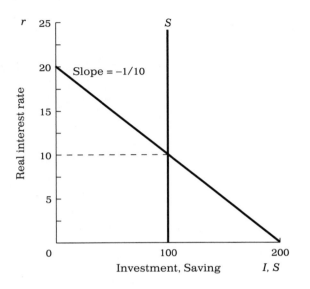

 d. public saving = –50; private saving = 150; national saving = 100

7. **a.** fall; 50; 50; left; 50

 Graph 3-8

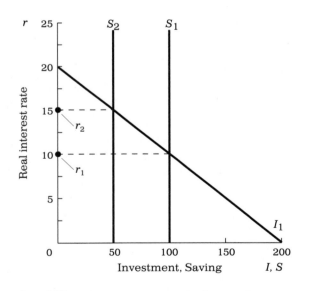

 b. fall; 50; 50; movement along; rise; $r = 15$

 c. decrease; increase; decrease

 d. increase; 965; decrease; 85; left; 15; fall; 15; 85; movement along; rise

e. right

Graph 3-9

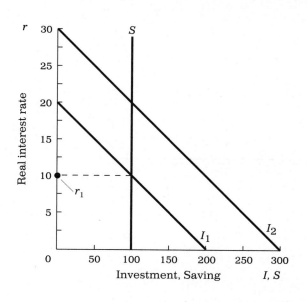

remain constant; not shift; rise; 100

f. positive; right; increase

Graph 3-10

8. **a.** decrease; left
    Graph 3-11

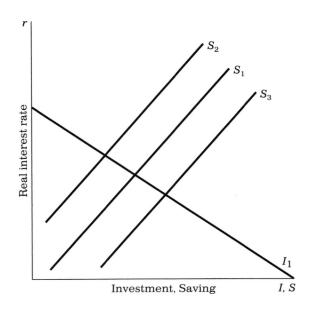

rise; fall; negative

b. increase; right; see Graph 3-11; fall; rise; negative

c. right; increase; left; decrease; positive

d. negative; positive

Problems

1.   Graphs for Problem 1

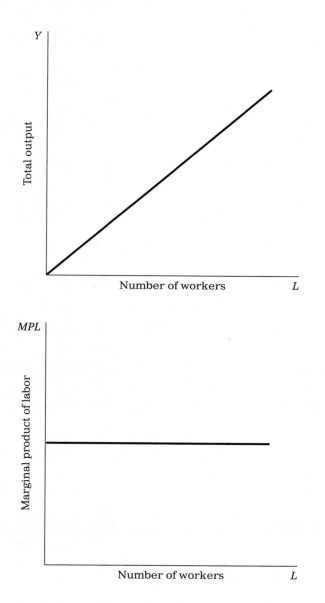

2.   **a.** The profit-maximizing rule sets the real wage equal to the marginal product of labor. The average products of labor in California and Florida could be very different even if the marginal products of labor were equal.

b. Once again, the average products of labor in California and Florida could be very different even if the marginal products of labor were equal. If all groves are maximizing profits, then the *MPL* is the same in all groves. Thus, the movement of a worker from Florida to California would reduce output in Florida by the same amount that output increased in California, resulting in no change in total orange production.

3.　a.　$Y = 960$; $Y = 1{,}920$; $Y = 2{,}880$. When all of the inputs were doubled, output doubled. When all of the inputs were tripled, output tripled. Consequently, these results illustrate the property of constant returns to scale.

　　b.　$MPL = 40K^{1/3}L^{-1/3} = 40(K/L)^{1/3}$

　　c.　$MPL = 80$; $W/P = 80$

　　d.　$MPK = 20K^{-2/3}L^{2/3} = 20(L/K)^{2/3}$

　　e.　$MPK = 5$; $R/P = 5$

　　f.　total real labor payments $= 640$;

　　　　total real payments to capital $= 320$;

　　　　labor's share $= 640/960 = 2/3$;

　　　　capital's share $= 320/960 = 1/3$.

　　g.　Since $W/P = MPL$ and $R/P = MPK$, $(W/P)L = (MPL)L$ and $(R/P)K = (MPK)K$.

　　　　$(MPL)L = 40(K/L)^{1/3}L = 40(K^{1/3}L^{2/3}) = (2/3)Y$.

　　　　$(MPK)K = 20(L/K)^{2/3}K = 20(K^{1/3}L^{2/3}) = (1/3)Y$.

　　h.　$(W/P)L + (R/P)K = (MPL)L + (MPK)K = 40(K/L)^{1/3}L + 20(L/K)^{2/3}K =$

　　　　$40(K^{1/3}L^{2/3}) + 20(K^{1/3}L^{2/3}) = 60K^{1/3}L^{2/3} = Y$.

4.　a.　The deficit would fall.

　　b.　Disposable income would fall by the full amount of the tax increase. Since consumption would fall by only a fraction (MPC) of this amount, private saving would also decrease. Public saving would increase by the amount of the tax increase plus the reduction in government spending. Consequently, national saving would increase.

　　c.　S would shift right to S_2. I would not shift. Consequently, the real interest rate would fall and investment would rise.

　　　　Graph for Problem 4c

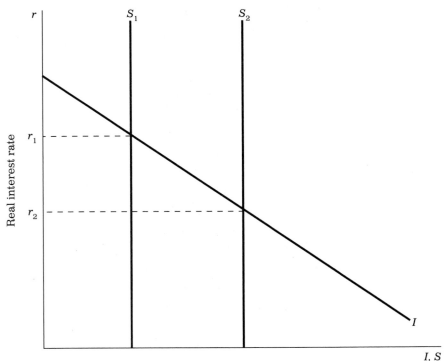

Investment, Saving

5. **a.** Real GDP will be unaffected because it depends on K and L, which are assumed to be relatively unaffected.

   b. Social Security benefits are transfer payments. Recall that net taxes T = gross taxes – transfer payments. Thus, if transfer payments fall by $100 billion, net taxes T will rise by $100 billion. Public saving T – G will also rise by $100 billion.

   c. Private Saving = (Y – T) – C. If Y is unchanged and T rises by $100 billion, disposable income will fall by $100 billion. Consumption will fall by MPC × $100 billion = $75 billion and private saving will fall by $25 billion.

   d. National saving, which is equal to public plus private saving, will rise by $100 billion – $25 billion = $75 billion.

   e. Since national saving is equal to investment, investment would rise by $75 billion.

   f. The increase in national saving will shift the Saving curve to the right. This will reduce the real interest rate and increase the amount of investment. Graph for Problem 5f

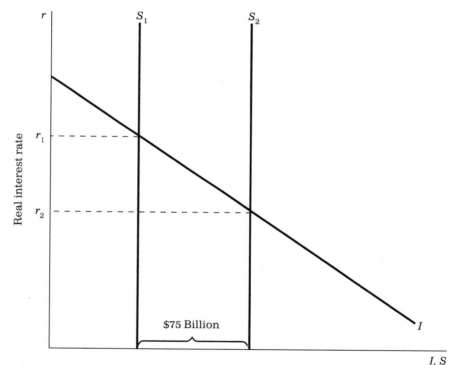

6. **a.** If both taxes and government purchases were reduced by equal amounts, the government budget surplus $T - G$, and hence public saving, would remain unchanged (at a negative value). The reduction in net taxes, however, would increase the amount of disposable income, $Y - T$, at the full employment level of GDP, $\overline{Y}$, by the full amount of the tax cut. Consequently, the level of consumption would increase at $\overline{Y}$ by $MPC \times (\Delta T)$, since consumption rises with disposable income. Since $MPC < 1$, some of the additional disposable income will go toward increasing private saving. Alternatively, note

that $S_{PR} = (Y - T) - C$. Disposable income at $\overline{Y}$ rises by the full amount of the tax decrease while consumption rises by only a fraction of the increase. Thus, the level of private saving would increase at $\overline{Y}$, along with the level of national saving S. This shifts the S curve to the right below. As a result, the equilibrium level of the real interest rate would fall and investment would rise.

6. Graph for Problem 6b

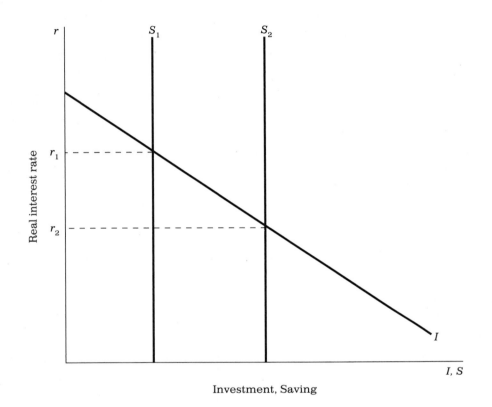

Investment, Saving

c. The increases in consumption and private saving at $\overline{Y}$ following an equal reduction in taxes and government purchases depend on the value of the marginal propensity to consume. The increase in disposable income at $\overline{Y}$ will equal the full amount of the tax reduction regardless of the value of *MPC*. If the *MPC* is large, that is, close to 1.0, the increase in consumption will be large, and the increases in private and national saving will be small. Consequently, the saving curve will shift only slightly to the right, the decline in the real interest rate will be small, and investment will rise by only a small amount. If, on the other hand, the *MPC* is small, the increase in consumption will be smaller and the increase in private saving will be larger. This will result in a large increase in national saving, a big shift to the right in the saving curve, a large decline in the real interest rate, and a big increase in investment.

7. **a.** The government surplus fell by the increase in government spending plus the reduction in taxes.

   b. Disposable income rose by the full amount of the tax reduction. Consumption rose by MPC times the reduction in taxes, and private saving rose by (1 − MPC) times the reduction in taxes. Public saving fell by the increase in government spending plus the reduction in taxes. Consequently, national saving fell by the increase in government spending plus MPC times the reduction in taxes.

   c. S shifts left to S_2. I does not shift. Consequently, the real interest rate rises and investment falls.
   Graph for Problem 7c

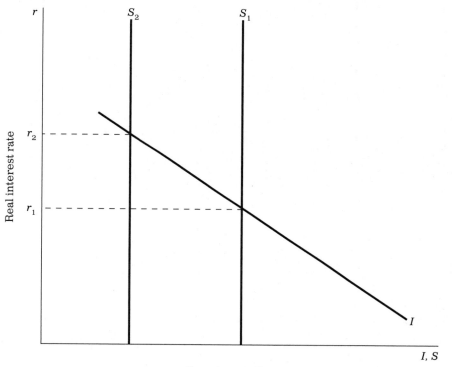

8. The increase in saving would shift the S curve right. The real interest rate would fall, and the amount of investment would rise.

Graph for Problem 8

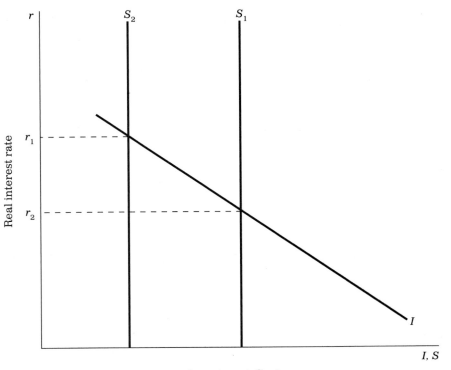

Investment, Saving

CHAPTER 4

Fill-in Questions

1. Money; store of value; unit of account; medium of exchange (last three terms in any order)
2. double coincidence of wants
3. fiat money
4. commodity money; gold standard
5. money supply; central bank; Federal Reserve
6. monetary policy; Federal Reserve or central bank; open-market operation
7. $M1$; currency; demand deposits; $M2$
8. balance sheet
9. reserves; 100-percent-reserve banking
10. fractional-reserve banking
11. reserve–deposit ratio; currency–deposit ratio
12. financial intermediation
13. bank capital
14. leverage

15. capital requirement
16. monetary base; high-powered money
17. money multiplier; currency–deposit ratio; currency–deposit ratio; reserve–deposit ratio
18. open-market operation; reserve requirements; discount rate
19. excess reserves
20. quantitative easing; interest on reserves

Multiple-Choice Questions

1. d	2. c	3. d	4. b	5. c	6. a	7. d
8. c	9. b	10. c	11. c	12. a	13. d	14. d
15. c	16. b	17. d	18. a	19. c	20. d	21. b
22. b	23. d	14. c				

Exercises

1. a. 1,000; 3,000; 25; reserve requirements
    b. 10; Reserves = $260 million; Deposits = $1,010 million; Loans = $750 million
    c. 25; 25; 10; 7.5; Reserves = $252.5 million; Deposits = $1,010 million; Loans = $757.5 million
    d. 7.5; 7.5; Reserves = $257.5 million; Deposits = $1,007.5 million; Loans = $750 million
    e. 25; 25; 7.5; 5.625; Reserves = $251.875 million; Deposits = $1,007.5 million; Loans = $755.625 million
    f. 5.625; 5.625; Reserves = $255.625 million; Deposits = $1,005.625 million; Loans = $750 million
    g. 3,023.125; 1,000; 3,000; 23.125
    h. 0.25; 40
    i. 10; exactly; more than
2. a. 500; 480; 20
    b. 20; 500; 4
    c. 500; 20; 25
    d. 490; 480; 10; 5; 50
    e. 480; 480; 0
    f. 20; 500; 4; were; 10; 490; 2.04; were not
3. a. deposits; reserves
    b. 3; 2; 1.6; 1; 1; 5
    c. decrease; decrease; 1.0; equal to; 1/*rr*; deposits
4. a. purchase; increase; greater than; increases; greater than; fall
    b. purchase; increase; sale; decrease
    c. increase; increase; decrease
    d. more; rise; increase; increase

Problems

1. **a.** store of value, medium of exchange, and unit of account
   b. store of value and medium of exchange
   c. store of value

2. **a.** 6
   b. 12
   c. $n/(n-1)$, where n equals the number of goods

3. **a.** $10,000; In this model $cr = 0$. Thus, the money multiplier $= 1/rr = 10$

4. The value of State Bank's capital would fall to –$10.

5. The capital ratio is calculated as Capital/Assets. If the value of bank assets were reduced to reflect more realistic market valuations, both capital and assets would fall by the same dollar amount. Since Capital is less than Assets, the capital ratio would fall.

6. The two are equal to each other.

7. **a.** $m = 2$
   b. $m = 1$; This is an example of a 100-percent-reserve banking system, in which there are no loans. Any increase in the monetary base leads to an equal increase in the money supply, either in the form of currency held by the public or deposits.

8. **a.** $dm/d(rr) = -(cr + 1)/(cr + rr)^2 < 0$
   b. $dm/d(cr) = (rr - 1)/(cr + rr)^2 < 0$ unless $rr = 1.0$

CHAPTER 5

Fill-in Questions

1. inflation
2. hyperinflation
3. quantity equation; transactions velocity of money; quantity theory
4. income velocity of money
5. real money balances
6. money demand function
7. seigniorage
8. nominal interest rate; Fisher equation; real interest rate; nominal interest rate; Fisher effect
9. *ex ante* real interest rate; *ex post* real interest rate
10. shoe-leather cost; menu cost
11. real variables; nominal variables
12. classical dichotomy; real variables; real variables; monetary neutrality

Multiple-Choice Questions

1. b	2. d	3. c	4. a	5. b	6. c	7. d
8. a	9. c	10. d	11. b	12. b	13. d	14. d
15. c						

Exercises

1. **a.** 1.6538

   b. $MV = \$9,120.8$ billion $\times 1.6538 = \$15,084$ billion

   $PY = 1.133 \times \$13,313$ billion $= \$15,084$ billion

   c. **Table 5-1**

(1) Period	(2) M	(3) % Change in M	(4) V	(5) % Change in V	(6) P	(7) % Change in P	(8) Y	(9) % Change in Y
1	100		2.0		1.0		200	
		4		1		3		2
2	104		2.02		1.03		204	

   % Change in M + % Change in V = 4 + 1 = 5

   % Change in P + % Change in Y = 3 + 2 = 5

   d. **Table 5-2**

(1) Period	(2) M	(3) % Change in M	(4) V	(5) % Change in V	(6) P	(7) % Change in P	(8) Y	(9) % Change in Y
1	100		2.0		1.0		200	
		8		− 4.8		6		− 3
2	108		1.904		1.06		194	

   % Change in M + % Change in V = 8 − 4.8 = 3.2. This is approximately equal to the % Change in P + % Change in Y = 6 − 3 = 3.

2. a. 0; 3; 3

b. and c.

Table 5-3

(1) Period	(2) M	(3) % Change in M	(4) V	(5) % Change in V	(6) P	(7) % Change in P	(8) Y	(9) % Change in Y
1	100		2.0		1.0		200	
		3		0		0		3
2	103		2.0		1.0		206	
		−5		0		−8		3
3	97.85		2.0		0.92		212.18	
		4		0		1		3
4	101.76		2.0		0.93		218.55	

d. Period 2: $P = MV/Y = 103(2)/206 = 1.0$

Period 3: $P = 97.85(2)/212.18 = 0.922$

Period 4: $P = 101.76(2)/218.55 = 0.931$

3. a. **Table 5-4**

(1) Real Interest Rate (%)	(2) Nominal Interest Rate (%)	(3) Inflation Rate (%)
6	10	4
2	10	8
−2	10	12
4	7	3
−2	12	14
3	8	5
−2	7	9

$r + \pi$

b.   3.5

Table 5-5

(1) % Change in P	(2) % Change in M	(3) Inflation Rate (%)	(4) Real Interest Rate (%)	(5) Nominal Interest Rate (%)
0	3	0	3	3
1	4	1	3	4
2	5	2	3	5
−1	2	−1	3	2
5	8	5	3	8

4. a. π; $E\pi$

b.   **Table 5-6**

(1) Nominal Interest Rate (%)	(2) Expected Inflation (%)	(3) *Ex Ante* Real Interest Rate (%)	(4) Actual Inflation (%)	(5) *Ex Post* Real Interest Rate (%)
8	3	5	3	5
8	3	5	5	3
8	3	5	1	7
2	−1	3	1	1

c.   **(i)** equal to   **(ii)** lower than; lower than; borrowers; lenders   **(iii)** higher than; higher than; lenders; borrowers

5. a.   21,000; 12,000; 9,000; 3; 3

b.   21,000; 6; 18,000; 3,000; 1; 1

6. a.   **Table 5-7**

(1) Nominal Interest Rate i	(2) $i^{-0.1}$	(3) Real Output Y	(4) Real Money Demand $(M/P)^d$
0.12 (= 12%)	1.236	100	123.6
0.08	1.287	100	128.7
0.05	1.349	100	134.9
0.03	1.420	100	142.0
0.01	1.585	100	158.5

increases

b. **Graph 5-1**

c. **Table 5-8**

(1) Nominal Interest Rate i	(2) $i^{-0.1}$	(3) Real Output Y	(4) Real Money Demand $(M/P)^d$
0.12 (= 12%)	1.236	150	185.4
0.08	1.287	150	193.1
0.05	1.349	150	202.4
0.03	1.420	150	213.0
0.01	1.585	150	237.8

d. right

e. left

7. a. 142

b. 142

c. 8; 128.7

d. 1.103; an increase

8. a. **(i)** 6 **(ii)** 9; 2

b. 6; 4; 4; 4; 0

c. increases; stays constant; 9; 6; 6; 7; −1

d. decrease

e. 3,700; 2,800; 900; 32.1; 135; 765; 27.3

f. 3,310; 3,266; loss; 44; 1.6; 135; 3,147; loss; 163; 4.9

Problems

1. 2% per year

2. 1,381 Zimbabwean dollars

3. 4

4.   **a.**   As prices rise, the real value of the dollars people hold in their wallets falls. When the government prints new money for its use, it makes the old money in the hands of the public less valuable.

      b.   It is a tax in that, solely as a result of inflation, people have to give up some real resources to maintain the same level of real money balances. It is not a tax in that people don't explicitly "pay" the government.

      c.   Holders of money pay for the inflation tax.

5.   **a.** $\ln(M) + \ln(V) = \ln(P) + \ln(Y)$.

      b. $dM/M + dV/V = dP/P + dY/Y$. Hence, for small percentage changes, % Change in M + % Change in V = % Change in P + % Change in Y.

      c.   If V is constant, % Change in $V = 0$, and for small changes, % Change in P = % Change in M – % Change in Y. Since % Change in Y in the long run is determined by population growth, technology, and other exogenous factors, changes in the money supply lead to equal percentage changes in the price level, that is, to inflation.

6.   **a.** $[d(M/P)/dY][Y/(M/P)] = 1$

      b. $[d(M/P)/di][i/(M/P)] = -0.1$

7.   **a.** $3

      b.   2.0

      c. $1/1.0 = $1; $3/2.0 = $1.50

      d.   ($1.50 – $1)/$1 = 50%

CHAPTER 6

Fill-in Questions

1. net exports
2. Net capital outflow
3. net capital outflow; net exports; trade balance
4. small open economy
5. world interest rate
6. nominal exchange rate
7. real exchange rate; nominal exchange rate
8. purchasing-power parity
9. trade surplus; trade deficit; balanced trade

Multiple-Choice Questions

1.	c	2.	a	3.	b	4.	d	5.	d	6.	d	7.	c
8.	b	9.	c	10.	d	11.	d	12.	b	13.	a	14.	c
15.	b	16.	b	17.	c	18.	c	19.	d	20.	d		

Exercises

1. a. **Table 6-1**

(1)	(2)	(3)	(4)
Group	Purchases of Goods and Services Produced in the U.S. ($ in billions)	Purchases of Goods and Services Produced Elsewhere ($ in billions)	Total Purchases ($ in billions)
U.S. households	$C^d = \$3,100$	$C^f = \$400$	$C = \$3,500$
U.S. businesses	$I^d = \$\ 600$	$I^f = \$200$	$I = \$\ 800$
U.S. governments	$G^d = \$\ 900$	$G^f = \$100$	$G = \$1,000$
Total	$\$4,600$	$\$700$	$\$5,300$

  b. 4,600
  c. imports; 700
  d. 5,300
  e. 700; $C = 3,500$; $I = 800$; $G = 1,000$; Exports = 900; Imports = 700; $Y = 5,500$
  f. 200
  g. $C^d = 3,100$; $I^d = 600$; $G^d = 900$; Exports = 900; $Y = 5,500$

2. a. surplus; positive; positive; lend; positive; greater
  b. negative; negative; borrowing

  c. **Table 6-2**

(1)	(2)	(3)	(4)	(5)	(6)	(7)	(8)	(9)	(10)
							($ in billions)		
Case	Y	C	I	G	NX	T	Private Saving	Public Saving	National Saving
1	5,000	3,000	700	1,000	300	900	1,100	−100	1,000
2	5,000	3,200	900	1,000	−100	900	900	−100	800
3	5,000	3,200	900	900	0	1,000	800	100	900

  d. 300; 300; −100; −100; 0; 0
  e. −100; 100

3. a. 950; 100; 150; 0; 0
  b. 1,100; 150; −50; 100; 0; 0

c. **Graph 6-1**

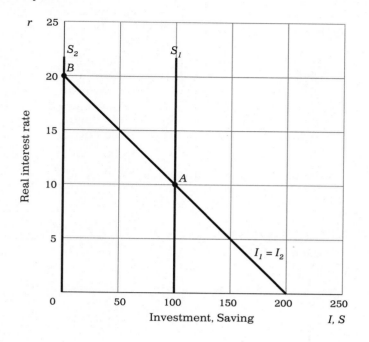

d. left; 100; not shift

e. 0; 0; 20

f. 100; −100; −100; fall; 100

g. increase; decrease; does not change; does not change; down; deficit

h. right; not shift

Graph 6-2

−50; −50

i. increase; decrease; 50; not change; 50; 50

4. **a.** **Table 6-3**

(1) Nominal Foreign Exchange Rate (euros per dollar)	(2) Price of IBM Computer in the U.S.	(3) Price of IBM Computer in Germany	(4) Price of Siemens Computer in Germany	(5) Price of Siemens Computer in the U.S
1.0	$10,000	10,000 euros	15,000 euros	$15,000
1.5	$10,000	15,000 euros	15,000 euros	$10,000
2.0	$10,000	20,000 euros	15,000 euros	$7,500

b. increases; decrease

c. remains constant; decreases; increase

d. exports; imports; decrease

e. decrease

5. **a.** **Table 6-4**

(1) Nominal Foreign Exchange Rate (euros per dollar)	(2) Price of IBM Computer in the U.S.	(3) Price of IBM Computer in Germany	(4) Price of Siemens Computer in Germany	(5) Price of Siemens Computer in the U.S.
1.5	$10,000	15,000 euros	15,000 euros	$10,000
1.5	$12,000	18,000 euros	15,000 euros	$10,000

b. equal to; greater than; decrease

c. **Table 6-5**

(1) Nominal Foreign Exchange Rate (euros per dollar)	(2) Price of IBM Computer in the U.S.	(3) Price of IBM Computer in Germany	(4) Price of Siemens Computer in Germany	(5) Price of Siemens Computer in the U.S.
1.50	$10,000	15,000 euros	15,000 euros	$10,000
1.25	$12,000	15,000 euros	15,000 euros	$12,000

20; 20; remain equal to; not change

d. 0.67; 1.0; 1.0; 1.2; 1.33

e. decrease; increase; decrease; increases; increases; decreases

6. a. decreases

b. Graph 6-3

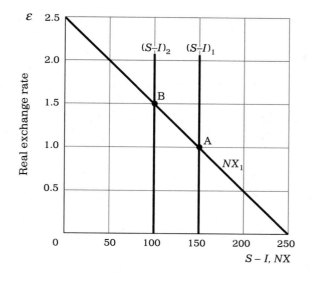

c. 150; 150; 1.0

d. decrease; 50; remains the same; decrease; 50; 100; left; 50; decrease; borrowing; decrease; 50; 100; 1.5; increase

e. Graph 6-4

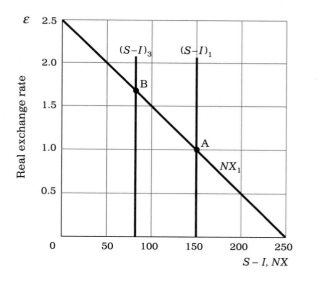

increase; decrease; increase; decrease; left; decrease; decrease; rise

7. a. % Change in $\varepsilon + \pi^* - \pi$; decrease; depreciate; increase; appreciate

b. 20; 100; 5

c. 40; 100; fall; 2.5

d. 200; increase; 10

e.   **Table 6-7**

(1) Long-Run Nominal Foreign Exchange Rate (zlotys per dollar)	(2) U.S. Price Level	(3) Polish Price Level	(4) Long-Run Real Foreign Exchange Rate
5.0	20	100	1.0
2.5	40	100	1.0
10.0	20	200	1.0

1.0; horizontal

f.   1.0; 0; $\pi^* - \pi$; all

8.   a.   more; less; more; less; fall

  b.   fewer; more; fall

9.   a.   fall; 20; 1/5

Graph 6-5

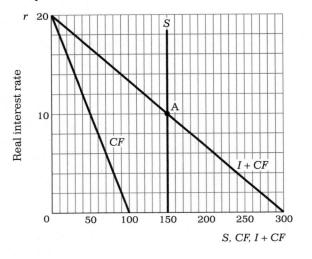

  b.   vertical

  c.   300; 15; 20; 1/15; flatter

  d.   150; 150; 10; 100; 50

  e.   50

10. **a.** **Graph 6-6**

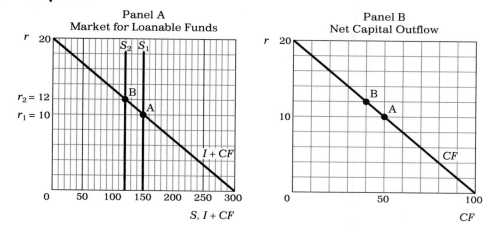

Panel A
Market for Loanable Funds

Panel B
Net Capital Outflow

Panel C
Market for Foreign Exchange

    b. 150; 150; 10; 50

    c. 1.0

    d. falls; 30; 120; left; 30

    e. 12; 80; 40

    f. rises; 1.5

    g. decrease; increase; decrease; decrease; decrease; increase

    h. shift right; not shift; rise; decrease; rise

Problems

1. **a.** U.S. investment would be low relative to our trading partners because relatively low U.S. saving would lead to a relatively high U.S. real interest rate, which would dampen U.S. investment.

    b. Net capital outflow has been negative—the United States has borrowed from abroad and has had a trade deficit.

2. **a.** The U.S. tax cuts and increased defense spending decreased world saving and, thereby, increased the world real interest rate.

   i. As r^* increases, investment in Europe and Japan falls.
   ii. Since national saving in Europe and Japan remains constant, as investment falls, $S - I$ increases, and European and Japanese net capital outflow rises.
   iii. Recall that $S - I = NX$. As European and Japanese net capital outflow increases, their trade surpluses NX increase (or their trade deficits decrease).
   iv. For their trade surpluses to increase, the real exchange rates in Europe and Japan must decrease.

   b. The high Belgian budget deficits have had no effect on:

   i. investment elsewhere in Europe and Japan.
   ii. net capital outflow elsewhere in Europe and Japan.
   iii. the trade balances elsewhere in Europe and Japan.
   iv. the real exchange rates elsewhere in Europe and Japan.

   c. The U.S. tax cuts and increased defense spending increase the world real interest rate because the United States is a "large" country in that it supplies a major part of total world saving. The Belgian budget deficits do not affect the world real interest rate because Belgium is a "small" country. It supplies a much smaller part of total world saving.

3. **a.** Purchasing-power parity does not imply anything about the nominal exchange rate between any two countries. It can take on any value.

   b. It implies that the real exchange rate between any two countries will always equal 1.0.

   c. Purchasing-power parity assumes that almost all goods are freely and easily tradable among countries. Consequently, if the real exchange rate deviates from 1.0, all consumers will prefer to buy all commodities from one country and none from the other. This, of course, cannot occur. If the real exchange rate cannot deviate from 1.0, the answer to Part a follows directly from the definition of the real exchange rate $\varepsilon = eP/P^*$ and the fact that P/P^* can take on any value.

4. **a.** According to purchasing-power parity, the long-run real foreign exchange rate will eventually approach 1.0 and stay there. In the long run, according to the classical dichotomy, it is unaffected by nominal variables, such as the growth of the money supply.

   b. According to the Quantity Theory, velocity is constant in the long run and the long-run rate of inflation is equal to the growth of the money supply minus the long-run growth rate of real output (real GDP). Thus, a reduction in the growth rate of the money supply would reduce the rate of inflation in the United States below that prevailing abroad. The real foreign exchange rate can be written as:

   $$\varepsilon = e(P/P^*).$$

The percentage change in the *nominal* foreign exchange rate can be written as:

$$\%\Delta e = \%\Delta\varepsilon + \%\Delta P^* - \%\Delta P.$$

According to purchasing-power parity, in the long run $\%\Delta\varepsilon = 0$. Thus, if foreign inflation exceeds domestic inflation, the nominal U.S. foreign exchange rate will increase.

5. **a.** According to the quantity equation, $MV = PY$.
Taking percentage changes of both sides yields
% Change in M + % Change in V = % Change in P + % Change in Y.
If the money supply grows at 3 percent per year, velocity remains constant, and real GDP grows at 3 percent per year in the long run, then
3% = % Change in P + 3%, or $\pi = 0\%$. If money supply growth rises to 10 percent per year, $\pi = 10\% - 3\% = 7\%$, that is, it rises by 7 percentage points per year.

b. According to the classical dichotomy, real variables, like the real interest rate, are not affected by nominal variables, like the money supply, in the long run. Instead, the real interest rate is typically determined by investment and saving. Consequently, the real interest rate would remain unchanged.

c. Recall $i = r + \pi$. Because r remains constant in the long run and inflation rises by 7 percentage points, the nominal interest rate will also rise by 7 percentage points.

d. Following the classical dichotomy, the real exchange rate will remain unchanged in the long run. This is also true if purchasing-power parity prevails.

e. Because $\varepsilon = e\,(P/P^*)$,
% Change in ε = 0 = % Change in e + % Change in P - % Change in P^*, or
% Change in e = % Change in P^* - % Change in P.
If foreign inflation is unaffected and U.S. inflation rises by 7 percentage points per year, the percentage change in the U.S. nominal exchange rate will fall by 7 percentage points per year.

f. Because investment is a function of the real interest rate, which is unchanged, investment will also be unchanged.

g. In the long run, real GDP is a function solely of technology and the amount of factor inputs, such as labor and capital. Because these are unchanged, real GDP will not be affected by the increase in money growth in the long run.

6. **a.** $\varepsilon = e\,(P/P^*) = 6.32$ yuan/\$1 × (\$4.20/Big Mac)/(15.42 yuan/Big Mac) = 1.72.

b. **i.** According to purchasing-power parity, the real exchange rate will eventually be 1.0. At any other real exchange rate, desired trade would theoretically go in only one direction.

ii. Recall $\varepsilon = e\,(P/P^*)$. Thus, if $\varepsilon = 1.0$,
1.0 = e (\$4.20/Big Mac)/(15.42 yuan/Big Mac)
e = 15.42 yuan/\$4.20 = 3.67 yuan per dollar.

7. Recall $\varepsilon = e\,(P/P^*)$.

    Thus, % change in ε = % change in e + % change in P – % change in P^*.

    Since both Germany and Italy use the euro, % change in $e = 0$. Thus,

    % change in ε = % change in P – % change in P*.

    The Italian real exchange rate relative to Germany has risen because Italian inflation (that is, % change in P) exceeded German inflation (% change in P^*).

8. **a** $\varepsilon = e\,(P/P^*)$, where

    ε = China's real exchange rate

    e = China's nominal exchange rate

    P = the domestic (China's) price level

    P* = the foreign (U.S.) price level

    b.   % change in ε = % change in e + % change in P – % change in P*.

    If China doesn't change its nominal exchange rate, % change in $e = 0$

    If Chinese inflation is 4% and U.S. inflation is 1.5%,

    % change in ε = 0% + 4% – 1.5% = 2.5%

    Thus, China's real exchange rate would rise by 2.5% per year. Since net exports are inversely (negatively) related to a country's real exchange rate, the increase in China's real exchange rate will reduce its net exports, i.e., reduce its trade surplus.

9. **a.**   In Germany net capital outflow would decrease, the German trade surplus would decrease, and the German foreign exchange rate would increase.

    b.   As German government spending increases, German saving would decrease, thereby decreasing net capital outflow and the German trade surplus even more, and increasing the German foreign exchange rate further.

10. **a.**   In the long run, the tax increase will decrease disposable income by ΔT. Consumption will fall by $MPC\,(\Delta T)$. Private saving will fall by $(1 - MPC)\,\Delta T$. Public saving $T - G$ will rise by the increase in taxes plus the reduction in government spending. Thus, national saving will rise by the reduction in government spending plus MPC times the increase in taxes.

b. Graph for Problem 10b.

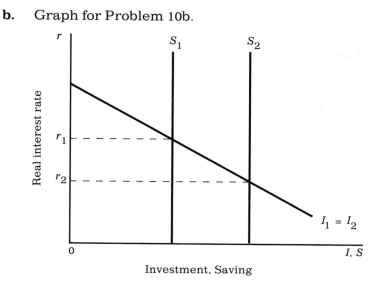

The increase in T and reduction in G would both shift the national saving curve to the right, from S_1 to S_2. In a closed economy $I = S$. Because the investment curve would not shift, the real interest rate would fall and the level of investment would rise.

c. Graph for Problem 10c.

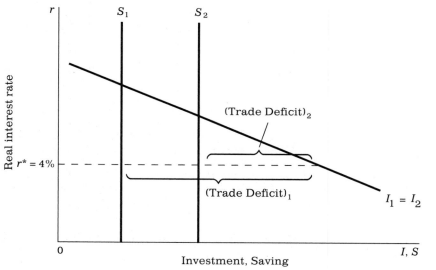

d. See graph for Part b.

In a small open economy, the real interest rate is unaffected by saving and investment decisions within the country. Although national saving will still increase, leading to the same shift in S to S_2, as in Part b, the real interest rate and the level of investment will remain constant. Consequently, $S - I$ will rise and the trade deficit will fall.

e. In the following graph, the $S - I$ curve shifts to the right following an increase in S. Consequently, the real exchange rate would fall, thereby increasing the quantity of net exports.

Graph for Problem 10e.

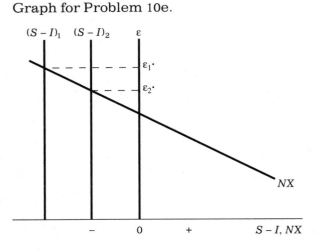

11. In a closed economy, saving and investment are equal. Consequently, investment will be low in a country with low saving and high in a country with high saving. In a small open economy, the levels of saving and investment are theoretically independent because a country can borrow unlimited amounts from abroad to finance any gaps between investment and saving at the world real interest rate. In a large open economy, a country can borrow more from abroad only if it raises its domestic real interest rate, which tends to reduce domestic investment. Consequently, low national saving will be associated with low investment.

13. **a.** Since both plans eliminate projected budget deficits that would occur in their absence, public saving $T - G$ will rise to zero in each plan.

$$\text{Private saving} = (Y - T) - C, \text{ where } C = f(Y - T).$$
$$\text{In the long run } Y = \overline{Y}.$$

In the Democratic plan, both Y and T are unaffected. Consequently, disposable income, consumption, and private saving are unaffected. In the Republican plan, taxes are cut, so disposable income is higher, and consumption rises by MPC times the increase in disposable income. As a result, private saving rises by MPS times the increase in disposable income.

In the Democratic plan, national saving will rise by the full amount of the deficit reduction. In the Republican plan, national saving will rise by this amount plus the increase in private saving.

b. If the United States were a closed economy, $I = S$ (see following graph). Consequently, both plans would shift the saving curve to the right, reduce the real interest rate r, and increase the amount of investment. Since S rises more in the Republican plan, r would fall by more, and the amount of investment would increase by more.

Graph for Problem 13b

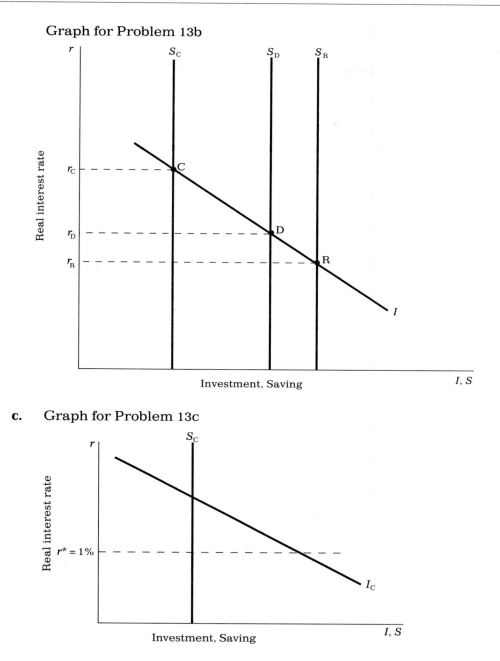

c.   Graph for Problem 13c

d.   If the United States were a small open economy, the increase in national saving would have no effect on either the real interest rate r^* or the amount of investment. Since S rises by more under the Republican plan, both $S - I$ and NX would increase by more.

Graph for Problem 13d

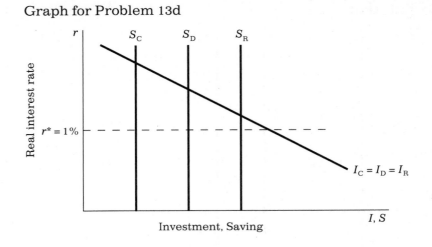

e. $S - I = NX$. In both plans $S - I$ and NX increase; consequently, both plans lead to a reduction in the real exchange rate. In the Republican plan $S - I$ and NX rise by more, so the real exchange rate falls by more.

Graph for Problem 13e

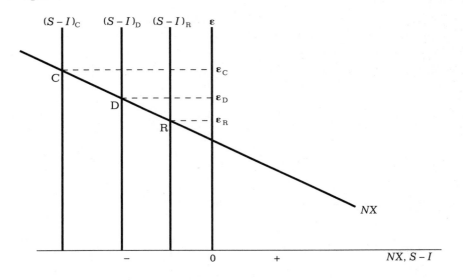

14. a. and b. The increased demand for Chilean wine will shift its NX curve to the right. Since neither S, I, nor $(S - I)$ has changed, this would merely result in an increase in Chile's real exchange rate and no change in Chile's trade surplus.

Graph for Problem 14a and b

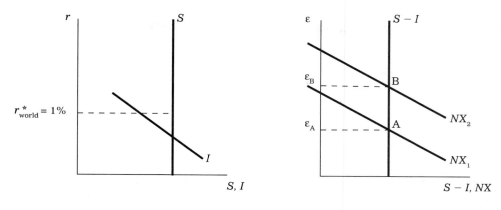

c. To keep Chile's real exchange rate unchanged the government could increase national saving by increasing taxes. The real interest rate would remain unchanged at the world real interest rate and Chilean investment would not change. Consequently, net capital outflow = $S - I$ would increase along with the trade surplus.

Graph for Problem 14c

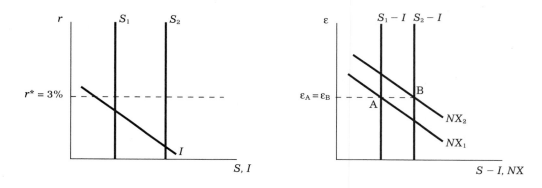

15. a. i. Because real GDP in the long run is a function solely of technology and factor inputs, it will be unaffected.

    ii. Public saving = $T - G$. Thus, public saving will fall by the reduction in taxes plus the increase in G.

    iii. Private saving = $(Y - T) - C$.

        Disposable income $Y - T$ will rise by the reduction in taxes.

        Consumption will rise by MPC times the reduction in taxes.

        Thus, private saving will rise by $(1 - MPC)$ times the reduction in taxes.

    iv. National saving is the sum of public saving, which will fall by the reduction in taxes plus the increase in G, and private saving, which rises by $(1 - MPC)$ times the reduction in taxes. Thus, national saving falls by the increase in G plus MPC times the reduction in taxes.

b. In a small open economy, the real interest rate is fixed at the world real interest rate r^*. The tax cuts and increase in government spending will shift the S curve left and saving will fall. Neither the real interest rate nor investment (which depends on r) will be affected.

Graph for Problem 15b

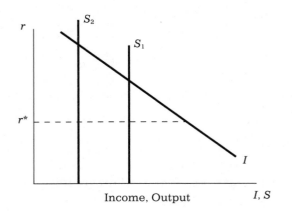

c. As S falls, $S - I$ also falls. Thus, the $S - I$ curve shifts left. This increases the real exchange rate and reduces net exports.

Graph for Problem 15c

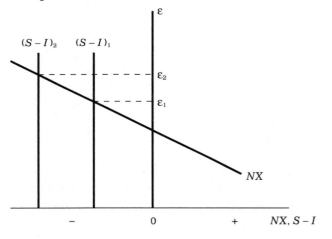

d. In the large open economy, a reduction in S raises the domestic real interest rate, which reduces both investment and net capital outflow. The reduction in CF increases the real exchange rate and reduces net exports. Graph for Problem 15d

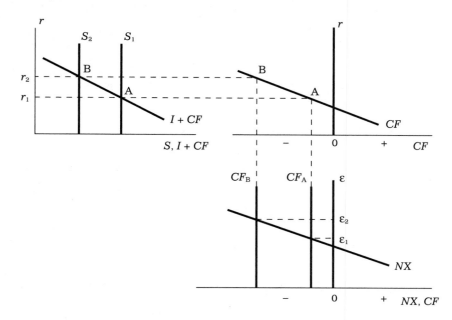

16. a. Since purchasing-power parity (PPP) holds at every moment in the past, present, and future, the real exchange rate will always equal 1.0, and will not change.

b. If the expected real interest rates are equal, the difference in nominal interest rates must reflect differences in expected future inflation rates of $1.8 - 0.6 = 1.2$ percentage points. Thus, U.S. inflation was expected to exceed Swiss inflation by 1.2 percentage points per year.

c. Recall $\varepsilon = e\,(P/P^*)$.

Thus, % change in ε = % change in e + % change in P - % change in P^* and % change in e = % change in ε + % change in P^* - % change in P.

If PPP holds and the real exchange rate always equals 1.0, % change in $\varepsilon = 0\%$.

From Part b we know % change in P^* - % change in $P = -1.2\%$.

Thus, the U.S. nominal exchange rate was expected to fall by 1.2 percent per year.

17. The initial equilibrium is represented by Points A in Panels A, B, and C below.
Graph for Problem 17

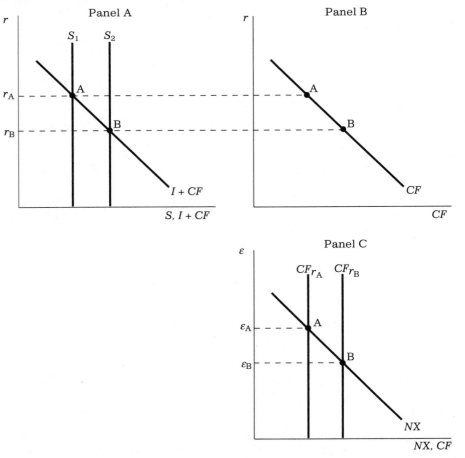

The increase in taxes and reductions in government spending would increase
national saving and shift the S curve right to S_2 in Panel A. The $I + CF$ curve
would not shift, so the domestic real interest rate would fall to Point B.
Consequently, the level of net capital outflow would rise in Panel B. Since net
capital outflow equals the trade surplus, the latter would also rise, implying a
decrease in the trade deficit. As NX rises, the real exchange rate will fall. As the
domestic real interest rate falls, investment will also rise.

19. The reduction in the perceived marginal product of capital will shift the
A Investment curve to the left. National saving and the CF curves are unaffected.
Consequently, the real interest rate will fall to r_B. As r falls, the amount of CF will
increase to B. This increase will result in a reduction in the real exchange rate
and an increase in the amount of exports. Although the reduction in the real
interest rate would tend to increase investment, the I curve originally shifted
left. Investment will fall because saving $S = I + CF$ did not change, and net capital outflow CF has risen.

Graph for Problem 19

20. a. Real GDP will be unaffected because it depends on K and L, which are assumed to be relatively unaffected.

Social Security benefits are transfer payments. Net taxes T = gross taxes – transfer payments. Thus, if transfer payments fall by $100 billion, net taxes T will rise by $100 billion. Public saving $T – G$ will also rise by $100 billion. Private saving = $(Y – T) – C$. If Y is unchanged and T rises by $100 billion, disposable income will fall by $100 billion. Consumption will fall by $MPC \times$ $100 billion = $80 billion and private saving will fall by $20 billion. National saving will rise by $100 billion – $20 billion = $80 billion.

b. The increase in national saving will shift the S curve in the U.S. to the right. This will reduce the U.S. real interest rate and increase the amount of net capital outflows (as well as the amount of investment). The real exchange rate will fall and the trade deficit will also fall as the trade surplus rises.
Graph for Problem 20b

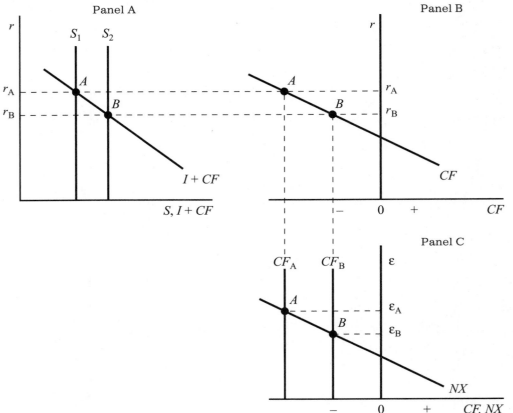

c. Since the U.S. is a large economy, its increase in saving will also increase world saving and reduce the real world interest rate. Since Norway's national saving is unaffected and the amount of Norwegian investment will rise, $S - I$ in Norway will fall. This will raise the real exchange rate in Norway and reduce its trade surplus.
Graph for Problem 20c

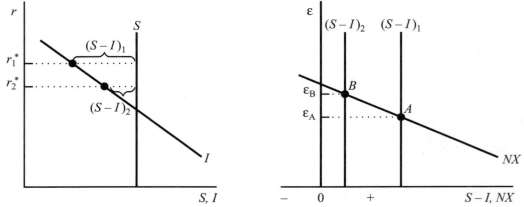

21. As investors increased their purchases of U.S. assets, the U.S. *CF* curve shifted left (since *CF* is equal to domestic purchases of foreign assets minus foreign purchases of domestic assets). This shifted the *I* + *CF* curve left, too. Since the *S* curve did not shift, the U.S. real interest rate fell, thereby increasing investment. The decline in net capital outflow (since *S* remained constant and *I* rose) led to a reduction in U.S. net exports and an increase in the U.S. real exchange rate.

Graph for Problem 21

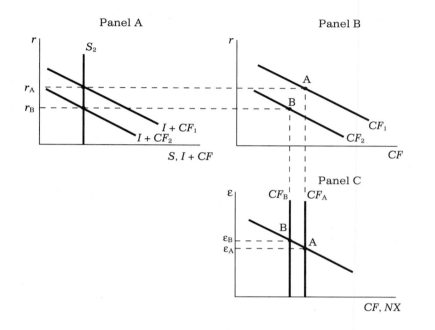

CHAPTER 7

Fill-in Questions

1. labor force
2. steady state; unemployment rate; natural rate of unemployment
3. sectoral shift
4. frictional unemployment; unemployment insurance
5. Wage rigidity; structural unemployment
6. insiders; outsiders
7. efficiency wage
8. discouraged workers

Multiple-Choice Questions

1. b	2. a	3. d	4. c	5. b	6. d	7. b
8. d	9. b	10. d	11. d	12. c	13. d	

Exercises

1. **a.** **(i)** 46   **(ii)** 46   **(iii)** 46; 46; 200; 46; 46; 2,300   **(iv)** Because the flows into and out of unemployment are equal, and the unemployment rate is constant from one period to the next.

    b. 2,500

    c. 8 percent

    d. $s/(s + f) = 0.02/(0.02 + 0.23) = 0.08 = 8$ percent

2. **a.** **(i)** 40   **(ii)** 69   **(iii)** 229; 2,271   **(iv)** 9.16

    b. **(i)** 46   **(ii)** 68   **(iii)** 229; 46; 68; 251; 2,271; 46; 68; 2,249   **(iv)** 10.04

    c. 13.0%

Problems

1. **a.** By allowing unemployed people to search longer before accepting a job and by cushioning the loss of income from unemployment, unemployment insurance reduces the probability of finding a job. Because employees and firms know that people who are laid off will receive unemployment benefits, firms' reluctance to lay off workers may be reduced, thereby increasing the probability of being separated from a job.

    b. **i.** By giving income to those who have recently experienced a sharp decline in their income and by easing the emotional pain of unemployment.

    ii. By allowing unemployed workers to wait until they find a job that fully utilizes their skills.

2. **a.** If the demand for low-wage workers is inelastic, total wage income accruing to low-wage workers will increase following an increase in the minimum wage; if demand is elastic, it will fall.

    b. Policymakers are more likely to support higher minimum wages if demand for low-wage workers is very inelastic because the reduction in employment would be small, and the increase in income accruing to low-wage workers would be large.

    c. Teenagers are less likely to be the primary wage earners in the family, and they "pay" for some kinds of on-the-job training by accepting low wages now for high wages after they are trained.

    d. **i.** If employers respond to the subminimum wages by firing adults and hiring teenagers, adult employment could fall.

    ii. If adults and teenagers are complements, a reduction in the price of teenage labor via the subminimum wage for teenagers would increase the demand for adult workers. If adults and teenagers are substitutes, a reduction in the price of teenage labor would decrease the demand for adult workers.

4. **a.** $du/df = -s/(s + f)^2 < 0$. As f increases, u decreases.

    b. $du/ds = f/(s + f)^2 > 0$. As s increases, u increases. As a greater percentage of those employed lose their jobs, the unemployment rate increases.

5. As we shall see in later chapters, the natural rate of unemployment is the rate toward which we should aim when using macroeconomic stabilization policies. It is also the rate toward which the economy is heading in the long run.

7. The quantity of labor supplied depends on the after-tax wage rate. An increase in the income tax rate will reduce the after-tax wage rate. If the supply of labor is elastic, the labor supply curve is flat, and a reduction in the after-tax wage rate will lead to a large reduction in the quantity of labor supplied. If labor supply is inelastic, the labor supply curve is steep, and a reduction in the after-tax wage rate will lead to a small reduction in the quantity of labor supplied

8. Unions may increase the natural rate of unemployment if nonunion employers raise their wages to prevent their workers from joining a union.

9. a. The higher minimum wage in San Francisco would raise the real wage, thereby reducing employment and increasing unemployment.

   b. If the price level in San Francisco is 60 percent greater than the average price level in the United States, the real wage in San Francisco is equal to $10.24/1.6 = $6.40, which is less than the federal minimum. Consequently, the amount of structural unemployment and the resulting unemployment rate would be lower in San Francisco.

CHAPTER 8

Fill-in Questions

1. Solow growth model
2. steady state
3. level effect
4. growth effect
5. Golden Rule level of capital

Multiple-Choice Questions

1. a	2. d	3. c	4. b	5. b	6. d	7. c
8. a	9. a	10. b	11. a	12. b	13. d	14. a
15. c	16. b	17. c	18. b	19. a	20. b	21. c
22. d	23. b					

Exercises

1. **a.** doubles

   b. −1/2; 1/2; 1/2

   c. **Table 8-1**

(1) Capital per Worker k	(2) Output per Worker $y = k^{1/2}$	(3) Consumption per Worker c	(4) Investment per Worker i	(5) Depreciation per Worker δk	(6) Change in Capital per Worker Δk
0	0	0	0	0	0
4	2.0	1.6	0.4	0.2	0.2
12	3.464	2.771	0.693	0.6	0.093
16	4.0	3.2	0.8	0.8	0.0
20	4.472	3.578	0.894	1.0	−0.106
36	6.0	4.8	1.2	1.8	−0.6

   d. **Graph 8-1**

   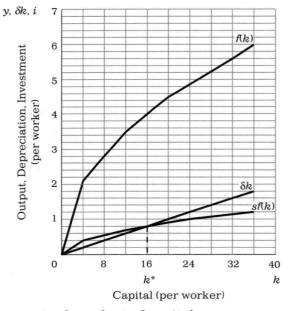

   marginal product of capital

   e. 20; 0.8; 80; see Table 8-1

   f. sy; 0.2; see Table 8-1 and Graph 8-1

   g. 20; 0.05; see Table 8-1 and Graph 8-1

   h. 0.05; $0.2(k)^{1/2}$; $0.05k$; see Table 8-1

   i. 0; 16; 4; 3.2; 0.8; less than; falls; greater than; rises

   j. 16

   k. upward; greater than; rise; rise; increase; higher; remain constant; have no effect on; lower; have no effect on

2. a.

Table 8-2

(1) Year	(2) Capital per Worker k	(3) Output per Worker y	(4) Consumption per Worker c	(5) Investment per Worker i	(6) Depreciation per Worker δk	(7) Change in k Δk
1	25	5	4	1.0	1.25	−0.25
2	24.75	4.975	3.980	0.995	1.238	−0.243
3	24.507	4.950	3.960	0.990	1.225	−0.235
.						
.						
.						
30	20.063	4.479	3.583	0.896	1.003	−0.107
31	19.956	4.467	3.574	0.893	0.998	−0.105
.						
.						
.						
100	16.657	4.081	3.265	0.816	0.833	−0.017
101	16.640	4.079	3.263	0.816	0.832	−0.016
.						
.						
.						
∞	16.000	4.0	3.2	0.8	0.8	0.0

b.   25; 0.25; 24.75

c. and d. see Table 8-2

e.   0

f.   16

3. **a.**   increases; 1/2

    b.   0.05

Table 8-3

(1) Capital per Worker k^*	(2) Output per Worker $f(k^*) = k^{*1/2}$	(3) Depreciation per Worker δk^*	(4) Consumption per Worker $c^* = f(k^*) - \delta k^*$	(5) Saving per Worker $sf(k^*)$
0	0	0	0	0
4	2.0	0.2	1.8	1.0
16	4.0	0.8	3.2	2.0
36	6.0	1.8	4.2	3.0
64	8.0	3.2	4.8	4.0
100	10.0	5.0	5.0	5.0
121	11.0	6.05	4.95	5.5
144	12.0	7.2	4.8	6.0

c.   **Graph 8-2**

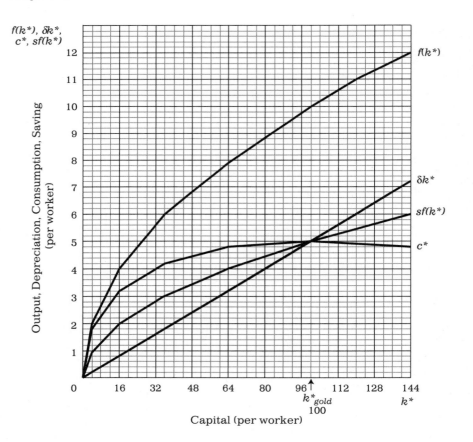

100; 100

d. 5; 10; 0.5; increase

e. higher; higher; greater; less

f. 0.05; greater; increases; less; decreases; greater; 0.05; 0.05

g. 0.05; 100; 100; 10; 101; 10.0499; 0.0499

h. 0.5; equal to

i. up; high; down; low

4. **a.** 0.5; 100; 10; 5

b. 16; 4; 4; 3.2; increase

c. 3.2; 5

d. 2; fall

e. decrease; 0.8; 2; 0.8; 2; 0.8; 17.2; 4.15; 4.15; 2.075

f. fall; increase; rise

g. increase; greater; fall

h. 400; 20; 20; 0; 10; higher; lower; increase; fall

i. rise; fall; higher

5. **a.** 2; −2; 2; 2

b. **Table 8-4**

(1) Capital per Worker k	(2) Output per Worker $f(k) = k^{1/2}$	(3) Investment per Worker $sf(k)$	(4) Break-even Investment per Worker $(\delta + n)k$	(5) Change in Capital per Worker $sf(k) - (\delta + n)k$
0	0	0	0	0
4	2.0	0.4	0.28	0.12
8	2.828	0.566	0.56	0.006
16	4.0	0.8	1.12	−0.32
36	6.0	1.2	2.52	−1.32

c. **Graph 8-3**

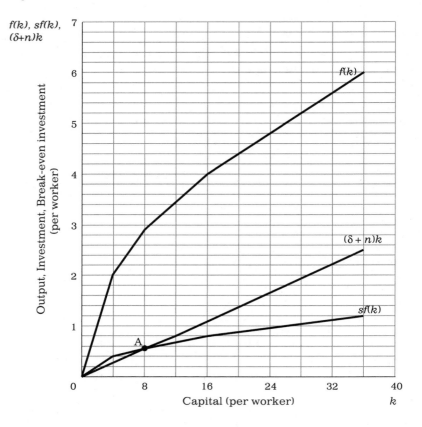

d. 0; $(\delta + n)k$; 8.16

e. shift up; not shift; decrease; lower; lower

f. 0.07; δ; n; increases; increases; decrease

Problems

1. $k = 256$; $y = 40$; $c = 34.88$; saving per worker $= i = 5.12$; $\delta k = 5.12$.

2. a. $sf(k) = (\delta + n)k$

   b. consumption per worker

   c. $MPK = \delta + n$

3. **a.** An increase in the saving rate would shift the $sf(k)$ curve up and increase the steady-state level of capital per worker.

Graph for Problem 3a

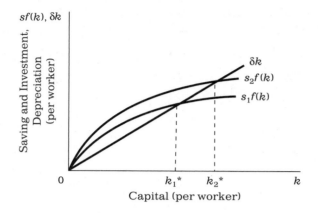

b. Since k^* rises, the steady-state level of output per worker will also rise.

c. In the new steady state, the amount of capital per worker will remain constant, so the amount of output per worker will also remain constant, and the steady-state growth rate of output per worker will remain equal to zero.

d. The Golden Rule level of capital per worker is independent of the saving rate (although only one saving rate will move the economy to the Golden Rule level), so it will not change.

e. In the initial steady state, the rate of growth of output per worker is zero. Since the level of output per worker is higher in the final steady state, the rate of growth of output per worker will increase during the transition to the final steady state.

4. **a.** Graph for Problem 4a

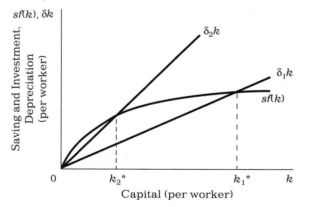

The steady-state level of capital per worker falls.

b. The Golden Rule level of capital per worker falls because as δ rises, MPK must also rise, and this requires a reduction in k^*_{gold}. Alternatively, at the old Golden Rule level, too much output must now be devoted to replacing the existing capital stock.

5. **a.** If the saving rate fell, the $sf(k)$ curve would shift down. By itself, this reduction in s would lower the steady-state level of capital per worker k^*. In addition, however, the reduction in the rate of depreciation δ will reduce the slope of the δk line. By itself, this reduction in δ would increase k^*. When the two changes occur simultaneously, however, the net effect on k^* is ambiguous. It could fall, rise, or stay the same. In the following diagram, k^* could fall to k_2^* or rise to k_3^*.
Graph for Problem 5a

b. At the initial Golden-Rule level of capital accumulation k_{gold}^*, the marginal product of capital, which is the slope of the production function $f(k)$, is equal to the rate of depreciation δ. When δ falls, therefore, the MPK at the new k_{gold}^* must also be lower. Given the shape of the $f(k)$ curve, this must occur to the right of the initial equilibrium, and k_{gold}^* must rise. (Note that the shape of $f(k)$ is unaffected when the saving rate falls.)
Graph for Problem 5b

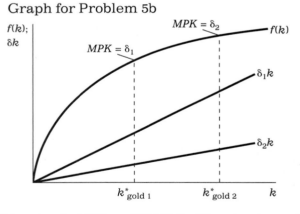

6. In Chapter 3, $MPK = dY/dK$. In Chapter 8, $y = Y/L = f(k)$, where $k = K/L$. Thus, $Y = Lf(k)$. Using the chain rule, $dY/dK = Ldf(k)/dK = Lf'(k)(L/L^2)$ [since $k = K/L = f'(k)$.

7. **a.** When $d(c)/dk = 0$, $f'(k) = \delta = 0.02$. This occurs when $2.5(k)^{-3/4} = 0.02$, or when $k_{\text{gold}}^* = 625$.

b. $y = 50$; $\delta k = i = 12.5$; $s = 0.25$; $c = 37.5$

8. $dk = d(K/L) = (LdK - KdL)/L^2 = dK/L - (dL/L)(K/L)$.
    Since $dK/L = i - \delta k$ and $dL/L = n$, $dk = i - \delta k - nk$.

9. **a.** The saving rate must rise.

    b. In the short run, consumption per worker will fall; in the long run, it will rise above its initial level.

    c. tax incentives to save, increases in the interest rate, or a tax on consumption

10. **a.** **i.** The amounts of capital per worker and output per worker will be higher in the final steady state.

    ii. The growth rates of both capital per worker and output per worker will be zero in both steady states.

    b. during the transition between the initial and final steady states, the growth rates of both capital per worker and output per worker will be positive.

11. a. Total output is a function of the amounts of capital and labor. If the capital stock is unaffected and the number of workers falls by half, total output will also fall (but by less than half).

b. Output per worker is a function of the amount of capital per worker k. Since the capital stock is unaffected and the number of workers falls by half, k will double, thereby increasing the amount of output per worker.

Graph for Problem 11c

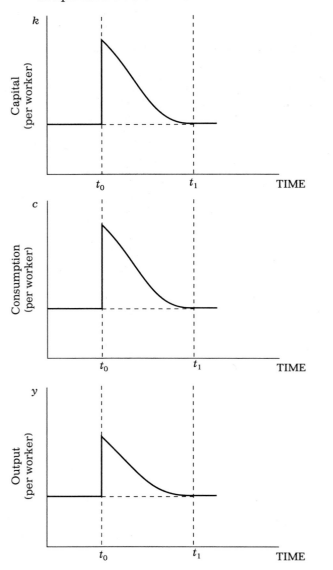

12. **a.** A reduction in China's saving rate would shift the *sf(k)* curve down. An increase in China's population growth rate *n* would shift the $(\delta + n)k$ line up. As a result *k** would fall, which would also reduce the steady-state level of output per worker.

    Graph for Problem 12a

    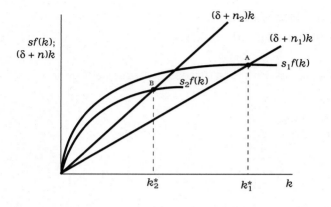

    b. In the graph below, the $(\delta + n)k$ line shifts up, as in part a. The *f(k)* curve, however, does not shift. Consequently, the *MPK* at the new k^*_{gold} must rise, which occurs at a lower level of *k*.

    Graph for Problem 12b

CHAPTER 9

Fill-in Questions

1. labor-augmenting technological progress; efficiency of labor
2. efficiency of labor
3. effective workers; efficiency of labor
4. labor-augmenting technological progress
5. Human capital
6. labor-augmenting technological progress; human capital
7. technological externality
8. endogenous growth theory
9. creative destruction

Multiple-Choice Questions

1. a	2. c	3. a	4. b	5. a	6. b	7. c	8. d
9. d	10. a	11. a	12. d	13. b	14. b	15. a	16. c
17. a	18. d	19. c	20. d	21. d	22. c		

Exercises

1. **a.** n; g
   b. 0; 1; −1; 1; 1
   c. Table 9-1

Table 9-1

(1) Capital per Effective Worker k	(2) Output per Effective Worker $f(k) = k^{1/2}$	(3) Investment per Effective Worker $sf(k)$	(4) Break-even Investment per Effective Worker $(\delta + n + g)k$	(5) Change in Capital per Effective Worker $sf(k) - (\delta + n + g)k$
0	0	0	0	0
4	2.0	0.4	0.32	0.08
6	2.45	0.49	0.48	0.01
8	2.83	0.57	0.64	−0.07
16	4.0	0.8	1.28	−0.48
36	6.0	1.2	2.88	−1.68

d. Graph 9-1

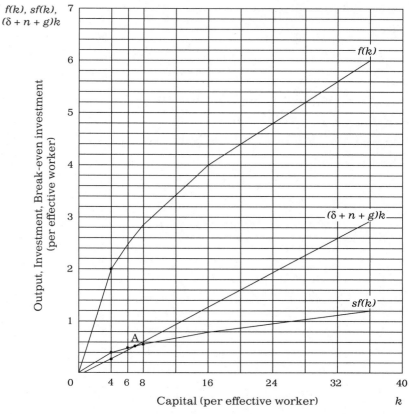

e.   0; 0.08k; 6.25

f. g; technological change

g. n; g

2. a. $\delta + n + g$; δ ; n; g

  b. n; g

  c.   decreases; increase; increasing

  d.   decreasing; decreasing

3. a. Y/K

  b.   % Change in K; $\Delta Y/Y$; $\Delta K/K$

  c. sY/K; δ

  d.   A

  e. sA; δ

4. a.   0.9; 4; 0.9; 8; 2; 7.59

  b.   0.1; 0.1, 10

  c.   14.4; 28.8; 8; 15.18

  d.   doubled

  e.   double

  f.   double; constant

  g.   10; increase; increase

5. **a.** 0.3; 0.7

    b. % Change in $Y - 0.3 \times$ (% Change in K) $- 0.7 \times$ (% Change in L)

    c. 3.4; 1.0; 1.2; 1.2

Problems

1. **a.** $y = f(k) = 10k^{1/4}$

    b. $k^* = 16$; $y = 20$; $c = 17.44$; saving per effective worker $= i = 2.56$; $\delta k^* = 1.6$

    c. They all grow at $g = 2$ percent per year.

    d. They all grow at $n + g = 6\%$ per year.

2. **a.** Graph for Problem 2a

b. Graph for Problem 2b

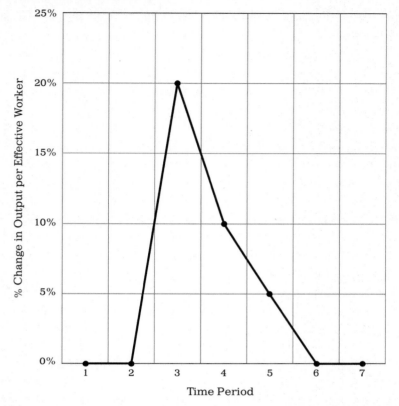

3. a. $sf(k) = (\delta + n + g)k$ In the steady state the amount of saving per effective worker equals the amount of capital per effective worker times the sum of the rates of depreciation, population growth and technological progress.

b. consumption per effective worker in the steady state.

c. $MPK = \delta + n + g$

4. a. $y = f(k) = 10k^{1/4}$

b. $k^*_{gold} = 39.0625$; $s = 0.25$

c. $y = 25$; saving per effective worker $= i = 6.25$; $c = 18.75$

5. In Chapter 3, $MPK = dY/dK$. In Chapter 9, $y = Y/EL = f(k)$, where $k = K/EL$. Thus, $Y = ELf(k)$. Using the chain rule, $dY/dK = ELdf(k)/dK = ELf'(k)(1/EL) = f'(k)$.

6. a. $y = f(k) = 10k^{1/4}$

b. $MPK = f'(k) = 2.5\ (k)^{-3/4}$

c. $f'(k^*_{gold}) = (\delta + n + g)(k^*_{gold})$; $k^*_{gold} = 39.0625$

7. a. $dk = [(EL)dK - k(EdL + LdE)]/E^2L^2$

$\quad = dK/EL - (K/EL)(dL/L) - (K/EL)(dE/E)$

Since $dK/EL = i - \delta k$, $dL/L = n$, and $dE/E = g$,

$dk = i - \delta k - nk - gk$

8. **a.** An increase in the saving rate will shift the *sf(k)* curve up and increase the steady-state capital stock per effective worker.

Graph for Problem 8a

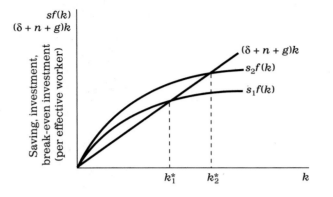

b. Graphs for Problem 8b

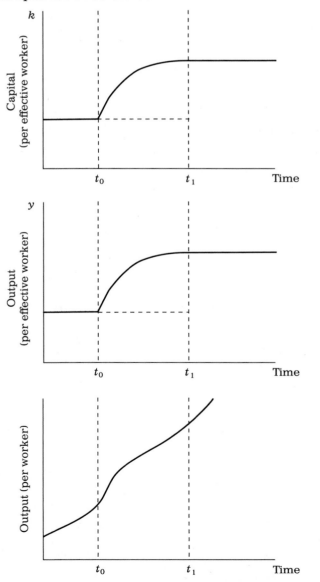

9. **a.** k^* will fall.

   b. The growth rates of k and y will become negative.

   c. They all equal zero.

   d. All the growth rates rise from the old rate of technological progress to the new rate of technological progress.

10. **a.** Graph for Problem 10a and 10c

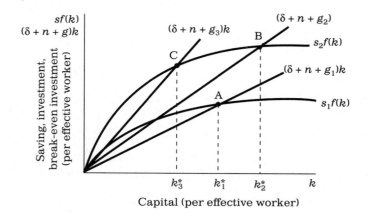

   b. At the steady state, the growth rates of capital per effective worker, output per effective worker, output per worker, and total output are 0, 0, g, and $n + g$.

   c. If both the saving rate and the rate of technological change increased, the steady-state level of capital per effective worker might rise (Point B) or fall (Point C).

   d. and e. The Golden-Rule level of capital accumulation per effective worker k^*_{gold} would definitely fall.

   Graph for Problems 10d and 10e

11. **a.** $MPK - \delta = .10 - .04 = .06$; $n + g = .04 + .03 = .07$

Since $MPK > \delta$, $n + g$, the level of k is greater than the Golden-Rule level.

b. $MPK - \delta = .09 - .05 = .04$; $n + g = .04$

Since $MPK - \delta = n + g$, the level of k is equal to the Golden-Rule level.

12. **a.** 3 percent

b. 3.3 percent

CHAPTER 10

Fill-in Questions

1. recession
2. Okun's law
3. index of leading economic indicators; recession
4. sticky wages and prices
5. aggregate demand
6. aggregate supply; aggregate demand
7. Stagflation
8. stabilization policy
9. supply shock; demand shock

Multiple-Choice Questions

1. c	2. a	3. b	4. a	5. d	6. c	7. d
8. c	9. b	10. a	11. d	12. b	13. b	14. a
15. c	16. c					

Exercises

1. **a.** 0; 3
   b. 1; 1; 1; 2; −1; 1
   c. 3; −2; −2; 4; 7

2. **a.** **Table 10-1**

(1) M	(2) V	(3) PY	(4) P	(5) Y
1,000	2.0	2,000	2.0	1,000
1,000	2.0	2,000	1.5	1,333
1,000	2.0	2,000	1.0	2,000
1,000	2.0	2,000	0.8	2,500
1,000	2.0	2,000	0.5	4,000

b.   Graph 10-1

c.   rises

d.   1,500; 2,000; 3,000; 3,750; 6,000

f.   the same; increase; right

g.   500; 667; 1,000; 1,250; 2,000

i.   the same; decrease; left

3.   a. and **b.**   2,000

Graph 10-2

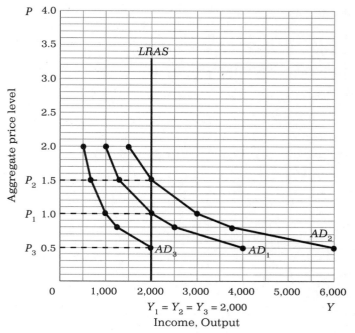

    c.   right

    d.   vertical; increase; not change; increase; 1.5

    e.   left

    f.   decrease; decrease; not change

4. **a.**   2,000

Graph 10-3

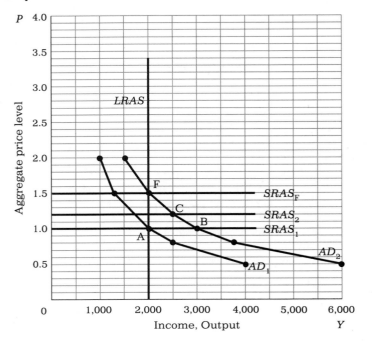

    b.   sticky

    d.   right

    e.   increase; not change; 3,000; 1.0

    f.   exceeds; increase; 2,500; 1.2

    g.   exceeds; increase; shift upward; 2,000; 1.5

    h.   decrease; not change; decrease; less than; downward; 2,000; decreased

    i.   output; the price level

5. **a.**   upward

Graph 10-4

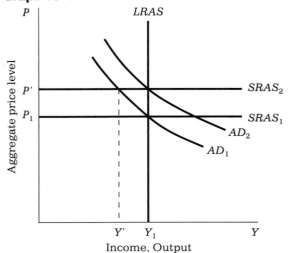

b. decrease; increase; stagflation

c. increase; right

d. higher; higher

e. decrease; lower; higher

Problems

1. **a.** The reduction in the money supply would shift the aggregate demand curve to the left (from AD_1 to AD_2) in the short run. Output would decrease, while the aggregate price level would remain constant as the economy moved from point A to point B.

   Graph for Problem 1a

   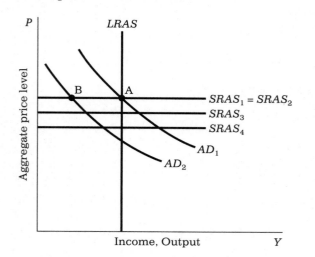

   b. If there were no further reductions in the money supply, the aggregate demand curve would not shift any further. Over time, however, the short-run aggregate supply curve would shift down (to $SRAS_3$, $SRAS_4$, etc.). Output would rise toward its natural level and the price level would fall.

   c. The long-run aggregate supply curve is vertical. Hence, the contractionary monetary policy would have no effect on output in the long run. It would, however, reduce the long-run price level.

2. $MdV + VdM = PdY + YdP$. Along a stationary aggregate demand curve, $dV = dM = 0$, so $YdP = -PdY$, or $dP/dY = -P/Y < 0$.

3. Those economists who believe that sticky wages and prices make the movement to the natural level a long drawn-out process generally believe that stabilization policies have an important role to play so that the economy need not languish for long periods of time below full employment. Those economists who believe that prices and wages are sufficiently flexible to move the economy to its natural level rapidly are less enthusiastic about the use of stabilization policy for several reasons: the policy effects and their timing are often unpredictable, policymakers may not act in the best interest of the economy, and the public's expectations of policy changes may reduce their effectiveness.

5. **a.** If velocity is stable, the Federal Reserve can easily ascertain the shape and position of the aggregate demand curve. Once the Fed located the position of the new short-run aggregate supply curve, it could implement the appropriate policy change to shift the aggregate demand curve and keep output stable.

   b. If velocity is unstable and unpredictable, it will be difficult for the Federal Reserve to ascertain the exact shape and position of the aggregate demand curve. Consequently, it would be difficult to determine the required change in the money supply even if the new short-run aggregate supply curve can be located precisely.

CHAPTER 11

Fill-in Questions

1. Actual expenditure; Planned expenditure
2. Keynesian cross
3. Keynesian cross; multiplier
4. *IS* curve
5. *LM* curve
6. *IS* curve; *LM* curve
7. liquidity preference theory

Multiple-Choice Questions

1. a	2. b	3. d	4. a	5. d	6. d	7. c
8. b	9. b	10. d	11. c	12. d	13. b	14. c
15. b	16. d	17. d				

Exercises

1. **a.** the amount by which consumption increases when disposable income increases by $1; 0.75; 125; 0.75

   b. 50; 0.75

Graph 11-1

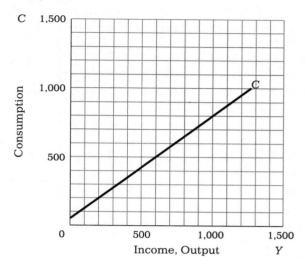

50; 0.75; −100; less than

c. **Graph 11-2**

Graph 11-3

d. **Graph 11-4**

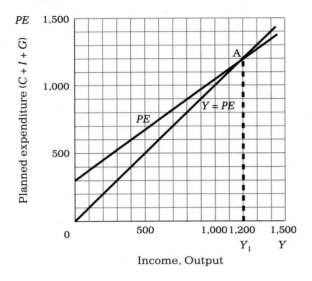

e. 50; 100; 150; 300; 0.75; 0; 0; 0.75

f. 300; 0.75

g. 1.0; 1,200

h. 1,500; 1,500; 100; lay off; decrease; fall; 1,200; 0

i. 1,050; 1,050; −50; hire more; increase; rise; 1,200; 0

2. a. 150; 151; 1

b. 1

Graph 11-5

Graph 11-6

c. 301; 0.75

d. 301; 0.75; 1,204

e. 4

f. MPC^2; MPC^2; MPC^3; MPC^3; 0.75; 0.75; 4

3. a. 0.75; 0.75; 0.75

b. 300.75; 0.75

c. 300.75; 0.75; 1,203

Graph 11-7

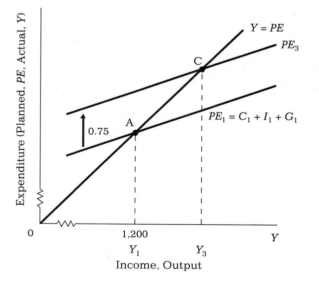

d. 3

e. MPC^2, MPC^2; MPC^3; MPC^3; 0.75; 0.75; 0.75; 3

f. $MPC/(1 - MPC)$

g. upward; 1; downward; 0.75; upward; 0.25; rise, larger; 4; 3; decrease; 3; increase; 1

4. a. 10

Table 11-3

(1) Interest Rate (%)	(2) Planned Investment	(3) Equilibrium Level of Income
0	200	1,600
5	150	1,400
10	100	1,200
15	50	1,000
20	0	800

Graph 11-9

b.   400; 0.75; 10

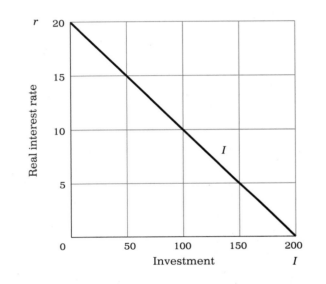

c.   400; 0.75; 10; 1,600; 40

d.   100; 1,200

e.   50; 50

Graph 11-10

50; 50; 0.75; 50; 0.75; 200

f. rises; upward

g. **Graph 11-11**

5. **a.** 100; 1,200; 0.75; 4; 1,204

   b. **Graph 11–12**

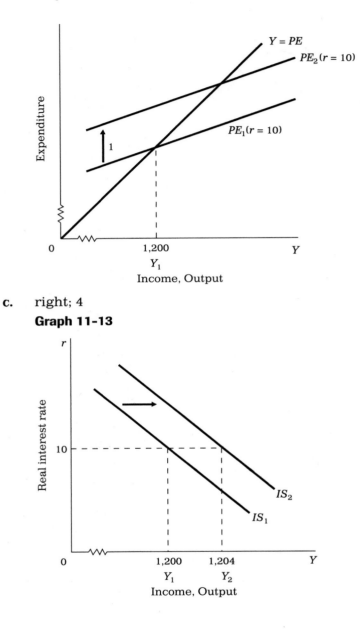

   c. right; 4

   Graph 11–13

   d. right; left; government-purchases multiplier

   e. smaller; larger; larger; larger; larger

   f. 1; 0.75; 0.75; 3; 1,203

Graph 11-14

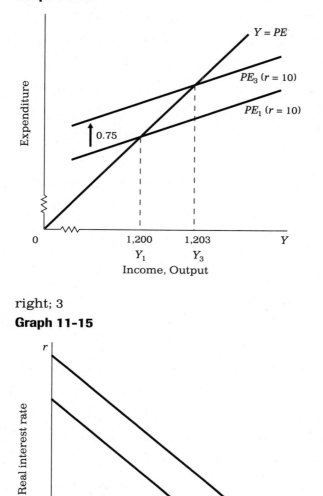

g. right; 3

Graph 11-15

h. right; left; tax multiplier
i. larger; smaller; larger; larger; larger; larger; flatter

6. a. **Graph 11-16**

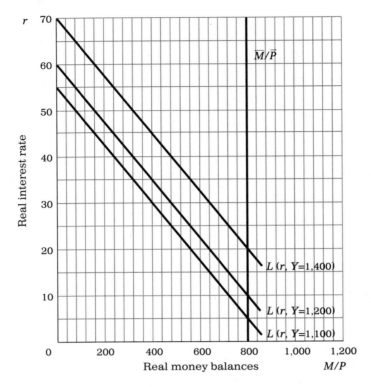

b. 0; 480; 720; 800; 880

c. 5

d. 0; 160; 560; 800; 880; right; rises; 10

e. 0; 320; 720; 960; 1,120; right; rises; 20

f. 800; 5; 10; 20

Graph 11-17

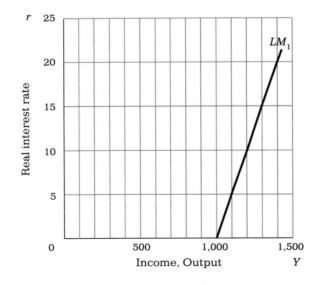

g. increase; rise

h. 800; 800; −50; 0.05; −50; 0.05

7. a. −50; 0.05

Graph 11-18

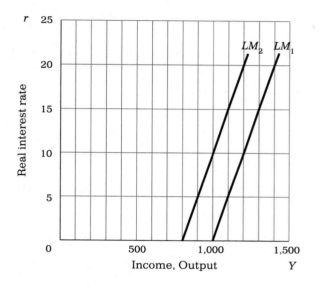

b. −40; 0.05; equal to; greater than; left (upward)

c. increase; decrease; left (upward); right (downward)

8. a. 40; −0.025

Graph 11-19

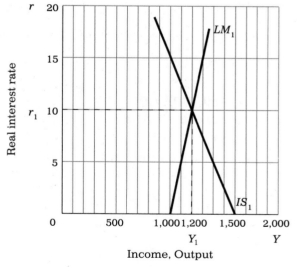

b. −50; 0.05

c. 1,200; 10

Problems

1. **a.** 0.8
   b. Graph for Problem 1b

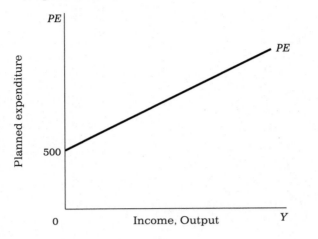

slope = 0.8; y intercept = 500

   c. 2,500
   d. 100

2. **a.** 2,500
   b. **i.** The planned expenditure curve shifts upward by 10.
      ii. The equilibrium level of income increases by 50.
      iii. The level of consumption rises by 40.
      iv. The government budget deficit rises by 10.
   c. **i.** The planned expenditure curve shifts downward by 8.
      ii. The equilibrium level of income decreases by 40.
      iii. The level of consumption decreases by 40.
      iv. The government budget deficit decreases by 10.
   d. **i.** The planned expenditure curve shifts upward by 2.
      ii. The equilibrium level of income increases by 10.
      iii. The level of consumption remains constant.
      iv. The government budget deficit remains unchanged.

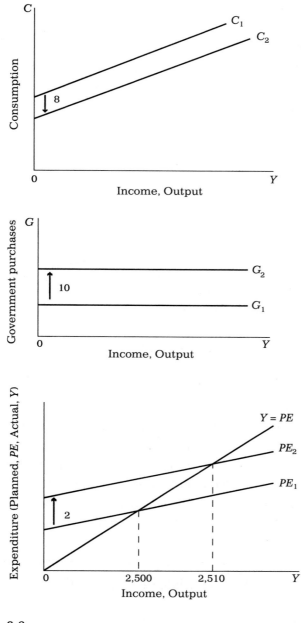

3. **a.** 0.6

   b. 100

   c. 1,500

   d. 2.5

   e. 50/2.5 = 20

5. **a.** $Y = 1,250 - 10r$

   b. $Y = 980 + 8r$

   c. $r = 125 - (1/10)Y$ (*IS* curve equation)

   $r = -122.5 + (1/8)Y$ (*LM* curve equation)

Graphs for Problem 5c

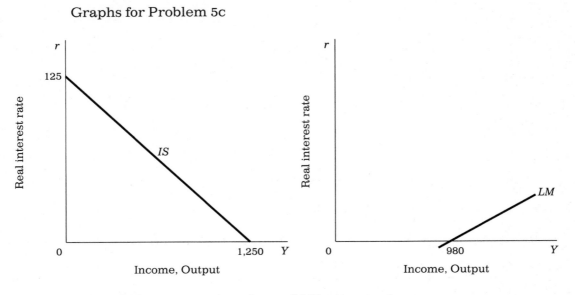

slope of *IS* curve = –1/10; slope of *LM* curve = 1/8

d. $r = 15$ (percent); $Y = 1,100$; $I = 40$; $C = 710$

e. –150

7. The money demand curve would shift to the right and the LM curve would shift to the left.

8. **a.** The *IS* curve becomes flatter.

b. The *IS* curve becomes flatter.

9. **a.** The planned expenditure curve shifted up by the increase in government purchases plus *MPC* times the reduction in net taxes *T*. Net taxes fell by the reduction in Social Security taxes plus the increase in unemployment benefits. The equilibrium level of *GDP* increased by the government purchases multiplier times the increase in *G* plus the tax multiplier times the reduction in *T* (or, by the shift in the planned expenditure curve times the government purchases multiplier).

b. The *IS* curve shifted to the right by the government purchases multiplier times the increase in *G* plus the tax multiplier times the reduction in *T*. The *LM* curve did not shift.

CHAPTER 12

Fill-in Questions

1.   monetary transmission mechanism
2.   shocks to the *IS* curve; shocks to the *LM* curve
3.   federal funds rate
4.   Pigou effect
5.   debt-deflation theory
6.   liquidity trap; zero lower bound

Multiple-Choice Questions

1. b	**2.** a	**3.** d	**4.** c	**5.** d	**6.** d	**7.** d
8. d	**9.** c	**10.** d	**11.** a	**12.** c	**13.** b	**14.** d
15. a	**16.** a	**17.** d	**18.** c	**19.** b	**20.** c	**21.** d
22. d	**23.** b					

Exercises

1. **a.**   1,200; 10

    b.   upward; 100; right; 400

    Graph 12-1

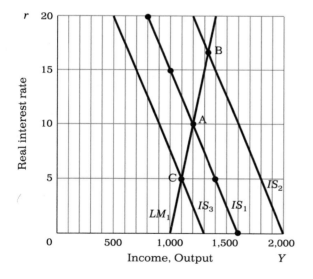

c.   rises; increase; decrease; less

d.   downward; 75; left; 300

e.   falls; decrease; increase; less

f.   downward (to the right); fall; rise; lower; increases; increases

Graph 12-2

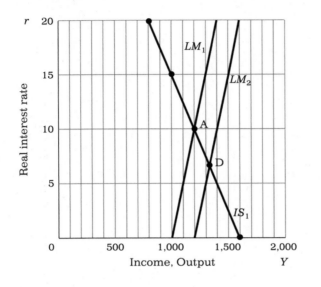

upward (to the left); rise; fall

g.   *IS*; right; rise; rise; *IS*; left; fall; fall; right; *LM*; upward (to the left); fall; rise

2. **a.** downward (to the right)

Graph 12-3 and **Graph 12-4**

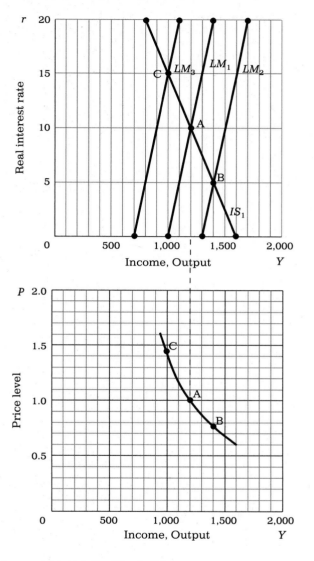

b. upward (to the left)

c. 1.0; 1,200

d. 0.77; 1,400

e. 1.43; 1,000

f. increase; *LM*; downward (to the right); decreases; increases; increases

3. a. 1.0; 1,000; 1,600; 1,300

Graph 12-5 and **Graph 12-6**

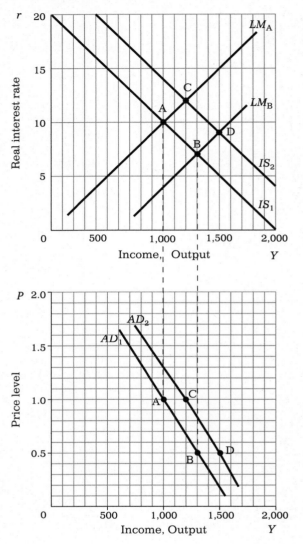

b. 4; right; 400

c. less

e. higher than; equal to; higher than; equal to

f. right; right; right; right

4. a. 1.0; 1,000

Graph 12-7

Graph 12-8

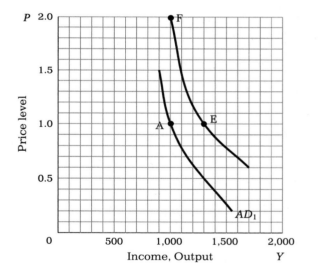

b. 1,600; downward (to the right)

c. higher than; equal to; right; left

d. 800; 1,000

5. **a.**   **Graph 12-9**

Graph 12-10

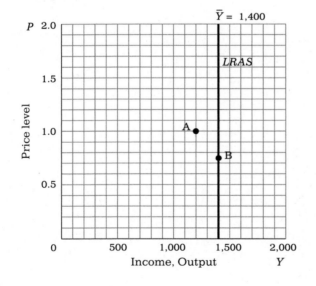

   b.   −50; 0.05

   c.   1,200; 10

   d.   less; sticky; horizontal

   e.   flexible; fall; increase; downward (to the right)

   f.   5; 1,040; 0.77

   g.   rise; *LM*; upward (to the left)

6. a. **Graph 12-11**

b. 1,200; 10; 10

c. 10; 17.5; higher; 10; 10; 10; −7.5; 2.5; 7.5; downward; 7.5

d. 1,100; 5

e. decrease; decrease; 10; 0; 10; 5; −7.5; 12.5; rises

7. a. 50; 50; 50; 0.75; 200

b. 0.9; 10; larger

c. 10; 500; larger

d. 5; 200; 500; larger; larger; flatter

e. 10

f. 20; more; flatter

Graph 12-12

     g.   100

     h.   10; 4; 200; 20; 100; 100; 400; flatter

8. **a.**   more; more; steeper

     b.   128; 128; 8; 160; 160; 10; more; steeper

     c.   16; 32; more; flatter

     d.   128; 128; 8; 128; 4; less; steeper

Problems

1. **a.** $Y = 1{,}250 - 10r$

     b. $Y = 980 + 8r$

     c. $r = 125 - (1/10)Y$ (*IS* curve equation)

         $r = -122.5 + (1/8)Y$ (*LM* curve equation)

         Graphs for Problem 1c

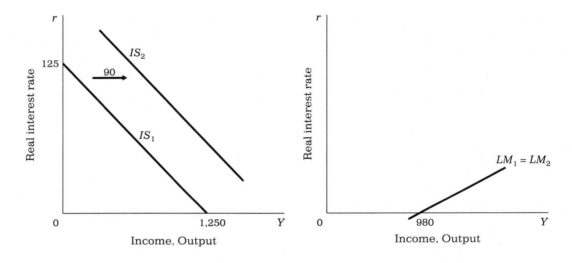

         slope of *IS* curve = $-1/10$; slope of *LM* curve = $1/8$

     d. $r = 15$ (percent); $Y = 1{,}100$; $I = 40$; $C = 710$

     e. -150

     f.   The *LM* equation remains unchanged. The new *IS* equation is $Y = 1{,}340 - 10r$.

     g.   The shift in the *IS* curve is equal to 90. The *LM* curve does not shift.

     h. $Y = 1{,}140$; $r = 20$; $I = 20$; $C = 734$

     i.   54

     j.   Government purchases are higher in Part h. Since taxes and output are the same as Parts h and i, consumption is also the same. Since the interest rate is lower in Part i, investment is higher. Advocates of expansionary fiscal policy may argue that the United States is badly in need of public spending in areas like education, defense, and infrastructure. Advocates of expansionary monetary policy, on the other hand, would tout its effect on investment, which might spur economic growth as the capital stock grows.

2. a. The *IS* curve would shift left to IS_2. Both Y and r would fall.

Graph for Problem 2a

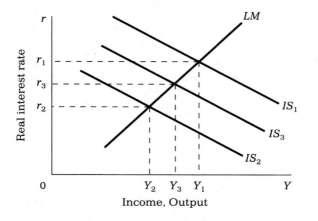

b. Since part of transfers are saved, the reduction in G would dominate. The *IS* curve would shift left (to IS_3) by a smaller amount than in Part a. Both Y and r would fall.

c. The reductions in Y and r would be smaller in Part b than in Part a.

3. a. By reducing household wealth, the stock market decline would shift both the consumption and total planned expenditure curves downward.

b. Consequently, the *IS* curve would shift to the left, and both Y and r would fall.

Graph for Problem 3b

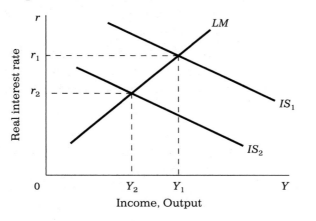

5. **a.** When the *MPC* is large, *ceteris paribus*, the slope of the planned expenditure curve will be large, and the multiplier will be large, resulting in a flatter *IS* curve in Country A. Intuitively, as *r* falls, investment rises and GDP increases via the direct effect on investment and multiplier effects on consumption. The latter will be larger when *MPC* is bigger, since people will then consume a greater fraction of the increase in disposable income in each successive round. The shape of the *LM* curve is unaffected by the *MPC*. Graph for Problem 5a

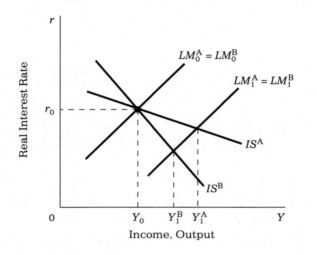

   b. Monetary policy will be more effective in changing *Y* in Country A, where the *IS* curve is flatter.

6. **a.** The *LM* curve would remain stationary. The economy would move along a stationary *LM* curve in response to shifts in the *IS* curve. GDP would rise when private spending increases and would fall when private spending decreases. Graph for Problem 6a

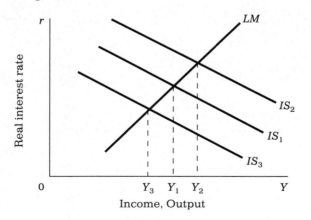

b. As Y increases in response to a shift in the IS curve to the right, the money demand curve would shift to the right. To keep the interest rate constant, the money supply would have to rise, shifting the LM curve downward (to the right).

Graphs for Problem 6b

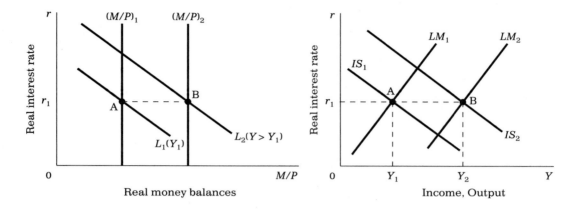

c. As Y decreases in response to a shift in the IS curve to the left, the money demand curve would shift to the left. To keep the interest rate constant, the money supply would have to fall, shifting the LM curve upward (to the left).

d. In Parts b and c, the Federal Reserve's policy exacerbates the fluctuations in Y following shifts in the IS curve. Consequently, a stable money supply would better stabilize the economy if the disturbances stem primarily from shifts in the IS curve.

7. a. An increase in G and cut in net taxes T shift the IS and AD curves to the right. The $SRAS$ and LM curves do not shift in the short run.

Graphs for Problem 7a

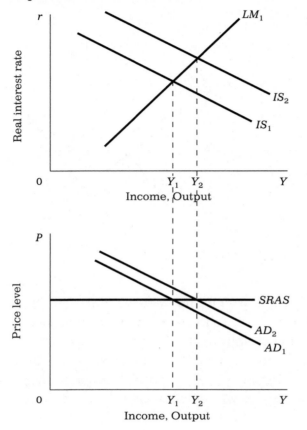

The equilibrium levels of Y, r, and C all rise. The equilibrium level of I falls, and G and P do not change in the short run (given the horizontal $SRAS$ curve of Chapter 10).

b. The Federal Reserve increased the money supply at the same time as government spending rose and taxes fell. Consequently, both the IS and LM curves shifted to the right. This shifted the AD curve even farther to the right.

Graphs for Problem 7b

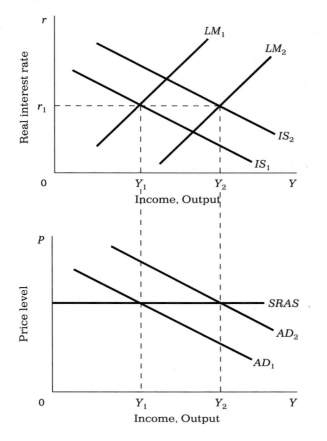

The levels of Y and C rise by more in Part b than in Part a. The remaining variables, r, I, G, and P remain constant.

8. The Federal Reserve should increase the money supply (which would shift the LM curve downward, or to the right), and the government should simultaneously reduce G and/or increase T (which would shift the IS curve left). Real GDP could remain unchanged, but the reduction in the real interest rate would increase investment.

Graph for Problem 8

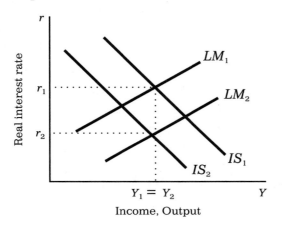

9. **a.** If consumption rises as the interest rate falls, the *IS* curve would be flatter because now both consumption and investment would increase when *r* falls. The *LM* curve is unaffected.

b. A flat *IS* curve will enhance the short-run effectiveness of monetary policy. (See Graph for Problem 5a.)

c. A flat *IS* curve will flatten the slope of the *AD* curve.

10. **a.** Graphs for Problem 10a

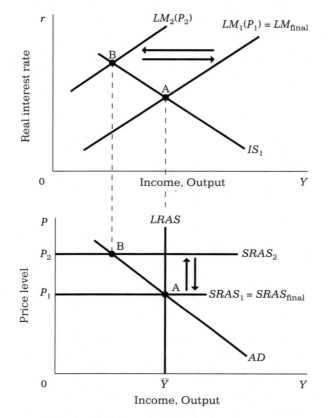

b. In the short run, the *SRAS* curve shifts upward. This increases *P* and thereby shifts the *LM* curve upward (to the left). Since output falls below its natural level, the *SRAS* curve will shift downward in subsequent periods. As it does, *P* will fall and the *LM* curve will shift back downward (to the right) until it reaches its initial position, at which point *Y* and *P* will also reach their initial levels. (This assumes that the natural level of output is unaffected.)

11. At the initial equilibrium the nominal interest rate is almost zero. If the announced monetary expansion increases expected inflation, the real interest rate would fall by the full amount of the increase in expected inflation at each level of the nominal interest rate. Consequently, the *IS* curve would shift upward by the increase in expected inflation. As the Fed increases the nominal money supply, the *LM* curve will also shift right. The equilibrium levels of *i* and *Y* would rise and the equilibrium level of *r* would fall.

Graph for Problem 11

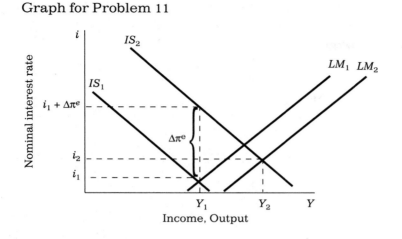

12. The sharp increase in stock prices during the 1990s increased household wealth and thereby increased consumption, shifting the *IS* curve to the right. The optimistic perceptions of the profitability of new technologies increased investment, shifting the *IS* curve further to the right. As a result, *Y* would increase substantially, as it did during the 1990s.

Graph for Problem 12

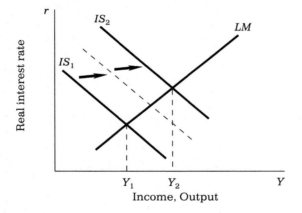

15. **a.** The *IS* curve would shift to the right by the change in government spending times the government purchases multiplier *plus* the reduction in taxes times the tax multiplier, or by:

$$(\text{Change in } G) \times 1/(1 - MPC) + (\text{Reduction in } T) \times MPC/(1 - MPC)$$

b. As illustrated below, the *IS* curve would shift right and the *LM* curve would not shift. Both output and the interest rate would rise.

Graph for Problem 15b

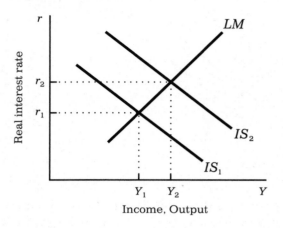

c. If the Fed acted to reduce the federal funds rate at the same time, the *LM* curve would shift right at the same time as the *IS* curve shifted right. Output would rise even more. Although the interest rate could theoretically rise or fall, the Fed acted to ensure that it fell.

Graph for Problem 15c

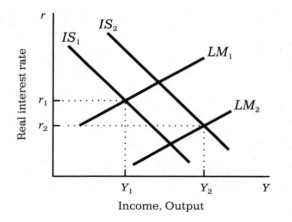

CHAPTER 13

Fill-in Questions

1. floating exchange rate
2. fixed exchange rate
3. fixed exchange rate; floating exchange rate
4. devaluation; revaluation
5. Mundell–Fleming model; devaluation; revaluation
6. fixed exchange rate
7. speculative attack; fixed exchange rate
8. currency board
9. Dollarization
10. impossible trinity; fixed exchange rate

Multiple-Choice Questions

1. c	2. d	3. c	4. c	5. a	6. b	7. a
8. b	9. d	10. c	11. b	12. d	13. d	14. a
15. b	16. c	17. d	18. c	19. b	20. d	21. b
22. d	23. d	24. b	25. d			

Exercises

1. **b.** 2; 50; 400; 0.75; 10
   c. 40; 0.025

   Graph 13-1

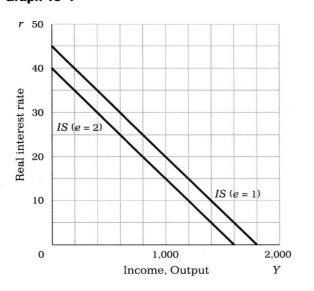

   d.   depreciation; rise; 1; 100; 45; 0.025

   e.   depreciation; increase; upward; right; 50; upward; 50; right; 50; 4; 200; appreciation; decrease; downward; left

2. a.   50; 1,200

Graph 13-2

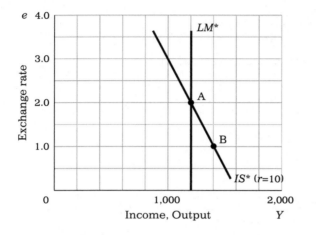

   b.   1,400; rise; upward; increases

   d.   2; 1,200; A

3. a.   2; 1,200

Graph 13-3

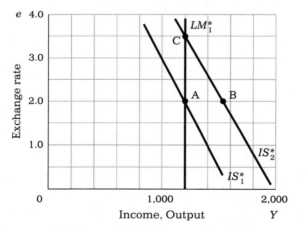

   b.   increasing; decreasing; increase; right

   c.   greater than; decreases; increase; rises; decrease; increase; rises above; increases

   d.   has no effect on; increases; fall; has no effect on; decreases

e. right (downward); rise; right;

Graph 13-4

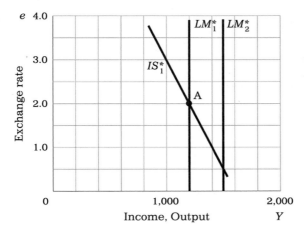

increases; decreases; rise

f. increase; the interest rate; out of; depreciate; increases

4. a. 2

Graph 13-5

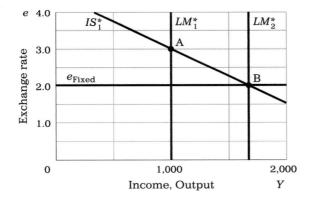

b. greater than; 3; 3; 3; 1.50

c. increases; right; increase; right

d. less than; 1; 1; 2

Graph 13-6

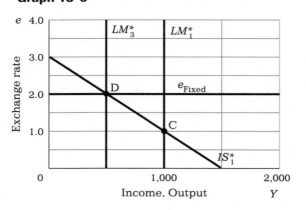

e. decreases; left; decrease; left

5. a. **Graph 13-7**

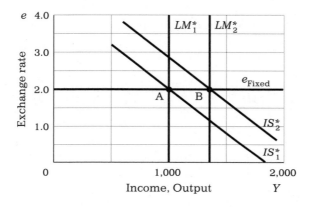

right

b. have no effect on; increase; increase; right; 2; increase; have no effect on

c. right

Graph 13-8

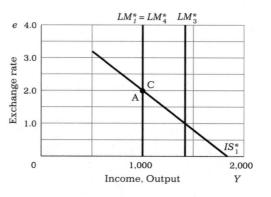

increase; decrease; falls below; selling; buying; decrease; left; 2; have no effect on; have no effect on; equal to; remain constant

d. buying; selling; increase; right; increase; left; decrease

6. **a.** higher
   b. rises; decrease; left
   c. decrease; right
   d. depreciation; increase
   e. increases; LM^*; left; decrease; LM^*; left; LM^* left

   Graph 13-9

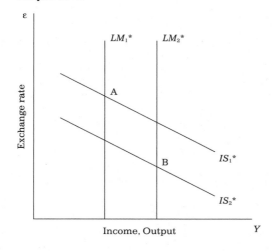

7. **a.** less than; remain constant
   b. downward; fall; rise

   Graph 13-10

Graph 13-11

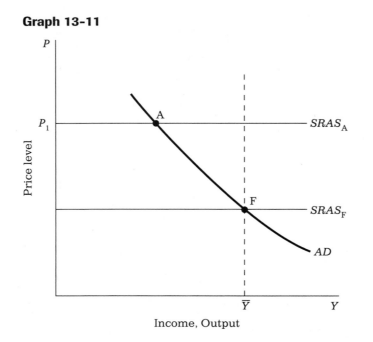

c. increase; supply; LM^*; right; fall; rise; rises; rise; remains the same; remains the same

8. a. increases; increases

   b. rises; rises; increase; increase; depreciation

   c. increase; increase; more; flatter

Graph 13-12

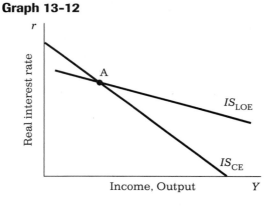

   d. more; less

Problems

1. As the money supply begins to contract, the domestic interest rate will begin to rise above the world interest rate. Capital flows into the domestic economy as both foreigners and domestic investors wish to buy additional domestic bonds and assets. This will push the foreign exchange rate above the initial fixed exchange rate. Arbitragers will then sell foreign currency to (and buy domestic

currency from) the central bank. As a result, the domestic money supply will rise until the foreign exchange rate and the domestic interest rate fall back to their initial levels, at which point the money supply and real income will be equal to their initial levels.

2. If Greece had its own currency and central bank, it would regain control over the use of monetary policy for stabilization purchases. Consequently, it could pursue expansionary monetary policy to alleviate its recession. Expansionary fiscal policy was not an option because of the high government debt. As prices rose, the real value of its debt would also fall. Policymakers who opposed such a move did so for a variety of reasons, many of which are not discussed in Chapter 13. One argument is that Greece's abandonment of the euro would remove a mechanism that provided useful discipline to Greek monetary authorities. It would also increase uncertainty regarding future exchange-rate movements. And it might lead to the bankruptcy of Greek and other banks and financial institutions that owned Greek debt.

3. Participating countries have lost their ability to conduct independent monetary policies.

4. During a recession, actual output is presumably less than the natural level of output. Consequently, over time the domestic price level will fall. This will increase the real money supply and shift the LM^* curve to the right. As a result, the real exchange rate will fall, and the trade balance will rise along with national output.

5. The export restrictions will shift the NX curve to the left. Consequently, the IS^* curve will shift to the left.

    a. If the country has a floating exchange rate, the LM^* curve is vertical. Consequently, the exchange rate will fall, but real GDP will remain unchanged.

        Graph for Problem 5a

    b.   If the country has a fixed exchange rate, the LM^* curve will also shift to the left to keep the exchange rate constant. Consequently, real GDP will fall. Graph for Problem 5b

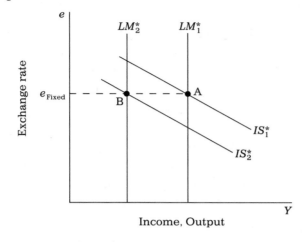

6.   A crisis in confidence will raise a country's risk premium. Consequently, the domestic interest rate will rise. This will shift the IS^* curve to the left and the LM^* curve to the right (to LM_2^*). If, however, the country has a fixed exchange rate, it will be compelled to sell foreign currency and shift its LM^* curve to the left of its original position (to LM_3^*). This will reduce real GDP.
Graph for Problem 6

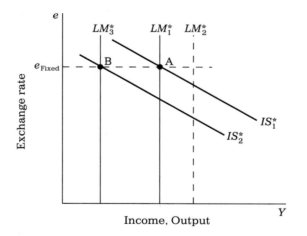

7.   Renewed stability would reduce these countries' risk premiums. Consequently, their domestic interest rates would fall. This would shift the IS^* curve to the right and the LM^* curve to the left. Under a regime of floating exchange rates, the countries' exchange rates would rise while real GDP would fall. (In reality, other developments have helped these countries increase their real GDP.)

Graph for Problem 7

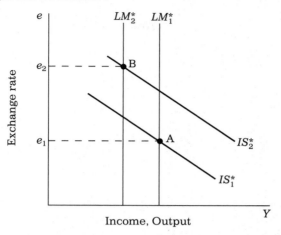

8. **a.** The shift in Argentina's net export curve would also shift its *IS** curve to the left. If Argentina kept the initial dollar–peso exchange rate of 1:1, it would have to buy pesos, thereby shifting its *LM** curve to the left. Consequently, its real GDP would fall. Since Argentina is being treated as a small open economy, its interest rate would remain at the world interest rate:

Graph for Problem 8a

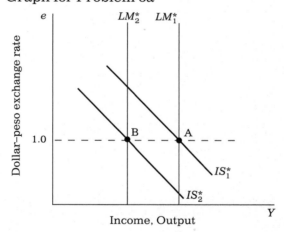

   b. Once again, the shift in the net export curve would shift the *IS** curve to the left. If Argentina abandoned its fixed dollar–peso exchange rate, however, it would have fallen (i.e., the peso would have depreciated) to point B and there would have been no effect on real GDP:

Graph for Problem 8b

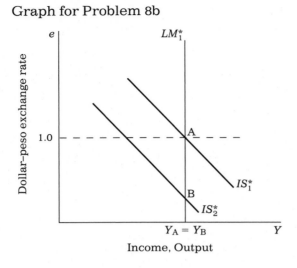

9. The reduction in consumer confidence will shift the *IS* curve to the left. Consequently, the domestic real interest rate will fall. As a result, net capital outflow will increase along with net exports. The foreign exchange rate will decline and net exports will rise, cushioning the decline in GDP.

Graphs for Problem 9

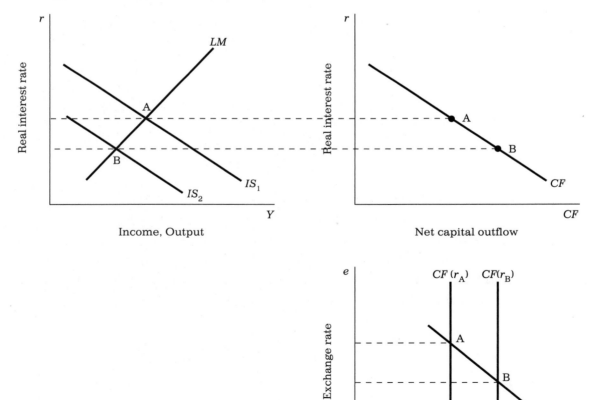

10. a. The net capital outflow curve will shift right as foreigners wish to buy fewer U.S. assets and lend less to U.S. borrowers at any given interest rate. Graphs for Problem 10

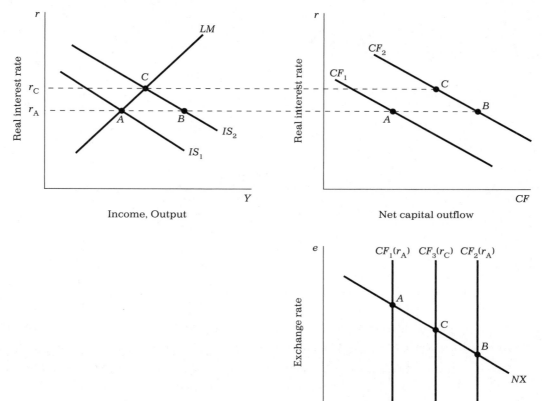

b. At the original real interest rate, the U.S. trade balance will increase (to Point B in the graph) and the foreign exchange rate will fall.

c. Since the decline in the exchange rate (and increase in net exports) occurred at the original interest rate, the *IS* curve will shift right to Point B. The *LM* curve will not shift.

d. The domestic real interest rate rises to Point C.

e. As the real interest rate rises, we move along CF_2 to Point C. Comparing Points A and C, the levels of net capital outflow and net exports have increased.

f. U.S. national income and output have risen (although other factors may affect them adversely).

11. To keep the real exchange rate constant, *CF* must not change, which will occur only if the real interest rate does not change. To increase Y without changing r, the Fed must increase the money supply while the government simultaneously pursues expansionary fiscal policy by increasing G or cutting T. This will shift both the *IS* and *LM* curves to the right.

Graphs for Problem 11

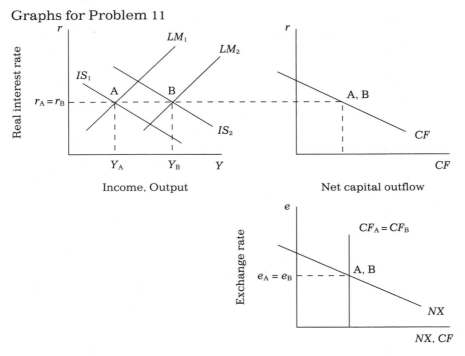

Income, Output

Net capital outflow

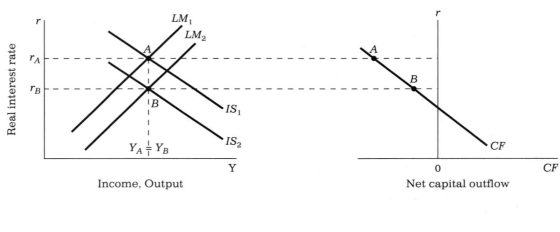

Net exports, net capital flow

12. To reduce the trade deficit, the exchange rate would have to fall. Policymakers could reduce the exchange rate without changing real GDP by an appropriate mix of expansionary monetary policy (such as an open-market purchase) and contractionary fiscal policy (such as a tax increase or a reduction in government spending), as the following graphs depict:

Income, Output

Net capital outflow

Net exports, net capital outflow

CHAPTER 14

Fill-in Questions

1. sticky-price model
2. imperfect-information model
3. sticky price; imperfect information
4. Phillips curve
5. NAIRU
6. demand-pull inflation
7. cost-push inflation
8. adaptive expectations
9. rational expectations
10. sacrifice ratio; rational expectations; adaptive expectations
11. natural-rate hypothesis
12. Hysteresis

Multiple-Choice Questions

1. d   2. c   3. c   4. a   5. b   6. b   7. a
8. b   9. b   10. a   11. d   12. d   13. a   14. a
15. c   16. d   17. a   18. a

Exercises

1. **a.** equal to; greater than

   b. **Graph 14-1**

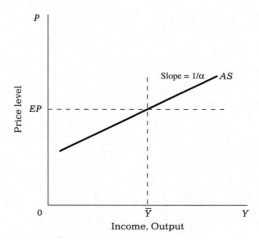

   slope = $1/\alpha$

   c. upward (to the left); downward (to the right); increase

2. **b.** rise; raise; increase; increase

   c. 0; equal to; greater than; decreases; increases; decreases; decreases; flatter; horizontal; 1; all

3. **b.** $1; 1; 1; 100

    Graph 14-2

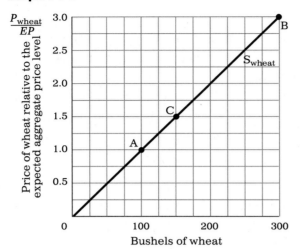

    c. $3; 1; 3; rise; 300

    d. $1; 1; 1; 100

    e. 200; 200; 100; 2; 2; 1.5; 150

    Graph 14-3

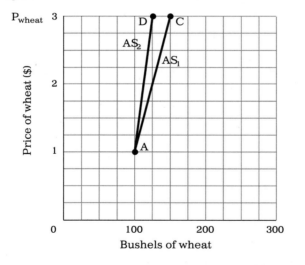

    f. 1; greater; less

    g. 200; 200; 140; 2.4; 2.4; 1.25; 125; steeper; steep; 1; 100; vertical

4. **a.** increase; *LM*; downward (to the right); increases; rises above; flexible; equal to

    b. equal to; 1

    c. increase; decrease; increase; 1; 1,400; 1.4

    d. greater than; increase

e. 1.4; 1.4; upward; 1.4

Graph 14-4

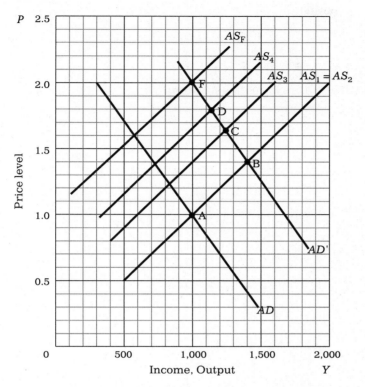

f. approximately 1,220; approximately 1.65; fallen; risen

g. greater than; increase; 1.65; 1.65; upward; 1.65

h. greater than; increase; upward; greater than; 1,000; 2; 2

i. no change; an increase

j. more; more

5. a. positive; less

b. 10; 0.4; equal to

Graph 14-5

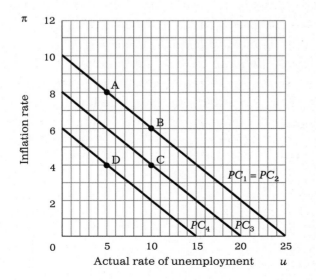

c. decreasing; increasing; decreasing; 8; right

d. 10; 6

e. less than; fall; downward

f. 6; 6; 6; 8; 0.4

g. 10; 4

h. less than; fall; downward; 4; 4; 4; 6; 0.4

i. 5; 4; equal to; stay the same; remain stationary

j. 4; 5; 5; 10; 4; 4; 2.5; 5; sacrifice

k. more; more; lower

l. 5; 8; 15; 4; 4; 4; 6; 0.4;

Graph 14-6

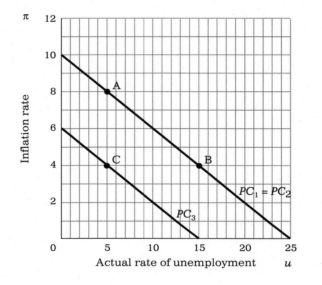

5; 4; equal to; 10; 4; equal to

m. shift upward

Problems

1. As the fraction of firms that have flexible prices becomes greater, the short-run aggregate supply curve becomes steeper because prices will adjust more quickly whenever real GDP deviates from its natural level. Monetary and fiscal policy changes affect real GDP by shifting the aggregate demand curve. If the aggregate supply curve is steep, shifts in the aggregate demand curve will have smaller short-run effects on output and bigger effects on the price level. Thus, as the fraction of firms with flexible prices becomes greater, the power of monetary and fiscal policy to change real GDP becomes weaker.

2. Graph for Problem 2

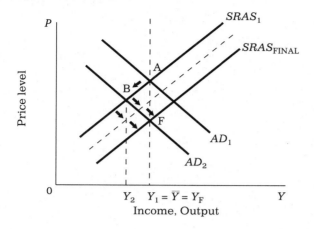

3. **a.** If expectations were rational, people would probably lower their expectations of future price levels more rapidly. Consequently, the *SRAS* curve would move toward its final position at Point F more rapidly.

   b. If a greater fraction of firms have flexible prices, the short-run aggregate supply curve would be steeper than that depicted in the Graph for Problem 2. As a result, the price level would fall by more in the short run following a decrease in aggregate demand. Consequently, the expected price level would also fall more rapidly, and the economy would move toward its final position at Point F more quickly.

4. $d[(1 - s)a/s]/ds = -a/s^2 < 0$. When the fraction of firms with sticky prices s rises, the slope falls and the short-run aggregate supply curve flattens.

5. If real GDP falls (or unemployment rises) along with an increase in inflation, this probably represents a supply shock or an upward shift of the Phillips curve. Since the economy began at the natural level of output, there is no reason for expected inflation or the expected price level to rise suddenly. Consequently, we could characterize the inflation as cost-push. If real GDP rises (or unemployment falls) along with the increase in inflation, this probably results from a shift in aggregate demand or a movement along a Phillips curve. Consequently, we could characterize the inflation as demand-pull.

6. **a.** The natural rate of unemployment is 0.04, or 4 percent.

b. Graph for Problem 6b

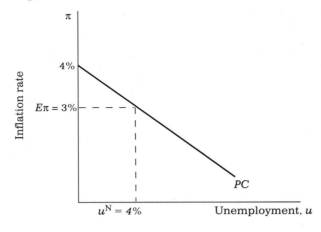

c. 8

7. Your answer will depend on the most recent unemployment and inflation data and whether the economy is experiencing a supply shock. Most economists believe that the natural rate of unemployment lies between 5 and 6 percent. If the most recent unemployment rate is below this range and there are no supply shocks, the actual inflation rate would exceed the expected inflation rate. Consequently, expected inflation would increase over time, thereby shifting the Phillips curve up, and unemployment would move toward its natural rate. If the most recent unemployment rate is above this range and there are no supply shocks, the reverse would be true.

8. According to the hysteresis theory, the natural rate of unemployment may rise during a recession, leading to a reduction in the natural level of output. This would shift the long-run aggregate supply curve to the left.

CHAPTER 15

Fill-in Questions

1. natural rate of interest
2. random variable
3. Taylor rule
4. predetermined variable
5. impulse response function
6. Taylor principle
7. Taylor principle

Multiple-Choice Questions

1. d	2. d	3. c	4. d	5. a	6. c	7. d	8. d	9. c	10. d
11. d	12. a	13. d	14. a	15. b	16. d	17. c	18. a	19. c	20. a
21. d	22. d	23. c	24. d	25. a	26. a	27. c	28. d	29. b	30. b

Exercises

1. **a.** fall; more

   b. $t + 1$; t

   c. 2

   d. t

   e. π_t; increasing; decrease; increasing; decrease; decrease; ρ

   f. falls; decreases; decreases

   g. $Y_t = \overline{Y}_t - [\alpha\theta_\pi/(1 + \alpha\theta_Y)](\pi_t - \pi_t^*) + [1/(1 + \alpha\theta_Y)]\varepsilon_t$

   h. falls

   i. increases; more than; rises; increase; reduces

   Graph 15-1

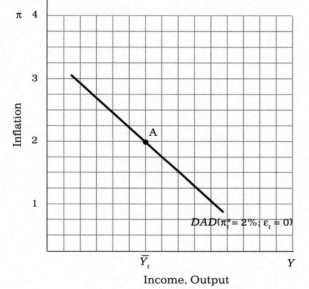

   k. rise; upward (to the right)

   l. increase; upward (to the right); decreasing; lower; decrease; right

   m. equal to; right

2. **a.** 2; 2

   b. 0; 2:2:0; 4; rises

   c. 1; rises; increases

d. and **e.**

Table 15-1

(1) Inflation (%)	(2) Actual GDP ($ billions)	(3) Natural Level of GDP ($ billions)	(4) GDP gap (%)	(5) Nominal Federal Funds Rate (%)	(6) Real Federal Funds Rate (%)
2	100	100	0	4	2
3	100	100	0	5.5	2.5
2	106	100	6	7	5
2	94	100	−6	1	−1
4	96	100	−4	5	1

minus

f. 1.5; rose; 0.5

3. **a.** $t-1$; t

b. falls below

c. negative

d. 2; 2.25; 1.75; 3; 3.25

e. 2; 1; 2.25; 1; 1.75

Graph 15-2

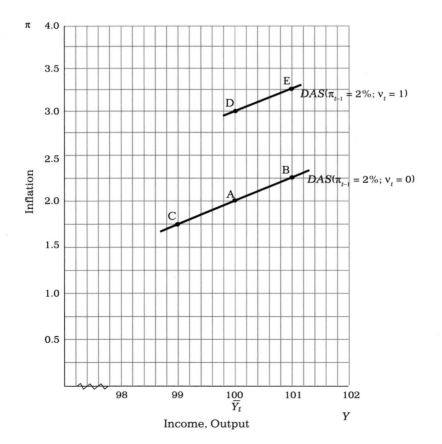

    f.   0.25; φ; rise; bigger; steeper

    g.   3; 3.25; upward; 1

    h.   3; 3.25; 3; 3.25; upward; 1; downward (to the right)

    Graph 15-3

    i.   100; 3; 110; 0; 3

4.   **b.** $\overline{Y}_t$

    c.   ρ

    d. π_t^*; target rate of inflation; π_t^*; target

    e. π_t^*; target rate of inflation

5.   **a.**   natural level

    b.   upward (to the left); equal to; the natural level of output

    c. $\overline{Y}_{t-1}$

Graph 15-4

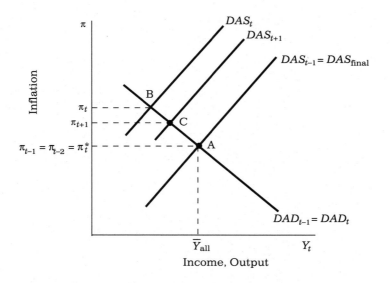

d. upward (to the left); decreases; increases
e. 0; increases; decreases
f. fall
g. lower; higher

6. **b.** 100; 1/3; 2; 2/3; 0.25; 100
   c. 100; 2
   d. 2; 0.25; 100; 2; 100; 100; 2
   e.

Table 15-4

(1) Period	(2) Supply Shock v	(3) Demand Shock ε	(4) Inflation in Preceding Period	(5) Output Y	(6) Inflation π
t − 2	0	0	2	100	2
t − 1	0	0	2	100	2
t	1	0	2	99.692	2.923
t + 1	0	0	2.923	99.716	2.852
t + 2	0	0	2.852	99.738	2.787
t + 3	0	0	2.787	99.758	2.762

   2; 1; 0; 99.692
   f. 2; 99.692; 1; 2.923
   g. 2.923; 2.923; 0; 0; 99.716; 2.923; 0.071; 0; 2.852
   h. 2.852; 2.852; 0; 0; 99.738; 2.852; 0.0655; 0; 2.787
   i. 1; falls; 99.692; 0; rises; 99.716; 0; 99.738; falls; rise
   j. rises; fall

Graph 15-5

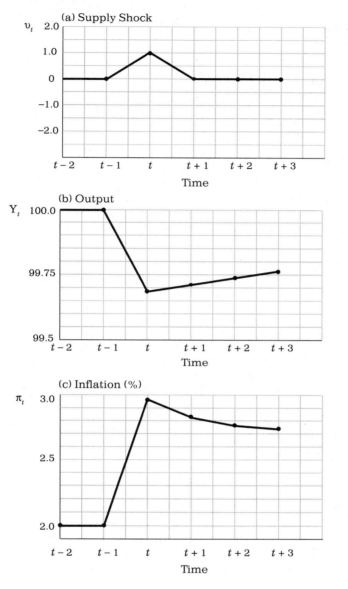

7. **a.** increase; right

    b. increased; increased

    c. 1; rise; upward (to the left); decreased; increased; increasing

    d. rise; upward (to the left); decrease; downward (to the right); target rate of inflation; natural level of output

Graph 15-6

8.   a.   **Graph 15-7**

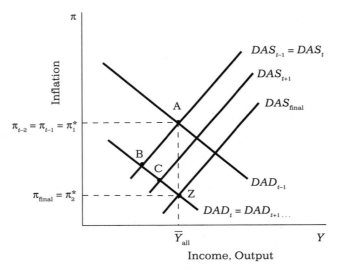

downward (to the left); decreases; decreases

b.   downward (to the right); increases; decreases

c.   downward (to the right); equal to

d.   quickly

9.   a.   **Graph 15-8**

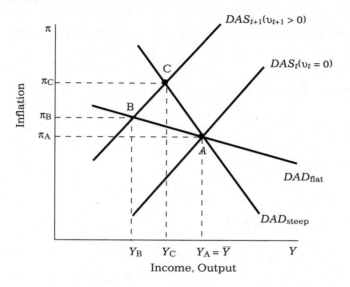

flat; steep

   b.   equal to: $[(1 + \alpha\theta_Y)/\alpha\theta_\pi]; - [(1 + \alpha\theta_Y)/\alpha\theta_\pi]$ (or negative)

   c.   large; small; flat; small; large; a lot; low; high

   d.   large; large; steep; large; small; a little; high; low

10.   **a.**   increase; more than; increase; decreases; negative

   b.   less than; decrease; increase

   c.   **Graph 15-9**

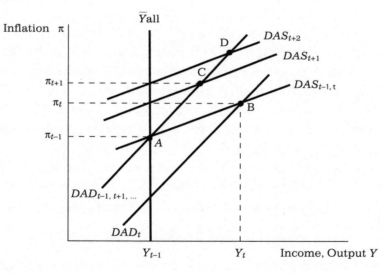

increasse

   d.   increase; upward; increases

   e.   increase; upward; increased

   f.   upward; rise

   g.   negative; more than; rises; positive

Problems

1. **a.** The size of α is determined primarily by the sensitivity of investment and consumption to changes in the real interest rate. If investment and consumption are very sensitive to changes in r, α will be large.

   b. If α is large, an increase in r (in response to an increase in inflation) will lead to a big reduction in the demand for goods and services. Thus, the DAD curve will be flatter.

   c. Graph for Problem 1c

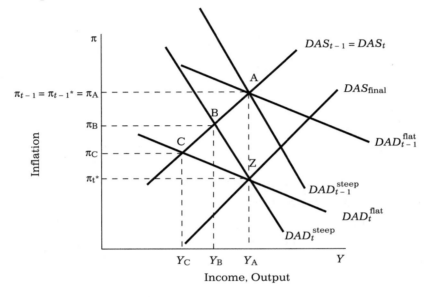

Income, Output

When the central bank reduces its target for the inflation rate, the DAD curve will shift down vertically by the change in the target. If the DAD curve is flat (and α is large), the short-run decline in output will be bigger (from Y_A to Y_C), as will the immediate decline in inflation (from π_A to π_C) than if the DAD curve is steep (and α is small). In the long run, there will be no differences in the responses since inflation will fall to the new target and output will be at its natural level at Point Z.

2. **a.** The recommended nominal federal funds rate = 8 percent, and the recommended real federal funds rate = 4 percent.

   b. The recommended nominal federal funds rate = 2.5 percent, and the recommended real federal funds rate = 1.5 percent.

3. **a.** –8 percent

   b. The recommended nominal federal funds rate = –1.5 percent, and the recommended real federal funds rate = –2.5 percent.

   c. The Fed could increase the money supply to generate inflation and increase inflation expectations so that they both exceed 2.5 percent. At that point, a low nominal federal funds rate would result in a negative real federal funds rate.

4. Inflation expectations would change more slowly and the economy would return more slowly to its long-run equilibrium following a temporary supply shock.

5. **a.** $\pi_t = \pi_{t-1} + (1/4)(Y_t - 100) + v_t$

Substituting for π_t in $Y_t = 100 - (1/3)(\pi_t - 2) + (2/3)\varepsilon_t$ yields

$Y_t = 100 - (1/3)[\pi_{t-1} + (1/4)(Y_t - 100) + v_t - 2] + (2/3)\varepsilon_t$

$(13/12)Y_t = 109 - (1/3)\pi_{t-1} - (1/3)\,v_t + (2/3)\varepsilon_t$

$Y_t = 100.6154 - (4/13)\pi_{t-1} - (4/13)\,v_t + (8/13)\varepsilon_t$

6. **a.**

Table 15-5

(1)	(2)	(3)	(4)	(5)	(6)
	Supply Shock	Demand Shock	Inflation in Preceding	Output	Inflation
Period	v_t	ε_t	Period	Y_t	π_t
$t-2$	0	0	2	100	2
$t-1$	0	0	2	100	2
t	0	1	2	100.6154	2.1539
$t+1$	0	1	2.1539	100.5681	2.2959
$t+2$	0	0	2.2959	99.9090	2.2731
$t+3$	0	0	2.2731	99.9160	2.2521

Graph for Problem 6

(a) Demand Shock

(b) Output

Graph for Problem 6 (continues)

Time

(c) Inflation (%)

Time

7. **a.** Let $a = [\alpha\theta_\pi/(1 + \alpha\theta_Y)]$ and $b = [1/(1 + \alpha\theta_Y)]$

Then $Y_t = \overline{Y}_t - a\pi_t + a\pi_t^* + b\varepsilon_t$, and $\pi_t = \pi_t^* - (1/a)(Y_t - \overline{Y}_t) + (b/a)\varepsilon_t$. Substituting for a and b yields $\pi_t = \pi_t^* - [(1 + \alpha\theta_Y)/\alpha\theta_\pi](Y_t - \overline{Y}_t) + (1/\alpha\theta_\pi)\varepsilon_t$

b. Slope of $DAD = d\pi_t/dY_t = -[(1 + \alpha\theta_Y)/\alpha\theta_\pi]$

c. $d(\text{slope})/d\theta_\pi = -[-\alpha(1 + \alpha\theta_Y)/(\alpha\theta_\pi)^2] = (1 + \alpha\theta_Y)/\alpha\theta_\pi^2$

Since α, θ_Y, and θ_π^2 are always positive, the derivative will be positive. Thus, the value of the slope will get bigger (less negative), and the DAD curve will become flatter.

d. $d(\text{slope})/d\theta_Y = -1/\theta_\pi$, which is always negative. Thus, the value of the slope will get smaller (more negative), and the DAD curve will become steeper.

e. $d(\text{slope})/d\alpha = 1/(\alpha^2\theta_\pi)$, which is always positive. Thus, the slope will get bigger (less negative), and the DAD curve will become flatter.

8. As shown in the following graph, a steep DAD curve will lead to a bigger reduction in both inflation and output. A flat DAD curve will lead to smaller reductions in both inflation and output.

Graph for Problem 8

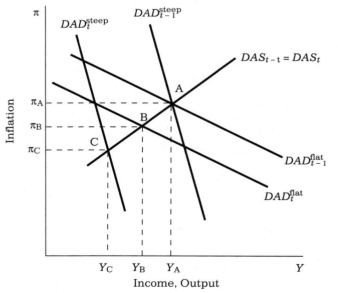

CHAPTER 16

Fill-in Questions

1. marginal propensity to consume
2. average propensity to consume; average propensity to consume; life-cycle hypothesis (or permanent-income hypothesis); permanent-income hypothesis (or life-cycle hypothesis)
3. budget constraint
4. intertemporal budget constraint
5. discounting
6. indifference curve
7. marginal rate of substitution
8. normal good
9. income effect; substitution effect
10. income effect; substitution effect
11. borrowing constraint
12. life-cycle hypothesis; precautionary saving
13. permanent-income hypothesis; Permanent income; transitory income
14. random walk
15. Behavioral economics

Multiple-Choice Questions

1. b	2. d	3. b	4. a	5. c	6. c	7. b
8. b	9. c	10. b	11. b	12. d	13. d	14. d
15. c	16. d	17. d	18. a	19. a	20. c	21. d
22. c	23. d					

Exercises

1. a. **Graph 16-1**

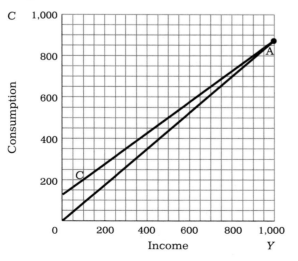

    b.   the fraction of each additional dollar of disposable income that households spend on consumption; 0.75; remains constant; 0; 1

    c.   0.75; 125; 0.75; 125; 1.25; 0.75; 125; 1; 0.75; 125; 0.875; decreases

    d.   875; 875; 1,000; 0.875; *APC*; *APC*; decreases

2. **a.**   0; 1; decreases

    b.   decrease; remain constant

    c.   0; 1; decreases; remain constant; 0

    Graph 16-2

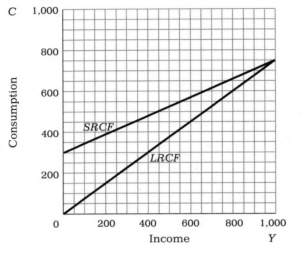

3. **a.**   105

    b.   105; 100

    c.   110.25

    d.   110.25; 100

    e. $FV_T = \$100 \, (1 + i)^T$; $PV = FV_T/(1 + i)^T$

4. a. 12; 12; 12; 0.50; 12; 30; 1.5

Graph 16-3

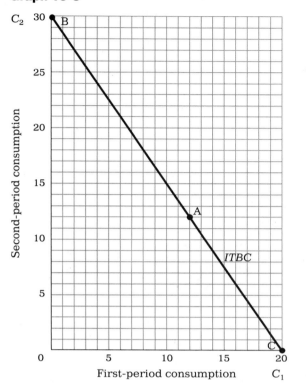

b. 0.50; 1.5; 1.5; 50

c. 12; 0; 12; 0; 12; 12; 12; 0.50; 12; 30; 0; 12; 12; 1.5; 20

---

5. a. **Table 16-1**

	(1)	(2)	(3)	(4)	(5)	(6)	(7)	(8)
C_1		8.0	9.0	10.0	11.00	12.0	14.0	16.0
C_2		18.0	16.0	14.4	13.09	12.0	10.3	9.0
$U = C_1 C_2$		144.0	144.0	144.0	144.00	144.0	144.0	144.0

b. **Graph 16-4**

144

c. **Table 16-2**

(1)	(2)	(3)	(4)	(5)	(6)	(7)	(8)
C_1	8.00	9.00	10.0	11.00	12.0	14.0	16.00
C_2	18.75	16.67	15.0	13.64	12.5	10.7	9.38
$U = C_1C_2$	150.00	150.00	150.0	150.00	150.0	150.0	150.00

d. **Table 16-3**

(1)	(2)	(3)	(4)	(5)	(6)	(7)	(8)
C_1	8.00	9.0	10.0	11.00	12.0	14.0	16.0
C_2	20.25	18.0	16.2	14.73	13.5	11.6	10.1
$U = C_1C_2$	162.00	162.0	162.0	162.00	162.0	162.0	162.0

e. right (upward); increase; marginal rate of substitution

g. 12; 12; $IC_{U=144}$; 144

h. $IC_{U=150}$; 150; 2; 3; 12; 3; 15; 10; 15; 150; right (above)

6. **a.** 31.17; 1.5

Graph 16-5

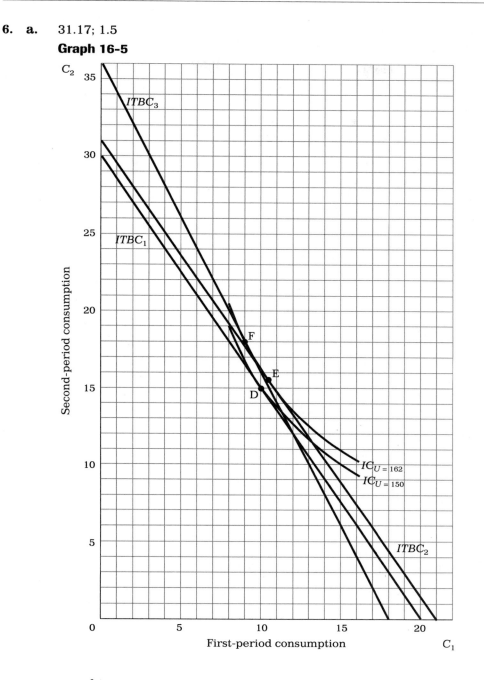

equal to

b. 162; 162; 15.59; increased

c. 12; 12; 12; 36; 2; 162; 162; 18

d. income; substitution; decreasing; increasing

e. increases; increases; decreases; increases; increase; decreases

7. **a.** R; T

b. 60; 45; 15; 40,000; 45; 60; 30,000; 30,000; 3; 4; 10,000; 1; 4; 0.75; 75

c. 40,000; 45; 1,800,000; 1,800,000; equal to

Graph 16-6

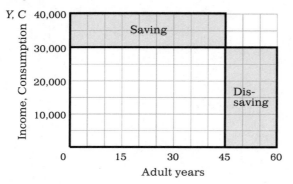

d. *R*; *T*; *T*; 60; 45; 0.75; 0.0167; 1.67

Graph 16-7

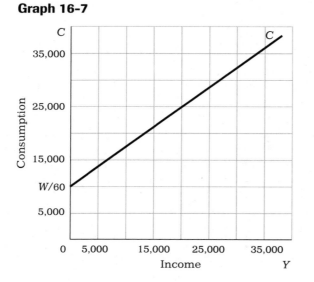

0.0167; 0.75

e. 0.75; 0.0167; 0.75; 0.0167; $120,000; $40,000; 0.80; 0.75; 0.0167; $120,000; $80,000; 0.775; falls; 0.85

f. 0.80

8. a. 75

b. **Table 16-4**

(1)	(2) Y^P	(3) $C = 0.75Y^P$	(4) Y	(5) $APC = C/Y$	(6) Y^T
College professor	$80,000	$60,000	$80,000	0.75	$0
Artist in a good year	$80,000	$60,000	$100,000	0.60	$20,000
Artist in a bad year	$80,000	$60,000	$60,000	1.00	−$20,000

c. not change; not change; decrease; not change; increase

d. decrease; decrease

e. increase; decrease

    f.   decrease; saved; permanent; consumed

    g.   remain constant

Problems

1. **a.** $MPC = 0.8$; $APC = (100/Y) + 0.8$

    b.   If $Y = 100$, $MPC = 0.8$ and $APC = 1.8$

        If $Y = 200$, $MPC = 0.8$ and $APC = 1.3$

        As Y rises, the MPC remains constant and the APC decreases.

2. $1136.16; $885.84; bond present values and prevailing interest rates move in opposite directions.

3. **a.**   Graph for Problem 3a

    Note: We have assumed that the substitution effect is larger than the income effect.

    e.   if the income effect is bigger than the substitution effect

5. **a.** $MPC = b$; $APC = (a/Y) + b$

    b. $d(MPC)/dY = 0$; $d(APC)/dY = -a/Y^2 < 0$

7. The life-cycle and permanent-income models of consumption imply that consumption is relatively stable from one year to the next. Consumption is not as volatile as current income because people do not respond very much to temporary changes in income. Consequently, private spending will be relatively stable (since consumption is by far its largest component), and policy activism will usually be unnecessary.

8. **a.** $C = (1/25)W + (2/5)Y$

    b. $C = $30,000$

9. A reduction in tax rates has two effects on current saving. The substitution effect reduces current consumption and increases current saving. The income effect, on the other hand, increases consumption in each period and, hence, reduces current saving. Consequently, the net effect of a reduction in tax rates on interest and dividends is ambiguous and depends on the relative sizes of the income and substitution effects.

11. **a.** According to the Keynsian consumption function, the tax cuts had their biggest effects on future rather than current disposable income. Consequently, they would change both disposable income and consumption by relatively small amounts in 2001–2002.

    b. According to the permanent income hypothesis, current consumption depends on permanent disposable income, which was substantially increased by the tax cuts when they were passed by Congress. Consequently, consumption in 2001–2002 would also rise substantially. The 5–10 year deferral would reduce the effects on permanent income, but by a much smaller amount.

    c. Even if one accepts the permanent income hypothesis and people wanted to increase current consumption in response to these large increases in permanent income, those who were subject to borrowing constraints would not be able to borrow to do so, and they might not be able to increase their consumption in 2001–2002.

    d. According to adherents of the Ricardian equivalence proposition, the tax cuts would not affect consumption at all, regardless of their timing, as long as they did not change people's expectations of future government spending. People would assume that at some point in the future, taxes would have to be raised by an amount equivalent to the Bush tax cuts.

12. **a.** According to the Keynesian consumption function, an acceleration of the tax cuts would increase current disposable income and thereby have a large effect on consumption in 2002.

    b. According to the permanent income hypothesis, permanent income would be only slightly affected by the acceleration of the tax cuts because people already expected their taxes to be cut within the next few years. Consequently, the main effects of the acceleration would be to increase transitory income, and the effects on consumption in 2002 would be small.

13. According to the life-cycle hypothesis, households would have spread the increase in consumption evenly over the remainder of their lifetime. They would have also increased their consumption when the rebate was passed and not when it was received. Instead, households spent a disproportionately greater portion of their tax rebate within the first 3 months of receiving it. They also increased their consumption only after they received their rebate even though everyone knew at the beginning of the year they were getting a rebate.

14. It would appear that the man's behavior is consistent with the Keynesian consumption function and a marginal propensity to consume out of current disposable income of 0.80. On the other hand, the man will enjoy the services provided by the car for the remainder of his working life. Consequently, he has, in effect "spread" his increase in consumption over the remainder of his (working) life. In this sense, his behavior is also consistent with the life-cycle hypothesis.

CHAPTER 17

Fill-in Questions

1. Residential investment; business fixed investment; inventory investment
2. neoclassical model of investment
3. depreciation
4. real cost of capital
5. net investment; depreciation
6. neoclassical model of investment; real cost of capital
7. corporate income tax
8. corporate income tax
9. investment tax credit
10. Tobin's q
11. stock market; Tobin's q
12. efficient markets hypothesis
13. financing constraints
14. subprime
15. production smoothing; inventories as a factor of production; stock-out avoidance; work in process

Multiple-Choice Questions

1. d	2. c	3. a	4. b	5. d	6. b	7. c
8. a	9. b	10. b	11. a	12. c	13. b	14. d
15. b	16. b	17. b	18. d	19. d	20. b	21. d

Exercises

1. **a.** 20; 15; 10; 5; 20

Graph 17-1

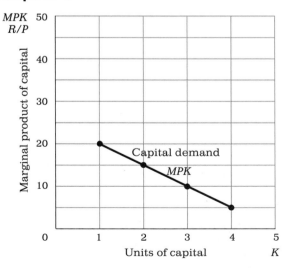

b. 2; 4; more

c. **Graph 17-2**

10

d. right; fall; higher; right; increasing; right; increasing

2. a. 0.03; $10; $15; $12; $22; $44

b. increase; decrease; increase; quickly; shorter

c. 0; 5

d. increase; increase

3. a. equal to; r; δ; r; δ; add to; positive; subtract from; negative

b. equal to; zero; decrease; increase; decrease; increase; add to; increase; rises; similar to; fall

c. have no immediate effect on; increase; add to; increase; added; fall

d. increase; decrease; increase

4. a. zero

b. right

Graph 17-3

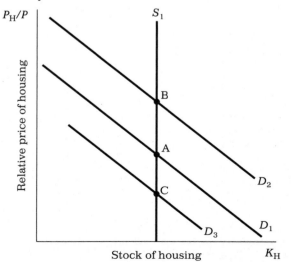

increase; increase; increase; right; fall

c.   left; decrease; decrease

Problems

1. **a.**   Graph for Problem 1a

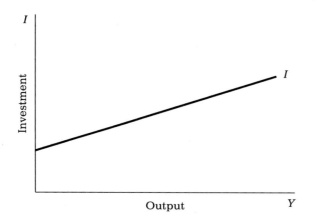

b.   Investment might rise as real output rises because investment may be linked to sales or sales expectations that rise with Y. This is especially true for inventory invesment.

c.   **i.**   The slope of the planned expenditure curve would become steeper. Now when Y increases, both consumption and investment will increase.

  ii.   The government-purchases multiplier will increase. When government purchases increase by $1, there will now be multiplier effects on both consumption and investment. Increases in government purchases will consequently lead to additional spending (and output) in each round.

  iii.   The IS curve will become flatter; the slope of the LM curve is unaffected.

  iv.   The AD curve will become flatter; the slope of the $SRAS$ curve is unaffected.

2. **a.** $2,300

  b. $4,100

3.   The (nominal) cost of capital $= P_K[i - \Delta P_K/P_K + \delta]$, where the second term $\Delta P_K/P_K$ represents the rate at which capital prices are changing. If capital prices are rising at the same rate as the aggregate price level, $\Delta P_K/P_K = \pi$, and the cost of capital becomes $P_K[i - \pi + \delta] = P_K[r + \delta]$. If $\pi > \Delta P_K/P_K$, $(i - \pi) < (i - \Delta P_K/P_K)$ and the use of the real interest rate will underestimate the true cost of capital.

4. **a.** $MPK = 64(K)^{-2/3}$

  b.   64; 16; 7.11; 4

Graph for Problem 4b

c. $MPK = 4(L/K)^{2/3} = 100(K)^{-2/3}$; $MPK = 100; 25; 11.11; 6.25$

5. a. The *IS* curve would shift to the right, increasing both the equilibrium levels of output and the real interest rate. The increase in the real interest rate would increase the real cost of capital, reduce the profit rate from owning capital, and thereby decrease investment according to the neoclassical (cost of capital) theory of investment

b. The *IS* curve again shifts to the right, increasing both the equilibrium levels of output and the real interest rate. While the increase in the real interest rate would tend to decrease investment by raising the real cost of capital, the increase in output would tend to increase investment. As a result, investment could rise, fall, or remain constant.

6. According to the efficient markets hypothesis, the price of one share of Google stock quintupled between August 2004 and February 2006 because of unexpected increase in the actual and expected future profitability of Google between those two dates. According to Keynes's "beauty contest" theory, the stock price quintupled because investors believed that Google would become increasingly attractive to stockholders, for reasons extending beyond reasonable expectations of future profitability.

7. As the baby-boomers retire and move to warmer climates, the demand for housing, relative price of housing, and investment in housing in the South will all increase, while they will all decrease in the North.

8. The demand for housing would shift to the left, reducing the relative price of housing and investment in housing. The profits of home builders would fall in the short run.

CHAPTER 18

Fill-in Questions

1. inside lag
2. outside lag
3. inside lag; outside lag
4. Automatic stabilizers
5. Lucas critique
6. political business cycle
7. time inconsistency
8. Monetarists
9. Automatic stabilizers
10. inflation targeting

Multiple-Choice Questions

1. b	2. d	3. c	4. b	5. b	6. d	7. c
8. d	9. a	10. c	11. d	12. b		

Exercises

1. **a.**   less than; less than
    b.   fall; downward; equal to

    Graph 18-1

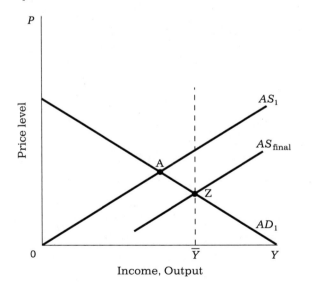

    rise; fall
    c.   increase; increase; decrease; right

Graph 18-2

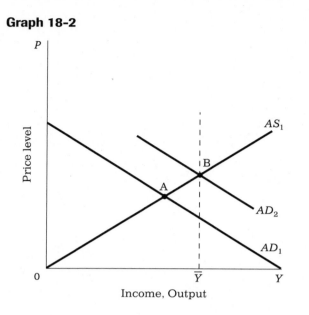

rise; rise

d. greater than; shorter

e. more; more; less

f. inside; outside

2. **a.** 6; 0.2; below

b. 0; 5; 0; 5; –5; 0; 7; 6

c. 0; 5; 0; 5

d. 5; 5; 6; equal to

e. quickly

3. **a.** 0; 3; 0; 3

b. 3; 3; increased; 4; decreased; 2

c. decrease; increase

Problems

1. **a.** If the unemployment rate were 6.1 percent (which is close to our estimate of the natural rate), it is probably better not to change either fiscal or monetary policy. The economy will soon correct itself, and the considerable lags in policy mean that they might take effect after the economy reaches the natural rate of unemployment, which will cause further fluctuations in output and unemployment.

b. If the unemployment rate were 10.1 percent, it is probably better to pursue expansionary monetary and/or fiscal policy. In the absence of any policy changes, the unemployment rate would eventually return to its natural rate, but it might take a long time. Although economic forecasts are unreliable and policy lags exist, it is probable that the economy will still be far from its natural rate when the policies do take effect.

2. The acceptance of rational expectations may reduce the need for policy activism because it tends to shorten the amount of time it takes for the economy to return to the natural rate of output. If prices are sticky, however, the economy will not immediately move back to the natural rate of output, and policy activism may be desirable.

3. **a.** Democratic administrations must be pursuing more expansionary monetary and/or fiscal policies during their first or second years. These policies will shift the aggregate demand curve to the right.

   b. If people have rational expectations and the imperfect information model of the economy is correct, prices are flexible, and output would be affected only by unexpected changes in monetary policy.

4. According to the Phillips curve, in the long run the economy will be at its natural rate regardless of the rate of inflation. Therefore, while more independent central banks may choose lower inflation rates, they will have no effect on the long-run rate of unemployment.

5. **a.** According to the best measures of GDP available in each time period.

   b. According to the best measure of GDP that is available for both time periods.

   c. It is generally acknowledged that macroeconomic stabilization measures have become more widely used since World War II. If the economy has also become more stable, this would support the continued use of these policies. If the economy has not become more stable, the effectiveness of these policies would be questionable.

7. **a.** After the election, people expected future tax cuts, resulting in higher expected future disposable income. As a result, consumption would immediately rise.

   b. By the time the tax cut was eventually passed by Congress, households had already incorporated the tax cuts into their expected future disposable incomes. Consequently, their consumption would not increase any further.

   c. According to the Lucas critique, traditional methods of policy evaluation do not adequately take into account the impact of policy on expectations. A traditional model that investigated the effects of the tax cut by looking only at its effects after the tax cut was enacted would erroneously conclude that the tax cut had no effect on consumption.

8. Recall that the real interest rate is equal to the nominal interest rate minus the inflation rate, that is, $r = i - \pi$. Central banks cannot reduce the nominal interest rate below zero. Consequently, the real interest rate can fall below zero only if inflation is positive.

9. **a.** Optimal $\pi = 0$.

   b. In the long run, unemployment will be at its natural rate since $\pi = E\pi$.

CHAPTER 19

Fill-in Questions

1. government debt
2. government debt
3. capital budgeting
4. cyclically adjusted budget deficit
5. traditional view of government debt
6. Ricardian equivalence

Multiple-Choice Questions

1. c	2. d	3. a	4. a	5. c	6. b	7. a
8. d	9. b	10. c	11. d	12. b	13. c	14. b
15. d	16. a	17. a	18. b	19. d	20. d	21. b
22. c						

Exercises

1. **a.** 60; 0.13; 260
    b. 0; 200; 0.13; 260; 200
    c. 0; 2,000; 2,000; 200; 2,200
    d. 1; 1.1; 2,000; 1; 2,000; 2,200; 1.1; 2,000; equal to; 0; overstate
    e. 0.03; 3; 0.03; 60; 60; 200; 60; 260; 0
2. **a.** *IS*; right; increase; increase; increase; fall; investment
    b. remain constant; appreciation, remain constant; increase; net exports; increase; increase; increase
    c. an increase; an increase; flatter; smaller
    d. decrease; increase
    e. decrease; decrease; fall
3. **a.** increasing
    b. 1,100; 1,100; 1,100; equally well off; have no effect on; remain constant
    c. have no effect on; remain constant
4. **a.** decrease; decrease; increase; left
    b. deficits; surpluses
    c. would not; would not

Problems

1. According to the traditional view, households' current and expected future disposable incomes would fall and current consumption would fall. According to the Ricardian view, the current tax increase would be offset by an expected future reduction in taxes, resulting in no change in consumption.
2. **a.** Current consumption would remain unchanged because people would expect future taxes to rise.

b. Current private saving would rise by $100 billion because current dispos-able income rises by $100 billion and consumption remains unchanged.

c. Current national saving remains unchanged. Private saving rises by $100 billion, but public saving falls by the $100 billion tax cut.

3. For the prospective emigrant, a tax reduction in the current year represents an increase in income because the expected future tax increase will not have to be paid by either the emigrant or her descendants. Thus, the current consumption of the prospective emigrant will increase. In the whole economy, however, a tax reduction represents no change in the sum of current and expected future income, and current aggregate consumption is unaffected.

6. a. The value of the Treasury securities in the Social Security Trust fund is not included in measures of the net debt because it represents money that the government owes to itself.

b. Some observers believe that these securities belong in measures of the government debt because they reflect (a small) part of the benefits that the government has promised to pay future Social Security beneficiaries.

7. a. In the short run, President Obama's fiscal stimulus package would shift the *IS* and *AD* curves to the right. The expansionary monetary policy would shift the *LM* and *AD* curves to the right. The combined effect would be a shift of the *AD* curve to the right, which would increase real GDP and the price level in the short run. As the U.S. price level rises, the real value of the Chinese dollar-denominated assets would decline.

Graph for Problem 7a

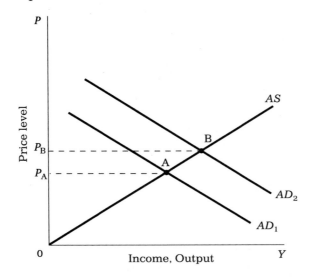

Since the United States is a large open economy, the rightward shift of the *IS* and *LM* curves would have an ambiguous effect on the U.S. interest rate in the short run and thus an ambiguous effect on the U.S. exchange rate. If there was a substantial increase in the risk premium on dollar-denominated assets, the dollar would depreciate and the value of Chinese holdings of dollar-denominated assets would fall in terms of the Chinese currency, the renminbi.

b. In the long run, the expansionary monetary policy would increase the price level and thereby reduce the real value of the Chinese dollar-denominated assets. The expansionary fiscal policy would reduce national saving and, since the United States is a large open economy, it would increase the U.S. real interest rate. This would result in an appreciation of the dollar, contrary to the Chinese Premier's concern.

Graph for Problem 7b

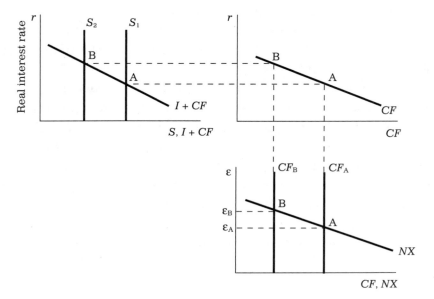

On the other hand, if the perceived risk premium of dollar-denominated assets rose, the dollar might depreciate and the value of Chinese holdings of dollar-denominated assets would fall in terms of the Chinese currency, the renminbi.

8. a. According to the simple Keynesian consumption function, current consumption is a function of current disposable income. Therefore, consumption will begin to be affected by the tax cut only when it takes effect, four years from now. Yet the plan still provides for an eventual reduction in the deficit.

b. According to the forward-looking view of consumption (which we called the permanent-income hypothesis or the life-cycle hypothesis in Chapter 16), current consumption depends on the sum of current and expected future income. Since the future tax increase will decrease future income, it will also decrease *current* consumption, along with the eventual budget deficit.

c. According to the theory of Ricardian equivalence, the future tax increase will affect the official deficit when it takes effect, but it will not affect consumption. According to the government budget constraint, people will merely expect a tax decrease sometime in the future (after four years), and they will dissave in order to maintain their levels of consumption.

d. If people have borrowing constraints, the future tax increase will still reduce consumption when it takes effect even if Ricardian equivalence is valid. The tax increase will reduce disposable income when it becomes effective. Although people may wish to dissave and maintain consumption, they may not be able to do so if they do not have the resources and cannot borrow.

9. If Brazil does not default on its debt, the U.S. guarantee will probably have no effect on the U.S. budget deficit. One might, however, argue that the U.S. guarantee increases the riskiness of U.S. government debt. As a result, U.S. government borrowing costs and U.S. government budget deficits might both rise.

10. a. Increases in government purchases will shift both the *IS* and *AD* curves to the right in the short run. Although the increase in real GDP will also increase tax revenues, the budget deficit will increase along with r, Y, and P. Thus, higher deficits will be associated with higher prices and higher interest rates. (Although the increase in P will also shift the *LM* curve upward a bit, both Y and r will still rise.)
Graphs for Problem 10a

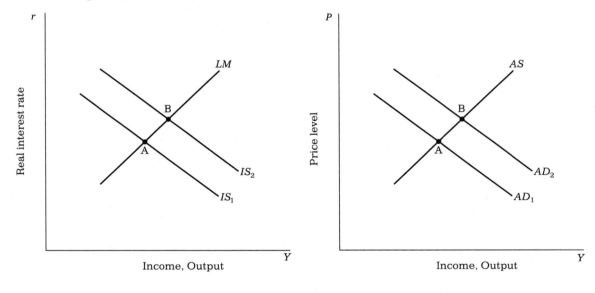

b. Declines in consumer or business confidence will shift the *IS* and *AD* curves to the left, reducing *r*, *Y*, and *P*. As *Y* falls, income tax revenues fall, and the budget deficit will increase. In this case higher deficits will be accompanied by *lower* prices and lower interest rates. (Although the decrease in *P* will also shift the *LM* curve downward a bit, both *Y* and *r* will still fall.)

Graphs for Problem 10b

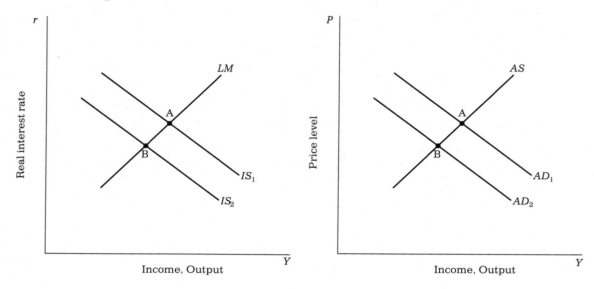

CHAPTER 20

Fill-in Questions

1. financial intermediaries; financial system
2. bond; stocks; financial markets
3. debt finance; equity finance
4. risk averse
5. diversification
6. mutual funds
7. idiosyncratic risk; systematic risk
8. asymmetric information
9. adverse selection
10. moral hazard
11. financial crisis
12. speculative bubble
13. leverage
14. fire sale
15. liquidity crisis
16. lender of last resort
17. shadow banks

Multiple-Choice Questions

1. b	2. c	3. a	4. b	5. c	6. c	7. d
8. a	9. b	10. b	11. d	12. d	13. d	14. d
15. c	16. b	17. c	18. a			

Exercises

1. **a.** 1; 2
   b. 4; 2; –$2; 1
   c. 4; 2; –$2; $4; –$2; 1
   d. 1; 1
   e. decrease

Problems

1. **a.** The FDIC charges banks a premium in return for insuring that savers receive the full value of their bank deposits if the bank becomes insolvent.

   b. Moral hazard occurs when an imperfectly monitored person or institution concludes a transaction and then acts in a dishonest or otherwise inappropriate way. In the case of the FDIC, depositors (who know that their deposits are safe) will insufficiently monitor the quality of the investments and loans made by the bank, leading the banks to take excessive risks or make bad loans.

   c. Depositors with more than $250,000 have the ability and incentive to monitor the bank's investments and mitigate the problem of moral hazard. Therefore, they don't need as much protection as depositors with smaller amounts.

   d. Although FDIC insurance creates a problem of moral hazard, most economists believe it plays an important role in preventing bank runs during financial crises that would endanger the entire financial system.

2. **a.** If people with serious illnesses are more likely to apply for life insurance, insurance companies may have to raise everyone's premiums because their customers will be sicker than average.

   b. To mitigate this problem of adverse selection insurance companies often require applicants to submit a complete medical history and take a medical exam. They could then refuse to insure sick applicants or charge them a higher premium.

3. **a.** Conventional banks typically don't make micro-loans because they are considered to be unprofitable. The small amounts and duration of the loans may be considered inadequate to justify the costs of assessing the creditworthiness of the borrowers and the costs of servicing the loans.

   b. Villagers who think that they, too, may someday apply for a micro-loan may put pressure on their neighbors who currently have loans so the microfinance bank will remain solvent and able to make new loans in the future.

    c. Moral hazard may be present for borrowers who already have loans. If they think they will not need any future loans, they may take excessive risks or work insufficiently hard to avoid default. The pressure from their neighbors will discourage such actions.

4.   **a.** A leverage ratio of 50 means that the ratio of the value of a bank's assets to its bank capital is 50. A bank's assets are the things it owns or the things others owe it. A bank's capital is the owner's equity, calculated by subtracting the value of its liabilities (the things it owes to others) from the value of its assets.

    b. Bank Capital = $100 – $98 = $2

    Leverage Ratio = $100/$2 = 50

    c. New value of assets = $98

    New value of bank capital = $0

5.   **a.** Banks are considered to be too big to fail if government policymakers and regulators believe that their failure would result in a national financial crisis.

    b. If a bank is considered too big to fail, its creditors might insufficiently monitor the bank's investments because they believe the government or the Federal Reserve will bail them out if the bank runs into financial difficulty.

    c. Banks considered too big to fail will be able to borrow at lower interest rates, giving them an unfair economic advantage over small banks that are not too big to fail.